STUDIES IN EARLY MODERN CULTURAL,
POLITICAL AND SOCIAL HISTORY

Volume 11

AN ENLIGHTENMENT STATESMAN IN WHIG BRITAIN

LORD SHELBURNE IN CONTEXT, 1737–1805

Studies in Early Modern Cultural, Political and Social History

ISSN: 1476–9107

Series editors
Tim Harris – Brown University
Stephen Taylor – University of Reading
Andy Wood – University of East Anglia

Previously published titles in the series
are listed at the back of this volume

AN ENLIGHTENMENT STATESMAN IN WHIG BRITAIN

LORD SHELBURNE IN CONTEXT, 1737–1805

Edited by

Nigel Aston and Clarissa Campbell Orr

THE BOYDELL PRESS

First published 2011
The Boydell Press, Woodbridge

ISBN 978–1–84383–630–8

The Boydell Press is an imprint of Boydell & Brewer Ltd
PO Box 9, Woodbridge, Suffolk IP12 3DF, UK
and of Boydell & Brewer Inc.
668 Mt Hope Avenue, Rochester, NY 14620, USA
website: www.boydellandbrewer.com

A catalogue record for this book is available
from the British Library

The publisher has no responsibility for the continued existence or accuracy of URLs for external or third-party internet websites referred to in this book, and does not guarantee that any content on such websites is, or will remain, accurate or appropriate.

Papers used by Boydell & Brewer Ltd are natural, recyclable products made from wood grown in sustainable forests

Printed in Great Britain by
CPI Antony Rowe, Chippenham and Eastbourne

Contents

Illustrations

Figures

Tables

Contributors

Nigel Aston is Reader in Early Modern History at the University of Leicester, and a specialist in the religious and political history of eighteenth-century France and Britain. His books include *The French Revolution 1789–1802: Liberty, Authority and the Search for Stability* (Palgrave, 2004) and *Christianity in Revolutionary Europe 1750–1830* (Cambridge University Press, 2002). He has contributed to several collections of essays including 60 biographical essays for the *Oxford Dictionary of National Biography* (Oxford University Press, 2004), and 'Church and State in Continental Catholic Europe' in the *Cambridge History of Christianity, Vol. VII, Enlightenment, Reawakening and Revolution 1660–1815*, ed. Timothy Tackett and Stewart J. Brown (Cambridge University Press, 2006). *Art and Religion in Eighteenth-century Europe* (Reaktion Books) was published in 2009. He is currently working on an edition of the correspondence of James Boswell with the Rev. W.J. Temple, vol. 2, 1777–1795, for Yale University Press, and two articles on Shelburne's family and politics.

Clarissa Campbell Orr is Reader in Enlightenment, Gender and Court Studies at Anglia Ruskin University, Cambridge Campus. She has edited and contributed to *Queenship in Britain 1660–1837: Royal Patronage, Dynastic Politics, and Court Culture* (Manchester University Press, 2002), and *Queenship in Europe 1660–1815: The Role of the Consort* (Cambridge University Press, 2004). Other works include 'Aristocratic Feminism, the Learned Governess, and the Republic of Letters', in *Women, Gender & Enlightenment*, ed. B Taylor S. Knott (Palgrave, 2005), and 'The Late Hanoverian Court and the Christian Enlightenment', in *Monarchy and Religion*, ed. Michael Schaich (German Historical Institute/Oxford University Press, 2007). She contributed the chapter 'Mrs. Delany and the Court' to *Mrs Delany and her Contemporaries*, ed. Mark Laird and Alicia Weisberg-Roberts (Yale University Press, 2009), and is writing a biography of Mrs Delany for Yale University Press. She is also currently working on a study of Queen Charlotte.

John Cannon, CBE, is Professor Emeritus of Modern History at Newcastle University. His publications include *The Fox-North Coalition: Crisis of the Constitution* (1970); ed., *The Whig Ascendancy* (1981); *Aristocratic Century* (1984), and *Samuel Johnson and the Politics of Hanoverian England* (1994). He contributed the entry on Lord Shelburne for the *Oxford Dictionary of National Biography* (2004).

Emmanuelle de Champs is Maître de Conférences in English (Université Paris 8) and a member of the Centre Bentham (Université Paris 10). She has published on Bentham's political theory (*La déontologie politique: ou la pensée constitutionelle de J. Bentham*, Geneva, Droz, 2008) and co-edited, with Jean-Pierre Cléro, a volume on the reception of Bentham's thought in France (*Bentham et la France: Fortune et infortunes de l'utilitarisme*, Oxford, SVEC, 2009–09). She works on intellectual and cultural transfers between France and Britain in the late eighteenth century, especially on Etienne Dumont's editorship of Bentham's manuscripts.

G.M. Ditchfield is Professor of Eighteenth-Century History at the University of Kent, Canterbury. He has published extensively on eighteenth-century British political and religious history, with particular reference to religious issues in parliamentary and popular politics, the history of the House of Lords, Protestant Dissent, and the emergence of Unitarianism. He is the author of *The Evangelical Revival* (1998) and *George III. An Essay in Monarchy* (2002), together with numerous journal articles and chapters in edited collections. He is editor of *The Letters of Theophilus Lindsey. Volume I: 1747–1788* (2007). He is currently completing the second volume of *The Letters of Theophilus Lindsey* and will then undertake an edition of the correspondence of Archdeacon Francis Blackburne.

Edmond Dziembowski is Professor of Modern History at the Université de Franche-Comté (Besançon, France) and Director of the LSH (Laboratoire des Sciences Historiques) EA 2273. He is the author of *Un nouveau patriotisme français, 1750–1770. La France face à la puissance anglaise à l'époque de la guerre de Sept Ans* (Oxford, Voltaire Foundation, 1998, Studies on Voltaire and the Eighteenth Century, 365) and *Les Pitt. L'Angleterre face à la France, 1708–1806*, (Paris, Perrin, 2006). He is currently working on the French official press in the second half of the eighteenth century.

Robin Eagles is a senior research fellow in the House of Lords (1660–1832) section of the History of Parliament. Previous publications include *Francophilia in English Society, 1748–1815* (2000), '"No More to Be Said"? Reactions to the Death of Frederick Lewis, Prince of Wales', *Historical Research* 80 (2007) and '"The Only Disagreeable Thing in the Whole": The Selection and Experience of the British Hostages for the Delivery of Cape Breton in Paris, 1748–9', in *British French-Exchanges in the Eighteenth Century*, ed. K.H. Doig and D. Medlin (2007).

Frank O'Gorman is Professor Emeritus in the University of Manchester. Frank O'Gorman has published extensively on the origins and development of political parties in England in the eighteenth and nineteenth centuries and is the author of *Edmund Burke: His Political Philosophy* (1973). The development of his interests from party to electoral history was a natural transition and in 1989 it yielded *Voters, Patrons and Parties: The Unreformed Electoral System of Hanoverian England, 1734–1832*. His major synthesis of the history of Britain during the Hanoverian period appeared in 1997: *The Long Eighteenth Century: British Political and Social History 1688–1832*. He is at present writing a book on the operation of political ritual in Britain during the long eighteenth century.

John Orbell is a business archivist and business historian. He spent most of his career as Archivist of Baring Brothers, later ING Bank London Branch, and is now a trustee of The Baring Archive Trust. He has published on banking and shipping history and on business archives and his thesis covers the history of grain milling. He has just published 'A Guide to Tracing the History of a Business' (Phillimore, 2009) and is completing a bibliography of British business history to be published in 2012 in print and, with the Business Archives Council, online.

Martyn J. Powell is Senior Lecturer in Modern British History at Aberystwyth University. He has published widely on eighteenth-century Britain and Ireland, and his latest book *Piss-Pots, Printers and Public Opinion in Eighteenth-Century Dublin* was published by Four Courts Press in 2009.

Andrew Stockley is the Dean of Law at the University of Auckland in New Zealand. He was previously Head of the Law School at the University of Canterbury in New Zealand and has published widely on constitutional law issues. He examined the role of Lord Shelburne in the peace negotiations of 1782–3 when studying for his doctorate at the University of Cambridge and is the author of *Britain and France at the Birth of America* (University of Exeter Press, 2001).

Richard Whatmore is Professor of Intellectual History and the History of Political Thought at the University of Sussex and Director of the Sussex Centre for Intellectual History. He is the author of *Republicanism and the French Revolution* (Oxford University Press, 2000), has co-edited two volumes of essays on British intellectual history since 1750 (*Economy, Polity and Society* and *History, Religion and Culture*, both Cambridge University Press, 2000), in addition to *Advances in Intellectual History* (Palgrave, 2006), and *Geneva: An English Enclave* (Slatkine, 2009). He has written widely on French, Swiss and British eighteenth-century and early nineteenth-century intellectual history. *Against War and Empire: Geneva, Britain and France in the Eighteenth Century* will be published by Yale University Press in 2012.

Acknowledgements

All but one of the chapters in this book were originally given in July 2007 at a symposium called 'Begetters of Revolution? Shelburne and the Bowood Circle Reappraised' organized by the co-editors at Sherborne School. Thanks are owed to others who gave papers or chaired sessions: Craig Beeston, Cyprian Blamires, Toby Barnard, Stephen Conway, Rachel Hammersley, Bob Harris, Linda Kirk, Peter Marshall, John Phibbs, Patrick Pilkington, Martin Fitzpatrick and John Stevenson. School staff, led by the Domestic Bursar, Eve Arnold, were splendid hosts, with Derek Jarrett's successor, the current Head of History, Huw Ridgeway, his immediate predecessor, Jeremy Barker, and another former master, Peter Currie, particularly helpful and assistive before, during, and afterwards. Thanks are also due to the Headmaster, Simon Elliot, the Secretary to the Old Shirburnian Society, John Harden, and the Assistant Secretary, Janey Goddard. We were also generously entertained at Bowood House by the Marquess and Marchioness of Lansdowne on the only sunny Saturday in July – a memorable coincidence.

The symposium was dedicated to the memory of Derek Jarrett, radical schoolmaster and historian, who died in 2004, and it was a great privilege to have his widow, Betty Jarrett, present with us throughout those days. Jarrett was an eighteenth-century British historian who had a finely attuned sense of the inter-connectedness of British and European political culture in the second half of his century. He put Lord Shelburne and the 'Bowood Circle' at the heart of that many-faceted nexus. Indeed, he may be said to have coined that term in the process of writing his Oxford B.Litt. thesis (supervised by John Bromley) on the subject. Jarrett's finest work was probably his 1973 publication *The Begetters of Revolution: England's Involvement with France, 1759–1789*, an astute and persuasive essay in comparative history founded on Jarrett's prescient perception that 'Politics in England and France during these thirty years were too closely interwoven for the history of either country to be intelligible on its own'. This insight has become axiomatic for historians but it never quite received the recognition it deserved in its own time, probably because so little comparative history of any quality was produced in the 1970s. The Sherborne colloquium of 34 years later was partly conceived as an attempt to correct that injustice. Jarrett returned to this approach later in his career with his *Three Faces of Revolution: Paris, London and New York in 1789* (1989), another important and excessively neglected book. He was at all times a diligent writer who produced accessible and well-received studies of William Hogarth's England

and Pitt the Younger, as well as a textbook on *Britain 1688–1815* for sixth-formers. Sadly, it was not by itself capable of making the long eighteenth century a popular curriculum choice for GCE A Level History teachers in the 1960s or, indeed, at any point thereafter.

After coming down from Oxford, Jarrett taught at Sherborne School in Dorset in 1952, becoming head of department three years later. It was, as his former pupil Tim Heald put it, in his obituary notice for *The Independent* (1 April 2004) an 'ancient and deeply conventional establishment' and the unorthodox and slightly raffish Jarrett stood out sharply in the 1950s and early 1960s. However, he was a superb teacher who delivered top quality results for his supportive headmaster and the majority of the boys found his approach much to their taste. This part of his career was commemorated at the 2007 conference with appreciative speeches and witty reminiscences from several of his former pupils. He remained at the school until 1964 when he took a post in higher education, at Goldsmiths College, London, where he remained until retirement. Thereafter he brought to completion a four-volume edition of Horace Walpole's *Memoirs of the Reign of King George III* for Yale University Press, despite his unconcealed absence of personal sympathy for Walpole: that 'dreadful man' as he dubbed him. Professionally, Jarrett has been under-appreciated. At this distance in time, however, recognition should no longer be withheld.

The editors would like to thank the Marquess of Lansdowne for generously waiving the reproduction fee for pictures owned by the estate, and for his support for this project; the Trustees of the Bowood Estate for access to the Archives at Bowood House and for permission to quote from them; and the Archivist, Kate Fielden, for all her help with material in the collection. We would also like to thank a private collection for the reproduction of Figure 6. Anglia Ruskin University generously supported Clarissa Campbell Orr's research as well as contributing to production costs. Marlene Buick, Carol Thomas, Paul Broomfield, Gareth Long and John Walsh at ARU also gave invaluable help on technical matters in editing the text.

Finally we would like to thank Peter Sowden at the Boydell Press for his enthusiastic sponsoring of this book.

Abbreviations

BA	Baring Archive
BHA	Bowood House Archives
BL	British Library
Bod. Lib	Bodleian Library
CHOP	*Calendar of Home Office Papers of the Reign of George III 1760 to 1775* (4 vols, London, 1878–99)
Diary	Diary of Lady Sophia, Countess of Shelburne, Bowood House Archives
Fitzmaurice, *Shelburne*	Edmond George Petty-Fitzmaurice, Baron Fitzmaurice, *Life of William, Earl of Shelburne, afterwards First Marquess of Lansdowne*, 2 vols (London, 1912)
Fitzmaurice, *Shelburne*, 1875–6	Edmond Fitzmaurice, *Life of William, Earl of Shelburne, First Marquess of Lansdowne, with extracts from his papers and correspondence*, 3 vols (London, 1875–6)
Fortescue	J.W. Fortescue, ed., *The Correspondence of King George III, 1760–1783*, 6 vols (London, 1928)
HMC	Historical Manuscripts Commission
HMSO	Her Majesty's Stationery Office
JRL	John Rylands Library
LPL	Lambeth Palace Library
ODNB online	*Oxford Dictionary of National Biography*, online edition, 2004–
Price Correspondence	*The Correspondence of Richard Price*, ed. D.O. Thomas and W. Bernard Peach, 3 vols) Durham, NC and Cardiff, 1983–94)
TNA	The National Archives
Walpole Correspondence	*The Yale Edition of Horace Walpole's Correspondence*, ed. S. Lewis, 47 vols (New Haven, CT, 1937–83)
Walpole Correspondence with Deffand	W.S. Lewis and W.H. Smith, ed., *The Yale Edition of Horace Walpole's Correspondence: Horace Walpole's Correspondence with Madame du Deffand and Wiart* [hereafter], 6 vols (New Haven, CT, 1939)

TABLE 1. PETTY FITZMAURICE (LANSDOWNE) FAMILY

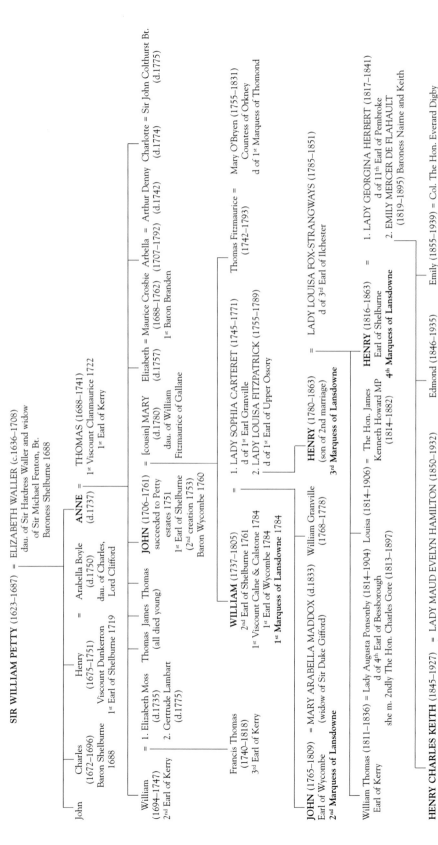

Beatrix Frances =1. Henry de la Poer Beresford (1875–1911) 6th Marquess of Waterford
(1877–1953)   2. Osborne de Vere Beauclerk (1874–1964) 12th Duke of St Albans

Evelyn Mary = Victor Cavendish **HENRY WILLIAM EDMUND** = ELIZABETH HOPE
(1870–1960)   (1868–1938) 9th Duke (1872–1936) Earl of Kerry (1885–1964)
              of Devonshire **6th Marquess of Lansdowne** she m. 2ndly Lord Colum Mount Stewart (1886–1957) son of 3rd Marquess of Bute

Charles George (1874–1914) Mercer Nairne 1914 killed in action, Ypres

Lady Violet Elliot (1889–1965) d of 4th Earl of Minto she m. 2ndly Col. The Hon. John Astor (1886–1971) 1st Baron Astor of Hever

Elizabeth (b. 1927) = Maj. Charles Lambton (1921–2004)

Edward Norman (1922–1944)

Katherine = Edward Clive Bigham (1906–1979) (1912–1995) 3rd Viscount Mersey — Baroness Nairne 1944

Henry Maurice (1913–1933)

CHARLES HOPE (1917–1944) Earl of Kerry **7th Marquess of Lansdowne** killed in action, Italy

GEORGE JOHN CHARLES (1912–1999) **8th Marquess of Lansdowne** = 1. BARBARA DEMPSEY CHASE (1918–1965)
2. The Hon. (Selina) Polly Eccles (b.1937) d of 1st Viscount Eccles
3. Gillian Morgan (d.1982)
4. Penelope Eve Bradford (1940–2007) widow of her husband's half-brother, The Hon. John Astor

(Mary) Margaret = Lt. Col. Ririd Myddelton (1910–2003) (1902–1988)

Robert Mercer Nairne = Jane Gordon (b.1947)   (b. 1950)

Georgina = 1. Guy Hamilton m. diss. 2. Robert Miller (b. 1950)

CHARLES MAURICE (b.1941) Earl of Shelburne **9th Marquess of Lansdowne** = 1. LADY FRANCES ELIOT (1943–2004) d. of 9th Earl of St. Germans
2. Fiona Mary Merritt (b.1954)

Caroline (1939–1956)

Rachel = James Spickernell (b.1968) (b.1965)

SIMON HENRY GEORGE (b. 1970) Viscount Calne & Calstone **Earl of Kerry**

William = Rebecca Sansum (b. 1973) (b. 1982)

Arabella = Rupert Unwin (b.1966) (b.1965)

Benjamin (b. 15.9.94)   Frederick (b. 16.10.96)   Olivia (b. 4.3.99)   Jemima (b. 3.5.01)

Abraham (b. 15.11.96)   Gala (b. 11.8.98)   Evie (b. 25.1.01)

Zara (b. 1.11.06)   Isla Mary Rose (b. 30.08.08)

TABLE 2. CARTERET AND FERMOR FAMILIES

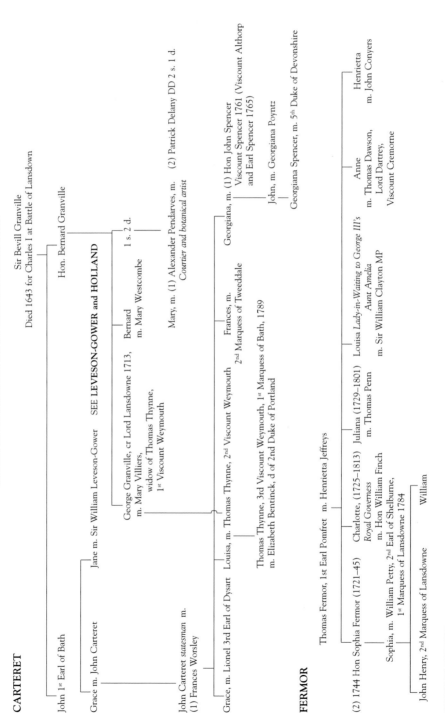

CARTERET

Sir Bevill Granville
Died 1643 for Charles I at Battle of Lansdown

Hon. Bernard Granville

John 1st Earl of Bath

Jane m. Sir William Leveson-Gower SEE LEVESON-GOWER and HOLLAND

Grace m. John Carteret

George Granville, cr Lord Lansdowne 1713, m. Mary Villiers, widow of Thomas Thynne, 1st Viscount Weymouth

Bernard m. Mary Westcombe

1 s. 2 d.

John Carteret *statesman* m. (1) Frances Worsley

Mary, m. (1) Alexander Pendarves, m. *Courtier and botanical artist* (2) Patrick Delany DD 2 s. 1 d.

Grace, m. Lionel 3rd Earl of Dysart

Louisa, m. Thomas Thynne, 2nd Viscount Weymouth

Frances, m. 2nd Marquess of Tweeddale

Georgiana, m. (1) Hon John Spencer Viscount Spencer 1761 (Viscount Althorp and Earl Spencer 1765)

Thomas Thynne, 3rd Viscount Weymouth, 1st Marquess of Bath, 1789 m. Elizabeth Bentinck, d of 2nd Duke of Portland

John, m. Georgiana Poyntz

Georgiana Spencer, m. 5th Duke of Devonshire

FERMOR

Thomas Fermor, 1st Earl Pomfret m. Henrietta Jeffreys

(2) 1744 Hon Sophia Fermor (1721–45)

Charlotte, (1725–1813) *Royal Governess* m. Hon William Finch

Juliana (1729–1801) m. Thomas Penn

Louisa *Lady-in-Waiting to George III's Aunt Amelia* m. Sir William Clayton MP

Anne m. Thomas Dawson, Lord Dartrey, Viscount Cremorne

Henrietta m. John Conyers

Sophia, m. William Petty, 2nd Earl of Shelburne, 1st Marquess of Lansdowne 1784

John Henry, 2nd Marquess of Lansdowne

William

SEE FITZMAURICE

TABLE 3. FOX AND LEVESON-GOWER FAMILIES

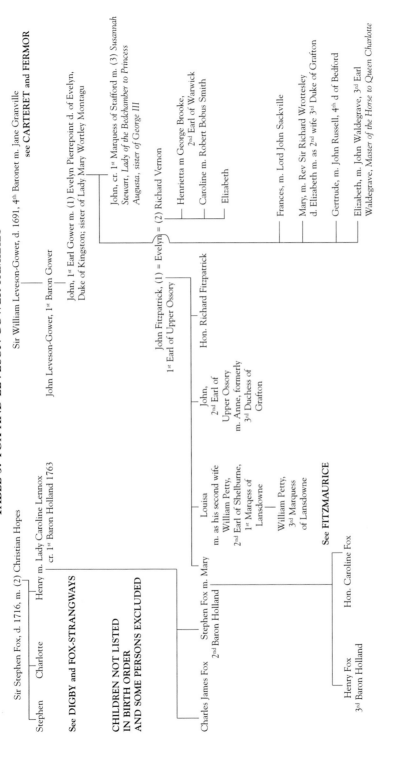

Sir Stephen Fox, d. 1716, m. (2) Christian Hopes

Sir William Leveson-Gower, d. 1691, 4th Baronet m. Jane Granville
see CARTERET and FERMOR

Stephen Charlotte Henry m. Lady Caroline Lennox
cr. 1st Baron Holland 1763

See DIGBY and FOX-STRANGWAYS

CHILDREN NOT LISTED
IN BIRTH ORDER
AND SOME PERSONS EXCLUDED

John Leveson-Gower, 1st Baron Gower

John, 1st Earl Gower m. (1) Evelyn Pierrepoint d. of Evelyn,
Duke of Kingston; sister of Lady Mary Wortley Montagu

John, cr. 1st Marquess of Stafford m. (3) Susannah
Stewart, Lady of the Bedchamber to Princess
Augusta, sister of George III

John Fitzpatrick, (1) = Evelyn = (2) Richard Vernon
1st Earl of Upper Ossory

Henrietta m George Brooke,
2nd Earl of Warwick

Caroline m. Robert Bobus Smith

Elizabeth

Hon. Richard Fitzpatrick

Frances, m. Lord John Sackville

Mary, m. Rev Sir Richard Wrottesley
d. Elizabeth m. as 2nd wife 3rd Duke of Grafton

Gertrude, m. John Russell, 4th d of Bedford

Elizabeth, m. John Waldegrave, 3rd Earl
Waldegrave, Master of the Horse to Queen Charlotte

Charles James Fox Stephen Fox m. Mary
2nd Baron Holland

John,
2nd Earl of
Upper Ossory
m. Anne, formerly
3rd Duchess of
Grafton

Louisa
m. as his second wife
William Petty,
2nd Earl of Shelburne,
1st Marquess of
Lansdowne

William Petty,
3rd Marquess
of Lansdowne

See FITZMAURICE

Hon. Caroline Fox

Henry Fox
3rd Baron Holland

TABLE 4. FOX STRANGWAYS, DIGBY, AND FOX FAMILIES

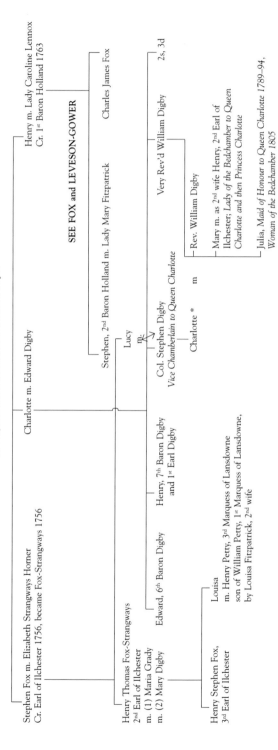

Sir Stephen Fox, d. 1716, m. (2) Christian Hopes

Stephen Fox m. Elizabeth Strangways Horner
Cr. Earl of Ilchester 1756, became Fox-Strangways 1756

Charlotte m. Edward Digby

Henry m. Lady Caroline Lennox
Cr. 1st Baron Holland 1763

SEE FOX and LEVESON-GOWER

Henry Thomas Fox-Strangways
2nd Earl of Ilchester
m. (1) Maria Grady
m. (2) Mary Digby

Edward, 6th Baron Digby

Henry, 7th Baron Digby
and 1st Earl Digby

Stephen, 2nd Baron Holland m. Lady Mary Fitzpatrick

Charles James Fox

Lucy
m.

Col. Stephen Digby
Vice Chamberlain to Queen Charlotte

Very Rev'd William Digby

2s, 3d

Henry Stephen Fox,
3rd Earl of Ilchester

Louisa
m. Henry Petty, 3rd Marquess of Lansdowne
son of William Petty, 1st Marquess of Lansdowne,
by Louisa Fitzpatrick, 2nd wife

Charlotte *   m

Rev. William Digby

Mary m. as 2nd wife Henry, 2nd Earl of
Ilchester; *Lady of the Bedchamber to Queen
Charlotte and then Princess Charlotte*

Julia, *Maid of Honour to Queen Charlotte 1789–94,
Woman of the Bedchamber 1805*

**CHILDREN NOT LISTED
IN BIRTH ORDER AND
SOME PERSONS EXCLUDED**

**SEE HOLLAND and LEVESON-GOWER
AND FITZMAURICE**

* Charlotte Digby was Maid of Honour to Queen Charlotte, 1802

Introduction

Nigel Aston and Clarissa Campbell Orr

William Petty, 2nd Earl of Shelburne, created 1st Marquess of Lansdowne in 1784, is the least studied statesman of the reign of George III. The only modern monograph on him was written in 1963 by John Norris, and concentrated on Economical (i.e. administrative) Reform.[1] This dearth is in part a tribute to the longevity of the three-volume biography written by Shelburne's descendant, the minor Liberal politician Lord Edmond Fitzmaurice (later created 1st Baron Fitzmaurice), based securely on the family archives.[2] That there is such an abundance of archival sources makes the omission the more glaring. The William L. Clements Library at Ann Arbor bought a selection of papers when they were sold in the 1920s. Access to what remained at Bowood was, admittedly, for a while problematic despite the papers being xeroxed by the Bodleian Library. After the death of the 6th Marquess, there was a further sale to the British Library with a relatively small residue being left with the family at Bowood. The essays in this book are based squarely on these unpublished sources. They are a contribution toward his systematic reassessment, and reflect new perspectives on political life, gender, and the Enlightenment, that have developed since Norris's work was published. They are intended to provoke new debate and further research. Selected aspects of Shelburne's life and career receive fresh attention in this collection; other avenues for further exploration are also suggested in this introduction. There are several conceptual frames through which the life and career of Lord Shelburne can be examined. The most obvious is his role in high politics.

The Context of High Politics

Shelburne somehow missed the Namierite high-tide of British post-war scholarship despite his dismissive attitude to 'party' which rather reflected the essential Namierite devaluation of it. Historians of this period were still drawn first and foremost to study the Rockingham Whigs, with their more

---

[1] John Norris, *Shelburne and Reform* (London, 1963).
[2] The revised two-volume edition of this biography was published in 1912.

positive view of connection and faction. The Marquess received a biography in 1973, the same year that Paul Langford published his Oxford Historical Monograph on the first Rockingham administration of 1765–6.[3] Sir Lewis's first apostle, John Brooke, had meanwhile established his reputation as far back as 1956 with a fine study of the Chatham government of 1766–8, but it is significant that this was not a straightforward biography.[4] These tended to be in short supply, possibly being relegated to the attention of those producing prosopographic volumes for the History of Parliament Trust. The overwhelming bulk of the Newcastle Papers in the British Library was an understandable deterrent to those contemplating a biography of the duke and, as to Lord North, the most significant work was by Ian R. Christie on the end of his ministry, and not a study of the Premier himself.[5] The only exception to this conspicuous eschewal of biography was John Derry's study of Charles James Fox, and a rather interesting and neglected study of 1967 by Peter Brown on *The Chathamites* that included chapters dedicated to some of Shelburne's supporters and followers such as Barré, Dunning, and Bishop Shipley.[6] Other than Norris's biography, Shelburne only received discrete treatment in a sparkling cameo essay by Charles Stuart in a festschrift for Hugh Trevor-Roper, while his ministry of 1782–3 was judiciously assessed by John Cannon in his classic study of 1969 on the Fox–North Coalition.[7]

At the same time as historians continued in the seventies and eighties to examine high politics, they were also broadening their understanding of political culture. Indeed, the study of politics, in the sense of the formation of ministries and their parliamentary behaviour, was itself subsumed into the notion of political culture. This embraced the whole ideological, social, parliamentary, and popular context in which the formation and execution of politics took place, including a better understanding of electoral behaviour and the role of the crowd. In deploying the term 'culture' historians

---

[3] Ross J.S. Hoffman, *The Marquis. A Study of Lord Rockingham 1730–82* (New York, 1973); Paul Langford, *The First Rockingham Administration 1765–6* (Oxford, 1973).

[4] John Brooke, *The Chatham Administration 1766–68* (London, 1956).

[5] Ian R. Christie, *The End of North's Ministry, 1780–82* (London, 1958). The Allen Lane/Penguin series of Political Biographies edited by Chris Cook in the 1970s, aimed at students and the general reading public, included a study of *Lord North* (London, 1976) by John W. Derry but for an Irish statesman chose Lord Castlereagh, not Shelburne (Peter D. Thomas, *Lord Castlereagh* [London, 1976]). Weidenfeld and Nicolson's similar series of Political Biographies commissioned Derek Jarrett to write on *Pitt the Younger* (London, 1974), not Lord Shelburne.

[6] John W. Derry, *Charles James Fox* (London, 1972); Peter D. Brown, *The Chathamites. A Study in the Relationship between Personalities and Ideas in the Second Half of the Eighteenth Century* (London, 1967).

[7] Charles Stuart, 'Lord Shelburne', in *History and Imagination. Essays in Honour of H.R. Trevor-Roper*, ed. Hugh Lloyd-Jones, Valerie Pearl, and Blair Worden (London, 1981), 243–53; John Cannon, *The Fox-North Coalition: Crisis of the Constitution 1782–4* (Cambridge, 1969).

were influenced by the work of social anthropologists, who sought to depict social structures and the meanings invested into them, and concentrated largely on peoples outside the developed world.

Seminal books include John Brewer, *Party Ideology and Popular Politics at the Accession of George III* (1976).[8] Brewer's motive was to reintroduce ideology back into the understanding of political faction, as well as to explore the link between high politics and popular politics. Brewer offered a critique of the Namierite paradigm of understanding later Georgian politics only in terms of aristocratic factions and connections, as if political beliefs and ideas had little influence on policy of behaviour. Party labels – more specifically, different groupings within the Whigs – were shown by Brewer to have ideological substance, and to reflect different interpretations of how the balanced constitution of the post-1688 settlement was meant to work. A shared language belied different interpretations, maintained at the time by political actors, on how executive power was supposed to operate, particularly in the formation and dismissal of ministries. In parallel with this, Quentin Skinner and the Cambridge school of historians of political thought argued that historians should avoid the intentionalist fallacy of believing that ideological articulations were sufficient to explain actions. However, Skinner's study of Bolingbroke showed that even if historians should not take at face value a politician's justifications for his actions and motivations, they can nevertheless be examined to show what kind of political ideas made sense for a politician to project, in order for him to persuade others to adopt his point of view.[9]

George III presented a particular challenge to mid-Hanoverian politicians. At his accession, he considered that his grandfather George II had been both the puppet of the politicians and too much dominated by petticoat power. He also deplored the libertine morals and cynical ambition of the era and wanted to establish a court with a high moral tone. Unfortunately in trying to restore the prestige and moral aura of the monarchy, George III fell into the trap of elevating – or seeming to elevate – a favourite, his Mentor and 'dearest friend', John Stuart, 3rd Earl of Bute, into a political prominence that rested almost exclusively on the monarch's personal support and, in so doing, undermine the Whig constitutional consensus on the operation of the royal prerogative under the Revolution settlement of 1688.

The biographies and essays on George III by Brooke, Hibbert, Bullion, Ditchfield, and Black have despatched the extreme Whig interpretation that alleges he was trying to restore the personal monarchy of his Stuart

---

[8] Cambridge, 1976.
[9] Quentin Skinner, 'The Principles and Practice of Opposition: The Case of Bolingbroke versus Walpole', in *Historical Perspectives: Studies on English Thought and Society in Honour of J. H. Plumb*, ed. Neil McKendrick (London, 1974), 159–89.

forbears.[10] These studies have traced the king's gradual political maturation, his acceptance that even worldly politicians like Henry Fox, or charismatic leaders like Pitt the Elder, were too well-established not to be tolerated by the sovereign, and then the emergence of greater stability in the hands of Lord North, whose family had been so closely associated with the 'Patriot' circle of George III's father, Frederick, Prince of Wales. Brewer's work was particularly important for analysing what it was that made Bute so unpopular, and emphasized the importance of being able to commence the respect, even the affection, of 'the people out of doors' – the artisans and wage-earners who were entitled to an urban vote and who rallied to politicians like John Wilkes, with one foot in the City of London and another in the nation at large. Brewer also explored the material culture of politics, including its rituals and commercialization, enabling historians to understand politics as a form of behaviour as well a matter of political office, executive decision-making, and electioneering. Subsequently, Frank O'Gorman's work on electoral behaviour, *Voters, Patrons and Parties: The Unreformed Electoral System of Hanoverian England*, deepened the historian's grasp of this aspect of the political process.[11]

Brewer's work coincided with further studies in popular behaviour, in keeping with the post-war commitment among Marxist historians, such as E.P. Thompson and Eric Hobsbawm, and their *Marxisant* sympathizers, to rescue the 'people' from the condescension of history. At the same time historians such as John Cannon, Michael Bush, and John Beckett continued to insist that the eighteenth century was an aristocratic century.[12] However, although the architecture and material culture of the eighteenth century continued to be examined outside the academy, particularly in the study of the country house and through debates on the case for its preservation, the trend within the academy remained engaged more with the labouring poor and the energetic crowd. Brewer's pupil Kathleen Wilson provided cogent analyses of corporation power and popular audiences in two cities, Newcastle and Norwich; Nicholas Rogers studied the crowd in Hanoverian Britain; E.P. Thompson traced the evolution from 'customs in common' to a more class-bound, consumerist culture; crime was decoded and the data from the

[10] John Brooke, *King George III* (London, 1974); Christopher Hibbert, *George III: A Personal History* (London, 1999); John Bullion, '"George, Be a King!": The Relationship between Princess Augusta and George III', in *Hanoverian Britain and Empire*, ed. S. Taylor, R. Connors, and C. Jones (Woodbridge, 1998), 177–97; G.M. Ditchfield, *George III: An Essay in Monarchy* (Basingstoke, 2002); Jeremy Black, *George III: America's Last King* (New Haven, CT and London, 2006).

[11] Oxford, 1980.

[12] E.g. John Cannon, ed., *Colloquies on Hanoverian England* (London, 1981); idem., *Aristocratic Century: The Peerage of Eighteenth Century England* (Cambridge, 1984); M.L. Bush, *English Aristocracy: A Comparative Synthesis* (Manchester, 1984); J.V. Beckett, *The Aristocracy in England, 1660–1914* (Oxford, 1986).

Old Bailey trials made available.[13] The middling sort was reinstated, both by understanding its composition and function, and tracing its representation in social and political discourse.[14] Their buying power and that of the better-waged artisan and tradesman were investigated through a new appraisal of the industrial revolution, emphasizing a consumer led rather than a technology led revolution.[15] The desire for greater inclusiveness by the historical profession of the marginal, the derided, or the working majority was admirable, and often entailed the imaginative use of legal records to recover diverse kinds of social experience and economic practice.[16]

But if 'history from below' has transformed a generation of historical research, it need not mean that the elite should now become the object of historical condescension – aside from the lives of aristocratic women who went off the rails, which have appealed so successfully to the wider reading public, as well as being expertly created by reputable scholars.[17] Any social group can and should be studied in its own right, as well as in order to understand the interaction between social ranks. This can sometimes be colourfully reconstructed in accounts of divorce proceedings, when maids' or ostlers' voices are heard as witnesses to the marital misdeeds of the Bon

[13] E.g. Kathleen Wilson, *The Sense of the People: Politics, Culture and Imperialism in England, 1715–1785* (Cambridge, 1994); eadem, 'Empire, Trade and Popular Politics in Mid-Hanoverian Britain: The Case of Admiral Vernon', *Past and Present* 121 (1988), 74–109; N. Rogers, *Crowds, Culture and Politics in Georgian Britain* (Oxford, 1998); E.P. Thompson, *Customs in Common*, (London, 1991); idem, *Whigs and Hunters: The Origin of the Black Act* (Harmondsworth, 1975); Denis Hay et al., *Albion's Fatal Tree: Crime and Society in Eighteenth-Century England* (Harmondsworth, 1975); Tim Hitchcock, *Down and Out in Eighteenth-century London* (London, 2004); V.A.C. Gatrell, *The Hanging Tree: Execution and the English People 1770–1868* (Oxford, 1994); Robert Shoemaker and Tim Hitchcock, ed., *Tales from the Hanging Court* (London, 2007); *The Proceedings of the Old Bailey, 1674–1913*, www.oldbaileyonline.org/, accessed 9 February 2010.

[14] E.g. Jonathan Barry and Christopher Brooks, ed., *The Middling Sort of People: Culture, Society and Politics in England, 1550–1800* (Basingstoke, 1994); Dror Wahrman, *Imagining the Middle Class: The Political Representation of Class in Britain, c. 1780–1840* (Cambridge, 1995). And see the latter's key recent text, *The Making of the Modern Self: Identity and Culture in Eighteenth-century England* (New Haven, CT, 2004).

[15] See especially the writings of Maxine Berg, *The Age of Manufactures, 1700–1820: Industry, Innovation, and Work in Britain* (2nd edn, London, 1994); *Luxury and Pleasure in Eighteenth-century Britain* (London, 2005).

[16] E.g. Craig Meldrew, *The Economy of Obligation: The Culture of Credit and Social Relations in Early Modern England* (Basingstoke, 1998); John Styles, *The Dress of the People: Everyday Fashion in Eighteenth Century England* (New Haven, CT and London, 2007).

[17] E.g. Stella Tillyard, *Aristocrats: Caroline, Emily, Louisa and Sarah Lennox* (London, 1995); Amanda Foreman, *Georgiana, Duchess of Devonshire* (London, 1998); Carola Hicks, *Improper Pursuits, The Scandalous Life of Lady Di Beauclerk* (London, 2001); Hallie Rubenhold, *Lady Worsley's Whim: An Eighteenth-century Tale of Sex, Scandal and Divorce* (London, 2008); and *Wedlock: How Georgian Britain's Worst Husband Met His Match* (London, 2009).

Ton, or more systematically examined in studies of domestic service.[18] In this book, a maid's letter describes Lord Shelburne's apoplectic fury at hearing of his brother's marriage from a family friend, Count Brühl (Chapter 1).

However, if the elite world of high politics attracted less and less attention among academic historians in the last thirty years, it is unsurprising in one respect that Shelburne, unlike Bute, North, Fox, Rockingham, Chatham et al., was left behind. For it was never easy to fit him into the earlier paradigm of elite politics and politicians. Although, as O'Gorman's chapter here explores, in some senses a Chathamite, he was still hard to pigeonhole neatly within the revised understanding of party politics in the age of George III. So his unpopularity in his own times was matched by his unattractiveness to historians. Yet as this collection of essays shows, investigating the popular dimension to later Georgian politics, following the practitioners of 'history from below', reveals some of the most salient features of Shelburne's strengths and weaknesses as a politician. Successful Hanoverian politicians, it can be argued, needed a variety of qualities: to combine a rapport with the monarch and perform well at court; to act within a functioning group or 'party' within Westminster, and the capacity to appeal to both county or urban voters in the family seats, as well as the 'people out of doors', especially in London. Shelburne scored unevenly on all counts. His inability to assimilate into a Whig connection meant he had a very inadequate power base in Parliament; he lacked the common touch; and he was sometimes maladroit in his dealings with the king, despite his useful court connections.

It may even be equally useful to regard Shelburne in his political prime during the early 1780s as aspiring to be the 'king's friend' – a minister unattached to party, but devoted to doing the king's business, a view of politics at odds with the doctrine articulated by the Rockinghams that a king had to appoint ministers as a group. This is the interpretation offered by Disraeli in *Coningsby*. Dziembowski argues in his essay that Shelburne's meeting in 1783 with the Abbé Morellet helped crystallize his view that kings needed to strengthen their executive power, and rule if necessary by restraint, not consensus. Brewer, Wilson, Jeremy Black, and Dziembowski himself have also demonstrated that politics 'out of doors' worked as much by rallying behind a charismatic personality – Admiral Vernon; Pitt the Elder; John Wilkes – as by supporting issues articulated by aristocratic factions.[19]

---

[18] E.g. Stella Tillyard, *A Royal Affair: George III and his Troublesome Siblings* (London, 2006); Rubenhold, *Lady Worsley's Whim*; Carolyn Steedman, *Labours Lost: Domestic Service and the Making of Modern England* (Cambridge, 2009); Kristina Straub, *Domestic Affairs: Intimacy, Eroticism, and Violence between Servants and Masters in Eighteenth-century Britain* (Baltimore, MD, 2009).

[19] Marie Peters, *Pitt the Elder* (London, 1998); Jeremy Black, *Pitt the Elder* (Cambridge, 1992); Edmond Dziembowski, *Les Pitt. L'Angleterre face à la France, 1708–1806* (Paris, 2006).

Shelburne's solitary private education and his incomplete studies at Oxford disadvantaged him from becoming the kind of clubbable and affable politician, such as Lord North, who could succeed in the later Hanoverian political system, while at the same time he lacked the manic charm of Pitt the Elder. Certainly Shelburne had a consistent horror of mob disorder. This may have been linked to his Irish background. John Seed's recent work on the 1780s underlines how Whig fear of a populist crowd such as that led by Lord George Gordon in 1780 against Catholics would steer Burke toward an explicit defence of aristocratic government and prepare the way for the *Reflections on the French Revolution*.[20] These fears governed Shelburne too, even though he was a patron of the utopian radicalism of Richard Price and Joseph Priestley.

Frank O'Gorman and John Cannon explore Shelburne's talents and limitations as a public man in their essays. O'Gorman makes plain that one cannot describe Shelburne as a 'Chathamite' without appreciable qualification. If the maverick one-time 'great commoner' was Shelburne's principal inspiration from the later 1760s, the two men were never on intimate terms and the policy overlap was seldom wholly correspondent. Nevertheless, it was the Chatham political following that Shelburne inherited in 1778 as well as the mantra of 'measures, not men' that may have been high principled but weakened him in terms of parliamentary arithmetic. The latter was never Shelburne's strongest suit as John Cannon makes clear in an authoritative cameo portrait of the ministry of 1782–3. But if Shelburne left too much to chance – and the Secretary to the Treasury, John Robinson – in making an assured majority in both Houses for his government an urgent priority, Cannon also contends that Shelburne (in the manner of Anthony Eden in the mid-twentieth century) might also be deemed a desperately unlucky politician. If a circumstance might conspire against him it usually did and Shelburne lacked that political thickness of skin to be able to respond quickly or creatively. His antennae in the Commons had always been Col Isaac Barré and the leading lawyer, John Dunning, but by the early 1780s age was catching up with Barré and death took Dunning (newly created Lord Ashburton) during the duration of Shelburne's ministry.[21] He had no supportive family members to fall back on in a public crisis: in 1783 his two sons were minors and his only brother, Thomas Fitzmaurice had left the Commons in 1780. Nigel Aston's essay explores the relations between the two brothers, and shows that their uneven relationship and divergent

[20] John Seed, "'The Deadly Principles of Fanaticism": Puritans and Dissenters in Gibbon's *Decline and Fall of the Roman Empire*', in *Reinventing Ancient History*, ed. James Moore, Ian McGregor Morris, and Andrew J. Bayliss (London, 2008), 87–112.

[21] The most up-to-date assessment of Barré, Dunning, and Shelburne's parliamentary following in the 1760s and 1770s is the fine 2006 Oxford D.Phil. dissertation "'Theorists and Politicians": the Earl of Shelburne and the Bowood Circle, c.1760–1783' by Craig Beeston.

ambitions contributed to a weakening of the fraternal axis both publicly and privately. Fitzmaurice has been a submerged character and in retrieving him from completely undeserved obscurity Aston discloses a pioneering aristocratic tradesman who, like his elder brother, followed an individualistic, even maverick course and yet failed to achieve his potential in business even as Shelburne did in politics.

Composite Monarchy, Court Society and Lineage Families

The Atlantic perspective on British History so popular in the Cold War, coupled with the need to understand why George III and his statesmen lost the American colonies, has meant that the four-nation approach, that has illuminated the understanding of the seventeenth-century civil war and Restoration, has proved less attractive than a transatlantic perspective to historians of the Long Eighteenth century.[22] There has also been the counter-attraction of exploring the Jacobite alternative to the Hanoverians, with its narrative of resistance and secret conspiracy – also attractive to the Cold War Era – rather than considering how the four nations worked together after 1688.[23] Irish and Scottish historians had tended more toward exploring their own respective histories, especially, in the case of Scotland, the nature of its Enlightenment. However, Linda Colley's *Britons* was both an influential and popular new synthesis offering a picture of increasing integration by the time of the Napoleonic Wars, and Stephen Conway has underlined the function of the mid-century wars as well as the American war in fostering this integration.[24] Arguably, until the Troubles in Northern Ireland subsided and the Celtic Tiger of the Irish Republic could rediscover its multiple identifies within the EU, it was also hard for historians of eighteenth-century Britain to look at Anglo-Irish relations in an holistic and non-teleological way, simply as a dimension of the eighteenth-century landowning elite of Great Britain, rather than as the prequel to nineteenth- and twentieth-century difficulties with Ireland. This lacuna has been filled in the last decade by the magisterial work of Toby Barnard and

---

[22] See especially J.C.D. Clark, *The Language of Liberty, 1660–1832: Political Discourse and Social Dynamics in the Anglo-American World* (Cambridge, 1994).
[23] E.g. Daniel Szechi, *The Jacobites: Britain and Europe 1688–1780* (Manchester, 1994); Bruce Lenman, *The Jacobite Risings in Britain 1689–1746* (London, 1980); Eveline Cruickshanks, ed., *The Stuart Courts* (Stroud, 2000); E. Cruickshanks and Jeremy Black, ed., *The Jacobite Challenge* (Edinburgh, 1988); Edward Corp, with others, *A Court in Exile: The Stuarts in France, 1689–1718* (Cambridge, 2004).
[24] Linda Colley, *Britons: Forging the Nation, 1707–1832* (New Haven, CT, 1992); Stephen Conway, *War State and Society in Mid-eighteenth-century Britain and Ireland* (Oxford, 2006); idem, *The British Isles and the War of American Independence* (Oxford, 2000).

others.[25] Barnard has recently revisited his work on Sir William Petty, Shelburne's great-grandfather, and suggested Shelburne 'may consciously have seen himself as an intellectual as well as legal heir'.[26]

The preoccupation with Atlanticism and Jacobitism also tended to obscure the perspective of historians of continental varieties of monarchy that emphasized crown-elite relations, and could be productive of more insights within British and Irish contexts. The Namierite legacy of the History of Parliament kept British historians focused on their own *sonderweg*, in which parliamentary institutions loomed larger than crown-elite relations. Yet in studying seventeenth- and eighteenth-century continental polities, the monarch's ability to deal with his or her elite is the most important concept for understanding the management of power, together with regarding states as legal, dynastic, and religious, not territorial, entities. This is a perspective that can also be usefully adapted to understanding the British state.[27] Some progress has been achieved toward revising our understanding of the Hanoverian connection.[28] Yet of course the British monarch was not only an Elector of Hanover, he was also a king of Scotland and of Ireland. Despite Colley's influential *Britons* there remains more work to be done to understand the monarch's multiple roles, and one avenue is to reassess the relations of Irish and Scottish elites both to the crown and to each other. McCahill's work on the Peerage has addressed some issues of how integrated the three peerages became.[29] Arguably, it is elites and their clients who now need to be rescued from the condescension of history: re-examining elites and high politics can and should complement history from below in understanding how Georgian institutions and society functioned. Campbell Orr's

---

[25] T.C. Barnard, *A New Anatomy of Ireland: The Irish Protestants 1649–1770* (New Haven, CT and London, 2003); *Irish Protestant Ascents and Descents 1641–1779* (Dublin, 2004).

[26] Toby Barnard, 'Sir William Petty, Landowner and Improver', in *Improving Ireland: Projects, Prophets, and Pioneers, 1641–1786* (Dublin, 2008), 41–72, quote at 71.

[27] E.g. Jeremy Black, *A Military Revolution? Military Change and European Society, 1550–1800* (Basingstoke, 1991); Mark Greengrass, ed., *Conquest and Coalescence: The Shaping of the State in Early Modern Europe* (London, 1991); Roger Mettam, *Power and Faction in Louis XIV's France* (Oxford, 1988); Jeremy Black, *Kings, Nobles & Commoners. States & Societies in Early Modern Europe. A Revisionist History* (London, 2004).

[28] E.g. Brendan Simms and Torsten Riotte, ed., *The Hanoverian Dimension in British History, 1714–1837* (Cambridge, 2007); Andrew C. Thompson, *Britain, Hanover and the Protestant Interest, 1688–1756* (Woodbridge, 2007). The end of the Cold War with its opening up of archives in the former Soviet bloc has refreshed our understanding of Central Europe (already established by R.J.W. Evans, *The Making of the Hapsburg Monarchy 1550–1700: An Interpretation* [Oxford, 1984] and Norman Davies, *God's Playground: A History of Poland in Two Volumes*, 2 vols [Oxford, 1991] and of the two German Personal Unions, Great Britain-Hanover and Saxony-Poland).

[29] M.W. McCahill, 'Peerage Creations and the Changing Character of the British Nobility, 1750–1830', *English Historical Review*, xcvi (1981), 259–84; ibid., *The House of Lords in the Age of George III (1760–1811)* (Oxford, 2009).

forthcoming study of Queen Charlotte examines this issue through the lens of Queen Charlotte's household, while the History of Parliament's work on the House of Lords promises to be a mine of information.

One reason why crown-elite relations have been a neglected aspect of understanding how the Hanoverians ruled is thus that until relatively recently the royal court has been neglected. Yet the rebirth of Court Studies has shown that courts were a prime locus for the management of elites by the crown, and, in Britain, for their integration within the four nations after 1688.[30] Furthermore, for families repenting their Jacobite antecedents, it could be easier to obtain a Royal Household appointment than a political one. Good examples of this were James, 2nd Earl Waldegrave (1715–63), and his brother and heir John, 3rd Earl (1718–84), whose father had been brought up in France in the household of his uncle, the Duke of Berwick, James II's illegitimate son. They both obtained Household appointments, the former as Governor to the future George III, the latter as Queen Charlotte's Master of the Horse from 1770 to his death in 1784. The 3rd Earl's wife was the aunt of Shelburne's second wife, Louisa Fitzpatrick (see Table 3) and his daughters kept their cousins, and thus Lord Shelburne, au fait with insider news of the Royal Household; so even though out of office for most of his career Shelburne generally had intelligence of what was transpiring at court from well-placed female insiders. Campbell Orr's essay explores how Shelburne's first wife, Sophia Carteret, was similarly very well-connected at court in the 1760s.

The two Celtic kingdoms had an asymmetric relationship with the English Crown and with each other. Ireland retained a parliament until 1800, while the union of Crowns with England and Scotland became an incorporated union in 1707. Although lingering Scottish sentiment for the exiled Stuarts might have suggested it would be more likely to resist assimilation to the new state of affairs, in fact the majority of the elite, from great magnates to the professoriate and lawyers, formed a consensus that Scotland needed to develop itself economically even as it tried to retain its distinctive kirk and legal system.[31] In Ireland, by contrast, any possible unity within the

---

[30] E.g. Hannah Smith, *Georgian Monarchy: Politics and Culture, 1714–1760* (Cambridge, 2006); Hannah Smith, 'The Court in England, 1714–1760: A Declining Political Institution?', *History*, 90:1, No. 297 (2005), 23–41; Clarissa Campbell Orr, *Queenship in Britain 1660–1832: Royal Patronage, Court Culture and Dynastic Politics* (Manchester, 2002); Clarissa Campbell Orr, 'New Perspectives on Hanoverian History', *The Historical Journal*, 52:2 (2009), 513–29; Nigel Aston, 'The Court of George II in the 1750s: Lord Berkeley of Stratton's Perspective', *The Court Historian*, 13:2 (2008), 171–93; R.O. Bucholz, and J. C. Sainty, *Officials of the Royal Household 1660-1837*, 2 vols (University of London, Institute of Historical Research, 1997); *Database of Court Officers 1660–1837*, http://www.luc.edu/history/fac_resources/bucholz/DCO/DCO.html; *Office-Holders in Modern Britain*, http://www.ihrinfo.ac.uk/office.

[31] E.g. Nicholas Phillipson, 'Culture and Society in the 18th Century Province: The Case of Edinburgh and the Scottish Enlightenment', in *The University and Society*, 2 vols,

elite based on a common landowning culture remained fractured by confessional divides, which were intensified after the Glorious Revolution. The post-1691 penal code discriminated harshly against Catholic landowners, while some of the confiscated land was awarded to the Anglo-Irish noble minority.[32]

In Shelburne's case, his ancestral kinsmen the earls of Kerry adhered to Catholicism until the late seventeenth-century and his cousin, the 3rd Earl of Kerry, married a Catholic widow, selling his estates in Ireland in order to live in France. Research on more of Shelburne's Irish kinship networks and their varied strategies in relation to the post-1688 settlement would be most illuminating, starting with Barnard's work on the Pettys specifically and the Irish landowning classes in general.[33] Shelburne's autobiography made it plain how much he associated the old school of patriarchal chieftain-ism with the feudal past of the two Celtic kingdoms. His own family was rooted in the far west of Ireland, the heartland of Kerry power: 'a county quite uncivilized, peopled by Catholicks, reduced by frequent rebellions' and ruled in tyrannical fashion by his grandfather. The Barons of Kerry could trace their prominence back to the thirteenth century, and it was the 22nd baron who became first Earl of Kerry. It is clear Shelburne wanted none of this legacy. In 1761, meeting the 1st and last Duke of Douglas, he considered him 'last of the feudal lords, like my ancestors' who told him 'he could neither read nor write without great difficulty'.[34] The duke's widow was apparently last of old Scottish society to be attended by an halberdier.[35] A peer had to be a modernizer, if nothing else, hence perhaps Shelburne's affinity with modernizing Scottish Whigs such as the 3rd Earl of Bute. Bute sold his town house to Shelburne after his retirement from politics in 1763, and as Orbell shows, was one of his creditors. Both were poor aristocrats on the rise who favoured living in the grand style. A topic deserving further exploration is the friendship and similarity between the Scot and the Irishman (despite

ed. L. Stone (Princeton, NJ and London, 1975), 2, 407–88; Richard B. Sher, *Church and University in the Scottish Enlightenment* (Edinburgh, 1985); Andrew Hook and Richard B. Sher, *The Glasgow Enlightenment: Studies in Eighteenth-century Scotland*, vol. 4 (East Linton, 1995).

[32] See the comprehensive recent overview by Sean Connolly, *Divided Kingdom: Ireland 1630–1800* (Oxford, 2008). Jim Smyth, *The Making of the United Kingdom 1660–1800* (London, 2001), is a recent introduction to the 'New British History'.

[33] See note 15; also Toby Barnard, *Improving Ireland*. Rosemary Raughter's planned biography of Lady Arbella Denny will fill in some of the gaps on the Fitzmaurice kin.

[34] Edmond George Petty-Fitzmaurice, Baron Fitzmaurice, *Life of William, Earl of Shelburne, afterwards First Marquess of Lansdowne*, 2 vols (London, 1912), 1, 5. Shelburne, contrarily, disliked the Douglas heir, who had been brought up in France, finding him over-Frenchified. The impression is unavoidable that Shelburne was a man uncomfortable in his own skin and not easy to please.

[35] GEC, *The Complete Peerage*, ed. G. Gibbs (1916), vol. 4, 440, note.

Shelburne's disclaimers to that identity), the latter being only marginally less unpopular than the former.

A fuller reassessment of eighteenth-century Anglo-Irish society and politics, to marry with the work going on within Irish history itself, can now be anticipated. More studies on the model of Proudfoot's investigation into how the dukes of Devonshire managed their Irish towns would be welcome.[36] A survey examining how many eighteenth-century English gentry, such as Shelburne's Digby relatives through marriage (Table 4) parlayed their way into the English peerage with a prior stage as Irish peers, is also a desideratum. Even where the careers of Westminster-based statesmen are explored, there are neglected aspects, including their roles in Ireland, or neglected statesmen. Ian McCracken, for example, has been researching the oversight of Irish affairs of Philip, 1st Earl of Hardwicke, who is otherwise familiar as Lord Chancellor and later Lord President, a core member of the Newcastle-Pelham ministry.[37] The publication of the *Dictionary of Irish Biography* as this book went to press will clearly be an essential aid in researching eighteenth-century Ireland. Toward redressing this imbalance, in this collection Martyn Powell re-examines Shelburne's role as an Irish politician within Ireland and shows him to be a figure of unsettling originality, unwilling to underwrite either Dublin Castle or the 'Patriot' cause. He was far from a typical absentee landlord, made the occasional visit to his scattered estates, and took an informed interest in them at all times, not least in the old Petty heartlands around Kenmare in the west. He had, Powell writes, a 'broader improving vision' for Ireland and his calculation that the Volunteering Movement would disturb the tranquillity of that kingdom was not one that endeared him to highborn Volunteers like Leinster and Charlemont who looked exclusively to the Rockinghams for Whig endorsement.

The Impact of Family History and Gender Studies

Court Studies provides an important context for understanding the family strategies of the elite, but family history is also significant in its own right, and for its intersection with other perspectives.[38] Chapters 1 and 2 of this book have drawn extensively on Bowood family papers still in the possession of the trustees and, when combined with sources readily available in

---

[36] L.J. Proudfoot, *Urban Patronage and Social Authority: The Management of the Duke of Devonshire's Towns in Ireland 1764–1891* (Washington, DC, 1995).

[37] Ian McCracken, 'Philip, Lord Hardwicke and the Governance of Ireland', paper given 1 February 2010 to Cambridge University History Faculty Modern English History Seminar; J.C.D. Clark, *The Dynamics of Change: The Crisis of the 1750s and English Party Systems* (Cambridge, 1982).

[38] *Family and Friend in Eighteenth Century England: Household, Kinship and Patronage* (Cambridge, 2001).

the British Library, the Bodleian Library, and the John Rylands University Library of Manchester, add a familial dimension to studies of Lord Shelburne in his family setting, which is indispensable to contextualizing and understanding his public activities and postures. Not least importantly, they restore a feminine dimension to his world (Shelburne probably got on better with women than men) in a manner that has been absent from almost every previous study.

As Aston's chapter shows, Shelburne's family background enabled his father to establish a secundigeniture of the ancient barony of Kerry on English soil, facilitated by the Petty inheritance and the crucially important award of the British barony of Wycombe in May 1760 which gave the right, much coveted among ambitious Anglo-Irish politicians and English peers who only had Irish titles, to sit in the British House of Lords. The rise of the Pettys from an Irish earldom to a British marquessate in a single generation was nothing less than astonishing;[39] Shelburne's father barely had time to make his mark as an English baron, before his son succeeded him in 1761. The elaborate monument by Scheemakers in All Saints Church, High Wycombe, stresses the Petty ancestry and virtually remakes the Fitzmaurices as of English descent.[40] This dynastic reinvention was continued by Shelburne, who could not identify with his Irish forebears and claimed that the intelligence in the family came from his Petty ancestress: his grandfather, he wrote, 'married a very ugly woman [Anne Petty], who brought into the family whatever degree of sense may have appeared in it'.[41] The touching monument he erected to his first wife, Sophia Carteret, also suggests his integration into the great Granville family, whose power base was in Cornwall, and it is significant that when elevated to the marquessate he chose a title, Lansdowne, which reflected this wife's ancestry and the lands near Bath which she brought to the marriage. Shelburne's identification with that neglected cosmopolitan statesman of George II's reign, John, 2nd Earl Granville, remains to be recovered but he was in a sense, just like his father-in-law, a politician set apart and distrusted by the Whig oligarchs of succeeding generations.

Of course, marriage to the right person and into the right family was crucial in the establishment of the Shelburne family on the English side of the Irish Sea. Shelburne was both fortunate and unfortunate in his wives: fortunate in that although both were marriages of advantage, they were also companionships of affection; but unfortunate in the short lives of both Sophia Carteret and Louisa Fitzpatrick, and the death of his and Sophia's second son. The work of Elaine Chalus has revivified the study of elites in politics by underlining their social and familiar character, which provided

[39] Nigel Aston writes elsewhere on this subject.
[40] Malcolm Baker, 'Lord Shelburne's "Costly Fabric": Scheemakers, Roubilliac and Taylor as Rivals', *The Burlington Magazine*, 131, no. 1053 (December 1990), 841–8.
[41] Fitzmaurice, *Shelburne*, 2.

a variety of roles for mothers, wives, siblings, and so on. This means that historians of high politics need to take the entire family dimension into account when examining political connection and behaviour.[42]

As an uxorious husband and, later on, as a conscientious uncle, Shelburne enjoyed being at home. Even the waspish Horace Walpole, one of whose main correspondents was Louisa Fitzpatrick's sister-in-law, Anne, Lady Ossory, granted that he had a good character in his domestic life. The marriage with Louisa was intended to facilitate a rapprochement with the Bedford Whigs, but this was never achieved, since George III was determined to remain as distant as possible from Louisa Fitzpatrick's wayward but attractive brother-in-law, C.J. Fox, prime crony of her own brother Richard Fitzpatrick, whose loyalty to Rockingham and Fox in due turn was unshakeable. Campbell Orr's chapter explores the reasons for Shelburne's choice of spouse but also underlines the role of aunts in his upbringing, marriages, and widowerhood.

Shelburne's family life also sheds light on the educational practices of the eighteenth-century peerage. He was intensely ambitious to educate his sons better than he considered he had been, and like many eighteenth-century parents with an experimental educational agenda, he succeeded in producing a reaction. He died alienated from his son by Sophia, but his grandson intermarried with the Digby/Fox relatives of his Fitzpatrick mother, so by the third generation a dynasty of impeccably Whig credentials was successfully founded, despite the biological bad luck and temperamental vagaries between the first two generations (see Table 1). In this at least Shelburne was to prove successful. The 3rd Marquess was a Chancellor of the Exchequer at 25, the 'Maecenas' of the Whigs, generous, clubbable, and enlightened, who would, in time, refuse a dukedom.

Gender studies have alerted historians to the performative character of sexual identity, and have examined the sources from which identity was constructed and validated. Shelburne's uneasy relations with his ambitious father, his repudiation of his Irish forbears and his inferiority complex over his education meant that he was unsure what style of masculinity to adopt.[43]

---

[42] Elaine Chalus, *Elite Women in English Political Life c.1754–1790* (Oxford, 2004); Judith S. Lewis, *Sacred to Female Patriotism: Gender, Class and Politics in Late Georgian Britain* (London, 2003).

[43] On eighteenth-century masculinity, see John Tosh, 'The Old Adam and the New Man: Emerging Themes in the History of English Masculinities, 1750–1850', and Michèle Cohen, 'Manliness, Effeminacy and the French: Gender and the Construction of National Character in Eighteenth-Century England' in *English Masculinities 1660–1800*, ed. Tim Hitchcock and Michèle Cohen (Harlow, 1999); Michèle Cohen, *Fashioning Masculinity: National Identity and language in the Eighteenth-Century* (London, 1996); Philip Carter, *Men and the Emergence of Polite Society: Britain 1660–1800* (Harlow, 2001); Lawrence Klein, 'Gender, Conversation and the Public Sphere in Early Eighteenth-Century England', in *Textuality and Sexuality*, ed. J. Still and M. Worton (Manchester,

On the same day in 1756 his father introduced him to Lord Granville and the 4th Earl of Chesterfield. Should his model become the plainer (but still sophisticated) style of his future father in law, Lord Granville, or the elaborate courtesy of Lord Chesterfield? Shelburne seems in some contexts at least to have adopted the francophile style of the latter. Campbell Orr (Chapter 2) shows that in his struggles to acquire a polite persona Shelburne felt he owed more to his aunt than to his parents. However, Shelburne's rapport with George III (who was his almost exact contemporary) in the first year or two after his accession, may well have been based more on the latter's respect for Shelburne's military prowess during the Seven Years' War than on his proficiency in politeness: the king always respected loyal and brave soldiers. Shelburne's military career is another neglected aspect of his life.

Political Geography and Material Culture

The ownership of an estate at High Wycombe, Buckinghamshire, twenty miles from London, was an important strategic asset for an ambitious politician, enabling him to combine metropolitan and country life very easily. It was also logical for Shelburne's father, a man with Irish roots and estates to purchase land in the West Country: hence the acquisition of Bowood. In his study, *The Making of a Ruling Class: The Glamorgan Gentry 1640–1790*,[44] Philip Jenkins has argued that south-west Wales, Bristol and its hinterland, and southern Ireland, can be regarded as a well-integrated region of Great Britain. Timothy Mowl and Brian Earnshaw have also emphasized the Irish link with Bristol in looking at the development of Irish rococo.[45] With Bowood as an additional power base, based on two more Parliamentary boroughs, the family could combine English, Irish, and Welsh political and economic horizons. Thomas Fitzmaurice's estate in Denbighshire had a similar geographical logic, since much of the passenger trade to Ireland went between Anglesey and Dublin, not Bristol and Dublin. His marriage to an heiress of an estate virtually opposite Windsor Castle also provided a useful strategic locale for anyone with ambitions to shine in London, whether at court or in Parliament, and Fitzmaurice became a serious landowner in his own right, albeit an indebted one, while using his county Sligo and Denbighshire properties for private industrial projects that reflected his links with Matthew Boulton.[46]

1993); Matthew McCormack, *The Independent Man: Citizenship and Gender Politics in Georgian England* (Manchester, 2005).

[44] Cambridge, 1983.

[45] T. Mowl and B. Earnshaw, *An Insular Rococo* (London, 1999).

[46] For the 'geographic turn', see Miles Ogborn and Charles W.J. Withers, *Georgian Geographies: Essays on Space, Place, and Landscape in the Eighteenth Century* (Manchester, 2004).

Shelburne's first marriage to Sophia Carteret made sense geographically, since the Granville family had been major power brokers in Cornwall, as well as owning estates in Wiltshire which were endowed on Sophia at her marriage. Her half-sister Louisa married Thomas Thynne, 2nd Viscount Weymouth (1734–95), the Longleat heir, courtier and politician, for whom the marquessate of Bath was created in 1789, more as a mark of amity and regard than as a political favour (see Table 2). Shelburne's second marriage to Louisa Fitzpatrick also made sense in terms of political geography. Her father and eldest brother (the 1st and 2nd Earls of Upper Ossory – another Irish honour) were based in Bedfordshire, again within relatively easy reach of London, but her sister Mary's marriage to Stephen, 2nd Lord Holland (brother of Charles James Fox) united her to a West Country cousinage of Digbys, Foxes, and Strangways (see Tables 3 and 4). The Digby seat was Sherborne in Dorset; the Holland estate was at Foxley, Wiltshire, and the Fox-Strangways cousins at Redlynch in Somerset. Thus, both marriages helped Lord Shelburne to develop a new West Country power base. This paid off handsomely in the third generation as cousins inter-married, and combined a Digby tradition of courtier service with the Foxite tradition of grand Whiggery at Holland House (see Table 4). Louisa Fitzpatrick's niece, the Hon. Caroline Fox, never married, and shared a house on the Bowood estate with Louisa's half-sister Elizabeth Vernon. They were regularly in Shelburne's company in the last two decades of his life and accompanied him to social events in town and country alike. Both Caroline Fox and Caroline Vernon, later Mrs Robert Smith (and thus sister-in-law of the Whig wit, the Rev. Sydney Smith) became custodians of family history: the former's letters and diaries included accounts of her relatives' political activities, while the latter and her husband were the first editors of a selection of Horace Walpole's correspondence.[47]

Improving country estates was an important occupation of great landowners, and Lord Shelburne was no exception, yet estate improvement is not always included in concepts of the English enlightenment, even though it is an obvious and practical example of the movement. A recent exception is David Wilkinson's *The Duke of Portland: Politics and Party in the Age of George III*.[48] Shelburne's estate management in England deserves as much study as his practices in Ireland, and Martyn Powell's discussion of

47 C.J. Wright, 'The Holland House Set (*act.* 1797–1845)', ODNB Theme, ONDB online, accessed 8 February 2010; idem, Fox, [*later* Vassall]. Henry Richard, third Baron Holland of Holland and third Baron Holland of Foxley (1773–1840), ODNB online, accessed 30 April 2007; V.E. Chancellor, 'Fox, Caroline (1767–1845)', ODNB online, accessed 3 April 2007; E.I. Carlyle, 'Smith, Robert Percy [Bobus Smith], (1770–1845), rev. Kathryn Prior', ODNB online, accessed 8 February 2010; Leslie Mitchell, *Holland House* (London, 1980).
48 London, 2003; see also John Gascoigne, 'Joseph Banks, Mapping and Geographies of Natural Knowledge', in *Georgian Geographies: Essays on Space, Place and Landscape in*

Shelburne's Irish dimension touches on this (Chapter 5). The Sherborne symposium benefited from the insights of John Phibbs, who has challenged interpretations of Lancelot Brown's landscapes offered by Tom Wilkinson.[49] Phibbs explored the cultural and political purpose of the landscapes at Bowood and Wycombe Abbey, arguing they are best understood in terms of what it meant to be English. Patrons of Brown, Lord Shelburne included, belonged to a group of 'improving' landowners who wanted to develop landscape in conjunction with improved pasture. This in turn enabled more horses to be bred and fed, which could be used in Britain's improving infrastructure of roads and carriage technology. This worked toward the improvement of agricultural yield and its exchange in a market economy.[50]

As well as his role as patron of Brown, Shelburne and his father were patrons of Robert Adam, both at Bowood and at Lansdowne House. This has been examined by Eileen Harris in her various studies of Adam, while Maria Perry has written the story of the House itself as a social history. Its library has been identified as a model for the King's Library in the British Museum.[51] Yet Lansdowne House, like Bowood, was not merely a masculine think-tank for an enlightened statesman and his protégés, but also a venue for the large scale entertaining of politicians and people of fashion of both sexes.

In parallel with Campbell Orr's research on Sophia Shelburne's intellectual and religious life, Amanda Vickery has explored her partnership with Lord Shelburne in furnishing and decorating an opulent interior to the town house.[52] This facilitates the intersection of family and cultural history with the new work on gender, taste, and material culture; the academy has discovered the domestic interior as a site of meaning and sociability, not simply an episode in the history of Georgian connoisseurship or polite consumption.[53] Lawrence Klein is currently exploring how Shelburne's type of politeness wound itself into his dealings with the artisans and tradesmen

---

the Eighteenth Century, ed. Miles Ogborn and Charles W.J. Withers (Manchester, 2004), 151–73, esp. 162–4.

[49] Tom Williamson, Polite Landscapes: Gardens and Society in Eighteenth Century England (Stroud and Baltimore, MD, 1995).

[50] Another matrix for this book was the York University Centre for the Eighteenth Century, 'Women and the Country House' project and conference in May 2004.

[51] E.g. Eileen Harris, Country Houses of Robert Adam: From the Archives of 'Country Life' (London, 2007); eadem, The Genius of Robert Adam: His Interiors (New Haven, CT and London, 2001); Tim Knox, 'The King's Library and its Architectural Genesis', in Enlightenment: Discovering the World in the Eighteenth Century, ed. Kim Sloan (London, 2003), 46–57. Maria Perry's study of Lansdowne House was privately published but the editors were able to consult a copy at Bowood House.

[52] Amanda Vickery, Behind Closed Doors: At Home in Georgian England (New Haven, CT and London, 2009).

[53] John Styles and Amanda Vickery, ed., Gender, Taste and Material Consumption in Britain and North America 1700–1830 (New Haven, CT and London, 2007).

who furnished his splendid new homes in town and country.[54] The Irish attitude to material culture has been studied comprehensively in Toby Barnard's
work, such as *Making the Grand Figure*, and he has also looked specifically
at the Caldwell family, who were advised by Shelburne's aunt Lady Arbella
Denny when they were furnishing their new home.[55] The lavish furnishing
of his Mayfair home by Shelburne's cousin, the 3rd Earl of Kerry, a connoisseur and friend of the Prince of Wales, has been investigated by Patrick
Pilkington, and the editors regret that space was too limited to include a
comparison between the two men's tastes and acquisitions.[56] The question
of how Shelburne's houses were financed is probed in this collection by John
Orbell in his important study of the friendship between Shelburne and his
banker, Baring. The acquisition of town and country properties reveals how
much of it was a result of excessive borrowing typical of the later Georgian
aristocracy, who habitually lived on credit. But Orbell's account is also part
of the larger context of trade and public finance (see below).

Confessional State, Enlightened Cosmopolitanism and the Bowood Circle

In 1985, with his *English Society 1688–1832: Ideology, Social Structure and
Political Practice during the Ancient Regime*, J.C.D. Clark challenged British
historians to rethink the secular commercial society of Brewer, Porter and
Langford as an *ancien regime* confessional state.[57] New work on the enlightenment has also argued that it could have a Christian dimension.[58] In this

---

[54] Lawrence Klein, 'The Radical as Aristocrat: The Second Earl of Shelburne, Sociability
and the Aristocratic Vocation', unpublished paper given to the Warwick Eighteenth-
Century Centre, 11 March 2009. The editors are indebted to Dr Klein for providing an
unpublished version of this paper.

[55] Toby Barnard, 'The Artistic and Cultural Activities of the Caldwells of Castle
Caldwell, 1750–1783', *Irish Architectural and Decorative Studies*, 10 (2007), 90–111;
idem, *A New Anatomy of Ireland: The Irish Protestants, 1649–1770* (New Haven, CT and
London, 2003).

[56] Patrick Pilkington, 'Thomas Francis Petty-Fitzmaurice, 3rd Earl of Kerry, 1740–1818:
The Extravagance of an Irish Émigré', dissertation submitted for M.A. Decorative Arts
and Historic Interiors 1660–1800, Birkbeck College, University of London, October
2005.

[57] Cambridge University Press, 1985, revised 2000 as *English Society 1688–1832:
Religion, Ideology and Politics*. Roy Porter, *English Society in the Eighteenth Century* (rev.
edn, London, 1991); John Brewer, below, note 41; Paul Langford, *A Polite and Commercial
People, England 1727–1793* (Oxford, 1992).

[58] Stewart Brown and Timothy Tackett, ed., *Enlightenment, Reawakening and Revolution,
Cambridge History of Christianity*, vol. 7 (Cambridge, 2006); Nigel Aston, *Christianity
and Revolutionary Europe, c1750–1830* (Cambridge, 2002); C. Campbell Orr, 'The Late
Hanoverian Monarchy and the Christian Enlightenment', in *Monarchy and Religion: The
Transformation of Royal Culture in Eighteenth-Century Europe*, ed. M. Schaich (Oxford,

volume, Grayson Ditchfield argues that whatever Shelburne's interests in Dissent and Dissenters, or even his tendencies toward scepticism, as an Anglican landowner he should be understood as a Latitudinarian Whig. He explores his ecclesiastical patronage and his intellectual associations with this wing of the Church of England, and its counterpart in Ireland, together with his parliamentary contribution to church reform and relief for Dissenters. He also explores Shelburne's anti-Catholicism and its Irish context. He concludes that Shelburne's non-dogmatic Protestantism is not adequately characterized by his association with rational Dissent alone, and that in a revolutionary era Shelburne valued an established Church. Campbell Orr shows that his philanthropy at the Bowood estate owed much to Lady Arbella Denny and her affinities with Selina Hastings, 9th Countess of Huntingdon. Both of Shelburne's wives took their religious duties seriously, Sophia Carteret more so than Louisa Fitzpatrick. Sophia was also one of visitors to Mrs Montagu's Bluestocking evenings, and her intellectual and scientific curiosity was strengthened by this as well as by her relationship to Mrs Delany. Lord Shelburne and Mrs Montagu also shared an interest in education and religion, and it was in her house that Shelburne first met Richard Price, the Dissenting minister and radical Utopian. Current perspectives on the Bluestockings have finally begun to acknowledge the importance of religion to them, and to weave them into an account of the English Enlightenment.[59]

Derek Jarrett's *The Begetters of Revolution. England's Involvement with France 1759–1789* (1973)[60] was the first work to attempt situating Shelburne into the context of the Enlightenment in general and the French Enlightenment in particular. One reason for his unpopularity in England may have been the endemic mistrust of the intellectual in politics: the man who seems

2007); B.W.Young, *Religion and Enlightenment in Eighteenth-Century England* (Oxford, 1998); K. Haakonssen, ed., *Enlightenment and Religion: Rational Dissent in Eighteenth-Century Britain* (Cambridge, 1996); Stefan Collini, Richard Whatmore, and Brian Young, ed., *History, Religion and Culture: British Intellectual History 1750–1950* (Cambridge, 2000). For more secular interpretations, see Roy Porter, *Enlightenment and the Making of the Modern World* (London, 2000), based on a 1980 essay; John Gascoigne, *Joseph Banks and the English Enlightenment: Useful Knowledge and Polite Culture* (Cambridge, 1994).

[59] Susan Staves, 'Church of England Clergy and Women Writers', in 'Reconsidering the Bluestockings', ed. N. Pohl and B. Schellenberg, *Huntingdon Library Quarterly*, 65:1–2 (2002), 81–104, does look more squarely, if somewhat tentatively, at the Anglican context, which is foregrounded more trenchantly by Karen O'Brien, *Women and Enlightenment in Eighteenth-Century Britain*, (Cambridge, 2009); C. Campbell Orr, 'The Queen of the Blues, the Bluestocking Queen, and Bluestocking Masculinity', in *Bluestockings Displayed: Portraiture, Performance and Patronage, 1730–1830*, ed. E. Eger (Cambridge, 2012); Sarah Knott and Barbara Taylor, ed., *Women, Gender and Enlightenment* (Basingstoke, 2005); Mark Laird and Alicia Weisberg Roberts, ed., *Mrs Delany and Her Circle* (New Haven, CT, 2009).

[60] London, 1973.

too clever by half finds it hard to succeed in English political culture, where popular appeal is essential to parliamentarians, in contrast with the readier acceptance of intellectuality across the channel. As the Acknowledgements explains, Jarrett's Anglo-French comparative perspective was a *leitmotif* of the symposium which engendered this collection of essays. Yet the symposium suggested that the Bowood circle was more untidy and various than Jarrett's helpful early work suggested. Eagles' essay demonstrates that Shelburne's encounter with French culture was relatively late and linguistically always rather uncertain. Richard Whatmore shows Shelburne's indebtedness to and patronage of francophone Genevan culture, which was distinctively different from the French enlightenment, and intensely wary of France's intellectual, political, and economic might. Emmanuelle de Champs explores the social codes of client–patron relationships, showing the different degrees of dependence and independence of Shelburne's protégés, and unpicking the complex relationship between Shelburne and Bentham. Shelburne's role as patron is also part of the larger story of Bentham's intellectual development, of Etienne Dumont's interpretation of his ideas, and of Anglo-French intellectual republicanism.[61]

Since Jarrett's pioneering work on Shelburne's patronage, Edward G. Andrew has included Lord Shelburne in his study *Patrons of Enlightenment*. As this is the most sustained recent effort to depict Shelburne as a patron, it is worth giving his book some consideration. Unfortunately, the author is a political scientist rather than an historian, and his main concern is how intellectuals today can remain autonomous in the face of the buying power of the great corporations. Therefore his *tour d'horizon* of eighteenth-century Scotland, England, and France is both inconsistent and, from the historical point of view, lacks social nuance. On the one hand, Enlightenment is reduced to a sociological category: 'Enlightenment is the use of plebeian talent for patrician objectives. Plebeians, such as Jean-Jacques Rousseau and Samuel Johnson, who were unwilling to be so used, were not parties to Enlightenment.' Such a bald assertion excises from the English Enlightenment non-plebeians such as the 2nd Duchess of Portland, a collector and naturalist as well as a patron, or the Lincolnshire landowner Sir Joseph Banks, the leading scientist and facilitator of research in George III's reign. On the other hand, plebeian becomes a catch-all category, and the social gradations of eighteenth-century Britain are ignored. It would surprise David Hume, product of old Scottish gentry, to find himself described either as a

---

[61] See Rachel Hammersley, *French Revolutionaries and English Republicans: The Cordeliers Club, 1780–1794* (Woodbridge, 2005); idem, *The English Republican Tradition and Eighteenth-Century France: Between the Ancients and the Moderns* (Basingstoke, 2010); and Cyprian Blamires, *The French Revolution and the Creation of Benthamism* (Basingstoke, 2008). Space precluded the inclusion of chapters by both authors, who contributed to the 2007 Bowood symposium.

plebeian, or as a social equal of the Genevan Rousseau, runaway apprentice, music copyist, and product of a socially uneven marriage between a skilled watchmaker with rights of citizenship and a mother of higher patrician urban status. Moreover, if the Enlightened are confined to plebeians, then university graduates such as Richard Steele and Joseph Addison, enjoying posts as officials, ministers, and diplomats, cannot be fitted into the Enlightened or the enlighteners either; nor can the lawyer Jeremy Bentham, or the Welsh Dissenting minister Richard Price, or the entrepreneurs and professionals of the Lunar Society, who are elsewhere in Andrew's book included among the men of Enlightenment with whom Shelburne associated.[62] Furthermore, William Hunter, Britain's leading gynaecologist and a notable natural historian, who attended Sophia, Lady Shelburne and inoculated her son and her black servant, would also disappear from this limited definition of the Enlightenment. Andrew's analysis is also fundamentally flawed because he misunderstands the word 'squarson', thinking it means the squire bestowing an Anglican living on his son, not a parson who is also a landowner and possibly – through inheriting from older brothers – a peer.[63] Yet Andrew's argument for the limited type of patronage available in England – the bestowal of Anglican livings on their younger offspring – hinges on this misinterpretation. But in any case, as well as appointing clergy to their livings, a patron can employ them as librarians, tutors, and bear leaders; and the latter roles can also be performed by Dissenting clergy – as was Joseph Priestley, tutoring Shelburne's son by his second marriage. The social diversity of the Enlightenment in Britain as a whole escapes the crude social categories of Andrew's analysis.

Rather than simply an Anglo-French comparative perspective, a broader context of Enlightenment cosmopolitanism is required for evaluating Shelburne fully as an Enlightenment figure.[64] Dziembowski puts Shelburne's ideas of executive power and Enlightened monarchy into this wider context. The friendship between Shelburne and Stanislas Augustus Poniatowski, King of Poland, and his Czartoryski relatives, who were entertained at Bowood and who in turn entertained the heir, Earl Wycombe on his Grand Tour, is part

[62] Edward G. Andrew, *Patrons of Enlightenment* (Toronto, 2006), 192; 129; 178.

[63] Nigel Aston, 'An 18th Century Leicestershire Squarson: Robert Sherard, 4th Earl of Harborough, (1719–99)', *Transactions of the Leicestershire Archaeological and Historical Society*, LX (1986), 34–46.

[64] M.C. Jacob, *Strangers Nowhere in the World: The Rise of Cosmopolitanism in Early Modern Europe* (Philadelphia, PA, 2006) explores the cosmopolitanism of literati, natural philosophers and Freemasons. Philip Mansel, *Prince of Europe, The Life of Charles-Joseph de Ligne, 1735–1815* (London, 2003) evokes aristocratic cosmopolitanism. In the British peerage, the Dukes of Richmond were also ducs d'Aubigny in the French peerage, and the Earls Harcourt were the cadet branch of the French ducs d'Harcourt – a cousinage recognized when the latter became émigrés from the French Revolution and stayed with their English relatives.

of this story and needs further examination, as does the latter's travels in Russia, facilitated partly by Jeremy Bentham's brother Samuel, a naval engineer in Catherine the Great's employment.[65] Shelburne, by then a Marquess, consoled himself for relative political inactivity (and it was much less than is commonly imagined) by using Wycombe as his eyes and ears both on the continent and in the United States as well as in Britain in the late 1780s and early 1790s.[66] It was a role that the heir was intelligent enough to play but became increasingly reluctant to do, seeing in it his father's desire for a personal, paternal control that, ironically, Shelburne had resented in his father, the 1st Earl.

Free Trade and Empire

One aspect of this Enlightened cosmopolitanism must be the influence of the Scottish Enlightenment. Shelburne became a proponent of Adam Smith's views when his brother was Smith's pupil in Edinburgh. A commitment to Free Trade may have been one of the tenets most consistently held by Shelburne. Stockley's chapter argues that it was instrumental in establishing a peace strategy with Vergennes in 1783, which gained effective traction as negotiations developed. Shelburne worked well with Rayneval and Vergennes in producing the Peace Preliminaries that Parliament rejected in 1783, partly because his apparent generosity to France fell foul of the resentment of the country gentlemen. Shelburne was widely seen as being ready to give too much away and yet Charles Fox, Foreign Secretary in the Coalition of 1783, ended up with broadly the same package despite his disapproving rhetoric in February. And Shelburne, of course, crucially transmitted his commitment to Free Trade to the Chancellor of the Exchequer in his government, Pitt the Younger. Whatmore shows how Shelburne's encouragement of a group of exiles from Geneva's constitutional struggles of the 1760s, is part of a larger context of how far a city-state such as Geneva can survive in world of free trade dominated by the rival 'commercial monarchies' of France and England. Shelburne was instrumental in trying to establish a colony of Genevan artisans at Waterford in Ireland. He also took a keen interest in the activities of the Lunar Society entrepreneurs and intellectuals who had both Genevan and Scottish connections.[67] Lord Shelburne's economic and financial enquiries, aided by papers written for him

---

[65] Richard Butterwick, *Poland's Last King and English Culture: Stanislaw August Poniatowski, 1732–1798* (Oxford, 1997).

[66] Nigel Aston writes elsewhere about Shelburne's public career after 1783.

[67] R. Whatmore, ed., *Geneva, An English Enclave, 1725–1814* (Geneva, 2009), including Whatmore, 'The Role of Britain in the Political Thought of the Genevan Exiles of 1782', 185–97, and C. Campbell Orr, 'Rousseau's Disciples at the Court of George III

by Baring, as Orbell shows (Chapter 4), are also part of the larger story of the interest taken in questions of public credit on both sides of the Channel in the eighteenth century, currently being researched by scholars such as Richard Whatmore, Istvan Hont, and Michael Sonenscher.[68]

The larger context of Imperial policy in the Caribbean, North America, and India is obviously crucial and in need of detailed research. Although Atlantic perspectives have became significant, with the emphasis on the first British Empire as an 'Empire of Goods', Shelburne's interest in trade and colonial issues has not led to his being factored very extensively into the trans-Atlantic debate on empire and the nature of the American revolution.[69] However, the editors are aware that the Atlantic historian, David Hancock of the University of Michigan, is researching a study of Shelburne and assume the imperial dimension will be a significant part of his forthcoming study.[70]

The Current State of Shelburne Studies Summarized

Shelburne's personal, financial, and intellectual resources as well as his political behaviour have cried out for reintegration, and these essays are a means to that very desirable end, based principally on archival scholarship and acute historical intelligence, for there were many pieces to Shelburne's world and a conventional high political straitjacket is not going to contain very many of them. Here a broader and yet a detailed view of things is projected, and if this serves to encourage more extended biographical coverage in addition to David Hancock's study, then the editors will have achieved an important objective. Two generations on from Derek Jarrett's pioneering investigation of Shelburne and the Bowood Circle, he is ripe for re-examination in a historical world that has taken a cultural turn to which all scholars are committed. It is still much too early given the current state of scholarship to expect authoritative answers but we can, meanwhile, take

and Queen Charlotte', 113–34; Jenny Uglow, *The Lunar Men: The Friends Who Made the Future, 1730–1810* (London, 2002).

[68] See references in Whatmore, Chapter 12; and also Istvan Hont, *Jealousy of Trade: International Competition and the Nation-state in Historical Perspective* (Cambridge, MA, 2005); Michael Sonenscher, *Before the Deluge: Public Debt, Inequality, and the Intellectual Origins of the French Revolution* (Princeton, NJ, 2009).

[69] E.g. John Brewer and Roy Porter, ed., *Consumption and the World of Goods* (London, 1994); John Brewer and Ann Bermingham, *Consumption of Culture 1600–1800: Image, Object, Text* (London, 1995); J.G.A. Pocock, ed., *Three British Revolutions, 1641, 1688, 1776* (Princeton, NJ, 1980); idem., *Virtue, Commerce and History, Essays on Political Thought and History, Chiefly in the Eighteenth Century* (Cambridge, 1985).

[70] The editors regret that invitations to a dialogue on mutual interests were not reciprocated.

stock of what these essays provisionally suggest at this early stage of reconstruction.

They are uncompromising in locating Shelburne within a complicated personal and familial milieu within which his relations with women were rather more satisfying than with his own sex and led him (in his remarkable fragment of 'Autobiography', c. 1800) to insinuate a range of critical and vitriolic comments about his forbears that have been uncritically received. Shelburne had a twisted and selective dynastic awareness (and perhaps a sense of destiny that grew soured) but it looks as if ancestral pride was limited to lauding the character and achievements of his Cromwellian ancestor, Sir William Petty, and was graphically demonstrated in his refusal to be buried in the mausoleum at Bowood that his father had constructed. Throughout his public career, certainly until the death of Louisa, Lady Lansdowne, in 1789, Shelburne lived the life of a grandee with two great estates in England, one of the most palatial London townhouses and a massive Irish acreage. Yet appearances were deceptive. Money problems connected to the family settlement were never far away and might well have overwhelmed him in the 1790s had it not been for the careful oversight of Sir Francis Baring. They undoubtedly affected and hindered his political impact in ways that still need to be reconstructed. And he was otherwise publicly hobbled. Thus after the most glittering start in the political world at the beginning of George III's reign, Shelburne took a tumble at the hands of Henry Fox in 1762–3 from which his reputation never wholly recovered. Thereafter, he exhibited a professional interest in (if not a matching competence for) the problems of government that arguably had no equal among the British nobility of the later eighteenth century. Scorched by his upbringing and experiences at the fag end of Lord Bute's administration, Shelburne distanced himself from his peers and came to see the royal prerogative wielded by an enlightened minister (preferably himself) as the best means of delivering efficient government.

Never entirely a convincing Pombal or even a Choiseul, Shelburne's reputation as a rather slippery King's Friend was born out of necessity as much of conviction and yet King George had little more time for him as an individual than any of the politicians. That is one paradox: another is that this accomplished parliamentarian and debater found it beyond his capacities to build up an extended political following; he lacked the skills and his interest was limited. Yet this weakness vitiated so much of his impact, nullified so many of his administrative aspirations. When he had an opportunity to stand firm as Premier in February 1783 (and might have been expected to stand firm given his proven courage as a soldier) Shelburne gave up the game in a semi-sulk from a far stronger parliamentary situation than Pitt the Younger found himself the following December. Yet, perhaps the complex and many dimensional character of British political culture in the late eighteenth century needs constantly to be borne in mind, before all reason for failure is laid at the feet of specific politicians. They had to operate in an imperial and composite monarchy, which was also in personal union with Hanover – always a complicating factor in foreign policy; they had to please the crown, both Houses of Parliament and the 'people out of doors'; and they often needed good luck to being policies to fruition at a time when both Britain and her main rival France were being profoundly changed by global trade and the Enlightenment. Shelburne did not always manage to operate equally effectively in all these contexts, and he may have been too cerebral and indecisive for sustained success, but his was surely a comprehensible failure.

Shelburne left for the continent in 1783 and then retreated to Bowood. It was always at Bowood that he found his friends, rather than at Westminster, but it would be useful if some reconstruction of the large numbers of guests who attended receptions in the London town house could be mustered. There was, however, no static Bowood Circle: it changed over time and was more a series of Circles than one steady state. If historians have over-emphasised the importance of Bentham, then they have also underestimated the contribution of Adam Smith's ideas to his intellectual formation, and they have not always distinguished between French intellectuals and the very specific francophone milieu of Geneva. Moreover, although his own personal religious convictions remain somewhat opaque, he must be seen as a landowner operating in an Anglican context in both England and Ireland, supplemented by the family philanthropy managed by his female relatives.

So much already appears apparent, although we are still a considerable distance from a fully informed and contextualised picture of Lord Shelburne. As this introduction suggests, any reassessment of a major British politician needs to deploy a very inter-disciplinary repertoire of approaches, and this is particularly the case for Lord Shelburne, given his combination of extensive intellectual engagement yet limited abilities in political management, together with his complex stance toward his roots in the Anglo-Irish ascendancy. These essays, meanwhile, show that the process of recovery is well underway and will offer both a more rounded and more accurate understanding of this key figure, in European and not just British political culture.

Part One

Family, Piety, and Finance

1

Petty and Fitzmaurice:
Lord Shelburne and his Brother

NIGEL ASTON

Prologue: Two Legacies

The focus in this chapter is primarily on the turbulent and unsatisfying relationship that persisted between Lord Shelburne and his younger brother, the Hon. Thomas Fitzmaurice (1742–93). They illustrate parallel paths in integrating themselves as an ancient Anglo-Irish family, more Irish than English and primarily resident in Ireland, into the British political and cultural establishment, with seats respectively in both British Houses of Parliament. Their dealings towards each other were characterized by a caution and often a distance that had its origins in early life and is symbolized by their different surnames: respectively, Petty and Fitzmaurice. For Thomas was no ordinary younger son: he was made the heir to many of the Fitzmaurice properties in Ireland which came to him in 1761 and 1780, whereas his brother, the 2nd Earl, acquired principally the Petty settled estates from his father. Shelburne's relations with his closest male family members were often awkward and strained and one might say that the multiple misunderstandings between the siblings nicely parallel the 2nd Earl's habitually awkward dealings with other members of the late eighteenth-century British political elite. Though Thomas in life had an equivalent share of disappointments and frustrations to Shelburne's, he was a pioneering gentleman industrialist and his career and character desperately need rescuing from the shadow of his elder brother's. This chapter is an initial attempt at recovery.

The seeds of fraternal disgruntlement were sown while William (the future 2nd Earl) (Figure 1) and Thomas (Figure 2) were boys being brought up in Ireland during the 1740s. Both were scions of one the oldest families in the kingdom, the Kerrys, being the two children of the Hon. John Fitzmaurice, and grandsons of Thomas, 21st baron of Kerry (1668–1742), of Lixnaw, county Kerry, to whom an Irish earldom had been granted in 1722/3 (Table 1). Thomas was named in honour of his grandfather (who died shortly before his conception) just as William had been christened after his maternal great-grandfather, Sir William Petty, the celebrated Surveyor

1. William Petty, 1st Marquess of Lansdowne by Jean-Laurent Mosnier, 1791, Trustees of the Bowood Estate

2. The Hon. Thomas Fitzmaurice, by Sir Joshua Reynolds, date unknown, Trustees of the Bowood Estate

General of Ireland under Cromwell. His names also echo his uncle the 2nd Earl of Kerry (1694–1747), his maternal grandfather Col. William Fitzmaurice, and his paternal great-grandfather, William, the 20th baron of Kerry. However, for Thomas any expressions of dynastic piety carried at first no particular presumption of material expectation: he was the younger son of a younger son, and would have to find his way in the world like others endowed with a small birthright. Then, quite suddenly, all that changed in April 1750 when the direct line of the Pettys failed through the death, without legitimate issue, of his uncle James Petty, Viscount Dunkerron, followed by the demise in April 1751 (without other surviving offspring) of the latter's father, Thomas's great-uncle Henry Petty (1675–1751), 1st and last Earl of Shelburne of the first creation (1719). Three elder brothers having predeceased him, William and Thomas's father the Hon. John Fitzmaurice (1706–61) thereupon succeeded to the Petty estates in Ireland and England and went to live in England. To confirm this acceptance, he changed his surname (and that of his eldest son William) to Petty, following the terms of his uncle Henry's will, and duly had the Irish earldom of Shelburne revived in his favour in 1753. Thomas, however, remained Fitzmaurice, since he stood to inherit some residual property of the Kerry family that came to his father John on the death of the 1st Earl of Kerry in 1742[1] as well as lands owned by his mother, Mary. She was her husband's first cousin and daughter of Col. the Hon. William Fitzmaurice of Gallane, County Kerry, younger brother of the 1st Earl of Kerry. Shelburne long nourished a sense of resentment that his brother had been excessively provided for whereas he, per contra, had been hemmed in by restrictive legal settlements that had been deliberately engineered by his father, the 1st Earl, and John Monck, the sole trustee of Henry, Lord Shelburne's estate. He considered he had been saddled with the settled estate while the more advantageous purchases made by the two boys' parents in the 1750s were to go to Thomas, 'the constant view both of my father & mother being to make a second family in the person of my brother'.[2] This was at the root of brotherly disaffection.

---

[1] According to Shelburne these holdings produced £3000 pa in 1760 and 40 years later were generating double that sum; Fitzmaurice, *Shelburne*, i. 5. The inheritance was bitterly contested by the dowager countess of Kerry on behalf of her son, the 3rd earl (a minor, to whom she stood executrix and sole guardian). The dispute lasted five years and went to the Irish House of Lords. See BHA, Box Lab 1/1/4: Property of the Lords of Kerry 1300–1800: 'Case of the Respondent: Francis Thomas, Earl of Kerry (a minor) by Lord Newport, his Guardian and next Friend, Appellant. John Petty, Lord Viscount Fitz-Maurice, Respondent, to be heard at the bar of the [Irish] House of Lords on [4 March 1752]; 7 printed pp.

[2] BHA, S. 89 'Papers concerning Henry Lord Shelburne's Trust and the settlement made by William Lord Shelburne in 1788', f. 108. Sir Gilbert Elliot reported in 1758: 'Lord Shelburn [the 1st earl] has an immence estate, and can afford if he pleases to settle ten thousand a year upon his second Son without at all hurting Lord Fitsmorris [*sic*], …'

Of course, if John, the 1st Earl, was excessively eager to make provision for the younger son it was surely because he had been one himself.

Divergent Educations

Looking back on his childhood and adolescence from the vantage point of 1800–01 (after a decade of wrangling with his own eldest son), Lord Shelburne (by then 1st Marquess of Lansdowne), discerned few expressions of adult love given him. According to this account, his father John had 'no notion of governing his children except by fear'[3] and, though he praised his mother's intelligence and drive, he did not write affectionately of her and, no less significantly, never mentioned his brother Thomas. The latter's experience of growing up appears to have been less troubled: from an early age, he was the favourite son (as well as the heir) of his mother, the 1st countess (d. 1780), and he was more willing than his brother William to be led by his father. After a private education in Dublin, in 1756 the eldest son quitted Christ Church, Oxford, for the army. This precipitate action (although it turned out in many ways to be the making of the young Viscount Fitzmaurice) vexed and disappointed his father and left William thereafter readily lamenting the deficiencies of his education.

By contrast, Thomas's formal education was altogether more suitable for a young person preparing to enter public life, probably more appropriate for a first rather than a second son. In 1755 he was sent to Eton where he remained for the next three years[4] and then, most unusually for the son of a non-Scottish peer, he was sent to the University of Glasgow, matriculating in 1759. His brother William was directly involved in this decision. Believing that Thomas would be as unhappy at Oxford as he had been, he asked the advice of David Hume's friend, the Scottish MP, literary patron, and follower of Lord Bute, Sir Gilbert Elliot, 3rd baronet of Minto (1722–77), who proposed sending him to study at Glasgow under the direction of Adam Smith. Elliot described Thomas to Smith as:

To Adam Smith, 14 November 1758, in *The Correspondence of Adam Smith*, ed. Ernest Campbell Mossner and Ian Simpson Ross (Oxford, 1977), p. 26.

Under his father's will, Thomas Fitzmaurice did indeed receive £10,000 on reaching 21 and an annual sum thereafter chargeable to the Petty estates. National Library of Ireland, D. 10,553 Last will and testament of 1st earl of Shelburne, 5 April 1756.

[3] Fitzmaurice, *Shelburne*, I, 6.

[4] His father reported him at school 'grown & very like an over-fed English clown'. Shelburne to Lord Fitzmaurice, 31 March 1757, BHA, S. 90, f. 41. According to Edmond Malone, Fitzmaurice at Eton was 'a light headed foolish boy'. *The Diary of Joseph Farington, 1747–1821*, ed. Kenneth Garlick and Angus Macintyre (New Haven, CT, 1978), ii, 494, 13 February 1796.

… a very good Scholar, very lively, and tolerably ungovernable, but probably will not give you much trouble, as you will have the total charge and direction without any controul. [5]

It proved to be a happy experience for all parties and Adam Smith early reported back to Shelburne that Fitzmaurice displayed ability and worked hard: 'There is not a poor boy in the college who is supported by charity and studies for bread that is more punctual in his attendance upon every part of College discipline.'[6] He benefited from the modernity of Glasgow's curriculum in relative contrast to Oxford's, taking classes in philosophy, modern and ancient languages, mathematics, moral philosophy, and even staying in residence during the vacations for further private tuition. The 1st Earl was delighted with Smith's endeavours. He wanted his son '… to be convinc'd, that it is His happiness and not my own, that I have in view. I wish him to become an honest and a Benevolent man; I wish him Punctual and Sober; a lover of Method, and so skill'd in Figures and the businesses of Life, as by Assisting me in my latter days, he may make me rejoice at my Labours in his early ones.' Thomas's father set store by the knowledge his son would gain of the Civil Law as a preparation for studying English law, thus facilitating a legal career south of the border, and assured Smith that 'it is upon Your Precepts and Example in Morality, that I depend for making him Happy'.[7] Nor did Fitzmaurice's higher education cease after he left Glasgow in 1761: his father entered him at St Mary Hall, Oxford the same year, where he impressed Sir William Blackstone. The latter wrote that October:

His points are lively, his apprehension quick and mixed with a solidity of judgment rarely to be found in so young a man. Free, affable, and unembarrassed in conversation, even among strangers, fondest of such subjects as may improve his understanding, yet pleasant and humorous upon common topics.[8]

Blackstone's impression of the nineteen-year-old undergraduate – with quite strikingly different traits compared to his elder brother – was substantially confirmed in later life. Fitzmaurice was a clubbable man with literary friends and was indeed in time elected a member of Samuel Johnson's celebrated Club; Shelburne lost whatever early taste he exhibited for club life and preferred to associate with dissenters and continental intellectuals. Thomas nevertheless left Oxford within a year without taking his degree and with any plans for the completion of his academic progress thrown into jeopardy by the 1st Earl's sudden demise in June 1761. Nevertheless, equipped

---

[5]   Elliot to Smith, 14 November 1758, in *Correspondence of Adam Smith*, ed. Mossner and Ross, 26–7.
[6]   Smith to Shelburne, 10 March 1759, in ibid., 29.
[7]   Shelburne to Smith, 26 April 1759, in ibid., 37, 38.
[8]   To Shelburne, 19 October 1761, quoted Fitzmaurice, *Shelburne*, I, 312.

with these advantages of education and inheritance, Thomas Fitzmaurice was well-placed to make his way in the world alongside his elder brother, now the head of the family. Yet that somehow never happened to the mutual advantage of the brothers. The death of their father, only a year after gaining his much sought-after British barony as Lord Wycombe, and when they were aged only twenty-four and nineteen respectively, conferred dynastic duties and responsibilities both might reasonably have preferred to defer for some years.

Diverging Politics

For a start, it took William off to the British House of Lords after only a few months as an MP. In 1761 he was still at a very early stage in forming a political connection and it was natural that he should look to his brother to join him in Parliament at the earliest opportunity. Indeed he was so desperate that Thomas Fitzmaurice became MP for Calne on 29 December 1762 still six months short of his legal majority. It was a dutiful response on the latter's part as the younger brother, though whether it coincided with inclination is open to question. Fitzmaurice came in when Shelburne had fallen out with Bute and Henry Fox and was struggling to realign himself in the often bitter factional jostling of the early years of George III's reign. In these circumstances, and possibly indicating his own unsettled political conviction, Fitzmaurice loyally if unenergetically followed Shelburne's lead.

Judged politically, it was an average performance. He is reported to have spoken only twice in the Parliament of 1761–8:[9] on 23 January 1765 he defended the conduct of Shelburne 'who ... did not retire to faction but adhered to his principles' and, four days later, spoke out against general warrants.[10] Significantly, although his brother was Secretary of State for the Southern Department during the Chatham administration of 1766–8, there is no evidence that Shelburne attempted to find a junior government post for Thomas. It was indicative of a degree of tension between the two brothers that was never completely resolved, and also suggested that the limits of their political cooperation had been reached. Having been somewhat unsettled by the premature death of a father whom he was accustomed to obeying, Thomas Fitzmaurice had charted an unsteady public track during

[9] He was, concurrently, MP for Co. Kerry on the Irish family interest, 1763–8, Edith Mary Johnston-Liik, *History of the Irish Parliament 1692–1800*, 6 vols (Belfast, 2002), iv, 174–5.

[10] Thomas Fitzmaurice may have found parliamentary speaking an ordeal in a way that Shelburne did not. William Baker reported on the latter occasion to a Mr Talbot, 4 February 1765, that 'Mr Fitzmaurice ... gave us a speech on I know not what which he had studied all the summer at his looking glass'. Baker mss quoted in Namier, *History of Parliament*, ii, 430.

his twenties. He had not settled to any profession, putting his name on the books at the Middle Temple in 1762, being called to the bar in 1768, and yet not practising. Neither did he start any business ventures in these years. Thomas was trying to manage on the proceeds of his Irish inheritances while living as a man about town and beginning to mix in literary circles. Moreover, his brother's felicitous first marriage and the birth of an heir to the earldom in 1765 negated whatever prospects had existed between 1761 and 1765 of Thomas consolidating the estates of both his parents in himself.

Not that he was entirely without political ambitions. Chafing at the constraints of being the 2nd Earl's torchbearer as MP for Calne, Fitzmaurice tried to establish an alternative and independent position for himself by standing as a candidate for the University of Oxford at a by-election caused by the death early in 1768 of one its two MPs, Sir Walter Bagot. It was a daring, slightly improbable venture: Fitzmaurice was trading on his brother's status as a Secretary of State in the rapidly disintegrating Chatham administration at the same time as he was attempting to emerge into the political limelight in his own right. Yet he had some advantages: Shelburne's estate at High Wycombe just over the county boundary in Buckinghamshire gave him a useful jumping-off base from which to cultivate University opinion; there was a growing respect for his character in metropolitan literary circles and he showed himself unwilling to upset Tory susceptibilities within the University in a manner that might not have been expected from Shelburne's brother. Unlike the earl, Fitzmaurice seems to have been permanently affected by the teaching and 'Church & King' loyalism of Dr William King and by the late 1760s this political maturation was in itself making it harder for the two brothers to present a united parliamentary front.[11]

Overall it was an attractive candidature. As W.R. Ward suggests:

> Shelburne's candidate therefore might attract Radical votes whether of nominally Tory or Whig origin and, if elected, would free the family borough at Calne for another candidate to support the earl at the new turn in his politics.[12]

Fitzmaurice elicited a range of support that suggested that, for the University, he was the right sort of candidate: well-educated, the younger son of a nobleman, and respectful of its institutional independency. The younger MAs of his own age liked him, as did the Tory friends and followers of Dr King, and others in All Souls and Magdalen Colleges. However, like the other candidates, Fitzmaurice pulled out of an unwinnable contest once Sir

---

[11] The Shelburne–King relationship is discussed in David Greenwood, *William King: Tory and Jacobite* (Oxford, 1969), 299–302.

[12] W.R. Ward, *Georgian Oxford: University Politics in the Eighteenth Century* (Oxford, 1958), 228. Full details of the two 1768 parliamentary are given in ibid., 226–36; L.S. Sutherland, 'Political Respectability 1751–1771', in *The History of the University of Oxford. Vol. 5. The Eighteenth Century*, ed. L.S. Sutherland and L.G. Mitchell (Oxford, 1986), 129–61 at 155–60.

William Dolben, a descendant of archbishops both of York and Canterbury, announced on 25 January 1768 that he would accept nomination for the vacancy. Fitzmaurice tried again to secure a University seat at the General Election but with no more success. He was therefore obliged to seek election once more with his brother's backing and he was returned unopposed for Calne in 1768. Though he voted regularly with the Opposition in the 1768–74 Parliament, he affected a show of independence from Shelburne that reflected the genuine political differences between them that were becoming more pronounced with every year. When coupled with his erratic attendance at the Commons, it reduced his parliamentary value to his elder brother almost to a nullity. If anything, Fitzmaurice may be classified as a Northite, a status underlined when Lord North awarded him an honorary DCL on the occasion of his installation as Chancellor of Oxford University in 1773.

How far Fitzmaurice had departed from Shelburne's perspective on the place of Church reform was graphically illustrated in 1772 when he spoke regularly in the Commons against attempts by dissenting ministers and teachers petitioning to obtain legislative relief from subscription to the 39 Articles as required under the 1689 Toleration Act.[13] This occurred precisely at the time that Shelburne's links with radical non-Anglicans were becoming more pronounced: in 1772 he had invited the French *philosophe*, the abbé Morellet, to England, asked the rational dissenter and chemist Joseph Priestley to be his librarian at Bowood, and was relying increasingly on the Arian minister Richard Price for advice on public finances.[14] The latter had even drawn up a careful case for relief that was sent to Chatham with Shelburne's in hopes (that were gratified) of encouraging him to speak for Sir Henry Hoghton's bill for relief from subscription in Parliament.[15]

---

[13] On 6 February, Fitzmaurice laced his speech claiming the petitioners denied 'the divinity of Christ' with quotations from *The Confessional* and Blackstone's *Commentaries*. Cavendish's 'Debates', BL Egerton MS 244, 214–20; Sir Roger to Lady Newdigate, n.d. [1772], marked 'Accounts of Debates upon Sir William Meredyths motions against the Church, 39 Articles etc', in 'The Correspondence of Sir Roger Newdigate of Arbury Warwickshire', *Publications of the Dugdale Society*, vol. 37, ed. A.W.A. White (Hertford, 1995), 177; Ward, *Georgian Oxford*, 248; Grayson Ditchfield, '"How Narrow Will the Limits of this Toleration Appear?" Dissenting Petitions to Parliament, 1772–1773', in 'Parliament and Dissent', *Parliamentary History*, ed. Stephen Taylor and David L. Wykes (Edinburgh, 2005), 91–106, at 95. Shelburne's speech in favour of extending the rights of dissenters is discussed in Craig Beeston, '"Theorists and Politicians": The Earl of Shelburne and the Bowood Circle, c. 1760–1783' (unpub. Oxford D.Phil., 2006), 133–4.

[14] 'An account of the Origin and Dissolution of Lord Shelburne's Connection with the Dissenters', *Gentleman's Magazine*, 53 (1783); Derek Jarrett, *The Begetters of Revolution. England's Involvement with France 1759–1789* (London, 1973), 130–5.

[15] Marie Peters, *The Elder Pitt* (Harlow, 1998), 214; Jeremy Black, *Pitt the Elder* (Cambridge, 1992), 287. Shelburne also spoke for the Bill which was lost in the Lords by 102 votes to 29.

It says much for the filial ties between the two and, perhaps, of Shelburne's sense of responsibility for his brother and of respect for his abilities, that the earl kept Fitzmaurice in Parliament in 1774, securing his return unopposed, this time for Wycombe. Shelburne, after all, only had three Commons seats at his disposal, two for Calne and one for Chipping Wycombe, both adjacent to his principal estates. And these were understandably earmarked for his supporters, not a term that any longer described Fitzmaurice. By 1774 Shelburne had established himself as a formidable presence on the opposition benches in the Lords and his talented lieutenants in the Commons, notably Isaac Barré and John Dunning, reinforced his importance as 'the protector of patriotic orators, political pamphleteers, and experimental philosophy'[16] in a way that mere numbers could not. Along with advisers like Price and Priestley, they constituted part of an emerging 'Bowood Circle' that was a key component of Shelburne's political clout. Fitzmaurice stood at a remove.[17] In the 1774–80 Parliament he proved himself to be so much deadwood, haphazard in his attendance and behaving not as a resourceful follower of his elder brother but more as a political independent.[18]

Different Family Strategies

Fitzmaurice's parliamentary inertia reflected his preoccupation with his personal affairs. These caused deterioration in his fraternal relationship at the same time as they apparently benefited him personally. He was still a bachelor in 1774, normally resident in London and leasing a substantial manorial property on the Isle of Wight at Knighton Gorges in the parish of Newchurch.[19] If the revenues generated by his Irish interests continued to be disappointing, Fitzmaurice was assured of the pecuniary support of his mother, Mary, the dowager countess of Shelburne who, despite failing health, remained a personal and financial force to be reckoned with in the family. From the late 1750s she had developed her estate at Ballymote,

---

[16] Anon., A Letter to the Right Honourable the Earl of Shelburne, on the motives of his political conduct, and the principles which have actuated the Opposition to the measures of the administration in respect to America (London, 1776), 1.

[17] For the Bowood Circle, see Jarrett, The Begetters of Revolution, passim; idem., 'The Bowood Circle, 1780–1793: Its Ideas and Influences' (unpub. Oxford B.Litt., 1955); Beeston, 'Theorists and Politicians', passim.

[18] Beeston, ibid., 32, crucially notes that many MPs who were nominally his followers in the 1768, 1774, and 1780 Parliaments, 'displayed a marked absence of loyalty in their parliamentary behaviour'. However, he exaggerates in classifying Fitzmaurice as one of those eleven men who formed 'The true kernel of the earl's support'.

[19] It was leased from the trustees of George Maurice (or Maurice George) Bisset (1757–1821) who was due to succeed to the estate in 1778; Hallie Rubenhold, Lady Worsley's Whim (London, 2008). He had also owned land in Shanklin.

County Sligo, by opening a factory for weaving and other manufacturing processes and took many of the rents on her estates not in cash but in raw linens. Since this was part of his own inheritance, Thomas Fitzmaurice became closely involved in the management of the Ballymote factory and it became the bedrock of his own schemes for generating wealth in a manner that would have pleased his aunt, Lady Arbella Denny, and his former tutor, Adam Smith. Mary, Lady Shelburne had always been closer to Thomas than William and the property disputes that followed on from the 1st Earl's death in 1761 further poisoned her affections for his successor in the title. After the death of Shelburne's first wife in 1771, Shelburne and his mother quarrelled and drifted further apart than ever. In Shelburne's own words '... nothing but a series of improprietys, & harsh Returns, could have effected that total alienation, which it must be own'd has taken place'.[20] He rarely attended her at her residence in Twickenham whereas Thomas was there regularly.

The earl's relation by marriage, Elizabeth, Lady Tweeddale (his late wife's half-sister, the widow of the 4th Marquess), implored him to make up their quarrel: '... I am sure you wou'd never forgive yourself if another fit wou'd carry her off in her <u>present situation</u>'. However, Shelburne found faults and initiative wanting on the other side, not his, writing 'I have withstood a great deal of provocation and shall continue to do so. As to them, I must leave them to act, as they think proper'.[21] The implication was clear: he saw Thomas and his mother acting in concert, with the younger son expecting to inherit the entire portion of his mother's properties and investments despite the growing encumbrances of the Petty estates. Shelburne had held back from litigation and yet his restraint had done nothing to make the family a more cohesive unit. The two brothers continued to exchange fairly jocular letters (at least on Fitzmaurice's side) and this was the best that they could do given their divergent financial interests and realization of their political mismatch.

Supported by his mother, Thomas next attempted to consolidate his status as an independent country gentleman with an interest in his own right by leasing an estate in north Wales at Lleweni Hall, Denbighshire, from Sir Robert Salusbury Cotton, 5th bt. (c. 1739–1809) in early 1776.[22] It had the convenience of being close to Holyhead, the most often used embarkation point for Ireland, while allowing scope for the small-scale industrial development that Fitzmaurice hoped would finally give him an assured income. Shortly afterwards, at Taplow Court on 21 December 1777, he wedded a woman he expected to be an heiress, Lady Mary O'Bryen (b. 1755), the only surviving child of Murrough, 5th Earl of Inchiquin (1726–1808) and

20 Shelburne to Lady Tweeddale, 28 October 1775, BHA, Correspondence M–Z, f. 111.
21 Lady Tweeddale to Shelburne, 13 October 1775, BHA, Correspondence M–Z, f. 110; Shelburne to Lady Tweeddale, 28 October 1775, BHA, Correspondence M–Z, f. 111.

Mary, 3rd countess of Orkney (c. 1721–91). She was heir in her own right to the earldom of Orkney, a Scottish creation of 1696 which could descend through either the male or female line. Inchiquin, a minor Irish politician and former army officer, had only five months earlier succeeded his uncle in the Irish earldom. The marriage was a considerable coup that Fitzmaurice effected without his brother's knowledge or consent as head of the family and it made Shelburne incandescent with anger in the mistaken belief that his mother had connived at it.[22] He twice stormed down to her house in Twickenham in early January 1778, and as the dowager's maid and house-keeper reported it, '... top full of furry [sic] & anger – he wondered much my Ly coud keep him at such a distancy not to say the least word of his Brother's marriage & to hear it from strangers in the park ...'.[23] All he could do was retaliate by promising to end his days as a widower and draw up a marriage settlement with Frances Molesworth, who had a fortune esti-mated at £40,000 and was the niece of Lady Lucan, a woman he knew his mother disliked. And even this plan came to nothing when she jilted him.[24] According to the same source writing to Fitzmaurice, '... she don't care all her comfort is now in your Honour & her Dear Lady Mary Heaven has particularly blest her ...'.[25] In total contrast to Shelburne's vexed consterna-tion that he had been ignored by all parties, Thomas Fitzmaurice told his fond mother that his new father-in-law, Lord Inchiquin, had been delighted at her reception of him at Twickenham, and went on to extol the delights of his new married state:

> Would you believe it, my Dearest Madam, When I spoke to you most sincerely that every hour seems to add to my happiness? But, how can it be otherwise when my dearest partner makes it her study to blend every agreeable with every usefull quality, & upon the whole to be every way contented. I won't say say 'to render the marriage state truly happy' because the newspapers are every day making one sick with such trash. But, this I will venture to say, that, for ev'ry bug-bear that my ingenuity or Fancy ever present'ed to my mind as attendant

---

[22] Fitzmaurice told his aunt, Lady Caldwell, that 'I assure you that not one of any family at this place [Lleweni] knew of anything having happened, at the time of my handing Lady Mary Fitzmaurice out of the coach at Llewenny Hall door. The whole of the neighbourhood here were in astonishment, and continued in that state, uncertain what to believe, for some days.' He had only introduced his mother the night before his marriage and asked her for her blessing '(which she gave with all <u>her heart and soul and mind</u>)'. BHA, S. 6 Family Correspondence, f.52 [in black ink, 1909 transcript] Llewenny Hall, 23 January 1778. The same letter reported: 'My mother is still mad with joy. My brother struck dumb with envy.'

[23] BHA, S. 6 Family Correspondence, f. 22, Mrs Diana Good to TF, Twickenham, 8 January 1778.

[24] In 1785 she married the future 2nd earl Camden.

[25] BHA, S. 6 Family Correspondence, f. 22, Mrs Diana Good to TF, Twickenham, 8 January 1778.

upon wedlock, I have a lovely woman now at my elbow who has banish'd them all & teaches me to acknowledge the actual enjoyment of a thousand of the most solid matrimonial pleasures, …[26]

It no doubt helped that the new Lady Mary Fitzmaurice, happily installed in the threadbare splendour of Lleweni, appeared ready to go along with a range of economies that would help her husband in the tedious business of balancing his books. He informed the dowager countess in a manner that bespoke both pleasure and disappointment:

Lady Mary's positive request, is that there shall be no new carriage bespoke of, in ev'ry thing, [she] seems resolv'd, that, no expence, of any kind whatsoever, shall be incurr'd on her account. This seems to be bringing one back to the golden age & is completely contradictory to ev'ry expectation I entertain'd.[27]

1778 was perhaps the happiest year of Thomas Fitzmaurice's life. In October the only child of the marriage was born, named John in honour of his paternal grandfather in a gesture that must have delighted the doting grandmother. The infant (styled Viscount Kirkwall after 1791) was heir presumptive to the earldom of Orkney, and also stood two rather than three lives removed from his uncle's earldom of Shelburne. 1778 by contrast was privately miserable for the 2nd Earl, seven years a widower and suddenly deprived of his own second son, the Hon. William Granville Petty, struck down aged ten, leaving only Viscount Fitzmaurice as heir apparent before the title and Petty estates would pass to Thomas and his descendants. Shelburne's response to his brother's change of status and his own personal loss was to speed forward plans to remarry, taking as his bride Lady Louisa Fitzpatrick, sister of the 2nd Earl of Upper Ossory, on 19 July 1779. Their son Henry (known as Lord Henry Petty) was born a year later and, if he lived, lessened the prospect of Thomas and his descendants succeeding to the main family estates at Bowood and Wycombe.

Fitzmaurice may have been newly established as a family man and estate owner in north Wales but problems were soon piling up for him again. He had an accumulation of debts; his Irish estates were inadequately productive; he could neither sell nor let his London house in Pall Mall; and his initially cordial relationship with his father-in-law, Lord Inchiquin, soon began to unravel when the latter (himself beset by creditors until his surprise marriage in 1792 to Sir Joshua Reynolds's niece, Mary Palmer) moved to guard against the possibility of Fitzmaurice leeching off Lady Mary's inheritance to offset the acquisition of Llewenni (which had really been beyond his means). With that route foreclosed, Fitzmaurice was resourceful enough

---

[26] BHA, S. 6 Family Correspondence, f. 24., TF to his mother, Llewenny Hall, 13 January 1778.
[27] Ibid., f. 25.

to set up as a linen merchant, and eventually built a large bleaching factory in his grounds at Llewenni for fabrics shipped across from the family estates in Ireland. He told Shelburne that his mother's estate in County Sligo was about the only portion of the Irish estates to yield its full rental and that was due simply to the linen business conducted on it. But taken as a whole the Irish arrears of himself and the dowager countess amounted to a huge £27,000. The prospects for improvement were good but, in the meantime, with '… every person I owe a shilling to clamouring for payment to an hour, I really scarce know how to keep my head above water'.[28]

These family problems shaded over into political ones. The crisis of the American War in the late 1770s does not appear to have galvanized him, and his brother's emergence as leader of the Chathamite branch of the Opposition in both Houses from 1778 did nothing to turn him into a reliable member of that connection. The following year he stopped attending the House of Commons altogether. Fitzmaurice's financial straits kept him in Denbighshire and made him neglect his political duties such as attending the mayoral election at High Wycombe in 1779, a key gesture towards keeping his constituents sweet. He was quite honest about it when Shelburne wrote to complain. The real cause of his absence was 'our situation with regard to Lord Inchiquin, wch, considering his connexions, as well as his residence, in that Neighbourhood [10 miles away at Taplow Court], render'd my going thither, at that time, altogether impracticable'.[29] From his elder brother's perspective, the loyalty of the voters of Wycombe could not be presumed and he tactfully told Fitzmaurice in January 1780 that, with a General Election looming, he had to do more there adding: 'I wish it were in my power to bring you in where attention might not be requisite, which your distance and possible avocations render inconvenient to you.' Despite the family wrangling, Fitzmaurice was not inclined to disagree. He knew that it was unfair to his brother's public importance to take up Commons space as '… an indolent clog upon your parliamentary interest'. Once the 1780 General Election was called, Fitzmaurice made it clear to Shelburne that he was ready to give up his seat at Wycombe and that he had neither the money nor the inclination to seek another elsewhere for the time being:

> Upon these accounts, as well as upon a much more material one, namely my very great distress for money, I cannot help being of opinion that the purchase of a seat for the ensuing Parliament would be except as to worldly appearance as useless as the advancement of a sum sufficient would … be embarrassing'.[30]

---

[28] Ibid., ff. 54–5, Fitzmaurice to Shelburne, 26 November 1779, Llewenny Hall.
[29] Ibid.
[30] Shelburne to Fitzmaurice, draft letter, January 1780; Fitzmaurice to Shelburne, 1 Febraury 1780, BHA, S. 6 Family Correspondence, ff. 58, 60. None of which prevented Fitzmaurice being for a second time a potential candidate for Oxford University at the General Election of 1780 though he eventually – and unsuccessfully – backed William

There was an honesty about this declaration that suggested the relations between the two brothers were moving at last on to a more even keel: both had the comfort of marriage and fatherhood to stabilize them while Shelburne, ever more prominent in Opposition to the North government, could secure the return of an MP for Wycombe who was at the forefront of the movement for economical and parliamentary reform. This was Lord Mahon, the brother-in-law of that other rising star who looked to Shelburne as his patron, William Pitt the Younger. This period of harmony lasted only a few months before it was curtailed by the death of Mary, the dowager countess of Shelburne on 9 December 1780. She left Thomas an inheritance that eased his immediate financial difficulties, kept at bay his most pressing creditors, but reawakened Lord Shelburne's easily kindled spirit of resentment at his parental treatment. He felt compelled to mount a legal challenge over the will that lasted until the end of 1781 and undoubtedly interfered with and lessened the time he could devote to public affairs as the American War reached its inglorious end.[31] This fraternal squabbling over their maternal inheritance led Shelburne to call it 'one of the subjects in life which has given me most uneasiness' as a matter that was 'uncreditable tiresome & expensive –'.[32] Yet he could not help himself pursuing Thomas towards the law courts, whatever the cost to their relationship. It was as though his accumulated sense of grievance burst over at this point and what he took to be a dispute motivated by equity could easily be read as one fuelled by resentment and a desire for revenge.

This latest aggravation between them was only just starting to heal over when Shelburne became Home Secretary in April 1782 and Fitzmaurice professed himself ready to make a new start: 'Matters 'twixt you & me, being now, thank God, put into as amicable & as equitable a train for adjustment as they will admit of, my wish & purpose are to embrace you very affectionately, …'[33] Fitzmaurice duly offered congratulations when Shelburne became Premier in July 1782 just when he was taking office as high sheriff of Flintshire wryly observing: 'Wch is the more important character,

---

Jones for the seat. See Jones to Viscount Althorp, 19 May 1780, in *The Letters of Sir William Jones*, ed. Garland Cannon, 2 vols (Oxford, 1970), i. 382.

[31] Shelburne submitted the complicated case to his political ally, John Dunning. The latter's legal opinion was dated 26 July 1781. BHA, S. 95. For Dunning's early associations with Shelburne, see Beeston, 'Theorists and Politicians', 39–43. Peter Brown in his three chapters on Dunning in his *The Chathamites. A Study in the Relationship between Personalities and Ideas in the Second Half of the Eighteenth Century* (London, 1967), 231–321, omits any mention of Dunning's legal dealings with Shelburne in a private capacity.

[32] Shelburne to Lord Fitzmaurice, Bowood Park, 22 May 1781, William Clements Library, University of Muchigan, Ann Arbor, USA, Shelburne Papers, Box SFL-4, Shelburne Family Letters.

[33] Fitzmaurice to Shelburne, Pall Mall, April 1782, BHA, S. 6 Family Correspondence, f. 68.

a High Minister, or a High Sheriff, it may be hard to determine, all I hope is, that, you are not already as sick of the one as I am, or am going to be, of the other, tho' perhaps you may tell me, & not without some reason, that yours is not altogether a bed of roses.'[34] Shelburne was out of office too speedily for there to be any possibility of brother Thomas benefiting from his patronage and, in any event, he seems to have asked for none.[35] The latter was by then mainly resident at Llewenni while Shelburne (created Marquess of Lansdowne in December 1784) had headed back to Bowood to bear his political banishment with as much grace as he could muster. Even if they were united by different disappointments, the two brothers barely saw each other for the last decade of Thomas's life: the breach had been repaired to some extent but there was no pretence at intimacy and their two wives –Lady Mary Fitzmaurice and Louisa, Lady Lansdowne – though both from similar backgrounds and of a similar age (both being born in 1755) never had a chance to get to know each other in person and thereby perhaps bring their husbands closer together.

The Final Decade

During the 1780s Fitzmaurice abandoned whatever hopes he nourished of returning to the House of Commons in favour of becoming a businessman. Financial necessity gave him little option; his last blundering excursion into political controversy none at all. After his estate purchase and marriage, Fitzmaurice concentrated on making himself a great man in north Wales, pushing himself into prominence in a manner that was often resented by the long-established gentry families of Denbighshire and Flintshire, especially those with Whig sympathies. These found him bent on challenging their prominence and obstructing a reformist commitment of the sort that was endorsed by Shelburne. Flintshire was the only Welsh county apart from Caernarvonshire to have an Association for Parliamentary Reform presided over by the Whig dean of St Asaph, William Davies Shipley. The latter's abrasive personality made it hard to keep the Flintshire Association together and caused real ructions with Fitzmaurice, who was necessarily involved as High Sheriff first of Denbighshire in 1781–2 and then of Flintshire, 1782–3.[36]

The imbroglio started when the Association initially approved a tract called *The Principles of Government, in a Dialogue between a Scholar and a*

---

[34] Fitzmaurice to Shelburne, Llewenny Hall, 4 August 1782, BHA, S. 6 Family Correspondence, f. 70.

[35] The letter of 4 August (supra) ended gracefully that as regards favours '(for it w'd be absurd to write to a Prime Minister without asking one of some kind)', Fitzmaurice hoped that it may be possible to make his and Lady Mary's compliments 'as acceptable as possible' to Louisa, Ly Shelburne and Ld Fitzmaurice.

[36] Brown, *The Chathamites*, 374–5.

Peasant published anonymously in August 1782 under the auspices of the Society for Constitutional Information and the radical reformer, Major John Cartwright.[37] This radical paper (composed by Shelburne's admirer, William Jones [1746–93], the lawyer and Oxford academic)[38] was read out publicly by Dean Shipley at the county meeting of 7 January 1783 and it caused consternation with its demystification of the state and calls for universal suffrage; those who had not read it but had endorsed it earlier were suddenly made aware of its political extremism and moved to distance the committee from granting its approval. The headstrong Shipley, however, would have none of it. Thinking that it would suffice to limit the *Dialogue's* incendiary dimension by substituting throughout the words 'gentleman' and 'farmer' for 'scholar' and 'peasant' he had a few copies of the amended tract reprinted by a Wrexham bookseller. Fitzmaurice then lost all sense of restraint. Propelled by his ultra-cautious Whiggism, his personal antipathy to Shipley and feeling that his authority as chairman of the Association and High Sheriff of the county was being ignored, Fitzmaurice turned on the dean. At a county meeting in March 1783, emerging in effect as leader of the Welsh anti-reformers, he castigated Shipley as a preacher of sedition, and travelled to London to request his prosecution by the government for seditious libel. The law officers refused to act but Fitzmaurice, undeterred, proceeded privately to prevent the further distribution of the pamphlet by acting in conjunction with his attorney, (another) William Jones of Ruthin, indicting Shipley in April 1783 for publishing a seditious libel to prevent the further distribution of the pamphlet.[39] The case went to Shrewsbury Assizes and then to King's Bench becoming a legal *cause célèbre*. It ended with Shipley being discharged by Lord Chief Justice Mansfield, as a free man. The news was well received in north Wales, with bonfires lit and houses illuminated when the dean returned triumphantly to north Wales in December 1784.[40]

Shipley's behaviour confirmed his character for rash judgment but Fitzmaurice emerged from the affair even less creditably. His animus towards the dean looked like a personal vendetta that embarrassed reformists in north Wales at a time when his own brother was first minister and is the more remarkable in that Dean Shipley was the son of Jonathan Shipley,

---

[37] Shelburne was not a member of the SCI in 1783 though his follower, James Townsend, MP for Calne, was. Eugene Charlton Black, *The Association. British Extraparliamentary Political Organisation 1769–1793* (Cambridge, MA, 1963), 196, n. 24.

[38] Jones had been Shelburne's first choice as under-secretary of state at the Home Office in April 1782 but he was away on circuit and could not be contacted; Michael J. Franklin, *Sir William Jones* (Cardiff, 1995), 71.

[39] Jones told Lloyd Kenyon, the Attorney-General, that 'Mr Fitzmaurice was unfortunate in seizing a ground, which he cannot possibly maintain; but I too was unfortunate in having, very undesignedly, given him an opportunity to seize any ground at all'. Letter of 28 March 1783, in *The Letters of Sir William Jones*, ed. Cannon, ii. 608.

[40] The Shipley affair is illuminatingly discussed in ibid., 72–8; Black, *The Association*, 197–200; Brown, *The Chathamites*, 373–82.

Bishop of St Asaph, who until they quarrelled in 1782, was Shelburne's favourite prelate.[41] Thus the elder brother was at odds with the bishop and the younger one with the dean. Yet, from whatever angle one looks at it, Fitzmaurice's behaviour had hardly been helpful and fraternal and he was, for different reasons, as much on the margins by 1784 as his brother was at Bowood. A political comeback even at county level after this date was nigh inconceivable. He was generally thereafter to be found either supervising his warehouse in Chester, transacting business in Liverpool, making occasional business trips to France or improving his estate at Llewenni with a bleaching works in his grounds on a grand scale that can only be compared with the mills that Richard Arkwright was erecting at Cromford. Fitzmaurice has no counterpart as a gentleman industrialist in the 1780s: in 1788 he was (rather optimistically) suggesting that he was finally within an ace of generating serious profit while also praising his own distinctive achievement in the field:

> I think I can now venture to assure you, that, my linen schemes are within a mere trifle of being <u>perfectly</u> accomplished & put upon a solid footing, for myself, & others after me, if so it pleaseth others; I do not mean the Boy [the Hon. John Fitzmaurice] I assure you.... Considering all the circumstances, the undertaking will, one day or other, be certainly consider'd as singularly wonderfull; taking Labour, perseverance, expense, extent of dissmissions into consideration.[42]

In this, Fitzmaurice was being acutely prophetic and Burke's disparaging reference to him as the 'Honourable Linnen Draper'[43] was a kind of backhanded recognition of his enterprise and energy.

Since, perhaps, there was so little prospect of their ever meeting, one finds a fresh note of apparent cordiality creeping into the occasional communications between the two brothers with Lansdowne even sending him news of manufacturing developments that he considered might be of interest. It no doubt helped that their mother was no longer alive to act as an agent of disharmony and, besides, Lansdowne's political ambitions in the 1780s were slowly moving from himself to his eldest son and heir, Earl Wycombe, and he was in no position to do much for Thomas Fitzmaurice were he actually inclined to do so. The latter, meanwhile, saw in his brother's fall from power a hubristic leveller between them and was ready to offer consolation rather than gloat at his public setbacks. Fitzmaurice had his own private discord-

---

[41] Ibid., 334–7.

[42] 26a. Fitzmaurice to Lansdowne, Liverpool, 20 November 1788, BHA, S. 6 Family Correspondence, f. 74. It was a sign of his continuing need for economies that he had recently sold his somewhat dilapidated house in Pall Mall to the Prince of Wales for £7000. *The Times*, 30 November 1787, p. 3 (issue 913).

[43] Edmund and Jane Burke to William Burke, 3 September 1792, *Burke Correspondence*, vii. 191.

ances to counter that could largely be traced back to his cash flow problems. His hopes that an advantageous marriage would give him the investment opportunities he craved were dashed by the blocking behaviour of his father-in-law, Lord Inchiquin, and permanently hindered Fitzmaurice from generating wealth enough to balance his books. These strains were enough in the last few years before his death in 1793 to weaken Fitzmaurice's health (he appears to have suffered a stroke in the winter of 1792–3) and drive him into depression and drinking[44] on a scale that fatally undermined his constitution: Fitzmaurice was less settled than his elder brother, less able to embrace retirement, but shared his melancholic strain. There was a brief flicker of expectation that events might at last work in Fitzmaurice's favour after Lady Mary succeeded her mother as Countess of Orkney *suo jure* in 1791 and, at last, Fitzmaurice had access to assured funds he could manage on his wife's behalf. Yet by 1792 they were leading semi-separate lives. The new Lady Orkney was living without him at Cliveden 'with great outward Pomp, and inward indigence'. Fitzmaurice had leased the house from his father-in-law's creditors and filled it with the late dowager Lady Shelburne's furniture. Since his behaviour could be both mean and bizarre, it was not altogether surprising that the marriage was in trouble. As his Buckinghamshire neighbour Edmund Burke reported it:

> After that act of munificence in the establishment of his cara sposa he left her without a Penny whilst she sufferd under the clamour of unpaid Butcher and Baker – and had solicited him, by as dunning Letters, for relief – to her no small astonishment one day her Ears were saluted with the full sound of a charming concert of Musick – Mr Fitzmaurices gallantry had delicately contrived without giving her Notice to send her a band of Musick in new rich Liveries.[45]

It appears that he was thinking of letting out his wife's estate at Cliveden (he was only occasionally resident there between 1791 and 1793 to balance his books if he could shortly before his death),[46] but was too sunk in drink, dropsy and depression to make much progress to that end. His nephew reported in April 1793: 'I think him on the whole dejected, and disgusted, not so much with the fatiguing business to which he is so unaccountably attached as with the world at large.... He told me that he rather wished for death, and that he thought his life was not to be of long duration.'[47] The

---

[44] '... that disposition to indulge in strong liquors which we all so much lamented'. Wycombe to Lansdowne, 13 July 1793, BHA, S. 141, f. 140.

[45] Edmund and Jane Burke to William Burke, 3 September 1792, *Burke Correspondence*, vii. 191

[46] His will was dated 21 June 1793 and provided for the sale of estates in Co. Kerry to pay his debts. BHA, S. 95, f. 138.

[47] Wycombe to Lansdowne, 10 April 1793, BHA, S. 141, f. 53. Wycombe reported the next day that his uncle was '... scarcely capable of managing himself or his affairs'. BHA, S. 141, f. 55.

end duly came on 28 October 1793. It had been an imperfectly fulfilled life. If Shelburne was ultimately a political failure, the same could be said of Fitzmaurice as a businessman. Certainly, he had been enterprising and resourceful as an entrepreneur, filling his Chester warehouse with goods estimated at £100,000 when he died and making an industrial bleaching works the centrepiece of his country estate. As one obituarist noted, his example played its part in persuading the local gentry to stop their 'silly prejudices' against taking part in trade.[48] Yet there was an absence of hard-headedness that cut down on his profit margins even as it reflected well on his character. As a landlord Fitzmaurice refrained from coming down hard on either his Irish or his Welsh tenants; he ran Ballymoat on decidedly philanthropic lines and seems to have over-staffed the Llewenni bleaching factory with two to three hundred of his poorest tenants. Nevertheless his achievements in business were recognized at death. As the same columnist noted in 1793:

> ... his love for the poor, for his country, for real improvements of every kind, his benevolence in general, and his uncommon skills in the management of the great concerns wherein he was engaged, were such as meet not often in one person; such virtues as these constitute true nobility, and rendered Mr F. the noblest ornament of his noble family.[49]

Praise indeed – and at the expense of the head of that family.

Coda: Parallel Frustrations

Lansdowne's reaction to his brother's illness and death is hard to discern. He was not with him during the decline of 1792–3 and had his doubts that Fitzmaurice's situation was quite as precarious as it was represented by Lady Orkney. Hid did, however, encourage Lord Wycombe to go down to Cliveden to see for himself and received regular reports from him. And in the years that elapsed down to Lansdowne's own passing in 1805, there is no sign of the lonely widower of Bowood attempting to comfort his widowed sister-in-law, the Countess of Orkney. On the contrary, there was renewed disagreement between them over the education and marriage plans of Thomas Fitzmaurice's only child, Lord Kirkwall. This distance had been typical of the fraternal relationship throughout: Fitzmaurice was not,

---

[48] See *The Times*, 31 August 1787, p. 3 (issue 838) reporting that Fitzmaurice's 'superb bleacheries' were losing their fascination for him: 'Though the encouragement of trade and manufactures is the duty and the honour of elevated stations, we cannot but express a wish, that the ell and the yard may be left to those who have learned their use and the counter.'

[49] *Gentleman's Magazine*, 63 (1793), 1053, 1147.

in maturity, willing to play the dependant and his brother, if not exactly freezing him out, responded by keeping Fitzmaurice at a distance. The resentments – spoken and unspoken – of the elder brother towards the younger one were quite formidable. In education, Thomas had made the most of Eton and Glasgow while Shelburne had left Christ Church without a degree; in terms of inheritance, Shelburne felt unfairly hedged around by the settlements of his uncle Henry and both his parents that had breached the principle of primogeniture and left Thomas with material advantages that were incompatible with his position as a younger son.[50] Curiously, Shelburne's disappointment over Thomas's politics appears less marked, and each can be accurately described as wayward, independent Whigs. The political differences between the two of them were publicly obvious from the time of the parliamentary debates on the religious Tests in the early 1770s though these do not appear in themselves to have caused family friction; this was one of the few political issues that energized Fitzmaurice and it was less that the brothers disagreed over his Tory sympathies than that Fitzmaurice was simply not much of a political animal. Shelburne was only slightly weakened in parliamentary terms by not having Fitzmaurice as a reliable member of his following in the Commons and it was not so much his politics as his unwillingness to cultivate his constituents that led to Fitzmaurice leaving Parliament for good in 1780. Moreover, it can be argued that functional, supportive political relationships between premiers and their brothers in the eighteenth century were thin on the ground, the Duke of Newcastle and Henry Pelham excepted, and even that one had moments of severe strain. Of course, Newcastle and Pelham were closer to each other than Shelburne and Fitzmaurice which makes it the more creditable that the latter two never finally broke with each other: when, in September 1793, Fitzmaurice sensed that his end was approaching, he told his nephew on the latter's departure to send his love to Lansdowne.[51]

This touching *nunc dimittis* could not conceal the fact that the brothers were awkward and angular men, restless in ways that worked against their securing lasting satisfaction either publicly or personally. And they undoubtedly had these characteristics in common. Those who saw Fitzmaurice at close quarters found him exhibiting similar, unattractive character traits that others found exasperating in his elder brother. Thus William Jones in 1783: '... I have long known the strange temper, not to say absurdity, of Mr Fitzmaurice, whom I have commonly seen at variance either with his brother Lord Shelburne or with himself, ...'[52] In its own way, Thomas Fitz-

---

[50] The issue of secundigeniture in eighteenth-century settlements is under-investigated but this case on the face of it appears untypical.

[51] Wycombe to Lansdowne, 24 September 1793, BHA, S. 141, f. 198.

[52] Jones to Lloyd Kenyon, 28 March 1783, in *The Letters of Sir William Jones*, ed. Cannon, ii. 608. Jones had earlier observed that Fitzmaurice was capable of an 'oracular

maurice's life was as sad and unsatisfied as William, Earl of Shelburne's, with one brother holding a mirror up to the other in a manner that both were too intelligent to deny. In that at least, they had much in common.

and inexplicit manner' – just like his brother. Jones to Lady Spencer, 16 June 1780, ibid., i. 417.

2

Aunts, Wives, Courtiers:
The Ladies of Bowood

CLARISSA CAMPBELL ORR

This chapter will look not only at Shelburne's female relations by birth and marriage but also relate these aristocratic networks to the royal court. This brings out a third element: the continuing Irish dimension in Shelburne's personal life, despite his drive to repudiate a backwoods Irish destiny.

As I have argued elsewhere, there are various reasons why we need to work harder at integrating our knowledge of the aristocracy and their political leadership with the role of the court.[1] Looking at courtier families leads naturally into looking at both women and men equally, as service in royal households was one of the few ways in which women could have a public, salaried career. The court was at the centre of British society and an important venue for political and social networking; successful ministers normally needed a good relationship with the monarch as well with aristocratic connections and the public. There can be no excuse, after Elaine Chalus's work on aristocratic elites, to overlook the social dimension of politics and women's role within it.[2] This alone makes it essential to look as the Bowood ladies if we are to re-appraise Shelburne's career.

Acknowledgements: My grateful thanks to Kate Fielden, Bowood Archivist, for guidance in the archive material and many helpful conversations; also to the Marquess of Lansdowne for his discussion of his family with me. To Nigel Aston, for suggesting I broaden my knowledge of Lord Shelburne's first wife into an exploration of his other female relatives, and to Dr Rob Evans for his teaching assistance while the book was going to press. Thanks also to Michèle Cohen, Naomi Tadmor, Mary Abbott, Toby Barnard, Larry Klein, and Hamish Scott, for stimulating comments, and to Sally Warwick-Haller, Martyn Powell, Anthony Malcomson, and C.J. Woods for advice on Irish sources. Finally, my grateful appreciation to Julie and Charles Hayward for their generous hospitality in Bath on several occasions, which enabled me to visit the Bowood archives, and to Gill Whelpton for house and cat-sitting in Cambridge during my absence.

1   Clarissa Campbell Orr, 'New Perspectives on Hanoverian History', *Historical Journal*, 52:2 (2009), 513–29.
2   Elaine Chalus, *Elite Women in English Political Life c.1754–1790* (Oxford, 2004).

Both his wives, Sophia Carteret (1745–1761), daughter of John Carteret, Earl Granville, and Louisa Fitzpatrick (1755–1789), daughter of John Fitzpatrick, 1st Earl of Upper Ossory, brought useful social connections to the court and to very different Whig political families. They were themselves distantly related, through the marriage of Sophia's great-aunt Jane Granville to Louisa's great-great-grandfather, Sir William Leveson-Gower (Tables * and *). Shelburne's women also kept him connected with Ireland. In addition the diaries and letters of the Bowood ladies give important glimpses into Shelburne's personality and the dynamics of his family life. Studying the ladies also yields insights into the role of female aristocratic education, religion, and philanthropy, and the challenge of conducting marriage in a libertine age.[3] In this chapter I particularly want to highlight the role of aunts, who could be especially important in an age of maternal mortality, as well as being the links to influential political dynasties, and often the brokers of marriages; and among the aunts none is more important to Shelburne than his father's sister, Lady Arbella Denny (Figure 3).

Lady Arbella Denny as Aunt and Exemplar

Shelburne was always very devoted to his aunt whom he recalled as the only person in his childhood who had shown him affection:

> It was to her alone I owed any alleviation of the domestic brutality and ill-usage I daily experienced at home ... I loved Lady Arbella Denny because she loved me. She inculcated into me a sense of duty toward God, the publick, and my neighbours, which has never quitted me.[4]

She had married the younger brother of the head an Anglo-Irish family, the Dennys, Earls of Coningsby, whose origins go back to the sixteenth century.[5] Arbella's husband, an Irish MP, army officer and squire, died when she was 35, and as her nephew put it, 'she had too much experience ever to become

---

[3] Cindy MacCreery, *The Satirical Gaze: Prints of Women in Late Eighteenth-Century England* (Oxford, 2004); idem, 'Keeping up with the Bon Ton: the Tête-à-Tête series in the Town and Country Magazine', in *Gender in Eighteenth-Century England: Roles, Representations and Responsibilities*, ed. Hannah Barker and Elaine Chalus (Harlow, 1997), 207–29; Kate Retford, ch. 5, 'The Battle of the Pictures', in *The Art of Domestic Life, Family Portraiture in Eighteenth-Century England* (New Haven, CT and London, 2006), 187–214.

[4] Edmond George Petty-Fitzmaurice, Baron Fitzmaurice, *Life of William, Earl of Shelburne, afterwards First Marquess of Lansdowne*, 2 vols (London, 1912), vol. 1, 8, 10.

[5] I am indebted to Rosemary Raughter for this point on their origins. It is worth speculating whether Disraeli knew of this connection when he wrote Coningsby (1844), and subsequently Sybil (1845), which includes an encomium of Shelburne as a true King's friend who helped the king resist the Venetian oligarchy of self-interested Whigs (see also Chapter 7).

3. Lady Arbella Denny, unknown artist, c. 1727, Trustees of the Bowood Estate

a slave again, and she refused two or three of the most respectable marriages Ireland afforded'.[6] Instead she devoted herself to a variety of philanthropic activities in Ireland. Shelburne intended to write an account of her charitable activities to inspire other women. He also praised her as hospitable and elegant in her household management: in other words, a mistress of the arts of politeness.[7]

6 Fitzmaurice, *Shelburne*, vol. 1, 9.
7 Ibid.

But this was not all. Her kindness and gentleness did not make her a doormat. She was in addition a remarkably resourceful and strong character. Her brother-in-law was, Shelburne said, a savage and a fool: from which it can be inferred that he harassed, or attempted to harass her sexually. To deal with this without setting her husband against his brother, she taught herself to become an excellent markswoman with a pistol, and then showed her errant brother-in-law how good she was at target practice, saying she would shoot him if he did not change his behaviour. He took the hint and stopped bothering her. Lady Arbella thus exemplified, Shelburne said, 'two qualities of mind which most adorn and dignify life – amiability and independence'.[8]

Shelburne's encomium of his aunt speaks volumes about what would now be called his sexual politics. He admired women who were nurturing but also immensely principled and strong, who could provide encouragement and training in the social graces, and who retained their femininity. This fitted in with prevailing expectations in the eighteenth century as notions of politeness developed that women had a central role to play as guardians and educators in manners and morals, and that they could assist boys to become gentlemen through their conversation and early influence in socializing them.[9] 'If it was not for her I should have had scarce known how to read, write, or articulate, to being able to do which I am indebted perhaps, for the greatest part of the little reputation I have lived to gain in the House of Lords.'[10] In the relatively fluid world of eighteenth-century Britain, with both downwardly mobile peers and gentry who lacked money, and the upwardly mobile 'quality' which included the newly moneyed who aspired to gentility, women helped to police the social hierarchy as well as to determine moral acceptability.[11]

Shelburne said his aunt's life deserved to be written about more than that of Mme de Maintenon, the pious second wife of Louis XIV, of Mme Roland, the able wife and martyr to liberty in the Jacobin terror of the Girondin Minister of Justice, or even of Catherine of Russia, leaving aside her 'vices and crimes'. Mme de Maintenon had been governess to Louis XIV's children by Mme de Montespan and founded a convent school for poor gentlewomen at St Cyr; her ideas about girl's education remained influential.[12] But what linked a pious gentry widow from the Irish Protestant Ascendancy and the usurping empress of Russia, who was at best a secularized Lutheran?

8 Ibid., 8–9.
9 Michèle Cohen, *Fashioning Masculinity: National Identity and Language in the Eighteenth Century* (London, 1996).
10 Fitzmaurice, *Shelburne*, I, 9.
11 For the Irish context, see Toby Barnard, *A New Anatomy of Ireland: the Irish Protestants, 1649–1770* (New Haven, CT and London, 2003), 71–80.
12 Clarissa Campbell Orr, 'Aristocratic Feminism, the Learned Governess, and the Republic of Letters', in *Women, Gender and Enlightenment*, ed. Sarah Knott and Barbara Taylor (Basingstoke, 2005), 306–25.

Shelburne's range of reference to Central and Eastern Europe is in itself telling. In a composite monarchy, the Anglo-Irish bear resemblance to their counterparts in Bohemia, where the Austrian monarchy encouraged conversion, this time from Protestantism to Catholicism, and rewarded its noble supporters with confiscated lands. Ethnic, linguistic, and religious differences could certainly subsist between the diverse Hapsburg nobilities in Bohemia and Hungary and their peasants, as they did between the Protestant Anglo-Irish and their Catholic, Gaelic-speaking tenants. Shelburne was also friendly with the anglophile Polish king Stanislas Poniatowski, who entertained Lord Wycombe on his Grand Tour in the 1780s; members of the Poniatowski and Czartoryski families had previously visited Bowood in 1768 and 1769.[13] Perhaps he identified with Poniatowski as a modernizing Polish aristocrat who had also been repelled by provincial politics and was crowned attired not in a Polish kaftan but modern French dress.[14] In Russia, likewise, Shelburne must have sympathized with Catherine's efforts to haul her subjects from out of economic and social backwardness. In making this comparison of his aunt to the Tsarina Catherine, Shelburne would also have known that Princess Dashkova, whom she had made President of the St Petersburg Academy of Sciences, visited Lady Arbella at her Dublin home in 1780 and commended her.[15] The respect was mutual: Lady Arbella told her friend Lady Caldwell she believed the Princess had been entirely innocent of involvement with the assassination of Catherine's husband, Tsar Peter III, even though her family was connected to the plotters.[16]

For the affinity between the Empress and Shelburne's aunt is not only the common determination of each woman to improve education, manners and morals of their respective countries, but also to improve them in the economic sense, including the better provision of technology and training. To appreciate how this applies to Lady Arbella the link in eighteenth-century Ireland between philanthropic and mercantilist initiatives needs consideration. After the Glorious Revolution, Dublin was developed rapidly as a capital city with an architectural and cultural infrastructure to support its political, judicial, and military role. Royal Barracks were erected in 1701; the castle, seat of the Lord Lieutenancy, was renovated between 1710 and 1717; the Library of Trinity College begun in 1712 and completed twenty

[13] *Diary*, entries for July 1767 and September 1768.
[14] Richard Butterwick, *Poland's Last King and English Culture: Stanisław August Poniatowski, 1732–1798* (Oxford, 1997); I am grateful to Dr Butterwick for discussing the Polish parallels with me and for supplying copies of mss letters from Stanisław August Poniatowski to Shelburne. A. Zamoyski, *The Last King of Poland* (London, 1992), discusses the coronation.
[15] *The Memoirs of Princess Dashkova*, trans and ed. Kyril Fitzlyon (London, 1958), 150–1.
[16] Letter 37, Lady Arbella Denny to Lady Caldwell, 26 November 1777, in Rosemary Raughter, ed., '"My Dear Lady C": Letters of Lady Arbella Denny to Lady Caldwell, 1754–1777', *Analecta Hibernia*, 41, Irish Manuscripts Commission (2009), 133–200.

years later. By this time the Protestant Ascendancy, political and clerical, were building handsome palazzi and terraced town houses in the city in locations such as St Stephen's Square, where Lady Arbella Denny and also the Dowager Lady Shelburne both had houses. In 1731 the Society of Arts was founded to improve technology, manufacturing and the decorative arts, and to bring them up to standards elsewhere in Europe.[17]

To assist Irish mercantilist aims, technical education and training was needed. With the encouragement of the Rev. Thomas Madden, the society offered premiums after 1740 rewarding sculpture, architecture, and painting, arguing that encouraging the luxury trades would incidentally give 'Bread and Industry to our Natives'.[18] Lady Arbella moved to Dublin in 1745, the year that Lord Chesterfield began his successful Vice-Royalty and encouraged the work of the Dublin Society, obtaining it an annual grant of £500 and its Royal denomination. The Society drew on French mercantilist and German cameralist models of state sponsorship for entrepreneurial endeavour, to a greater degree than in England where private initiative mistrusted state sponsorship.[19] The Irish Parliament also sponsored a variety of economic initiatives to improve infrastructure or develop mining and agriculture, financed not (as in England) by enabling local trusts to raise rates, but by appropriating revenues or granting bounties. The Irish Linen board was founded in 1711 to promote its manufacture.[20]

Chesterfield worked with the traveller, connoisseur and clergyman Richard Pococke, whom he appointed Archdeacon of Dublin and later Bishop of Ossory in Kilkenny, to found Protestant Charter schools to train boys and girls in artisanal skills. It became fashionable for the Dublin elite to visit the workshops and studies and to commission work to decorate private houses and public buildings. The involvement of senior clerics also reflected a peculiarly Irish configuration of Church and State within the Protestant Ascendancy; given that proportionately more of the lay peers were absentees, the episcopacy was prominent in its cultural patronage and in many cases their princely style of living. Building Episcopal seats or Dublin residences could be seen as job-creation opportunities as well as

---

[17] T. Mowl and B. Earnshaw, *An Insular Rococo: architecture, politics and society in Ireland and England 1710–1770* (London, 1999), 160–2.

[18] John Turpin, *A School of Art in Dublin since the Eighteenth Century* (Dublin, 1995), 10–11; also M. Dunleavy, 'Samuel Madden and the Scheme for the Encouragement of Useful Manufactures', in *Decantations*, ed. A. Bernelle (Dublin, 1992), 21–8, and James Livesey, 'The Dublin Society in Eighteenth-century Irish Political Thought', *Historical Journal*, 47:3 (2004), 615–40.

[19] Turpin, *School of Art*; cf. H. Hoock, *The King's Artists* (Oxford, 2003).

[20] Eoin Maginnin, 'Coal, Corn and Canals: Parliament and the Dispersal of Public Moneys 1695–1772', in *The Irish Parliament in the Eighteenth Century: The Long Apprenticeship*, ed. D.W. Hayton (Edinburgh, 2001), 71–86; Edith Mary Johnston, *Ireland in the Eighteenth Century* (Dublin, 1974), 90–4 summarizes the Linen Board's role.

increasing the dignity of the Protestant Ascendancy.[21] And since women were often expected to show more consistency in moral tone than their male counterparts, the role of pious laywomen in charity and industry is more readily understood.[22]

This was the context which enabled Lady Arbella to develop a life-long interest in the textile trades in Ireland. As Aston shows, her cousin, Shelburne's mother, shared these interests to a lesser degree. Lady Arbella however was what would now be called a major social entrepreneur. She not only supported charities for the poor and the sick, she also encouraged schemes that would create work and enable the poor to be self-sufficient. There was already a female side to this in the periodic encouragement of various Viceroys to 'buy Irish' when it came to dress.[23]

Other textiles benefited from Lady Arbella's taste. From 1752 the Dublin Society tried to stimulate carpet making by offering premiums for various kinds of carpet. One of the successful winners was a William Read, who had begun producing designs 'under the instructions' of Lady Arbella Denny. His tapestry carpet produced in 1757 with his partner John Long was purchased by the 4th Duke of Bedford, then the Lord Lieutenant, and won the 1760 premium.[24] The duke and his wife, Gertrude, were lavish entertainers and at least initially popular with Dublin society; Lord Shelburne would later marry Duchess Gertrude's niece Louisa Fitzpatrick. In 1767 and 1769 Lady Arbella was granted a premium from the Royal Dublin Society to encourage lace-making by the Foundling Hospital children; she presented gloves they had made to Queen Charlotte.[25] She was a patroness of the Royal Dublin Society's silk warehouse and introduced sericulture at her Blackrock villa; commented on the patterns proposed by one of the Charter School masters; encouraged the design of wool and worsted for the Portuguese market; and sent the Royal Dublin Society a paper on flax growing from a Col. Ramsay. Given all this activity it is not surprising, though it was still exceptional,

---

[21] Toby Barnard, '"Grand Metropolis" or "Anus of the World"? The Cultural Life of Eighteenth-century Dublin', in *Two Capitals: London and Dublin 1500–1840*, ed. P. Clark and R. Gillespie (Oxford, 2001), 185–210.

[22] Barnard, *New Anatomy of Ireland*, 33.

[23] Ibid., 65; S. Foster, 'Buying Irish: Consumer Nationalism in Eighteenth-century Dublin', *History Today*, xlvii (1996), 44–51.

[24] Ada K. Longfield, 'Some Eighteenth Century Dublin Carpet-Makers' *Burlington Magazine* vol. 82, no. 483 (1943), pp. 148–151

[25] Beatrice Bayley Butler, 'Lady Arbella Denny 1707–1792', *Dublin Historical Record*, 9:1 (December 1946–February 1947), 1–20, at 7–9; John Turpin, A *School of Art in Dublin since the Eighteenth Century* (Dublin, 1995), 64, shows Lady Bingham and Lady Elizabeth Fownes were also given patents; Lady Bingham sent patterns after visiting Chambéry in 1779. After 1777, Lady Louisa Conolly, sister of Emily Duchess of Leinster, began to interest herself in the poor in Cellbridge (the parish of her estate at Carton); the various enterprises included a chip-straw hat factory. Brian Fitzgerald, *Lady Louisa Conolly, 1743–1821: An Anglo-Irish Biography* (London, 1950).

that in 1766 she was elected the first woman member of the Royal Dublin Society.[26] In the later correspondence with her nephew preserved at Bowood it is clear she became, effectively, his eyes and ears for all kinds of enterprises to stimulate industry and assist the skilled working man.[27]

Meanwhile Lady Arbella had pursued more conventionally female kinds of philanthropy.[28] Like many women she took an interest in Dublin's several hospitals, which relied on public subscription and various fund-raising schemes. In 1745 Dublin had acquired a maternity hospital, founded by Dr Bartholomew Mosse and funded along entrepreneurial lines: lotteries, and other ticketed public entertainments provided the money to keep it going. Mosse acquired a large plot of land and started building a combined hospital and leisure complex, where the pleasure gardens behind the hospital, together with building plots leased for elegant housing, would pay for the maternity care. Parliament subsidized it with a grant; Dubliners subscribed to it and fashionable ladies and gentlemen visited – as they would later visit Thomas Coram's hospital in London. Lady Arbella became a member of its Ladies' Committee and took a particular interest in the needs of the blind.

In 1759 Lady Arbella began visiting the much longer established Foundling Hospital, which dated from 1704 and included a workhouse and provision for the mentally ill, and was funded by the Dublin rates. She put her organizational skills to work reforming its management. She offered cash rewards to wet nurses whose children survived and provided £4000 toward extending its buildings. The death rate dropped markedly and in 1764 the Dublin Parliament gave her a vote of thanks. The following year she was given the Freedom of the City of Dublin.[29] Perhaps prompted by her knowledge of the women who had been obliged to give up their babies to the Hospital, she founded her own institution in 1767, a 'Magdalen Hospital', whose remit was to provide training for 'fallen women' to become economically independent. These young women, aged below nineteen, and both Catholic and Protestant, were probably unfortunate girls seduced in domestic service as much as prostitutes. Some were the 'disgraced' genteel,

---

26 Butler, 'Lady Arbella Denny'; A. Peter, *Sketches of Old Dublin* (Dublin, 1907), 158–9 quotes the parliamentary resolution.

27 BHA, Letters from Lady Arbella Denny to Lord Shelburne, 1765–90.

28 Rosemary Raughter, 'A Discreet Benevolence: Female Philanthropy and the Catholic Resurgence in Eighteenth-century Ireland', *Women's History Review*, 6:4 (1997), 465–87 and idem., 'A Natural Tenderness: The Ideal and the Reality of Female Philanthropy', in *Women in Irish History*, ed. M.G. Valiulis and M. O'Dowd (Dublin, 1997), 71–88. Raughter is researching a biography of Lady Arbella Denny, and I am indebted to her for helpful corrections and comments. Among her discoveries is that Lord Shelburne gave Lady Arbella Power of Attorney on several occasions. Private communication, 25 February 2010.

29 Butler, 'Lady Arbella Denny'.

duped perhaps by promises of marriage.[30] They resided in the hostel for a year and were given a guinea premium on leaving, after a rigorous regime of prayer, Bible reading, needlework, and gardening, with a further incentive of two more guineas if they kept out of trouble for a year. Their needle-work included gloves and tassels which she encouraged her friends to buy.[31] The whole enterprise was funded by subscriptions to its regular activities, or to attend its charity sermons: the chapel could seat five hundred and was frequently full. Subscribers could also buy published editions of sermons by regular preachers.[32] Some of the guest preachers were inclined to Meth-odism, introduced through Lady Arbella's friendship with Selina, Countess of Huntingdon.[33] Thus when her nephew praised his aunt's role, he was surely not underestimating her influence as a power in the land.[34]

By contrast to this affectionate and enterprising aunt, Shelburne considered his mother to have been emotionally neglectful of him, albeit immensely ambitious to drive her husband into 'making his way in the world'.[35] 'If it had not been for her continual energy my father would have passed the remainder of his life in Ireland, and I might at this time be the chief of some little provincial faction' he wrote in 1800, also alluding to her 'boundless love of power'.[36] Women who were too overtly domineering or grasping therefore crossed an unacceptable boundary, as can be further illus-trated by his negative comments on the way Sarah Duchess of Marlborough handled the Churchill family's clients.[37] This suggests that for many men of Shelburne's generation, feminine power was only palatable if the velvet glove covered the iron fist: or if affection as well as drive was evident. He resented his parents' stern attitude, which made him temperamentally an *esprit contraire*.[38] He also recalled that when he came to London at about fifteen he was left to shift pretty much for himself, to the extent that he was dependent on two other paternal aunts, Charlotte, Lady Colthurst and

---

30 Barnard, *New Anatomy of Ireland*, 277, 304–5, 325 for Lady Arbella's work with the Magdalens, and ibid., ch. 10, passim for the context of the Irish poor and measures to deal with their problems.

31 *Diary*, 29 July 1770.

32 E.g. BHA, flyer for sermons by Rev. Mr Skelton, included in Letter 15 May 1784 from Lady Arbella Denny to Louisa, Marchioness of Lansdowne, née Lady Louisa Fitzpatrick. Skelton was the very conscientious Church of Ireland rector of Fintona, Co. Tyrone, as well as a man of enlightenment: Raughter, ed. 'My Dear Lady C', 170, note 150.

33 D. Hempton and M. Hill in *Women and Early Modern Ireland*, ed. M. MacCurtain and Mary O'Dowd (Edinburgh, 1991), 197–211.

34 The Magdalen Hospital was still going strong with 2337 residents in 1947 when B.B. Butler researched her article on Lady Denny, and there is still a Lady Arbella Denny Trust which inter alia funds research for the Irish government into adoption.

35 Derek Jarrett, *England in the Age of Hogarth* (St Albans, 1976), 88.

36 Fitzmaurice, *Shelburne*, I, 6.

37 Ibid., 21–2.

38 Ibid., 10.

Elizabeth, Lady Branden, and his cousins, for ready money[39] (Table 1). As Nigel Aston's chapter has shown, Shelburne felt that his mother preferred her younger son Thomas, with whom she stayed whenever she visited England after his marriage. Significantly aunt Arbella left Thomas a portrait of his mother, 'knowing he will always put a high value on it', while Lord Shelburne 'my nephew whom I have loved from an infant' was given her own diamond ring 'which I hope he will love for my sake'.[40]

Of course, it is impossible to know how far Shelburne really was neglected or bullied by his parents, and in any case siblings can react very differently to their parents. Certainly Shelburne *felt* neglected – which is what counts insofar as it shaped his character; and as his parents were often busy networking in Dublin or England while he grew up in Kerry, then they were certainly absent. Doubtless they would have said it was all for his own good, to help him establish a career in England. And it *was* absolutely crucial that his father was awarded his British barony just before he died in 1761, which qualified him to sit in the English House of Lords.

Although later Shelburne complained that not much thought had been given as to what to do with him when he arrived in London and before he went to Oxford, his father evidently thought that one thing he should do was to introduce him to elderly men of note whom he might not have other chances to meet. Thus in 1753 his father introduced him to two previous Lord Lieutenants of Ireland: Lord Carteret (who was now Lord Granville) and Lord Chesterfield.

> I was with them the same morning, and happening to go to Lord Chesterfield first, and being much struck with his wit and brilliancy and good breeding, I expected all the same in Lord Granville, but finding him quite plain and simple in his manner, and something both commanding and captivating, more in his countenance and general manner than in anything he said, I was much at a loss to account for the difference of impression.[41]

Perhaps Shelburne always remained puzzled about which style of manner to adopt, as he so frequently seems to have made a bad impression on his English contemporaries. Not having been at school with them, and when at Christ Church, Oxford, being outside the corps of Old Westminsters at the

---

[39] 'Soon after fifteen I came to London, where I was suffered to go about, to pick up what acquaintance offered, and in short had no restraint except in the article of money, of which I should not have had sufficient to answer he most common purposes, if it was not for old aunts again and cousins.' Ibid., p. 11. Both ladies were sisters of Lady Arbella and Lady Mary.

[40] Peter, *Sketches of Old Dublin*, citing Lady Arbella's will, now lost in the Four Courts fire.

[41] Fitzmaurice, *Shelburne*, I, 13. On Lord Chesterfield, see also Philip Carter, *Men and the Emergence of Polite Society: Britain 1660–1800* (Harlow, 2001).

heart of the college, he did not have the social codes in his bloodstream. But on one occasion Mary, Lady Rockingham, found his manner excessively elaborate, so he evidently opted in some situations for Chesterfield's rather than Carteret's style, though on others he could be quite curt.[42] In the army he was particularly friendly with James Wolfe, who certainly had no time for 'Showy men who are seen in palaces and the courts of Kings'.[43] Shelburne's inconsistent manner may have contributed to his reputation for slippery unreliability.

Sophia Carteret and Her Court Connections

In 1765, when Lady Arbella Denny was becoming well established as an economic patriot, arbiter of taste, and charitable entrepreneur, Lord Shelburne was getting established in marriage. His first wife, Lady Sophia Carteret (Figure 4), was the only daughter of John Carteret, 2nd Earl Granville, by his second marriage. Granville and his first wife Frances Worsley (1694–1743), had been a social success in Ireland as Viceroy and Vicereine, 1724–30, and Sophia was pleased, when she visited Ireland over thirty years later, to find people who had known them. Although Carteret had died two years before his daughter's wedding in 1765 there was a political lineage to this marriage. Without ever having established a strong political following, he had been highly influential and widely respected, and a mentor to Lord Chatham, with whom Shelburne was so long associated.[44] Sophia Carteret's mother was Sophia Fermor, a daughter of the 1st Earl of Pomfret and his literary wife, Henrietta, a bluestocking *avant la lettre*.[45] Sophia Carteret bequeathed to her daughter a number of interesting aunts, all with useful connections (Table 3).

Lady Charlotte Finch was appointed in 1762 to be Governess of the Royal Nursery. She had apartments at St James and Kew. Sophia frequently went to court, either informally to visit her aunt Charlotte, where she compared her children with the royal ones and borrowed patterns for their caps, or more formally, especially after her husband held ministerial office in 1766, when she attended drawing rooms, enquired after the queen's health after she gave birth, and was present at important occasions like the

---

[42] Fitzmaurice, *Shelburne*, I, 391–2.

[43] I am indebted to Nigel Aston, who plans to write more on Shelburne's military experience, for the point about Shelburne's unpredictability. Wolfe's comment is cited in William C. Lowe, 'Keppel, George, Third Earl of Albemarle (1724–1772)', ODNB online, accessed 10 November 2008.

[44] Basil Williams, *Carteret and Newcastle: A Contrast in Contemporaries* (Cambridge, 1943), 3.

[45] Richard Quaintance, 'Fermor [née Jeffreys], Henrietta Louisa, Countess of Pomfret (1698–1761)', ODNB online, accessed 4 November 2009.

4. Sophia, Countess of Shelburne and Viscount Fitzmaurice, by Catherine Read, 1766, Trustees of the Bowood Estate

proxy wedding of the king's sister Princess Caroline Matilda to the king of Denmark, on 1 October 1766, and the christening and formal lying in for the queen's eldest daughter, Charlotte Princess Royal, on 27 October.[46] In her turn Sophia received letters from Queen Charlotte and the Dowager Princess of Wales, congratulating her on the birth of her first son, which came at the same time as news of the death of the king's fifteen-year-old brother Frederick William.[47] The births, marriages, and deaths of the royal family punctuated the lifecycles of aristocrats such as the Pettys. Sophia was pleased that when her eldest son, styled Lord Fitzmaurice, was two and a half, he got on well with the royal princes George, William, and Frederick. The latter was only four months older than her boy. 'At one o'clock we came away having receive'd great honour from the Prince of Wales who is vastly civil & prettily behaved and leaving a very good impression of Lord Fitzmaurice behind us.'[48] This could lay the foundation for a subsequent position in a princely household when they gained separate establishments.

Another aunt was Lady Juliana, who married Thomas Penn, son of the Founder of Pennsylvania: their house at Stoke Park was near the Shelburne's Buckinghamshire seat at Wycombe. A third aunt, Lady Louisa, seems to have been instrumental in the marriage-broking, along with – perhaps surprisingly – the Dowager Lady Shelburne. Lady Sophia's diary recalls that the first approach to her candidature as bride had come from Lady Shelburne to Lady Louisa.[49] She was a Lady-in-Waiting to George III's aunt, Princess Amelia,[50] and the third wife of Sir William Clayton, MP for Bletchingley in Surrey, and subsequently for another family seat, Marlow in Buckinghamshire.[51] These connections all suggest that the marriage sprang out of the newly minted English links of Lord Shelburne. But there was a fourth aunt by marriage who had very significant Dublin links and may have been the starting point of his mother's approach to Lady Louisa. This was Lady Anne Dawson (1733–69), the youngest of the Fermor sisters, who married the Dublin banker Thomas Dawson, (1725–1814), later Lord Dartrey and

---

[46] *Diary*, entries for 1 October and 27 October 1766. Sophia records that there was a very full court on 2 October 1766, because of the two happy events of Princess Charlotte's birth (30 September 1766), the day before the Danish wedding.

[47] *Diary*, entry 29 December 1765.

[48] *Diary*, entry 21 June 1768.

[49] *Diary*, Appendix.

[50] Isabella Finch, a fellow Lady-in-Waiting to Princess Amelia, was sister-in-law to Lady Charlotte Finch, being the youngest sister of the latter's husband William, both children of Daniel Finch, 2nd Earl of Nottingham and 7th Earl of Winchilsea.

[51] William Clayton was a descendant of the financier Robert Clayton. Romney Sedgwick, ed., *The House of Commons 1715–54*, 2 vols, HMSO (London, 1970), vol. 1, 559. Lady Louisa lived in Windsor after her husband died and continued to be a familiar face in court circles.

Viscount Cremorne.[52] Lord Shelburne's private finances remain something of a mystery (Chapter 3) but there may have been banking connections to the Shelburne family, and a shared Dublin/Buckinghamshire axis may have been behind the arrangement of this first marriage.

The degree of arrangement behind this marriage need not suggest that Lady Sophia had no personal attractions for Lord Shelburne: to the contrary she was in many ways a very suitable bride for a clever man and aspiring politician. She had been educated by the French governess and educational writer Mme LePrince de Beaumont, who had been appointed Sophia's governess when her despairing maternal grandmother considered her excessively spoiled by the deference of a succession of governesses and servants, who had all emphasized that she was an heiress, and had let her do as she pleased. After taking charge of her, LePrince de Beaumont apparently turned her into a conscientious and socially responsible person, and she was to be the dedicatee of LePrince de Beaumont's *The Young Ladies Magazine*,[53] a book of dialogues for teenage young women, where she figures as the right thinking Lady Sensée.

Part of her governess' teaching was that women had the right to think; 'The science taught by Socrates, is called moral philosophy, and you will see clearly, my children, that it belongs as much to women as to men: for the prerequisite for learning philosophy, is to be thoroughly reflective.'[54] Her pupils were given a smattering of natural philosophy as well, together with geography and history. Religious knowledge and self-discipline remained central to the curriculum. The language of instruction was French, essential for a future Foreign Secretary's wife: she became especially friendly with the Sardinian ambassador Count Viry and his wife. And the method of instruction was conversational, giving young women the means to participate in the mixed-sex conversation of polite sociability.[55]

Mme Le Prince de Beaumont's pupils were also encouraged to read: indeed LePrince de Beaumont had put the fable of 'Beauty and the Beast' into its canonical modern version, and it will be remembered that a sign of the Beast's essential good nature is that he gives Beauty a library. When Sophia was still housebound after her first child was born Lord Shelburne read Thucydides with her: heavy duty history, maybe, but a book her education would have prepared her to understand. Her reading matter also included historical memoirs such as those of Louis XIV, and his morganatic

---

[52] Public Record Office of Northern Ireland, 'The Dartrey Papers', Anthony Malcomson, www.proni.gov.uk/records/private/dartrey.htm, accessed 20 April 2007.

[53] *Magasin des adolescentes: ou dialogues entre une sage gouvernante, et plusieurs de ses éléves de la premiére distinction. Par Made Le Prince de Beaumont ...*, 2 vols (London, 1760). Translations from this edition are my own.

[54] *Magasin des Adolescentes*, vol. 1, 82–3.

[55] L. Klein, 'Gender, Conversation and the Public Sphere in Early Eighteenth-Century England', in *Textuality and Sexuality*, ed. J. Still and M. Worton (Manchester, 1993).

wife Mme de Maintenon. Sophia remained friendly after her marriage with her governess's patron, Alicia, Lady Egremont, whose second husband, the Saxon minister Count Brühl, had been taught at Leipzig by Queen Charlotte's favourite German moralist, C.F. Gellert, and shared the king's fascination with horology. Lady Egremont herself was one of the queen's six Ladies of the Bedchamber and her first husband had been a Secretary of State.[56]

Sophia was in essence something of a Bluestocking and had an entrée to Bluestocking circles; her diary mentions her visits with Mrs Montagu, a near neighbour in London.[57] She also knew Margaret Bentinck, 2nd Duchess of Portland, the early patroness of Elizabeth Montagu and exemplar to the Bluestockings as a woman with wide interests in literature, history and above all, science. Sophia visited Bulstrode, the Buckinghamshire home of the Duchess of Portland, just after her marriage in 1765, and recorded London visits of the Duchess and of Mrs Delany, who each summer shared Bulstrode with the duchess after she was widowed in 1768.[58] Sophia's older half-sister, Louisa Carteret, married Thomas Thynne, 2nd Viscount Weymouth, who was a cousin of Mary Granville Delany, and whose seat, Longleat, was in easy reach of Bowood.[59] The son and heir, the 3rd Viscount Weymouth and 1st Marquess of Bath, married Elizabeth Bentinck, daughter of the Duchess of Portland. Sophia's diary mentions Lady Weymouth often as, like Lady Charlotte Finch, she was in Court service to Queen Charlotte as a Lady of the Bedchamber and then Mistress of the Robes, so regularly resident in London. Her husband shared the king's interest in astronomy, as well as being a hunting companion, and an ambitious politician. He was better than Shelburne at keeping the king's favour: he was Master of the Horse to Queen Charlotte 1763–5; Lord Lieutenant of Ireland 1765–8; and took over from Shelburne as Secretary of State for the Southern Dept when he resigned in 1768.[60]

Like the Duchess of Portland or Mary Delany, although on a more modest scale, Sophia made her own natural history collection, and in 1769 when her eldest son was recovering from his smallpox vaccination she took him into her closet and gave him her shells to amuse him when he was very feverish.

---

[56] H.M. Scott, 'Wyndham, Charles, Second Earl of Egremont (1710–1763)', ODNB online, accessed 23 February 2009; Anita McConnell, 'Brühl, John Maurice, [Hans Moritz], Count von Brühl (1736–1809)', ODNB online, accessed 26 February 2009. Diary entries, 12 July, 30 August and 2 September 1765 and 19 January, 23 July 1766 mention visits with either Count Brühl or Lady Egremont.

[57] E.g. *Diary*, entries 2 March 1766; 19 March 1766; 8 April 1766.

[58] E.g. *Diary*, entries 3 February 1765; 18 July 1766; C. Campbell Orr, 'Mrs. Delany at Court', in *Mrs. Delany and her Circle*, ed. Mark Laird and Alicia Weisberg-Roberts (New Haven, CT and London, 2009), 40–63. In Ireland she also met Mrs Vesey, another of the Bluestocking circle.

[59] The Thynnes also had Irish estates.

[60] H.M. Scott, 'Thynne, Thomas, Third Viscount Weymouth and First Marquess of Bath (1734–1796)', ODNB online, accessed 31 January 2008.

Sophia was keen on gardening and landscape design and followed enthusiastically Brown's works at Bowood. Once in Ireland she enthused over signs of landscape improvement exemplified by the picturesque and sublime gardens in the vicinity of Dublin, which she interpreted through the lens not of Edmund Burke but of the classical Longinus. She also noticed approvingly the canal bordering some of her husband's estates which had improved navigation to Dublin: improvement embraced not only the aesthetic but the utilitarian. These two facets combined in her search for the perfect dairy design: Mrs Vesey, the Irish bluestocking, gave her two plans.[61]

Sophia was also able to enter into her husband's interest in technology. In 1766 they made a visit to Birmingham and were shown around by the leading industrialist Samuel Garbett, whose enterprises included a button factory. Sophia listened intently to all explanations of industrial processes and asked her husband to supply a brief account for her diary of how and why Birmingham had become industrially pre-eminent. As well as the tour to Birmingham in 1766, the couple visited other factories in 1770, en route to Ireland, seeing carpets at Kidderminster, and porcelain at Worcester, where Sophia was also interested in the way a road was being built, comparing it in her mind to road-building then in train near Bowood.

In July 1770 Lady Sophia and her eldest son accompanied Lord Shelburne on a two-month visit to Dublin and his Irish estates. Sophia and her son stayed in a house just outside Dublin hired for them by Lady Arbella, Peafield, near her Blackrock villa, which Sophia admired for its elegance, while noticing it was furnished with 'manufactures of the country'.[62] Lord Shelburne stayed in his mother's St Stephen's Green house. Doubtless this facilitated his business, and doubtless it was also maintained that the suburban air was better for the young child; but there are also hints that Lord Shelburne tried to keep his children away from their grandmother, since when Sophia called on her, she extracted a promise that she would speak to her husband about her mother-in-law seeing more of her grandchildren. Lord Shelburne conceded that when she was in London she could see them whenever she asked.[63]

Sophia considered Ireland very backward compared with England:

The faces, clothing and manners of the Common-People wear an appearance of extreme Poverty & Indolence, which must make the living in the Country exceedingly disagreeable unless one had ye power of working a Great, General Reformation in ye Government of it, wch I am amaz'd the English can have so long & so Grievously Neglected.[64]

[61] *Diary* entry, 10 September 1770.
[62] Ibid., entry 21 July 1770.
[63] Ibid., entry 28 July 1770.
[64] Ibid., entry 23 July 1770.

Travelling with her husband to Lord Sidney's estate which was contiguous with her husband's, she remarked on the evidence of poor housing and diet, and spotted that many peasants were vassals of the landlords, which gave them little incentive to work. She realized that Ireland did not have the English Poor Law system or provision for workhouses. The Shelburnes' rural neighbour was an improving landlord who was trying to encourage the linen industry, like many eighteenth-century peers, who saw the utility in creating another source of tenant income so as to facilitate payment of rents. Lord Shelburne discussed with him the idea of subscribing to the Linen Board and of their joining in efforts to encourage the industry.[65]

Sophia's friendship with her husband's aunt must have been furthered by the fact that she was genuinely religious herself, as her diary attests. When she discovered one of her Tollemache nieces was not yet confirmed she promptly arranged for this to be done under the instruction of the Wycombe rector; similarly her young black house-servant was both baptized and inoculated.[66] Daily prayers were said in the Berkeley Square house and sermons read out loud. So Sophia was appreciative of Lady Arbella's philanthropic projects; she subscribed to the Magdalen Hospital, attended a sermon there, bought trimmings and ordered ruffles made by the residents. She also visited the Foundling Hospital and described its arrangements. There were 886 children in residence, most waiting to be fostered out. Lady Arbella's companion, Miss Katherine Fitzmaurice, a cousin's daughter whom she regarded as an adopted daughter, had devised an effective bottle to feed

---

[65] Ibid., entry 19 August 1770. See Barnard, *The New Anatomy*, ch. 9 for landlord efforts to stimulate rural industry. It is not clear who the Lord Sidney in question is, as there was no Lord Sidney alive in 1770, but Sophia records that the estates comprised 16–17,000 acres of the lands owned by 'the late Sir Peter Leicester' so they undoubtedly were referring to estates formerly owned by the earls of Leicester, whose name was Sidney. The second earl of Leicester, Robert Sidney [Sydney], was Lord Lieutenant of Ireland, 1640–1, and his son, Henry Sydney was created Earl of Romney and then Viscount Sidney (1704). He had no direct heirs, but lands descended to collateral members of the family, including the second earl of Leicester's second daughter Lucy. She married into the Pelham family, and one daughter became the progenitress of the Pelham-Holles Dukes of Newcastle, the other of the Townshend family. The lands referred to as 'Lord Sidney's', may have been acquired by Shelburne's contemporary, Thomas Townshend, an independently wealthy man, in memory of his ancestors. The title Viscount Sidney, spelt Sydney, was recreated for him in 1789. He was loosely connected to Chatham and the Rockinghamites, and became Shelburne's Home Secretary in 1782. His wife Elizabeth was a member of the extensive courtier family, the Brudenells of Deane, Northants, and became one of Queen Charlotte's Ladies of the Bedchamber in 1791. Ian K.R. Archer, 'Townshend, Thomas, First Viscount Sydney (1733–1800)', ODNB online, accessed 29 July 2009. The Diary notes that Lord Shelburne regretted his father had not purchased these lands when they were on the market: Diary, entry 19 August 1770: 'I believe he is sorry his father gave up his first intention of fixing here.' This second mention of the lands gives a figure of 18,000 acres.

[66] *Diary*, entries for April 1769.

those not yet assigned to a foster-mother.[67] Sophia also describes the craft training to spin, knit or make lace, and notes that they were taught to read. Lady Arbella gave young Lord Fitzmaurice a child's library, a catechism, a map of Ireland and a writing set, devised by her in conjunction with Dr Thompson, one of the Asylum guardians, for use by the Foundling children.[68]

Sophia's diary thus gives us examples of Lady Arbella in action as a philanthropist. But is also suggests that she must have been very enjoyable company – not just an earnest widow. She held a regular Thursday evening at home, and one September evening, a cold supper turned into an impromptu dance, and, assisted by Lord Charles Fitzgerald, she sang Irish songs until 2 a.m. Lord Charles was the fifteen-year-old third son of Emily, Duchess of Leinster, and lived with his siblings and their tutor, William Ogilvie, at Frescati, the neighbouring villa to Peasfield.[69]

Louisa Fitzpatrick and Her Whig Connections

Unfortunately for Lord Shelburne, Sophia did not live long enough to continue her role as cultured companion, able hostess, social networker, and engaged mother; she died in 1771, probably of some kind of chest infection.[70] Shelburne was disconsolate, and travelled abroad to get over it, with great profit to his intellectual life (Chapter 9). He left his two boys (aged six and three) in the care of his aunt: one cannot but wonder if they shared some of the open air regime of the Fitzgeralds nearby, who scrambled over rocks and bathed in the sea, following the Rousseauist ideas endorsed by their tutor. Lady Sophia too had read her Rousseau and evidently agreed with some of his ideas.[71] A charming glimpse of summer at Blackrock comes in a letter to Lord Shelburne in July 1773, mentioning that the children are eating strawberries, and getting better at riding.[72] To Lady Arbella, parenting was an art: to console the eleven-year-old Lord Fitzmaurice when he was upset at having to stay in London rather than accompany his father to Bowood,

---

[67] *Diary*, entry for 29 July 1770, 31 July 1770. On wet-nursing, see Valerie A. Fildes, *Breasts, Bottles and Babies: A History of Infant Feeding* (Edinburgh, 1986).

[68] *Diary*, entry 29 August 1770.

[69] *Diary*, entry 2 August 1770. On the Fitzgeralds, Brian Fitzgerald, *Emily, Duchess of Leinster, 1731–1814, A Study of Her Life and Times* (London, 1949); Stella Tillyard, *Aristocrats: Caroline, Emily, Louisa and Sarah Lennox 1740–1832* (London, 1994), 243–5. Irish elite interest in Irish traditional music was already evident by the 1770s: see W.J. McCormack, 'Introduction', in Maria Edgeworth, *The Absentee* (Oxford, 1980).

[70] Unfortunately, John Cannon ascribes her death to childbirth in idem, 'Petty, William, Second Earl of Shelburne and First Marquess of Lansdowne, 1737–1805', ODNB online, accessed 16 December 2004.

[71] For example, *Diary*, entry, 15 February 1765 and 29 July 1770.

[72] BHA, Letter from Lady Arbella Denny to Lord Shelburne, 14 July 1773.

she explained 'the paternal preceptor is the painter who must now and then do what is not pleasing to himself in order to make the subject he works on receive the beauties he wishes to bestow on it'.[73] Lady Arbella resided with her nephew for three years, mainly at Bowood, to look after the boys until they were of the age when, customarily, boys were transferred into masculine care. On parting with them she wrote to Lady Caldwell, 'The children here are lovely souls. My heart will ache at leaving them, I find. Lord S[helburne], I believe, will be one of the best fathers.'[74]

In 1773 Shelburne turned his attention to the poor and elderly on his Bowood estates, writing in a memorandum that their situation was 'a reproach to the owner' and that he wanted to 'encourage morals and industry'.[75] He decided a school was required: who better was there to advise on its management and regulations than Lady Arbella? She in turn enlisted the help of a widow, Mrs John, who according to the account he gave to Bentham:

> was a sort of dependent of Lord Shelburne's first wife; lives gratis in a little house … close by; is a Methodist; comes a-begging to great people for money to give to charity, is a conversable woman who has seen the world and has court connections. She has distributed money for the queen; and though she has the dress and appearance of an upper servant, has had correspondence with all manner of great people, and could be made use of occasionally to put news about.[76]

By the end of the 1770s, Shelburne was looking for another wife; when he remarried he confided to his second wife that he hated to be alone.[77] Meanwhile, ever one to make the grand figure, he took as his mistress the leading actress of the day, Mrs Abington, who had first really made her name in Dublin. She returned to London under the protection of an Irish MP, Needham. She created the part of Lady Teazle, which Sheridan wrote for her.[78] Shelburne seems to have remained in thrall to Ireland in his affairs of the heart, despite his efforts to transcend his background.

73 BHA, Letter Lady Denny to Lord Fitzmaurice, 19 April 1779.
74 Letter 32, Lady Arbella Denny to Lady Caldwell, 23 June 1774, in Raughter, ed., 'My Dear Lady C', 192.
75 BHA, 'Memorandum on the Bowood Poor', February 1773.
76 Fitzmaurice, *Shelburne*, II, 328, citing Jeremy Bentham, *Works*, ed . J. Bowring, vol. 10, 101, letter 14 September 1781. Also in *The Collected Works of Jeremy Bentham*, gen. ed. J.J. Burns, *Correspondence*, Vol. 3, ed. Ian R. Christie, 96. Sophia's *Diary*, 6 August 1770, indicates she deplored Methodism as a 'snare', so either Shelburne or Bentham was mistaken, or else Mrs John had developed methodistical inclinations after her patroness's death, or they were not overt enough to be objectionable.
77 BHA, Letter 2 August 1782, Lord Shelburne to Louisa, Countess of Shelburne: 'You know I don't like living alone, and you know too what resource it is to me to tell you my grievances.'
78 Alison Oddey, 'Abington, Frances (1727–1815)', ODNB online, accessed 30 April 2007.

When looking for a second wife, there were several Irish candidates; and once more the business was managed by various aunts. A false start came with his engagement in 1778 to Frances Molesworth, an Irish heiress with 30,000 useful pounds. His mother was opposed to this marriage,[79] and young Frances found unbearable his talking constantly of politics with, or more probably, *at* her, and cried into her soup over dinner in Berkeley Square. She begged her aunt Lady Lucan, who had brought her up, to help her break off the match.[80] Evidently Shelburne needed a clever wife, as Sophia Carteret had been, or at any rate someone with political savvy.

His late wife's aunt Lady Louisa Clayton then stepped in with advice, and a list of seven possible candidates, three of them Irish, and taking into account 'age birth and education'.[81] One suggestion was Lady Almeira Carpenter – later to become the mistress of the king's brother, the Duke of Gloucester, after his disenchantment with his wife, the Dowager Countess Waldegrave.[82] A second, Lady Frances Fitzwilliam, was pretty, modest, and liked to live quietly, though as a niece of Lord Rockingham, with whom Shelburne had an uneasy relationship at this point, Louisa recognized she might be somewhat unsuitable. A third suggestion, which proved the right answer, was Lady Louisa Fitzpatrick (Figure 5), niece of Gertrude, 4th Duchess of Bedford, who had been largely responsible for her upbringing after the death of Louisa's mother, Evelyn Leveson-Gower, Gertrude's younger sister. Lady Louisa Clayton noted that 'all those ladies that have married from the Duchess of Bedford, have behaved uncommonly well, & all have confor'd themselves to the taste of the persons they have married'.[83]

The father of 'these ladies' was John, 1st Earl Gower, later 1st Marquess of Stafford, who had produced eleven children in all, which resulted in a powerful web of connections (Table 3). He was an adroit courtier, whose Household positions included Master of the Horse, and Lord Chamberlain, as well as being an emollient Lord President of the Council, when Lord Shelburne was Prime Minister. The marquessate was secured from Pitt in 1786. Gower's third wife (m. 1768) was a particularly able (or pushy, depending on your point of view) female politician, Susanna Stewart, who had connections to the Bute interests and was also a Woman of the Bedchamber to

[79] BHA, Letter 8 January 1778 to Thomas Fitzmaurice from Mrs Diana Good (maid and housekeeper to Dowager lady Shelburne): 'my Lady dislikes her of all things and made very little answer to it She thinks her very Disagreeable but she don't care ...' I am indebted to Nigel Aston for this reference.

[80] Fitzmaurice, *Shelburne*, II, 137.

[81] BHA, Letter January 23 1778, Lady Louisa Clayton to Lord Shelburne

[82] Stella Tillyard, *A Royal Affair, George III and his Troublesome Siblings* (London, 2006), 312, 325, 328; Matthew Kilburn, 'William Henry, Prince, First Duke of Gloucester and Edinburgh (1743–1805)', ODNB online, accessed 3 November 2008.

[83] BHA, Letter January 23 1778, Lady Louisa Clayton to Lord Shelburne.

5. Lady Louisa Fitzpatrick as Countess of Shelburne, by George Romney, c. 1780, Trustees of the Bowood Estate

George III's sister, Princess Augusta, later Duchess of Brunswick.[84] So on her maternal side, Louisa brought Shelburne links to a formidable dynasty of men and women who were courtiers, politicians, and Enlightened improvers on their estates.

Louisa's father was the Irish peer, John, 1st Earl of Upper Ossory. Her brothers John, the second earl, and Gen. Richard Fitzpatrick, both served loyally in the Bedford political interest, the former being MP for Bedford-shire from 1767 to 1794, and Lord Lieutenant between 1771 and 1818; by the 1770s they had moved close to the Rockinghams. But their connections were as much of a liability as an asset to Shelburne (Tables 3 and 4). In the first place, his bride's sister-in-law was a divorcée. Born Anne Liddell, daughter of a Northumberland landowner, Henry Liddell, 1st Baron Ravens-worth, she first married the 3rd Duke of Grafton, from whom she separated because of his notorious liaisons, including one with the courtesan Nancy Parsons.

As Amanda Vickery has described, she insisted on a proper financial settlement that would enable her to live in appropriate style.[85] She then fell in love with Lord Ossory. Their union was legalized in 1769 after their son had been born, and by playing her cards adroitly with her husband's aunt Gertrude, the Duchess of Bedford, she achieved some semblance of social rehabilitation – though never reception at court.[86] Stuck in Bedfordshire, she relished her correspondence with Horace Walpole.[87]

It seems that Louisa was not considered to be morally contaminated by her sister-in-law, and stayed with her at the Ossory's English home, Ampthill from time to time, but she also lived in London with her aunt, and in Warwick with her younger half-sister, Henrietta Vernon, who had been married off at sixteen by her step-aunt Susanna to the 2nd Earl of Warwick. Henrietta and her two Vernon sisters, Caroline and Elizabeth were Louisa's half-sisters from her mother's second marriage to Richard Vernon[88]

---

[84] Sophia Petty's diary mentions visits with Princess Amelia, e.g. when Princess Amelia, entertained her and her husband on a visit to England, Diary, 17 January 1766. Lady Susanna was also a great friend of the Irish beauty, Elizabeth Gunning, successively Duchess of Argyll and of Hamilton, another Lady of the Bedchamber to Queen Char-lotte.

[85] Amanda Vickery, *Behind Closed Doors: At Home in Georgian England* (New Haven, CT and London, 2009). My thanks to the author for showing her work on the duchess of Grafton before publication.

[86] BHA, two letters from Anne, Countess of Upper Ossory to Gertrude, Dowager Duchess of Bedford, March 1769.

[87] *Walpoles Correspondence*, vol. 32, Preface; Matthew Kilburn, 'Fitzpatrick, [née Liddell] Anne, Countess of Upper Ossory, [other married name Anne FitzRoy, Duchess of Grafton] (1737/8–1804), Correspondent of Horace Walpole', ODNB online, accessed 23 October 2008.

[88] G. Le G. Norgate, rev. J.-M. Alter, 'Vernon, Richard (1726–1800)', ODNB online, accessed 19 January 2010.

(Table 3). As their mother died when they were infants it seems Gertrude Russell helped to bring them up as well.[89] We know less about Louisa's education than we do about Sophia's, but it is possible she was also brought up on Mme LePrince de Beaumont's series of conduct books for ladies in high stations, among other similar advice books. Jeremy Bentham commented she had 'the best, highest aristocratical education possible' – meaning of course a training in social graces as well as intellectual formation.[90] However she also knew Latin, and prepared her son Henry for Westminster School. Bentham remembered her as rather aloof and grand, but his willingness to crawl over the floor with young Henry on his back, and his accompaniment of her harpsichord playing with his violin, thawed her a little. He also played chess with her and Caroline Vernon. He became a close friend of the family and was one of the few who visited Louisa when she was the last stages of her illness. Although he tells us that at Bowood the ladies were very correct and 'gallantry' was discouraged, Bentham managed to keep up a kind of flirtatious, bantering conversation with them in person and by letter. As Emmanuelle de Champs, shows, however, Bentham misread the social codes and found himself frozen out[91] (Chapter 11).

Shelburne's second marriage in theory might have cemented a connection with the powerful Bedford group of Whigs, but this did not happen. For a start Lord Ossory was not unduly ambitious; his elopement had already put paid to the chance of the embassy to Spain. He supported North's admin-

---

[89] However, *Walpole, Walpole Correspondence*, vol. 32, 347 praised Lady Ossory for keeping her sisters in the country away from their Machiavellian aunt, where they lead a 'rational and agreeable life', Letter 26 January 1777. Bentham, who had much difficulty puzzling out how all these women were connected, observed 'Lady Shelburne was with old Gertrude for 9 years. What an exquisite brood that old hen has sat upon!' Bentham, *Correspondence*, vol. 3, 73. Other female cousins were daughters of Mary Leveson-Gower by Rev. Sir Richard Wrottesley, 7th Bart: Elizabeth, second wife of the deserted 3rd Duke of Grafton (1745–1822) and Dorothy, wife of Baron von Kutzleben, Minister to the Landgrave of Hesse-Cassel. Retford, *The Art of Portraiture*, discusses the 4th Duchess of Marlborough's representation in portraiture, and her reputation for domestic fidelity and probity, in her Conclusion, 215–34. See also Clarissa Campbell Orr, 'Queen Charlotte as Patron: Some Intellectual and Social Contexts', *The Court Historian*, 6:3 (December 2001), 183–212, for the cultural and patronage links of the 4th Duke and his sister, Lady Pembroke, to the crown.

[90] *Works*, ed. Browning, vol. 10, 115; also 117.

[91] In fact Bentham was smitten both by Caroline Vernon and also the young, pretty, buxom Caroline Fox. In the reports he sent the former about how Shelburne was adjusting to Louisa's death, he refers to them as the Queen (Caroline), the Vice-Queen (Elizabeth) and the Princess (Caroline Fox). The two Miss Vernons were also described as the 'two Minervas', suggesting an air of intellectuality and chaste reserve. After his brother Samuel had sent a present of an arctic fox to the Bowood menagerie, the ladies were sometimes called 'The White Foxes'. Bentham, *Correspondence*, vol. 3, 95 and 49; vol. 4, 98–110; ibid., 255 to C. Fox, late February 1791; also in Works, ed. Bowring, vol. 10, 118. See Chapter 11 in this volume.

istration until the American War when he sided with Fox. Later in 1780, just after his sister's marriage, he voted for Economical Reform, but did not organize a petition in Bedfordshire for it. In 1782 Shelburne canvassed his political support more actively. His sister tried to ginger him up, knowing that one thing her brother did want was a British peerage:

> It will be impossible for him to urge what you so much wish without the most distinct and avowed precious support, other wise we shall feel in a very awkward position.[92]

But he became more and more a Foxite supporter – until the French Revolution. Ossory was close to the titular leader of the Foxite Whigs, the 3rd Duke of Portland, and was one of those who successfully urged the duke to cooperate with Pitt. He duly received his reward in July 1794 when the Portland Whigs joined the government in the shape of his much coveted British barony of Upper Ossory.[93]

More obviously a political and indeed a moral liability was Lord Ossory's brother, Richard Fitzpatrick, one the great charmers of the age – according to *The Gentleman's Magazine*, 'Natural, easy, unaffected, supremely well-bred' – and also the principal gambling crony of Charles James Fox, who was his cousin by marriage[94] (Table 3). He sat for various seats in the Commons in the Bedford interest, but when his aunt Gertrude solicited George III for a place for him at court, the king replied 'I do not choose to fill my family with gamesters.'[95] He followed Fox into opposition over the American War, and during the Fox–North coalition, where he was briefly Chief Secretary for Ireland during the Duke of Portland's brief Lieutenancy, his relations with Shelburne became increasingly strained. During Shelburne's ministry Fitzpatrick opposed him, yet retained cordial personal relations with him. Shelburne observed to Louisa in 1785, 'Your brother Richard in high spirits. He's the only one of your family who keeps up with me.'[96] Thus, the political unity of the Opposition in 1779, when the marriage took place, did not really knit Shelburne firmly into the Bedford political interest, despite his devotion to his wife.[97]

---

[92] Cited in Sir Lewis Namier and John Brooke, ed., *The House of Commons 1754–90*, 2 vols (London, 1985), vol. 2, 431–3, at 432, letter 18 September 1782. He said to his uncle, Lord Gower, that the peerage was 'his only ambition'. Ibid.

[93] See Copy of Lord Ossory's Commonplace book in Bowood papers for further autobiographical sketch.

[94] Namier and Brooke, *House of Commons*, vol. 2, 433–5, citing obituary from the Gentleman's Magazine, 435.

[95] Ibid., including quotation from George III; he was MP for Okehampton, 1770–4, Tavistock 1774–1807, and Bedfordshire 1807–12.

[96] BHA, Letter 23 June 1785, Lord Shelburne to Lady Louisa, Countess of Shelburne.

[97] Fitzmaurice, *Shelburne*, II, 38, citing Shelburne, in Parliamentary History, 20, 1165.

Although Shelburne's second marriage was evidently the result of some judicious social introductions, it is plain from the letters of husband and wife that again there was an affectionate union. However, Louisa's rackety Fitzpatrick connections were of some concern to Louisa's half-sister Caroline Vernon when she married, for she realized that Louisa's elevation would mean she could lead a fast life at the centre of the London *Ton*. Caroline's father Richard Vernon was himself a fast-living crony of Charles James Fox and Richard Fitzpatrick, and one of the most successful horse-breeders and racing men of the day, who had converted his younger son's portion of £5000 into a £100,000 fortune from his racing and gaming.[98] So Caroline knew the pitfalls she was warning her half-sister against – though, as Horace Walpole had said to Lady Upper Ossory, Shelburne had made a good husband to Sophia Carteret and was not a gamester.[99]

On the eve of Louisa's marriage to him, Caroline Vernon wrote a letter of advice to Louisa, expressing her fears she might now neglect religious duties. She urged her simply not to reply to any counter-religious arguments, and to show her disapproval of anyone in her company who spoke slightingly of religion. Caroline believed religion was not a gloomy business, but designed to show mankind true happiness; and such happiness was more likely if the 'idle dissipations of the corrupt world' were despised and avoided. She urged her to make systematic and prompt charitable initiatives: 'To spend all your money upon baubles, cards and cloaths [sic] I must look upon in your situation to be not only a folly but a sin – and such a one as I flatter myself you are not capable of committing.' Above all she begged her to desist from the horrors of gaming, painting in how ghastly it would be if she were forced to ask her husband for extra money to cover her debts: 'Only arm yourself my sister against The Ton, The Fashion – and all the giddy Fools that will next winter be vying for who can best seduce a new, young, beautiful countess with dissipation & folly.'[100]

Caroline's fears were realistic: as well as Fox's notorious indebtedness, she must have known about the febrile Georgiana Duchess of Devonshire's gambling.[101] Louisa herself certainly came to know some very 'fast' people; even her Bedford aunt Gertrude had given her social approval to Louisa's attending the private parties held by the Duchess of Cumberland. The

---

[98] Norgate, 'Richard Vernon'.

[99] Horace Walpole commented to Lady Ossory, 'Lord Shelburne made an admirable husband to a wife, much less handsome, and apparently, for I did not know her, much less agreeable ...' Walpole, *Correspondence*, vol. 33, Letter July 20 1779, 115.

[100] BHA, Letters from Caroline Vernon, later Mrs Bobus Smith, to Lady Louisa Fitzpatrick, 1779–80.

[101] L.G. Mitchell discusses the gambling habits of the Whigs in *The Whig World* (London, 2005), 49–51, and C.J. Fox in particular, in idem., *Charles James Fox* (Oxford, 1992). See also Phyllis Deutsch, 'Moral Trespass in Georgian London, Gaming, Gender and Electoral Politics in the Age of George III', *Historical Journal*, 39:3 (1998), 637–56.

Duke, brother to George III, who had married the widowed Irishwoman Anne Horton, without his brother's knowledge or permission, had been reconciled to him in 1780. Duchess Anne ran a private faro bank, and her sister Elizabeth Luttrell was even more notorious as a gambler; their behaviour was exactly what Caroline Vernon deplored.[102]

It is impossible to know the character of Louisa's religious inclinations, as she left no diary. As she became more and more of an invalid, her letters to Shelburne show her affection and appreciation for his loving care of her, but never mention submission to divine Providence or any other type of religious sentiment.[103] Perhaps she did not think along these lines. However, she did pursue some systematic charity, either of her own accord, or with Caroline's warning or reminders in mind. And naturally enough she turned to the redoubtable Lady Arbella Denny for her advice.

In 1780 Shelburne's mother, aware she was approaching her death, had bequeathed the pension from the Irish civil list she had been granted by George II to be used for public charity, through Louisa's agency. Louisa in turn asked Lady Arbella to manage this annual sum for her, and although Lady Arbella was in her late seventies, she took on this trust and sent her niece by marriage an annual letter and account of how she had disbursed the money, which amounted to at least £175 p.a.[104]

These letters to Louisa, Countess of Shelburne, and her husband, in the 1780s, are extremely revealing of Lady Arbella's economic philosophy. She explained in 1784, 'I hope God in his mercy will raise some active spirit among the sensible of the nation, who may mark out the eligible paths of

---

[102] BHA Letter from Gertrude Duchess of Bedford to Louisa, Countess of Shelburne, 1784, approving she attend a private party at the Cumberlands – presumably this is now suitable as the king and his brother are reconciled. The Cumberland marriage prompted the 1772 Royal Marriages Act and also the Duke of Gloucester's owning up to his marriage to Maria, Dowager Countess Waldegrave. Anne Horton and Elizabeth Luttrell were the daughters of the ageing roué Lord Irnham. Their brother Henry Luttrell was Wilkes's opponent in the Middlesex elections. Sir Lewis Namier and John Brooke, ed., *The House of Commons 1754–90*, 2 vols (London, 1985), vol. 2, 65–6; A.F. Blackstock, 'Luttrell, Henry Lawes, Second Earl of Carhampton (1737–1821), Army Officer and Politician', ODNB online, accessed 10 November 2008. For the Duke of Cumberland, Matthew Kilburn, 'Henry Frederick, Prince, Duke of Cumberland and Strathearn (1745–1790)', ODNB online, accessed 10 November 2008; Tillyard, *A Royal Affair*. The 1780 Gordon Riots, the most serious public disorder of the century, prompted the king's brothers to show him their loyalty. Louisa wrote to her husband in Bowood about the camp in Hyde Park and the king's actions, urging him to visit court to show his loyalty rather than seem the odd man out. BWA, Letter June 16 1780, Lady Louisa, Countess of Shelburne, to Lord Shelburne.

[103] BWA, Folder of letters from Lady Louisa, Countess of Shelburne, to Lord Shelburne, 1780–9. Louisa was probably suffering from tuberculosis.

[104] BHA, Letter from Dowager Countess of Shelburne to Lady Louisa, Countess of Shelburne; Letter 18 December 1780, from Lady Arbella Denny to Lady Louisa, Countess of Shelburne.

industry, for in my mind they are very visible: agriculture, fisheries, manufactures would engage all our labouring hands …' Manufacturers needed employment in Ireland and customers from abroad. She felt dissatisfied with her efforts to apprentice some of the Foundling orphans to make cord fishing nets, because of guild restrictions of indentures to members' children, which reduced the productivity to the detriment of both workers and customers.[105] In her will she left some money to her nephew Sir John Colthurst to help him invest in his fishing net business.[106]

In 1780 Lord Shelburne was among those who had given money to unemployed weavers; in 1782 she asked him if he had any employment schemes for them, and told him how she had helped organize a meeting called in Dublin by the sheriff for the nobility and gentry to discuss ways of assisting. She also described to Lord Shelburne a new stove to be used for drying codfish instead of relying on sunshine. Various worthies, including the philanthropic Roman Catholic peer Lord Trimelston, were considering investing in it, and Lord Hillsborough, then Secretary of State for the South, approved but thought Parliament should subsidize it.[107] Perhaps impatient of waiting for male politicians to act, she also encouraged a female subscription to a fund to subsidize Irish fisheries and prevent French and Dutch encroachment.[108] And in the next year, 1783, she enclosed to Louisa a design for some 'Emblematical' silks subscribed by Irish ladies, under the direction of herself and the Dowager Duchess Emily of Leinster, who was Lord Hillsborough's sister-in-law. The pattern is of blue-grey pillars entwined by olive leaves, alternating with bunch of corn. The pillars, she explained, represented the ladies' support for the distressed manufactures; the olive branches, the peace of 1783; and the corn, 'plenty – the certain

---

[105] BHA, Letter 14 April 1784, Lady Arbella Denny to Lady Louisa, Marchioness of Lansdowne.

[106] See note 39.

[107] BHA, Letters 19 January 1770; 8 May 1782; 20 November 1782; 5 August 1779 Lady Arbella Denny to Lord Shelburne. Wills Hill, 2nd Viscount Hillsborough, was an Irish peer, courtier-politician, and legal expert; later Marquess of Downshire; President of Board of Trade, 1763–5, 1766, 1768–72; Secretary of State for Southern Department, 1779. Peter Marshall, 'Hill, Wills, First Marquess of Downshire, 1718–1793', ODNB Online, accessed 18 January 2010. Brother-in-law of Emily Lennox, after her marriage to the premier Irish peer, James Fitzgerald, Earl of Kildare, later Duke of Leinster. His daughter Mary had also been taught by Mme LePrince de Beaumont, and married James, 7th Earl and 1st Marquess of Salisbury, said to be given his post as Lord Chamberlain because of his wife's wit, grace, and intelligence. She had herself painted wearing his Order of the Garter, perhaps to indicate that she was the man of the family, or that women should be given these honours. George III certainly contemplated awarding the Garter to suitable women. Lady Mary was deployed by the Court party in elections as a counterpart to the febrile Georgiana, Duchess of Devonshire. Lord David Cecil, *The Cecils of Hatfield House* (London, 1973).

[108] BHA, Letter 15 June 1782, Lady Arbella Denny to Lady Louisa, Countess of Shelburne.

fruits of industry and public spirit'.[109] As well as these job-creation schemes, Lady Arbella spent Louisa's money on her charities: a birthing chair for the Lying-in Hospital; premiums for the wet-nurses at the Foundling Hospital; equipment for the new dispensary; a gift to the lunatics' wing; and some micro-lending to help three poor women to rent a shop, stock it with earthenware, and take in lodgers.[110]

Poignantly Louisa, since 1784 Marchioness of Lansdowne, died in 1789, just as she and the 1st Marquess were discussing the plans to send their son Henry (later the 3rd Marquess), to Westminster School, as recommended by Bentham. Making him an alumnus of this supremely political school was probably the best educational decision his father could have made, instead of trying to plan the perfect private education as he had done for Lord Wycombe. In this second widowerhood, Lady Louisa Clayton again stepped in to help, trying to sooth the tensions between Wycombe and his father after Louisa's death. In 1792, ever the matchmaker, she was even trying to introduce him to a suitable Miss H, with money, character and education – but not beauty.[111]

1792 was also the year of Lady Arbella's Denny's death after an unusually long life of enterprise and benevolence. The Ladies of Bowood, whether aunts, wives, or sisters-in-law, provided an element of intellectuality and culture which complemented in its distinctive way that of the much better known men of the Bowood circle. His first wife linked him with the Blue-stockings and the Carteret connections to the court, while his second wife's links were to the ever-ramifying Leveson-Gowers and their Whig and court connections. One of Shelburne's greatest misfortunes was to have married twice for both love and advantage, but to have been widowed each time so quickly. Finally, Ireland is never far away, through the continuity of his beloved aunt's long life, or the Irish dimension to both of his wives.

---

109 BHA, Letter 10 October 1782, Lady Arbella Denny to Lady Louisa, Countess of Shelburne.
110 BHA, Letters, 2 June 1781; 24 July, 1783; 9 March 1781, Lady Arbella Denny to Lady Louisa, Countess of Shelburne. These three letters account for the charitable outlay on Lady Louisa's behalf for their respective years.
111 BHA, Letter, 13 April 1792, Lady Louisa Clayton to Lord Shelburne. Bentham said Shelburne turned to Lady 'Betty' Clayton as his oracle on family matters. Bowring, ed., *Works*, vol. 10, 117.

3

A Christian Whig: Lord Shelburne and the Latitudinarian Tradition

G.M. DITCHFIELD

How important was religion to Lord Shelburne? For much of his life, his best-known religious connections were to be found among the leading figures of heterodox Dissent, notably Joseph Priestley, who served as his librarian and literary companion from 1773 to 1780, Richard Price, who became one of his closest confidants, and Thomas Jervis, a tutor to Shelburne's son between 1772 and 1783. All three were Dissenting ministers with highly unorthodox opinions, particularly over the doctrine of the Trinity. Moreover, Shelburne allowed himself to become identified publicly with support for Dissenting causes in Parliament. However, we would also remember that Shelburne was born into, was brought up in, and remained throughout his life a member of, an established Church, in England and in Ireland. For someone well known for imprecision, Shelburne was remarkably explicit in the Lords' debate on the union with Ireland on 19 March 1799 when he declared 'I am no dissenter, nor am I a Catholic'.[1] But within the Church of England in particular there was a wide range of doctrinal and ecclesiastical opinion and it may be worth asking where within that range Shelburne's own position may be located. It will be the suggestion of this chapter that he had a substantial measure of affinity with the Latitudinarian tradition, a tradition which historians such as John Gascoigne have identified as an important source of intellectual inspiration for the ideas of those whom Derek Jarrett

Acknowledgements: I am grateful the Marquess of Lansdowne for permission to consult the BL Bowood Papers at the British Library; to the Houghton Library, Harvard University, for permission to quote from the diary of Thomas Hollis; and to Lambeth Palace Library and Dr Williams's Library for permission to consult manuscripts in their possession. This chapter has benefited from the critical comments of those present at the 'Begetters of Revolution' conference; I am particularly grateful to Drs Nigel Aston, Martin Fitzpatrick, John Seed, and to Clarissa Campbell Orr.

[1] Cobbett, *The Parliamentary History of England from the Norman Conquest ... to the Year 1803*, 36 vols (London, 1806–20), XXXIV, 679.

deemed 'begetters of revolution'.[2] But this was an evolving tradition, and an examination of Shelburne's ideas in the context of Latitudinarianism may go some distance towards the elucidation of both.

I

When visiting France with Shelburne in 1774, Joseph Priestley observed that 'all the philosophical persons to whom I was introduced at Paris' were 'unbelievers in Christianity, and even professed Atheists', who 'had given no proper attention to it, and did not really know what Christianity was'. He added 'This was also the case with a great part of the company that I saw at Lord Shelburne's.'[3] And John Norris's very brief discussion of Shelburne's religion sees it primarily in secular, utilitarian terms.[4] But as a major landowner and politician, Shelburne could hardly avoid involvement in the formalities of the established Church. At Christ Church, Oxford, where he associated with the anti-Westminster element, his tutors were clergymen, while from the former Jacobite William King of St Mary Hall, he seems to have imbibed some measure of oppositional Toryism. He was well acquainted with Wiltshire clergymen, such as Dr Edward Popham, his exact contemporary at Oxford and rector of Chilton Foliatt from 1778 and a member of the influential Popham family of Littlecote, Wiltshire,[5] and with the poor-law commentator Joseph Townsend, rector of Pewsey.[6] One such clergyman, Osmond Beauvoir, vicar of Calne, and subsequently headmaster of the King's School, Canterbury, served as domestic chaplain to Shelburne's mother from 1764. Another, Frederick Dodsworth, vicar of Calne from 1767, became one of Shelburne's own domestic chaplains in 1768

---

[2]   John Gascoigne, 'Anglican Latitudinarianism and Political Radicalism in the Late Eighteenth Century', *History*, 70 (1986), 22–38.

[3]   *The Theological and Miscellaneous Works of Joseph Priestley*, ed. J.T. Rutt, 25 vols in 26 (London, 1817–32); the first volume, divided into two parts, consists of the life and letters of Priestley. Hereafter it is cited as *Works of Priestley*, ed. Rutt. This reference is to Vol. I (i), 198–9.

[4]   John Norris, *Shelburne and Reform* (London, 1963), 82–7.

[5]   See BL Bowood Papers B46, fol. 155, Charles Spencer to Shelburne, 2 August 1782, in which he referred to Edward Popham as 'your acquaintance and neighbour'. Popham matriculated at St Mary Hall in May 1755, Shelburne at Christ Church the previous March. Alexander Popham, MP for Taunton, voted for repeal of the Test and Corporation Acts in 1787 and 1789; William Popham, MP for Milborne Port, did so in 1789. See G.M. Ditchfield, 'Debates on the Test and Corporation Acts, 1787–90: The Evidence of the Division Lists', *Bulletin of the Institute of Historical Research*, L (1977), 72–6.

[6]   *The Correspondence of Jeremy Bentham*, Vol. 5, ed. A.T. Milne (London, 1981), 194–5. Joseph Townsend's brother James Townsend was MP for Calne, on Shelburne's nomination, from 1782 to 1787.

and was rewarded with a canonry of Windsor in 1782.[7] Shelburne's series of domestic chaplains also reflects his continuing links with Christ Church, Oxford, where his son, John Henry Petty, second Marquess of Lansdowne, was briefly an undergraduate.[8] Shelburne's circle and his broader range of acquaintances included many clergymen, Anglican as well as dissenting. And, in common with other eighteenth-century politicians, Shelburne received requests for ecclesiastical preferment. Although his opportunities for exercising it in a ministerial capacity were very limited, quite a number of letters were addressed to him on that subject in 1782–3, on this subject, including an unsuccessful application from his former Christ Church tutor, William Holwell.[9]

But at an informal level, we have Shelburne's own testimony that at Oxford he 'read by myself a great deal of religion'.[10] In so doing he came to embrace those two major principles of the Protestant Reformation, the fundamental authority of the Bible, and the right and duty to exercise one's reasoning capacities in order to interpret the scriptures for oneself.[11] Among the sermons which, according to the first Lady Shelburne's journal, he read to her in the late 1760s, was one by the non-subscribing Irish Presbyterian John Abernethy, an admirer of Bishop Benjamin Hoadly.[12] On 23 February 1766, she recorded 'I came home to Lord Shelburne, who read me a sermon out of Barrow against judging others, a very necessary lesson delivered in very persuasive and pleasing terms.'[13] The subject is probably significant, although in view of the renowned length of Isaac Barrow's sermons, this entry may be regarded as testimony to Lady Shelburne's patience. Shelburne showed continuing interest in the theological works of André Morellet, while *The Repository*, reflecting the views of Shelburne's circle, included in 1788 a favourable review of Jacques Necker's essay on the importance of religious opinions.[14] Shelburne's interest in theological heterodoxy is seen in his subscription to Joshua Toulmin's *Memoirs … of Faustus Socinus* in 1777.[15] Probably, however, he was not in the habit on his own initiative of subscribing to theological works; we know that he subscribed to Toulmin at Priestley's specific instigation.[16] He is not listed as a subscriber to the works

7   LPL, FV/1/XIV, fols 9r, 80r (Registers of Noblemen's chaplains).
8   LPL, FV/1XV, fols 20v, 155v, 185r.
9   See BL Bowood Papers, B36, fols 131–2 (Holwell to Shelburne, 8 July 1782). For other examples, see BL Bowood Papers, B36, fol. 88; and B46, fol. 132.
10 Fitzmaurice, *Shelburne*, I, 14–15.
11 Fitzmaurice, *Shelburne*, II, 348.
12 Fitzmaurice, *Shelburne*, I, 268.
13 Fitzmaurice, *Shelburne*, I, 270.
14 *The Repository*, no. VII (1 April 1788), 396–401.
15 Joshua Toulmin, *Memoirs … of Faustus Socinus* (London, 1777), 9.
16 *Works of Priestley*, ed. Rutt, I (i), 293–4.

of the Latitudinarian turned Unitarian John Jebb (1787), nor to those of other heterodox writers such as Nathaniel Lardner or William Enfield.

But, as Charles Stuart's elegant essay noted in 1981, rather than displaying hostility or even indifference towards Christianity, Shelburne evinced a classic Whig anticlericalism.[17] His notes on ecclesiastical ranks deplored clerical pretensions to power.[18] On 17 March 1778 in the Lords debate on the Franco-American treaty, he castigated what he called 'those drones of society, the church benefices ... the golden prebends, and those church officers who, having no parochial connection, lived a life of idleness'.[19] He retained a particular dislike for William Markham, whom he had encountered among the 'Westminsters' at Christ Church, and who, as archbishop of York from 1777, was a strong supporter of the American war.[20] While Secretary of State for the South in 1767 Shelburne displayed a complete lack of sympathy towards the proposal for a resident Anglican bishop in the North American colonies. Archbishop Secker noted in his *Autobiography*:

> Also this Spring [i.e. 1767] the ABp of York & I waited upon Ld Shelburne, Secretary of State, to recommend to him the Ecclesiastical Affairs of Canada, & the appointmt of Bps in America. We had a long Conversation with him. The ABp dwelt chiefly on the former Point, in which he seemed well disposed. I dwelt chiefly on the latter, but could make no Impression at all upon him.[21]

As Judith Jago put it drily, 'Shelburne ... was hardly likely to be a patron of episcopacy' and 'It was the misfortune of Secker and Drummond that Shelburne happened to be the southern division secretary at the time they sought him'.[22] When Robert Lowth, bishop of Oxford, objected to the Dissenters' relief bill in May 1772 because the Dissenters opposed the American bishopric, Shelburne is said to have retorted that his warning to Secker and Drummond in 1767 that an American bishopric would be most unwelcome to Dissenters had been ignored.[23]

---

[17] Charles Stuart, 'Lord Shelburne', in *History and Imagination. Essays in Honour of H.R. Trevor-Roper*, ed. Hugh Lloyd-Jones, Valerie Pearl, and Blair Worden (London, 1981), 250.

[18] Fitzmaurice, *Shelburne*, II, 347–8.

[19] Cobbett, *Parl. Hist.*, XIX, 925.

[20] See, for example, Shelburne's clash with Markham in the House of Lords on 30 May 1777, when he described the archbishop as 'a man who would not suffer the word "liberty" to be pronounced without a qualification'; Cobbett, *Parl. Hist.*, XIX, 350–1.

[21] *The Autobiography of Thomas Secker, Archbishop of Canterbury*, ed. John S. Macauley and R.W. Greaves (Lawrence, KS, 1988), 58.

[22] Judith Jago, *Aspects of the Georgian Church. Visitation Studies of the Diocese of York, 1761–1776* (Madison, NJ and London, 1997), 252. From January 1768 responsibilities for America were transferred from Shelburne to the newly-established third secretary of state for the American colonies, Lord Hillsborough.

[23] Fitzmaurice, *Shelburne*, I, 442; Horace Walpole, *Last Journals*, ed. A.F. Steuart, 2 vols (London, 1910), I, 94–5.

Shelburne's religious opinions were informed by a suspicion of ecclesiastical hierarchies, of spiritual tyranny, and of claims to the exclusive possession of religious truth. As his fellow Whig and anti-cleric Lord Holland put it, 'He was, from conviction, sincerely averse to all commercial restraints and all religious intolerance.'[24] This was entirely consistent with Shelburne's own observation when defending his peace preliminaries in the Lords on 17 February 1783: 'This seems to be the æra of Protestantism in trade. All Europe appear enlightened, and eager to throw off the vile shackles of oppressive ignorant monopoly; that unmanly and illiberal principle, which is at once ungenerous and deceitful.'[25] His distaste for the rigorous authority of creeds and articles, his wish to broaden the Church's theological boundaries to include other Protestants and his suspicion of *iuro divino* ecclesiastical authority were all firmly in alignment with the mentalities of late eighteenth-century Latitudinarianism. Emphasizing, in John Gascoigne's words, 'simplicity of doctrine', 'resolute anti-sacerdotalism' and 'the need to demonstrate the congruity between Christianity and human reason',[26] this was a tradition originally associated with late seventeenth-century figures such as Archbishop John Tillotson, and exemplified in the early eighteenth century especially by Benjamin Hoadly. In Shelburne's own lifetime it was well represented in Cambridge University, and personified by clergymen such as Edmund Law, Francis Blackburne, William Paley, Peter Peckard, and John Hey. The priority accorded in the Latitudinarian tradition to Protestant inclusivity, or comprehension, over doctrinal protectionism renders more comprehensible not only Shelburne's links with Dissenters but also, more specifically, with those Dissenters who had most in common with the Latitudinarian tradition in the Church. Evidence of active political co-operation, as well as the 'mutual admiration' noted by Dr Fitzpatrick,[27] between Latitudinarians and Dissenters, for example, over petitions for conciliation with the American colonies in 1775–6, is not difficult to find.[28] And Shelburne's opinions serve as a reminder that anticlericalism is not necessarily to be equated with irreligion.

---

[24] Lord Holland, *Memoirs of the Whig Party during My Time*, 2 vols (London, 1852), I, 41.
[25] J. Debrett, *The Parliamentary Register: or the History, Debates and Proceedings of the House of Commons [and Lords], 1780–1796*, 45 vols (London, 1781–96), XI, 67.
[26] John Gascoigne, 'Anglican Latitudinarianism, Rational Dissent and Political Radicalism in the Late Eighteenth Century', in *Enlightenment and Religion in Eighteenth-Century Britain*, ed. Knud Haakonssen (Cambridge, 1996), 238.
[27] Martin Fitzpatrick, 'Latitudinarianism at the Parting of the Ways: A Suggestion', in *The Church of England c.1689–c.1833. From Toleration to Tractarianism*, ed. John Walsh, Colin Haydon, and Stephen Taylor (Cambridge, 1993), 210.
[28] See James E. Bradley, *Popular Politics and the American Revolution in England. Petitions, the Crown and Public Opinion* (Macon, GA, 1986), especially chapter VI.

II

There was, of course, no axiomatic connection between Latitudinarianism and association with, let alone admiration for, Shelburne. In 1788 the arch-latitudinarian clergyman Samuel Parr, for example, while savaging Shelburne's conduct in seizing the highest office in July 1782, heaped praise upon the Fox–North coalition that supplanted him. Parr depicted the fallen prime minister as 'Doson', the name given in mockery to Antigonus, King of Macedon, 'as one ready to make, but backward in performing', promises, and 'full of insidiousness and treachery'.[29] It was a view shared by many of Shelburne's fellow politicians. Five years earlier Josiah Tucker, Dean of Gloucester, who was formerly associated with Shelburne and who shared his free trade sentiments, had launched a bitter attack upon him and his 'democratical' ideas in *Four Letters ... to the Earl of Shelburne*.[30]

But Shelburne's intellectual associations with Latitudinarian clergy and laity were demonstrably extensive. Among his early acquaintances was his father's adviser, Josiah Hort, in whose Dublin house he was born. Successively Bishop of Ferns and Kilmore, and from 1742 Archbishop of Tuam, Hort, in common with other adornments of the bench such as Archbishops Secker and Potter, and Bishop Butler, was educated at a dissenting academy, where one of his contemporaries had been Isaac Watts.[31] He married Shelburne's maternal aunt, Elizabeth Fitzmaurice and Shelburne subsequently showed considerable loyalty to his family, securing for his son, Sir John Hort, the post of consul-general at Lisbon, and using his influence with Bute to obtain a canonry of Windsor for Robert Hort in 1762.[32] With Francis Blackburne, archdeacon of Cleveland, author of *The Confessional* and a leading critic of compulsory subscription to the thirty-nine articles of the Church of England, Shelburne was on friendly, and perhaps even convivial, terms. Responding to a letter from Shelburne after a visit to him in Yorkshire by Lord John Fitzmaurice in September 1781, Blackburne wrote:

> Your Lordship's good opinion would be sufficient to flatter the vanity of a man of talents infinitely superior to those that have fallen to my share. It is more than enough for me to have merited your Lordship's approbation by meaning well, and

---

[29] Samuel Parr, *A free translation of the preface to Bellendenus; containing animated strictures on the great political characters of the present time* (London, 1788), 105.

[30] Josiah Tucker, *Four Letters on important national subjects, addressed to the right Honourable the Earl of Shelburne* (Gloucester, 1783).

[31] Fitzmaurice, *Shelburne*, I, 11–12.

[32] Fitzmaurice, *Shelburne*, I, 12; BL Bowood Papers, B36, fo. 157 (Robert Hort to Shelburne, 28 September 1761) and fo. 159–60 (Hort to Shelburne, 29 May 1767). Hort was a canon of Windsor from 1762 until his death in 1773; S.L. Ollard, *Fasti Wyndesorienses: The Deans and Canons of Windsor* (Windsor, 1950), 141.

expressing those sentiments with an homely freedom, to which the very few only of your lordship's generous and liberal turn of mind will pay the least attention.[33]

An associate of Blackburne in Yorkshire was the lawyer John Baynes, a pupil of the anti-trinitarian Latitudinarian Anthony Temple at the Richmond Grammar School. As a Cambridge mathematician, fellow of Trinity College, friend of the Cambridge reformer John Jebb, and a member of the Westminster Committee in 1782, Baynes helped to bring to Shelburne's circle the reforming ideas of Jebb and other Unitarian sympathizers from Peterhouse, presided over by Edmund Law.[34] Blackburne and Baynes both died in 1787, but many of Shelburne's later clerical contacts also belonged to the Latitudinarian tendency in the Church. He was friendly with William Bagshawe Stevens, the mentor of Sir Francis Burdett, who, after a conversation at Bath in 1795 recorded rather engagingly that Shelburne 'talks volubly and graciously and wreathes his Whiskered Smiles from side to side'.[35] He believed that only Shelburne could rescue Burdett from 'Seclusion and Solitude' and prepare him for a political career.[36] And the Holland House wit Sydney Smith spent two weeks at Bowood in December 1797 (partly to officiate at the marriage of his brother Robert Percy Smith ['Bobus'] to Caroline Vernon – the marriage took place in the great library at Bowood).[37] On 1 December 1797 Smith wrote from Bowood, 'It is dinner time and this Aristocrat or Democrat gives such good dinners, that they are by no means to be neglected, and especially not by such an Epicure as me.'[38] And Shelburne engaged in a lengthy correspondence with Christopher Wyvill, which revealed a common approach to religious, as well as parliamentary, reform of the constitution.[39]

Wyvill was a leading promoter of the Feathers Tavern petition for reform of clerical and undergraduate subscription to the thirty-nine articles in 1772. There is no surprise in that Shelburne's MPs Isaac Barré and John Dunning voted, albeit unavailingly, for the petition in that year.[40] It is true

---

[33] BL Bowood Papers, B25, fo. 112 (Blackburne to Shelburne, 13 September 1781).

[34] For Baynes and Shelburne, see Derek Jarrett, *Begetters of Revolution: England's Involvement with France, 1759–1789* (London, 1973), 259; see also Caroline Robbins, *The Eighteenth-Century Commonwealthman. Studies in the Transmission, Development and Circumstance of English Liberal Thought from the Restoration of Charles II until the War with the Thirteen Colonies* (New York, 1968), 371.

[35] *The Journal of the Rev. William Bagshaw Stevens*, ed. Georgina Galbraith (Oxford, 1965), 332.

[36] *Journal of the Rev. William Bagshaw Stevens*, 301.

[37] Peter Virgin, *Sydney Smith* (London, 1994), 38–40.

[38] *The Letters of Sydney Smith*, ed. Nowell C. Smith, 2 vols (Oxford, 1953), I, 11–12.

[39] This correspondence is published in Christopher Wyvill, *Political papers, chiefly respecting the attempt of the County of York ... to effect a Reformation of ... Parliament*, 6 vols (1794–1802), Vol. VI.

[40] Cobbett, *Parl. Hist.*, XVII, 296–7.

that Shelburne's brother, Thomas Fitzmaurice, MP for Calne, spoke against the petition, but it will be recalled that he had recently been a potential parliamentary candidate for Oxford University.[41] In the Lords, Shelburne himself voted for relief bills for Dissenting ministers and schoolmasters in 1772 and 1773.[42] He helped to bring into Parliament Henry Beaufoy, the mover of motions for repeal of the Test and Corporation Acts in 1787 and 1789; and he was regarded by Archbishop Moore as the surreptitious promoter of the repeal campaign.[43] To Wyvill Shelburne described the Test Act as 'a disgrace to the Church'.[44]

Anthony Page has illustrated John Jebb's disillusionment with Shelburne's brief administration – curiously, over the revival of ship money in Suffolk as well as the ministry's reluctance to grant immediate independence to America.[45] But the disenchantment experienced by Jebb and those who shared his reforming opinions was far exceeded when their former hero Fox entered into coalition with Lord North. Thereafter, Shelburne, at least until 1790, unlike Fox, could be seen in Latitudinarian and dissenting circles as a principled, if unsuccessful, champion of reforming ideas. Hence Theophilus Lindsey could write in the immediate aftermath of the general election of 1784:

> The Dissenters in London have taken a very warm and open part for Mr Pitt, of which I am told Ld Shelburne takes merit to himself and perhaps not without cause, as Dr Price in particular continues very much attached to and intimate with him.[46]

And some lingering influence of Jebb's campaign for educational reform in Cambridge is perhaps perceptible in Shelburne's warm endorsement of the proposals of his loyal supporter and former treasury secretary Thomas Orde for a second university in Ireland, and, in particular, his enthusiasm for Jebb's idea for annual public examinations.[47]

---

[41] W.R. Ward, *Georgian Oxford: University Politics in the Eighteenth Century* (Oxford, 1958), 226–35, 248; Fitzmaurice, *Shelburne*, I, 440, n. 1.

[42] G.M. Ditchfield, 'The Subscription Issue in British Parliamentary Politics', *Parliamentary History*, 7 (1988), 68.

[43] *Journals and Correspondence of William Eden, 1st Lord Auckland*, ed. Bishop of Bath and Wells, 4 vols (London, 1861–2), I, 406. Shelburne's MPs, Barré and Jekyll, voted for the repeal of the Test and Corporation Acts in 1789; Barré did so in 1787 as well; Ditchfield, 'Debates on the Test and Corporation Acts', pp. 72–6.

[44] Wyvill , *Political Papers*, VI, 346.

[45] Anthony Page, *John Jebb and the Enlightenment Origins of British Radicalism* (Westport, CT and London, 2003), 245–8.

[46] *The Letters of Theophilus Lindsey (1723–1808). Volume I: 1747–1788*, ed. G.M. Ditchfield, Church of England Record Society 15 (Woodbridge, 2007), 418.

[47] Page, *John Jebb*, 130–5; Shelburne's detailed manuscript comments on *Mr Orde's Plan of an improved system of education in Ireland* (Dublin, 1787) may be found in BL Bowood

It could be argued that Shelburne's principal connections of this sort involved unrepresentative, dissident (even maverick) Anglican clergy. In 1764, for example, he met Laurence Sterne at Scarborough and kept up what seems to have been a friendly, though largely non-surviving, correspondence until Sterne's death four years later.[48] Shelburne's note on clerical pretensions to which we have referred cited a work of William Frend, fellow of Jesus College Cambridge, who faced expulsion from the university following his expression of Unitarian opinions in the late 1780s and anti-war opinions in the early 1790s.[49] According to the *Memoirs* of Catharine Cappe, quoting Priestley, Shelburne expressed regret at Theophilus Lindsey's resignation from the Church in 1773, declared himself 'much affected' by Lindsey's *Farewell Address* and added that 'he [Shelburne] wishes to see him as soon as he comes to London'.[50] Indeed it is clear from Lindsey's letters that on more than one occasion he visited Shelburne's London house together with Priestley.[51] And Shelburne is listed as a subscriber of £100 to Lindsey's Unitarian chapel in 1776 – although twenty years later Lindsey wrote in that connection 'May 10 1796. L^d S ___ ne's promise was not realized'.[52] And, finally, when Thomas Fyshe Palmer, former fellow of Queens College, Cambridge, wrote to Shelburne in 1793 from the Tolbooth at Perth, he appealed to the former minister, as 'a friend to the liberties of your country', to help 'to put a stop to' what he called 'this despotism'.[53]

But Francis Blackburne offers an important reminder that the overwhelming majority of Latitudinarians, unlike Lindsey and Jebb, did not leave the Church, any more than Shelburne himself did. What Shelburne shared was the Latitudinarian willingness to engage with heterodoxy (especially heterodoxy over the doctrine of the Trinity) in terms of Blackburne's 'homely freedom' and on the basis of a shared Christianity, rather than thrust it, plague-like, beyond the limit of Christianity altogether. He remained convinced, moreover, that in moves for religious reform, there remained a necessity for Latitudinarian leadership, with Dissenters serving as what he called 'active and powerful assistants' rather than as principals.[54] And it was the radicalism – even the alleged infidelity – of Latitudinarianism, not the avowed separatism of Dissent, for which Shelburne was reputed.

Papers, B72, fols 38ff. Shelburne expressed his approval of the regular public examinations at the newly-founded Hackney College in his letter to Silver Oliver, 26 July 1786 (BL Bowood Papers, B42, fol. 10) and to Price, 29 November 1786; Price Correspondence, III, 93.

[48] See *Letters of Laurence Sterne*, ed. Lewis Perry Curtis (Oxford, 1935), 226, 234, 342–4.
[49] Fitzmaurice, *Shelburne*, II, 348, n. 1.
[50] *Memoirs of the Life of the late Mrs Catharine Cappe. Written by herself* (London, 1822), 166.
[51] *Letters of Theophilus Lindsey*, ed. Ditchfield, 206, 210.
[52] *Letters of Theophilus Lindsey*, ed. Ditchfield, 223–4.
[53] BL Bowood Papers, B41, fos 51–2 (Palmer to Shelburne, 5 November 1793).
[54] Wyvill, *Political Papers*, VI, 346.

That was why it could be rumoured in 1790 that Shelburne was the author of a pamphlet entitled *Hints addressed to the attention of the Clergy, Nobility and Gentry newly associated*, a work which proposed reform of the Church's liturgy. The author in fact was the 3rd Duke of Grafton, a committed Unitarian in later life.[55] It was even reported Shelburne had proposed the ultra-Latitudinarian Frederick Hervey, Bishop of Derry, as his peace negotiator at Versailles in 1782.[56] Hervey had expressed gratitude to Shelburne for assisting in his translation from Cloyne to Derry in 1768, and his visit to Bowood in August 1781 was recorded entertainingly by Jeremy Bentham.[57] Shelburne had more in common with the Latitudinarianism of Blackburne, Jebb, and Wyvill than that of Tillotson.

The bishops, indeed, with whom Shelburne could be expected to have some affinity were those appointed by Grafton in 1769, notably Edmund Law, John Hinchliffe, and Jonathan Shipley. Hence Andrew Kippis and other Dissenters could use him as a conduit to the Church of England hierarchy.[58] In July 1782 Shelburne wished to promote Hinchliffe, Bishop of Peterborough, to Salisbury; George III insisted on the choice of Shute Barrington instead. However, Barrington's elevation vacated Llandaff for the Cambridge Whig Richard Watson, originally Rockingham's preference for the bench, which Shelburne implemented. Watson had not been part of Shelburne's circle, and in the first place, Shelburne seems to have used him to strengthen his connection with the Duke of Rutland.[59] But Watson himself wrote of his promotion by Shelburne that it was the last occasion in this period when a clergyman whose 'thoughts, both religious and civil, were in perfect coincidence with those of Bishop Hoadly' was made a bishop.[60] It was unfortunate for Shelburne that the death of Archbishop Frederick Cornwallis on 19 March 1783 occurred one month after the defeat of the peace preliminaries. Nonetheless, he hoped to appoint the Chathamite, and protégé of Hoadly, Jonathan Shipley, to the primacy. He seems to have promised Shipley his support: on the very day of Cornwallis's death, Shipley thanked Shelburne for 'yᵉ generous & friendly warmth You show'd yesterday

---

[55] *Monthly Review*, II (July 1790), 343; Francis Kilvert, *Memoirs of the Life and Writings of the Right Rev. Richard Hurd, D.D.* (London, 1860), p. 179, n. †.

[56] *Walpole Correspondence*, vol. 25, 454–5.

[57] BL Bowood Papers, B26, fol. 66 (Hervey to Shelburne, 10 April 1768); also fol. 22 (Earl of Bristol to Shelburne, 13 January 1768, urging his brother's claim to Derry); for Hervey at Bowood in 1781, see *The Correspondence of Jeremy Bentham*. Vol. 3, ed. Ian R. Christie (London, 1971), 59.

[58] See, for example, BL Bowood Papers, B37, fols 189–212 (Kippis letters to Shelburne).

[59] Timothy J. Brain, 'Some Aspects of the Life and Works of Richard Watson, Bishop of Llandaff, 1737–1816' (unpublished PhD dissertation, University of Wales, Aberystwyth, 1982), 26–7; Peter Brown, *The Chathamites. A Study in the Relationship between Personalities and Ideas in the Second Half of the Eighteenth Century* (London, 1967), 336.

[60] Watson, *Anecdotes*, I, 155.

in my favour'.[61] But George III, in alliance with Hurd and Lowth, pre-empted both Shelburne and the incoming Fox–North coalition by securing the translation of John Moore from Bangor instead.[62] Shelburne's opportunities for the exercise of ecclesiastical patronage, and the promotion of Latitudinarian interests, thus came to an end at the very time when Latitudinarian influence within the Church was itself in decline.[63]

III

Turning to the issue of church reform, during the Lords debate over the commercial treaty with France on 1 March 1787, Shelburne made a characteristic observation in response to Bishop Watson. He declared, 'A right reverend prelate had said that our commercial system required no alteration, which, with great submission, he thought could not be said of anything; and, if the question was put to him, he believed he would not say it of the Church.'[64] There is some slender evidence that, particularly up to 1783, those with ideas for ecclesiastical reform thought Shelburne a likely sympathizer. He received proposals for such reform, including one in November 1766 from his former tutor William Holwell for the regulation of the Church's temporalities.[65] On Shelburne's return to office in 1782 there were brief hopes that he would introduce measures for the purification of the Church as well as the state. When in January 1783 Jonathan Shipley congratulated Shelburne on his peace preliminaries, he added, 'Yet allow me to look upon this as only y[e] first fruits of your Ministry. You have hitherto in every instance done more than You have promisd, & I am now usd to expect it.'[66] Richard Price also believed that peace, under Shelburne's leadership, would be followed by a reign of virtue.[67] The civic reformer and anti-slavery campaigner, Thomas Percival of Manchester, wrote to Shelburne in April 1782 expressing similar hopes.[68]

---

[61] BL Bowood Papers, B46, fol. 61, Shipley to Shelburne, 19 March 1783.

[62] Fitzmaurice, *Shelburne*, II, 262–3; HMC *Ailesbury Papers*, 15th Report, Appendix, pt vii, 227; *The Historical and Posthumous Memoirs of Sir Nathaniel William Wraxall 1772–1784*, ed. Henry B. Wheatley, 5 vols (London, 1884), III, 31–5.

[63] However, the death on 15 June 1782 of Jemmett Browne gave Shelburne the opportunity of nominating Joseph Deane Bourke, from 1792 Earl of Mayo, to the archbishopric of Tuam.

[64] Cobbett, *Parl. Hist.*, XXVI, 555; Fitzmaurice, *Shelburne*, II, 301.

[65] BL Bowood Papers, B36, fol. 124 (Holwell to Shelburne, 29 November 1766). See also BL Bowood Papers, B59, fols 1–2 ('Ignotus' to Shelburne, 10 January 1768).

[66] BL Bowood Papers, B46, fol. 57 (Shipley to Shelburne, 24 January 1783).

[67] *Price Correspondence*, II, 117, 165; William Morgan, *Memoirs of the life of Richard Price, DD, FRS* (London, 1815), 98, 100.

[68] BL Bowood Papers, B42, fol. 44 (Percival to Shelburne, 2 April 1782).

This, then, was the context in which Shelburne as first minister encountered Richard Watson's proposals for reform of some of the Church's revenues. Recognizing the new bishop as a kindred spirit, Shelburne approached
him with the suggestion that he might serve as his ecclesiastical advisor, as
Dunning was his advisor on legal matters.[69] Although declining to become
a formally committed Shelburnite, Watson believed that Shelburne encouraged him almost at their first meeting, to 'turn my thoughts' in the direction
of church reform.[70] Watson proposed a reform of the structure, rather than
the doctrine or liturgy, of the Church. His idea for the gradual equalization
of episcopal incomes and patronage, which was designed to reduce bishops'
incentives to seek richer sees and thus allow them a consequently greater
level of independence from Crown and ministry, had obvious appeal to an
Economical Reformer, that is to say, one who advocated a reduction in
the influence of the crown, a greater measure of regulation over patronage
and the expenditure of the central government, and an enhanced public
scrutiny of public accounts. His detailed plan for the augmentation of the
incomes of poorer clergy by a reduction of the Cathedral and collegiate
establishments blended with Shelburne's denunciation of these establishments in 1777 and was designed to minimize the Church's vulnerability
to its most severe critics.[71] Although Watson assured Shelburne that 'Your
Lordship will derive no discredit from supporting it, nor will the support
of it create any embarrassment to your Administration',[72] the beleaguered
minister temporized, urging Watson not to bring forward his scheme at
that stage. Arthur Burns in *Rethinking the Age of Reform* suggested that the
reasons why Shelburne did not pursue church reform were lack of will and
a weak parliamentary position.[73] Perhaps, in this instance at least, he should
be given credit for a measure of realism.

As Arthur Burns and others have pointed out, religious reform may legit-
imately be regarded as the equivalent of economical reform.[74] It may be,
as Timothy Brain's thesis on Watson suggested, that 'when Shelburne left
office in 1783 he took with him not only any hope of Church reform for at
least a generation, but also Watson's chances of further advancement'.[75] But

---

[69] *Anecdotes of the Life of Richard Watson, Bishop of Llandaff, written by himself* (London,
1817), 95.
[70] BL Bowood Papers, B50, fol. 82 (Watson to Shelburne, 10 November 1782).
[71] Brain, 'Richard Watson, Bishop of Landaff', 164ff.
[72] BL Bowood Papers, B50, fol. 82 (Watson to Shelburne, 10 November 1782). Watson
nonetheless published his ideas in his *Letter to the Archbishop of Canterbury* (London,
1783); there is a copy in the BL Bowood Papers, B50, fols 84–109.
[73] Arthur Burns, 'English "Church Reform" Revisited, 1780–1840', in *Rethinking the Age
of Reform. Britain 1780–1850*, ed. Arthur Burns and Joanna Innes (Cambridge, 2003),
149.
[74] Burns, 'English "Church Reform" Revisited', 149; Brain, 'Richard Watson, Bishop of
Landaff', 160–1.
[75] Brain, 'Richard Watson, Bishop of Llandaff', 29.

while it is true that Watson remained bishop of Llandaff for the rest of his life, it might be fanciful to suppose that Shelburne's fall represented a lost opportunity for Church reform. Dr Brain's thesis raised the possibility that Shelburne was reluctant to take immediate action over Watson's scheme because he planned to bring forward a scheme of his own.[76] A more serious possibility, however, is that there was some measure of continuity between Shelburne's ideas on religious reform and the ways in which Pitt's ecclesiastical policy took a cautiously pragmatic line towards the Church and did not follow a specifically Anglican agenda.[77]

Shelburne and Watson were never on close terms. But the continuing interest which Shelburne and his circle took in Watson's ideas is suggested in the strong support for Church reform published in *The Repository* of 16 February 1788, which cited Watson's scheme of 1783, and especially its concern for the lowest clerical incomes.[78] And Shelburne appears to have shared Watson's practical view of Christian charity and good works, which placed relief of the destitute above what the bishop saw as dogmatic squabbling.[79] Shelburne's support for local charities in Wiltshire – including those managed by the Baptist minister Isaac Taylor of Calne – was supplemented by a critical interest in the poor law and the work of Joseph Townsend.[80] He was convinced that the poor laws as constituted were 'daily destroying all natural subordination and affection',[81] and feared that the paternalistic role of independent men of property was being undermined. Perhaps this perception explains the otherwise curious remark in a letter of Joseph Jekyll, MP for Calne, to Shelburne in November 1796: 'Charles Grey said "Press Lord L. to get a County Petition from Wilts". I said it is a thing L[d] L[ansdowne] will not stir in as he does not mingle in County Politics. He [Grey] replied "He took up the Question of the Poor of Wilts[hire]."'[82] It is a reminder that Christian Humanism, as well as a determined Protestantism, contributed substantially to the Latitudinarian mentality.

Shelburne never formulated a detailed plan for the structural reform of the Church. However, some clues as to his aspirations may perhaps be deduced from his comments on the Church of Ireland. Those aspirations were informed partly by his Chathamite inheritance and partly by the spirit

---

[76] Brain, 'Richard Watson, Bishop of Llandaff', 165.

[77] G.M. Ditchfield, 'Ecclesiastical Legislation during the Ministry of the Younger Pitt, 1783–1801', in *Parliament and the Church, 1529–1960*, ed. J.P. Parry and Stephen Taylor (Edinburgh, 2000), 64–80.

[78] *The Repository*, IV, 197.

[79] Brain, 'Richard Watson, Bishop of Llandaff', 93.

[80] Fitzmaurice, *Shelburne*, II, 304–5, 306n; Marjorie E. Reeves, 'Protestant Nonconformity', in *VCH Wiltshire*, Vol. III, ed. R.B. Pugh and Elizabeth Crittall (London, 1956), pp. 137, 145–6.

[81] *The Correspondence of Jeremy Bentham*, Vol. III, January 1781 to October 1788, ed. Ian R. Christie (London, 1971), 45.

[82] BL Bowood Papers, B37, fol. 76 (Jekyll to Lansdowne, 14 November 1796).

of benevolence which, as Martin Powell shows, underpinned his ideas for agricultural, social and economic reform in Ireland. In a lengthy letter to the Irish MP Silver Oliver in 1786, Shelburne condemned the payment of tithes to the clergy of the minority established church, and set out his remedy for the questions of pluralities and non-residence:

> No man should be allow'd to hold Two Livings in a Country circumstanced as Ireland now is; all power of Dispensation should be abolish'd, and where Livings have neither a Church, or a House for the Clergyman, a Law should be pass'd to keep them vacant, and to apply the Revenues, in the first instance, to assist the building of both; at the same time I suppose that some Parishes might be conveniently consolidated, and those that are too large better divided.[83]

He added, ominously, that:

> The times are unfavourable to the Clergy both at home and abroad – & the House of Commons cannot in its nature be expected to be very favorable to Tythe – Foreign Intrigue will necessarily, after what has lately happen'd in America, mix in these disturbances ... Factions will inflame things, ambitious and disappointed People will as usual blow the Coals, whilst English Government will never hazard a War for such a motive. In the mean time the Church of England runs the risk of falling in Ireland and if great care is not taken all Property & Government will be endanger'd at the same time.[84]

An item in *The Repository* for June 1788, entitled 'A Letter taken from the Irish Volunteers Journal, March 1786. To Lord Viscount Mountgarrett', from 'A son of the Clergy' is in places an almost exact paraphrase of Shelburne's views as quoted in Fitzmaurice.[85] It repeated Shelburne's critique of pluralities and dispensations and expressed anxiety for order and property in the absence of reform. Although Shelburne stressed the profound differences between Ireland and England, vital motives for his interest in the Irish church included, in his own words, 'to make Ireland happy and united within itself'. This ambition could be brought within reach, he believed, by the mitigation of some of the harsher features of the rule of the Anglo-Irish Protestant Ascendancy, and by the kind of modest ecclesiastical reform which might render more defensible a beleaguered and vulnerable outpost of the Church of England. His overall objective, in which he had an obvious interest in the shape of his Irish property, was the preservation of the Anglo-Irish connection. Similarly, Shelburne, in common with other Latitudinarians, was always prepared to find fault with particular features of

---

83 BL Bowood Papers, B41, fols 6–7 (Shelburne to Silver Oliver, 26 July 1786).
84 BL Bowood Papers, B41, fols 7–8.
85 *The Repository*, 459–65; Fitzmaurice, *Shelburne*, II, 362–3.

Church establishments, but at heart he became increasingly committed to their survival on both sides of the Irish Sea.

IV

A characteristic of the eighteenth-century Latitudinarian tradition was its perception of Catholicism, and also by implication High Church Anglicanism, as a greater danger to the constitution and liberties enshrined in the post-1689 settlement than Protestant Dissent. Latitudinarians tended to equate Catholicism with superstition, persecution, divided political loyalties, and a threat to liberty and property. Anti-Catholicism, moreover, offered a meeting ground for Latitudinarianism and the eighteenth-century Commonwealth ideals, so memorably delineated by Caroline Robbins.[86] The Dissenter Thomas Hollis and his Latitudinarian friend and biographer Francis Blackburne vied with each other in their paranoid suspicion of 'Popish' subversion of the state, and in their energetic propaganda efforts to resist it. Hollis was a friend and admirer of Chatham, through whom Shelburne too was brought into personal connection with leading representatives of the Commonwealth mentality. According to his diary entry of 2 April 1764, Thomas Hollis sent to Shelburne 'a copy of Toland's life of Milton, elegantly bound'.[87] As Caroline Robbins demonstrated, the ranks of the Commonwealthmen included many Latitudinarians.

Even after the defeat of Jacobitism, there were widely expressed fears that Catholic numbers in England were increasing to a dangerous extent. Shelburne had been a secretary of state when, on 22 May 1767 Lord Radnor moved in the House of Lords for an address to the king urging a census of papists. It was Shelburne's responsibility to communicate directions for this survey to Archbishop Secker and it was to Shelburne in his official capacity that the bishops sent their returns.[88] With other Chathamites, he voted for Camden's motion to repeal the Quebec Act, 17 May 1775, a measure which, passed the previous year, had granted a measure of toleration and civic participation to Catholics in the newly-conquered territory of Canada as well as extending the boundaries of Canada to include the Ohio and Illinois areas. In June 1782 he told a delegation from the Protestant Association that he was still opposed to that measure.[89] Although he spoke in favour of the Catholic Relief Act of 1778,[90] and took no part in Lords debates of

---

[86] Robbins, *Eighteenth-Century Commonwealthman*, especially chapters VIII and IX.

[87] Diary of Thomas Hollis, Houghton Library, Harvard (microfilm copy consulted at the Seeley Library, Faculty of History, Cambridge).

[88] *Autobiography of Thomas Secker*, 60, 64; Colin Haydon, *Anti-Catholicism in Eighteenth-century England. A Political and Social Study* (Manchester, 1993), 190–2.

[89] *Sketch of a Conference with the Earl of Shelburne* (London, 1782), 14.

[90] Cobbett, *Parl. Hist.*, XIX, 1145.

1780 on the bill for the security of the Protestant religion, at the time of the Gordon Riots he was reputed to be strongly anti-Catholic.[91] In June 1780 Horace Walpole was not alone in believing that Chatham's former associates, Shelburne, Camden and Grafton were 'strongly anti-papistic',[92] while the *London Chronicle*, 1–3 June 1780, reported that Shelburne, with Camden and Bishop Hinchliffe among others, were treated with 'great respect' by the Gordon rioters. In 1782 indeed, while urging the Protestant Association to refrain from agitation against the Catholic Relief Act, he assured it 'that no one could suppose him a favourer of Popery. His affections to the Protestant religion were firmly rooted. His prejudices against Popery were particularly strong.'[93] In this respect he showed himself in his true Latitudinarian colours; like Francis Blackburne, he was their heir to a tradition which saw 'Popery' as a continuing threat, external and internal, to Britain (as well as to Ireland); and his remark to the Protestant Association was made at a time when Britain was still at war with two Catholic powers. And Shelburne's continuing reputation for anti-Catholicism is no doubt responsible for the wry note struck by the editors of the *Parliamentary Register* when Shelburne's inadvertent omission to take the requisite oaths at the beginning of the new parliament in 1796 necessitated a private Act of Indemnity to relieve him. They explained that the Act of 1696 prescribed that a peer who voted in Parliament without taking the oaths – as Shelburne had done – was to be considered a '*Popish recusant convict*', with all the attendant legal disadvantages.[94]

In common with that of many Latitudinarians, Shelburne based his anti-Catholic sentiments upon a combination of fear of Catholic encroachments, reinforced by its internationalism, upon the state in Britain and Ireland, and mistrust of Catholicism's intolerance.[95] However, he did not accept the traditional Protestant stereotype of a Catholicism which was unchanging and which by its very nature was incapable of change.[96] In 1786 an item in the *Leyden Gazette* which described some of the church policies of the Grand Duke of Tuscany led him to extol 'the liberal temper which is every Day taking place in the Roman Catholick Countries', though he added signifi-

---

[91] Haydon, *Anti-Catholicism*, 197.

[92] *Walpole Correspondence*, vol. 29, 63.

[93] *Sketch of a Conference*, 5.

[94] *The Parliamentary Register*, III, 59–60 (3 March 1797); italics as in the original. The Act which Shelburne inadvertently infringed was 7 & 8 William III (An Act for the Better Security of His Majesty's Royal Person and Government). The private Act of Indemnity for Shelburne (37 George III, c. 22) received the Royal Assent on 7 March 1797.

[95] See, for example, BL Bowood Papers, B41, fols 8–9 (Shelburne to Silver Oliver, 26 July 1786); and B72, fol. 67v.

[96] For examples of eighteenth-century anti-Catholic stereotyping, see Haydon, *Anti-Catholicism*, 3–14.

cantly, 'where there are no White Boys' (i.e. agrarian malcontents).[97] When speaking in support of English Catholics in the Lords debate on the Relief Act of 1791 he referred to his 'strict observance of their change of character and system in every part of the world' which led him to regard Catholics as no longer a danger to the state.[98] And his changing attitude towards Catholics is most sharply evident in his speech on union with Ireland on 19 March 1799, when he advocated their complete emancipation.[99]

This change of attitude reflected two intellectual currents in late eighteenth-century Britain. The first current was the realization that Catholicism was no longer the national enemy, that the fate of Pius VI (who died in French captivity in 1799 after Rome was overrun by the French revolutionary armies) despatched talk of 'Popery' to what was becoming the 'Ultra' margin of Protestantism and that the Catholic Church internationally, whatever its faults, stood for order, discipline, and obedience. The liberalization of the law in favour of Catholics could therefore be justified on pragmatic grounds. Although he had not shown much sympathy towards the plight of the French clergy in 1792,[100] this was part of Shelburne's argument in his speech on the union, when he advised those who still feared Catholicism 'to look at the state of the pope, and the state of France'. They would then appreciate 'that there was no fear from any body of men on account of the religion they professed'.[101] The second current was the evolution both of the Latitudinarian and Commonwealth mentalities from toleration exclusively for Protestants towards the concept of 'universal toleration' for all religions as a matter of principle. Although Shelburne arrived fairly early in life at a predilection for Protestant inclusiveness, derived in part from Hoadly, he gradually supplemented it with an enlightenment-inspired aspiration towards universal toleration – including full civil equality for Catholics. This was a tendency, as Dr Fitzpatrick has shown, articulated most effectively by Joseph Priestley,[102] and it was continued and applied by Christopher Wyvill, who, though resigning his rectory in 1806, never left the Church of England. Wyvill's petitioning campaign for the repeal of discriminatory religious legislation in the early nineteenth century made 'universal toleration' its centre-piece. It was a campaign in which Lord Henry Petty, subsequently third Marquess of Lansdowne, participated.[103] Well acquainted

97 BL Bowood Papers, B41, fols 9–10.
98 Debrett, *Parl. Reg.*, XXX, 253.
99 Cobbett, *Parl. Hist.*, XXXIV, 672–80.
100 *Memoirs of the Life of Sir Samuel Romilly, written by himself; with a selection from his correspondence.* Edited by his sons, 2nd edn, 3 vols (London, 1840), II, 14.
101 Cobbett, *Parl. Hist.*, XXXIV, 677.
102 Martin Fitzpatrick, 'Joseph Priestley and Universal Toleration', *Price-Priestley Newsletter*, no. 1 (1977), 3–30.
103 North Yorkshire Record Office, ZFW 7/2/193/13 (Wyvill of Constable Burton papers).

as he was both with Priestley and Wyvill, Shelburne stood at a turning point in the tradition of Latitudinarianism and its allies.

V

Unlike Pitt the Younger, Shelburne did not have a Tomline to seek to cast an Anglican glow over his memory in a laudatory biography. But far from being irreligious, Shelburne espoused a non-dogmatic Protestantism and belonged to a 'radical' tradition which was informed by religious values, and of which Dissent, although an important component, was far from the totality. His career serves as a model not only for the interdependence of 'enlighten-ment' and religion, but also for the strength of clerical enlightenment, ably delineated in its British context by B.W. Young.[104] But at the same time, Shelburne was confronted by the same dilemma as that faced by Latitudi-narians as a whole at the end of the century. In an age of revolutions, he, in common with many of them, fell back upon a more explicit defence of the principle of establishment – albeit on a substantially re-modelled basis – and the connection with the state. For Shelburne in particular the threat and reality of rebellion in Ireland as well as the French Revolution helped to reinforce an understanding of the importance of the established Church in England and Ireland as a valuable social institution. While it could not claim a monopoly of theological truth, its preservation was essential for order, morality, and good government. He observed in 1782 that 'Religion was very good for the lower sort of the people - and indeed among all sorts of people.'[105] By 1799 at the latest he became convinced that irreligion on the French model was worse than popery: 'The question is not what reli-gion you shall have but whether you shall be permitted to have any?'[106] If it were necessary to apply a label to Shelburne's religion, perhaps the most appropriate would be that of 'A Christian Whig', the pseudonym adopted by Richard Watson when writing in favour of the Feathers Tavern petition in 1772.[107] It was an appellation, one may suspect, to which Shelburne himself would not have objected.

[104] B.W. Young, *Religion and Enlightenment in Eighteenth-Century England. Theological Debate from Locke to Burke* (Oxford, 1998).
[105] *Sketch of a Conference*, p. 10; italics as in the original.
[106] Cobbett, *Parl. Hist.*, XXXIV, 677–8.
[107] See Brain, 'Richard Watson, Bishop of Llandaff', ch. III.

4

Lord Shelburne, Finance, and Sir Francis Baring

JOHN ORBELL

The personal associations of politicians and bankers, while pregnant with potential for historians, have been remarkably little explored. This is not altogether surprising as their essence was informality and discretion, so consequently they are poorly documented and hard to pin down. They were probably at their most intense in the eighteenth and early nineteenth centuries when banking was in the hands of private bankers acting in small partnerships and controlling their own capital. In charge of his destiny and possessing flexibility and discretion, the private banker was well placed to form associations with men of influence. Such relationships were not easily replicated in the era of joint stock banking which overhauled private banking as the nineteenth century progressed; here relationships were more rigid and formulaic.[1]

Acknowledgments: I am most grateful to Lord Lansdowne and to the Archivist at Bowood, Dr Kate Fielden, for access to the Bowood Papers at Bowood; to Moira Lovegrove, Archivist of The Baring Archive Trust, to Jane Waller, formerly Archivist, and to Clara Anderson, Assistant Archivist, for their extensive help; and to Tracy Earl, Archivist of Coutts & Co., for access to Lord Lansdowne's accounts in Coutt's registers. The Baring Archive (BA) holds correspondence exchanged between Lord Shelburne and Francis Baring between 1782 and 1803 as well as papers sent by Baring to Shelburne. These are handwritten copies made at about the end of the nineteenth century. There are also typescript copies of Baring's correspondence and papers, made in about the 1930s, as well as the original letters of Shelburne. The original letters and papers of Francis Baring are in the Bowood (Shelburne) Papers at the British Library.

[1] Lengthy runs of correspondence between banker and politician seem to be rare. Archives detailing the politician's use of banking facilities are less rare. These range across current/deposit account ledgers; memorandum books detailing credit standing, financial needs, and facilities received; security ledgers detailing investments; safe custody ledgers detailing articles in the banker's safe, etc. In themselves, individual transactions tell the historian little. When pieced together, they reveal a particular aspect of the man central to the rest of his life.

The relationship between politician and private banker was at its most complex, potent, and durable in the arena of merchant banking. The private merchant banker long outlived his high street equivalent and survived until well into the twentieth century. He had his origins in international merchanting, trading in commodities, and corresponding with a network of trusted merchant houses in trading centres around the world. The most successful and powerful merchants added trade finance – that is, financing the trade of other merchants – to their activities and emerged as merchant bankers. It was a short step from this to financing governments, businesses and individuals, either through loans or trade finance, or, increasingly from the late eighteenth century, by buying up and/or distributing bonds of governments and, later, businesses, in need of finance.

The client list of a leading merchant banker included governments and government agencies from all parts of the world; businesses of all descriptions including the precursors of central banks, transport, and especially railway companies, munitions businesses, and great international trading houses; and not least individuals – often associated with these other entities – such as heads of state, cabinet ministers, ambassadors, business leaders, wealthy travellers and the like, together with their relatives and, in due course, their descendants.

Potential links were wide-ranging. For his part, the merchant banker had much to bring to the relationship both officially and personally. Most obviously was his role in carrying out official government business when a government required a particular operation to be carried through, perhaps publicly, sometimes secretly. Such operations might include the purchase of goods or the remittance of funds, say, for the benefit of an allied government. His firm could be an instrument of government policy, say supporting an allied government through raising finance via a bond issue or by denying one to a government that was hostile. He was a source of expert advice on financial and trading issues of a quality not be found in government departments. Equally he was a source of intelligence about international markets, commodities, procedures, people, transactions and the like; this had obvious strategic value and was derived from his international correspondent network which was every bit as competent as a secret service. His privileged knowledge of the affairs of his government, corporate and even private clients was another source of intelligence, loaded with political usefulness although burdened with obvious conflict of interest. And then there was the personal association. For the politician, the banker was a source of advice on financial matters. He could, for example, provide assistance in the form of a loan, manage securities, give investment advice, provide current account and foreign exchange facilities and offer participation in one-off investment opportunities such as in the sub-underwriting of a securities issue.

For the banker, the politician was a source of influence in, say, obtaining contracts for the supply of goods and services to government departments. More important was the offer of financings such as bond issues, a source of immense profit for bankers in the eighteenth and for much of the nineteenth century. Less easy to pin down is the influence the politician could exercise on behalf of the banker, again informally, in areas such as the recovery of sovereign debts, perhaps resulting from a foreign government's default on its bonds, or the acquisition of approval for business with political ramifications such as a bond issue by a hostile or allied government to fund a military campaign. Another point of contact might be the sharing of privileged information and assessment of events likely to have impact on financial markets. More difficult still to pin down is the enhanced standing likely to be gained by the banker through his political associations. The receipt of government contracts or the provision of expert advice, either formal or informal, inevitably in the eyes of others blessed a banker with a prestige that could only promote his business prospects.

The above is a hypothetical scenario, but evidence can quite easily be found to support most aspects of it. The precise nature of these potential points of contact between banker and politician, intertwined as they are with a multiplicity of conflicts of interest, varied over time according to prevailing convention and, indeed, regulation. They are certainly worthy of detailed research notwithstanding the fact that much was never written down and that documentation is consequently scarce.

This chapter serves to highlight in somewhat general terms a connection between one banker and one politician and therefore has a somewhat tight and specific brief. It explores the relationship between Lord Shelburne and the banker, Sir Francis Baring, and is possible because a snatch of their correspondence has survived. Although insightful, this correspondence suffers both from incompleteness and brevity on account of the shortness of Shelburne's ministry. Moreover, as in most such relationships, it is clear that the essence of their communication was oral and characterized by conversations at Shelburne (later, Lansdowne) House.

I

In 1787 Francis Baring commissioned from Sir Joshua Reynolds, the most fashionable of London's painters, a triple portrait of his political friends as they would have appeared in 1783 at the close of Shelburne's ministry (Figure 6). They were Lord Ashburton, Chancellor of the Duchy of Lancaster, Colonel Isaac Barré, Paymaster General, and Lord Shelburne. If only because of its size – about five feet by seven – it was a work that was meant to impress. Yet it was kept far from the public eye. Reynolds never exhibited it, which was somewhat untypical of him, and Francis Baring commissioned no engraving of it until about 1805, the year of Shelburne's death. For Baring it was a private statement about personal relationships – relationships that were notable for achieving considerable depth over a remarkably short period. By 1787 Baring had known Shelburne and Barré

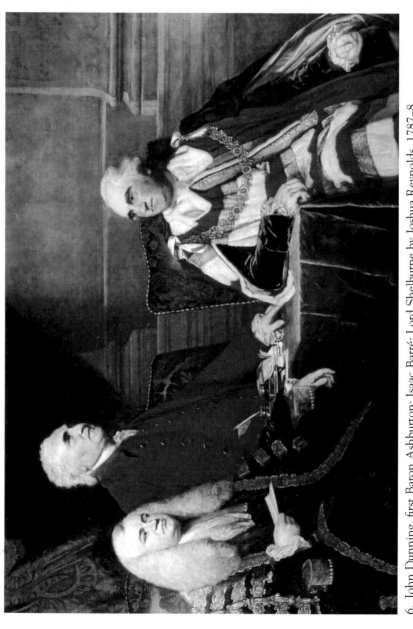

6. John Dunning, first Baron Ashburton; Isaac Barré; Lord Shelburne by Joshua Reynolds, 1787–8, Private Collection

for just five years, Ashburton for only slightly longer. It can scarcely be interpreted as a crude attempt to curry favour for by 1787 both Shelburne and Barré were well passed their best and Ashburton had been dead for four years.[2] Rather it is a personal tribute by Baring to his friends and perhaps an acknowledgment of the extent to which he thought himself in their debt.

Relative to Shelburne, little has been published about Francis Baring. Shelburne's biographers in particular have overlooked this banker who was perhaps Shelburne's closest friend in the last twenty-five years of his life. 'I have not words to express my feelings for the loss of a man whom I have loved as a brother & ever revered with all the affection due to a father', said Baring on Shelburne's death.[3] His affection received due acknowledgment at Shelburne's funeral where, according to *The Gentleman's Magazine*, the procession consisted of the hearse, three mourning coaches, the marquess's private carriage and Sir Francis Baring's chariot.[4]

This friendship was the more remarkable because the men's characters were markedly different. Baring stood no fools and could cut to the quick but was known for his good heart, integrity, loyalty, generosity, incisiveness, and, not least, ability to make allies and friends. Shelburne, whether rightly or wrongly, is reckoned quarrelsome, slippery, unpopular, unfocused, reckless, his own worst enemy. What they shared most, other than a similar age, was a liberal outlook; they were open-minded reformers. In commerce Baring preached laissez-faire by a different name and was fifty years ahead of his time in doing so.[5] He wholeheartedly supported American independence. Their contrasting personalities are etched in their correspondence. Baring's long and detailed letters were informed and reasoned and certainly opinionated. He had pace and could be cutting. Shelburne's, in stark contrast, lacked focus and had little to say about his ideas and the drift of his argument.

At the time of Shelburne's ministry, Baring had just started on his way up; his best days lay ahead of him. At the end of the 1770s he differed little from the thousands of merchants, brokers, and financiers who then made up the financial City of London; invariably they operated from tiny offices and lived above them. At that time, Baring's greatest asset was probably himself although, as the second son of an Exeter merchant, his origins were prosperous. His family's continuing influence in the West Country had enabled

---

2   David Mannings and Martin Postle, *Sir Joshua Reynolds. A Complete Catalogue of His Paintings* (New Haven, 2000). The picture is remarkably undocumented and this is the best source for it.
3   BA, NP1.B6.5, Baring to Lord Henry Petty, 7 May 1805.
4   *Gentleman's Magazine*, 75 (1805). I am most grateful to David Snoxell for this reference.
5   Ralph W. Hidy, *The House of Baring in American Trade and Finance* (Cambridge, MA, 1949), 18.

the election of his brother and sleeping partner, John, as member for Exeter in 1776.

An important leg-up from obscurity came in 1779 with Baring's appointment as a director of the East India Company, probably as a result of the influence of Lord Ashburton, a long-term adviser to the company. Ashburton, or John Dunning as he then was known, was a clever lawyer who had grown rich at the bar and influential in the Commons. Like the Barings, he came from the West Country and was proud of it. In 1780 the Baring family's links with him were consolidated through his marriage to Francis's sister Elizabeth. The Barings scented their opportunity. Until the marriage, Elizabeth's elder brother, John, had voted in the Commons consistently with the administration; immediately afterwards, he was allied to Shelburne and voted with the opposition.[6] Soon afterwards, Ashburton introduced Francis Baring to Shelburne.

At the end of July 1782, Shelburne wrote to Baring stating his need 'at the Treasury to have recourse from time to time to mercantile advice' to which Baring replied that 'in consequence of what Lord Ashburton acquainted me of your Lordship's wishes I have held myself ready to receive your Lordship's commands'.[7] The moment was not lost on Baring who annotated Shelburne's letter: 'The first ... I ever received from his Lordship.'[8] In terms of prestige and influence, if not capital, Baring had been propelled to the front rank of City merchants.

Baring served Shelburne, now a Marquess, with a devotion that was sometimes to border on the sycophantic. In December 1784, by way of example, he was moved to tell Shelburne that '... I esteem the friendship you have the goodness to offer me as the highest honour & gratification which I can receive' and that '... Your Lordship may be assured that I never will in the smallest instance, disgrace the confidence which you are pleased to repose in me'.[9] Baring also served Pitt as an adviser and had easy access to him but the two were never close. He did little for Pitt without Shelburne's knowledge and sometimes approval. In accepting Pitt's 1784 invitation to become a commissioner in regulating emoluments received for holding public office, he did so only with Shelburne's express permission.[10] Shelburne's esteem for Baring is best illustrated through the patronage he exercised in making available to Baring his parliamentary seats at Calne and Chipping Wycombe, both sometime represented by Barré.

---

[6]   Lewis Namier and John Brooke, *The History of Parliament. The House of Commons, 1754–1790*, vol. 2 (London, 1964), 48.
[7]   Baring Archive (BA), DEP 193.17.1, Baring to Shelburne, 31 July 1782; NP1.B1.3, Shelburne to Baring, 31 July 1782.
[8]   Ibid.
[9]   BA, DEP 193.17.1, Baring to Shelburne, 13 December 1784.
[10] BA, DEP 193.17.1, Baring to Shelburne, 4 December 1784.

II

The careful collection and analysis of intelligence about commodity and financial markets and about the economic and political issues and events that underpinned them were vital to the success of an international merchant banker such as Baring. His intelligence was gathered from agents and correspondents, customers and collaborators, family and friends around the globe. Baring was a master at networking and in the twenty years before meeting Shelburne, established corresponding relationships with leading houses in cities such as Paris and Madrid, Lisbon and St Petersburg, in trading centres along with northwest European coast and around the Mediterranean. By 1774 he was in contact with Robert Morris's house at Philadelphia. His intelligence was probably second to none and every bit as good as that emanating from diplomatic sources and espionage.

Baring was not slow in offering it to Shelburne. In 1782, for example, he reported on the perilous state of French government finance which had an obvious bearing on Shelburne's peace negotiations. 'The French loan which has been negotiating for some time is at last published', he told Shelburne in December. '… I can venture to assure Your Lordship that from the general scarcity of money in France and Holland that it will not be filled'.[11] A couple of months earlier he had passed on information about French stockjobbers in London whose activities in causing destabilization in stock prices had become a government concern.[12] And when Shelburne visited Amsterdam in mid-1784 Baring was much involved in planning his itinerary and creating introductions. 'The tenor of my letters [to friends at Amsterdam]', he wrote to Shelburne, is that 'Your Lordship's wishes were to be acquainted with men and manners; that as a citizen of the world it would be more agreeable to you to converse with natives than foreigners & that you are perfectly indifferent whether they were French, Dutchmen or English Dutchmen provided they spoke a civilized language & that parade & ceremony was avoided.'[13]

Intelligence was also gathered closer to home. Baring brought his networking skills to the political scene especially after his election to Westminster as member for Grampound in 1784; he was to sit in the Commons until 1805. He was an active parliamentarian making no less than forty speeches in his first year. With Dunning dead and Barré now debilitated by total blindness, Baring became Shelburne's trusted eyes and ears at Westminster, passing on all manner of fact and rumour. Much was matter of fact. A letter in July 1784 ranged across the Budget 'which gave satisfaction on the whole', an altercation on the civil list which 'was very warm', the

---

11 BA, DEP 193.17.1, Baring to Shelburne, 28 December 1782.
12 BA, DEP 193.17.1, Baring to Shelburne, 6 January 1783. Fitzmaurice, *Shelburne*, 1875–6, vol. 3, 292.
13 BA, DEP 193.17.1, Baring to Shelburne, 29 August 1783.

absence of Burke and Fox from the House, and Sheridan's 'very able' attack on Pitt 'about the numerous blunders in every bill of importance which had been brought in this session'.[14] Some was fanciful intrigue which smacked at winning favour. August 1783 found Baring at an audience with the king. 'The Duke of Portland & Mr Fox were at the Levée after which The Duke was immediately admitted [to the king's presence], then some other person, & afterwards myself, Mr Fox continuing in the anteroom', Baring reported to Shelburne, 'These circumstances may be trivial, or they may be important, but I mention them for Your Lordship's information.'[15]

Baring reported to Shelburne in three ways – by visits to Shelburne (later Lansdowne) House, by letter and by preparing researched papers. Visits were frequent and their most important channel of communication. In the early years researched papers accompanied several of Baring's letters. They often extended to above 3000 words and were well-informed, empirically-based, scientifically-reasoned and with clear conclusions. That said, Shelburne was not easy to influence. 'The greatest difficulty I have ever found in politics', he admitted to Baring in a rare character sketch of himself, 'is not to be persuaded out of my opinions or not to be discouraged when they happen not to be general'.[16]

It was as prime minister that Shelburne called for the first of Baring's papers; later ones were provided in the years immediately following Shelburne's ministry, when he had expectation of a return to office.[17] The early papers provided expert information on specific trade and commercial matters and helped shape policy; many touched on issues relating to the peace negotiations with America and her allies. In September 1782, for example, Shelburne sought information about Senegal as a source of slaves and about the Newfoundland fisheries. 'As to the first', wrote Shelburne, 'I wish to know the real importance of Senegal and whether any other place could be proposed to the French in lieu of it where they could be supplied without our interference' and as to the fishery 'I want to know particularly what advantage we derive from the north and west side of it.'[18] Others papers touched on Gibraltar, which Baring saw as having no commercial importance, commercial terms of the American peace treaty, Bank of England reform, army victualling and the like.

---

[14] BA, DEP 193.17.1, Baring to Shelburne, 24 July 1784.

[15] BA, NP1.B1.3, Shelburne to Baring, 29 August 1783.

[16] BA, NP1, B1.3, Shelburne to Baring, 1 November 1786.

[17] BA, DEP 193.17.1, Baring to Shelburne, undated, probably 1783. Baring wrote 'Supposing that Your Lordship should be induced to return into administration & accept of the lead or guidance of publick affairs …'

[18] BA, NP1. B1.3, Shelburne to Baring, 16 September 1782.

III

The need to sort out army victualling in North America and the West Indies had probably been the initial reason for Shelburne seeking Baring's advice.[19] It had grown hugely expensive as the war progressed and in opposition Shelburne and Barré had been scathing about the flawed procedures and corruption that underpinned it. Traditionally annual contracts had been placed on the basis of limited competition and as reward for services rendered to ministers and officials. Shelburne received advice on change from many quarters but Baring's was looked on the most favourably.

After a fashion, Baring recommended a solution based on a fixed-commission rather than a fixed-price – a surprisingly innovative feature at the time. A further recommendation was that, for the first time, the *entire* business should be placed in the hands of a *single* merchant with appropriate resources and experience. The selection process appears to be unrecorded but by October 1782 it was clear that the man to handle the 1783 contract was Francis Baring. The single contract, in place of the several contracts awarded in previous years, was massive and seemingly without precedent, involving an expenditure of some £540,000, equalling about 2.5 per cent of net government expenditure.[20]

When the news broke, there was a predictable outcry; Pitt, for one, protested to Shelburne.[21] Baring had done well for himself and Shelburne had probably made it possible. Yet in fairness to Baring, he had set himself a tough contract with innovatory features including penalties for late delivery and guarantees for supplier performance. And most importantly he saved money; if judged on Shelburne's and Barré's initial objective of containing costs, the contract was a success as a saving of around 10 per cent over 1782 was achieved without loss of quality and despite a rise in commodity costs.[22] Shelburne regarded it as a triumph, referring three years later to 'the great business of the contract', how it had made Baring's name in government circles and how he had benefited from being associated with it.[23] And although Pitt had disapproved of the contract's award to Baring, he nevertheless rehired him to dispose of unwanted stores – which constituted the

[19] Norman Baker, *Government and Contractors. The British Treasury and War Supplies, 1775–1783* (London, 1971). This provides an excellent account of Francis Baring's contract and is much used here.

[20] BA, DEP 193.17.2. This includes a memorandum on the contract drawn up by Francis Baring after its completion. Some of the data are at odds with that in Baker. Baring's data are used in this account. In 1783 British government net expenditure was around £24 million.

[21] John Norris, *Shelburne and Reform* (London, 1963), 228. He does not give his source.

[22] 1782 and 1783 costs were 5.5p and 4.96p per ration respectively.

[23] BA, NP1.B1.3, Shelburne to Baring, 11 November 1785.

bulk of the 1783 purchases – when the end of hostilities meant they were no longer needed.

All of that said, the contract had been put in the hands of a merchant with relatively small resources. For one thing, the business was handled privately by Baring and not by his firm, and, for another, he needed to borrow resource from a banker brother-in-law to carry it through.[24] Moreover, his commission was enormous relative, say, to the regular annual commission income of his firm. His commission, fixed at £75.33d per 1000 troops supplied, amounted to a sum of almost £5525 while a further £1500 was received for the disposal of stores after the cessation of hostilities.[25] Additional income accrued from interest on government money in his hands.[26] The upshot was a total income of over £11,000, more than double his firm's total commission income in a good year.[27] And it is with more than a touch of irony that Baring paid out of it the £3000 expenses he incurred in his election to parliament.[28] Baring may have carried this massive contract through effectively but his credentials for doing so had scarcely met those of the contract-givers at the time of the contract's award. Baring, it seems, had been well-favoured.

IV

The fall of Shelburne's ministry led to a less productive relationship between the two men although Baring remained optimistic about Shelburne's return to office and maintained fully his communication. Shelburne was not so sure, in April 1783 claiming to be 'intoxicated with my liberty' and 'detesting the idea of returning to state affairs'.[29] In the next two or so years their correspondence and Baring's papers in particular ranged over three subjects – the East India Company, United States trade and public finance. However, at the end of the day they had little of substance to show for it.

Their East India Company connection highlights Baring's role as Shelburne's listening post at East India House and as his lobbyist. Since his election to the court in 1779, Baring had rapidly extended his influence and devoted a huge proportion of his time to its affairs – 'I have been a prisoner

---

[24] DEP 193.40. Entry for 1784 – 'gained by the sale of stock which I borrowed from Martin & Co to enable me to execute the government business'.

[25] Ibid. Entries for 1784 and 1785.

[26] Ibid. Entry for 1785 – 'interest on money belonging to the government in my hands – £2250'.

[27] Philip Ziegler, *The Sixth Great Power: Barings, 1762–1929* (London, 1988), Appendix 3. DEP 193.40. Entry for 1785.

[28] DEP 193.40. Entry for 1785.

[29] BA, NP1.B1.3, Shelburne to Baring, 25 April 1783.

at East India house for the last ten days' he told Shelburne in April 1784.[30] Shelburne, himself, had long taken an interest in the Company's affairs and Baring now became the point through which he could exercise his influence. 'I think it is my duty to interfere knowing that it will facilitate the communication and confidence which ought to subsist ever between government and the company', Shelburne explained to Baring in July 1782 when asking him to work for the election of Nathaniel Smith as Deputy Chairman.[31] 'I have solicited in his behalf', responded Baring, '& shall continue my utmost efforts for his success'.[32]

When in December 1783 Fox sought to establish for the first time a bureaucratic framework for control of the company by Parliament and with it the administration of India, Baring vigorously lobbied a somewhat detached Shelburne, as well as Pitt and Henry Dundas, to oppose the bill. He condemned Fox's opportunism and urged Shelburne to rise up against it. Sidelined by Pitt and holed up at Bowood, Shelburne's isolation at this time is well-known. 'I hear little of what is passing in London and have no correspondent there who is au fait to the reports of the day', Shelburne complained to Baring in November, '... I shall be very glad to be favour'd with your observations on whatever is proposed'.[33] Thus Baring became both Shelburne's informant and interpreter as the crisis unfolded. 'It is such a system of influence & corruption as amazes me', he told Shelburne in November 1783, '... if no other proof existed of the abilities & ambition of C Fox, it will forever remain a monument to the boldest & most artfull effort ever attempted by any subject since the restoration'.[34]

The ideas of Shelburne and Baring for greater government influence over the Company's affairs chimed, albeit to differing extents. 'There can be no doubt but that reform, & very material reform is wanted: nor can there be the smallest doubt but that the power of the Crown should be encreased.'[35] Baring told Shelburne in underscoring his reformist views, but he went on to argue for the Company's commercial integrity. Galvanizing Shelburne into action on his behalf, however, proved hard work. 'All that I pretend to, & hope', coaxed Baring, 'is that I may touch a key or note which your Lordship may improve into a tune & which I can follow up when I perceive what may meet your own ideas.'[36] But Shelburne was not for tune-making and responded blandly if somewhat characteristically that government control was inevitable but best achieved with the consent of the proprietors.

30 BA, DEP 193.17.1, Baring to Shelburne, 26 April 1784.
31 BA, NP1.B1.3, Shelburne to Baring, 31 July 1782.
32 BA, DEP 193.17.1, Baring to Shelburne, 31 July 1782.
33 BA, NP1.B1.3, Shelburne to Baring, 16 November 1783.
34 BA, DEP 193.17.1, Baring to Shelburne, 20 November 1783.
35 BA, DEP 193.17.1, Baring to Shelburne, 23 November 1783.
36 Ibid.

Shelburne, a longstanding friend of America, was proactive in working to liberalize United States trade with Britain and its colonies, especially the West Indies. In the 1780s he found in Baring a powerful ally in formulating his arguments. Shelburne had apparently first asked his advice in 1782 on the commercial article of the preliminary peace treaty although on this occasion, and somewhat oddly in view of his later position, Baring favoured in large part the exclusion of American merchants from British and colonial markets. Whatever the cause, the Peace of Versailles had disappointed American trading ambitions.[37]

Out of office Shelburne campaigned for the lifting of restrictions on United States trade, setting up a 'Committee of Gentlemen' to sketch out a new commercial system between Britain and the United States and favouring the 1784 American Intercourse Bill.[38] In February 1784 he invited Baring to lay out the arguments in favour of freer trade in another research paper headed 'Thoughts upon on a Commercial Treaty with America'. This closely argued and transparently clear 3000 word document called for far freer trade on the basis that it would not damage Britain's prospects.[39] A couple of months later, with Shelburne muttering about 'a terrible narrowness somewhere'[40] and confounded by arguments of the other side, Baring restated his view:

> ... the two great objects for this country are, to check the Americans in their circuitous voyages to encourage our own shipping; & to prevent their interfering by every means in our power with the fisheries. These two points secured, I would give them almost the whole of what remains so long as they do not pretend to be a manufacturing country, & in the present situation of affairs, this would more than content America, as embracing even more than the object at present under contemplation.[41]

But it was much ado about nothing when the Intercourse Bill was thrown out.

The other subject of major concern to both of them was public finance but, as with other issues, they brought little influence to bear. This is an area where Shelburne was known to be shaky; he had long been influenced by the celebrated Dr Richard Price.[42] Baring, on the other hand, was more than full of himself. 'I never lose sight of our finances', he somewhat over-confidently advised Shelburne in November 1783, '... & I do not see any

---

[37] Hidy, *op cit.*, 18. I have not been able to locate this document.
[38] Robert C. Alberts, *The Golden Voyage. The Life and Times of William Bingham, 1752–1804* (Boston, MA, 1969), 134.
[39] BA, DEP 193.17.2.
[40] BA, NP1.B1.3, Shelburne to Baring, 26 May 1784.
[41] BA, DEP 193.17.1, Baring to Shelburne, 30 May 1784.
[42] J.E.D. Binney, *British Public Finance and Administration, 1774–92* (Oxford, 1958), 267.

difficulty that I should labour under to give Your Lordship an opinion upon almost any point that you wish to be informed about, provided that I could obtain official papers to enable me to be correct, as I have been accustomed to confine my ideas to the principle alone'.[43]

During Shelburne's ministry Baring's role in British government finance appears as marginal; indeed Shelburne generated little relevant legislation and no annual issue of loan stock was made although one, it seems, had been planned for. Rather, Baring was restricted to passing to Shelburne details of price movements in government stock and explanations for them. This distance, albeit fairly short-armed, from government financial policy was perhaps just as well as between 1780 and 1784 Barings Bank participated in annual issues of funded debt which generated very handsome profits of £19,000.[44] There is no evidence that Shelburne participated in these trans-actions although there is a passing reference to the bank handling one stock transaction for him, albeit in the late 1780s.[45]

At the end of the war widespread concern existed about the size of the national debt – both funded and unfunded, the burden its service placed on annual government revenue, the new tax regime needed to bolster revenue, and the extent to which investors had lost confidence in the stocks. Baring passed Shelburne a plethora of information and opinion on all these issues and Shelburne's reliance on him for technical advice is impressive. For example, when Shelburne rose in the Lords to debate the 1783 loan bill he was fully armed with Baring's arguments. He told Baring that 'I shall be entirely dependent on you ... for materials to compare with the present bargain, namely 1) Dr Price's plan, 2) a five per cent loan, 3) taking the whole out of the 4 per cents, 4) any other plan that can be suggested which might promote a plan of redemption.'[46] It was a tall order in which Shel-burne pitted Baring against his other expert, Price. The result was another weighty paper, some 4000 words long, but Shelburne seems to have achieved little despite it.

V

Away from public life Shelburne showed little hesitancy in asking Baring's help in his private financial affairs. Early tasks were straightforward. In 1782, for example, both Francis and his brother, John, were interceding on Shel-burne's behalf in the acquisition of land at Pewsham Forest, Wiltshire, while a year later Francis was summarily charged with disposing of Shelburne's

[43] BA, DEP 193.17.1, Baring to Shelburne, 30 November 1783.
[44] BA, Calculated from profit & loss account in general ledgers, 1780–4.
[45] BA, 100006 f. 50.
[46] BA, NP1.B1.3, Shelburne to Baring, 25 April 1783.

temporary country home at Streatham.[47] Other requests were for the supply of fabric samples for copying by the decaying Wiltshire textile industry in order to revive its prospects and relieve unemployment.

It was seemingly inevitable that Baring would be drawn into the tangle of Shelburne's financial affairs although not nearly to the extent that many believed. For one thing Shelburne's appetite for borrowing was prodigious, for another he had few qualms about doing so from friends. In 1768 when his cousin, Lord Kerry, declined to help him out 'with some very pressing demands that are at this time distressing me exceedingly', he felt betrayed and made the point that 'money matters is the touchstone of friendship'.[48]

Shelburne borrowed massively throughout his life through a mixture of mortgages, bonds, and bills for long-, medium- and short-term finance respectively. In 1773, for example, his debts totalled almost £160,000 against assets of £190,000.[49] By 1783 he owed at least £190,000 in respect of mortgages, bonds and bills alone and paid annual interest of almost £10,000.[50] His creditors at different times ranged from Lord Ashburton (£600) to his librarian, Joseph Priestley (£400), and from former Prime Minister, the Earl of Bute (£16,500), to his brother, Thomas Fitzmaurice (£32,600).[51] Another source was Coutts Bank, his banker from 1791, who granted him £20,000 mortgage and, later, lent £5000 against his bond. Many were badly treated. A Mrs Nesbitt of Norwood in 1783 lent him £8000 for 12 months against his bond and was still waiting for the return of the larger part of her money at the end of 1788.[52]

In such circumstances, Shelburne many times sailed close to the wind as in mid-1785. The City merchants Grove & Hood, perhaps on account of their Irish connections, for long played a vital role in Shelburne's affairs, remitting funds to his bank accounts and advancing funds at times of need. In June, with Shelburne having run up debts of £4000 against a permitted limit of £2000, their patience was almost at an end. John Smith, Shelburne's London lawyer, was sent round to smooth matters over. His affairs in 1781 had been no easier. Another creditor, Mr Sumner, wanted repayment of a £3000 debt and John Smith thrashed out an arrangement for 'paying £5,000 gradually in 21 months instead of paying £3,000 in six or seven months'.[53]

Francis Baring's firm provided Shelburne with no long-term banking arrangements although a very small and short-lived account once existed in

47 Fitzmaurice, *Shelburne*, 1875–6, vol. 3, 242; BA, DEP 193.17.1, Baring to Shelburne, 12 August 1783.
48 I am most grateful to Patrick Pilkington for this reference.
49 BHA, Box 98, Statement of assets and liabilities, 1773.
50 BHA, Box 98, Account of bonds, notes, etc., 1783.
51 BHA, Box 98, *passim*. Coutts Bank Archives, ledgers holding Lord Lansdowne's account.
52 BL, Bowood Papers, vol. 61, Shelburne's bond, 13 March 1783.
53 BHA, Box 97, John Smith to Lord Shelburne, 30 March 1781.

the name the Marquess of Lansdowne.[54] Jeremy Bentham, who was friendly with Baring, was certainly wrong in believing that, by the end of his life, Shelburne had borrowed heavily – perhaps the greater part of £300,000 – from Baring and the Dublin banker, Lord Daltrey, a relative of Shelburne's first wife.[55] Not a scrap of evidence exists for this in the books of Barings Bank or in Francis Baring's private accounts. Had such a commitment been made, it would have fallen not far short of the entire partnership capital of Barings Bank at the time of Shelburne's death. There may, however, have been guarantees; in 1797 Shelburne had requested a surety of £20,000 from Baring in respect of pressing creditors.[56]

That said, one quite extraordinary financial transaction stands out. For five years from 1783 Francis Baring made a £5000 5 per cent loan to Captain Leslie Grove of the City merchants, Grove & Hood, for Shelburne's benefit. The security, it seems, was Shelburne's bond originally in Grove's favour but now assigned to Baring. Details of the underlying transaction are obscure but in all probability it was a means of financing Grove & Hood's unwilling advances to Shelburne. Whatever the case they detested the arrangement, finding it by 1785, when already consumed with anger at Shelburne's treatment of them, 'more disagreeable than any other part of the business'.[57] More important, for Baring this loan represented an extraordinarily large commitment, representing almost 20 per cent of his personal wealth. The arrangement has the unmistakable feel of Shelburne calling in a favour following the award to Baring of the profitable 1782 victualling contract a year earlier.[58]

Baring's final service to Shelburne was the executorship of his estate. It proved to be a can of worms and Francis Baring was still sorting it out when he died five years later. Shelburne had lived well beyond his means using 'expedients of every sort & kind ... for the purpose of raising money' and 'must necessarily [be] supposed to have died insolvent'.[59] Within a month of Shelburne's passing, Baring had uncovered 'monstrous' debts of £92,000 and three month's later Shelburne's eldest son despaired of the estate as a 'heap of artifices, confusion and insolvency'.[60] Ever dutiful, Baring told Shelburne's second son, Lord Henry Petty, to 'consider me a temporary banker. I

[54] BA, 1000221, 1000222, 100223.

[55] John Bowring, ed., *The Works of Jeremy Bentham*, vol. 10 (Edinburgh, 1843), 116. I am most grateful to Clarissa Campbell Orr for this reference. Lord Dartrey's first wife was Anne Fermor, aunt of Sophia Carteret. See Chapter 2.

[56] BA, NP1.B1.3, Shelburne to Baring, 27 January 1797; DEP 193.17.1, Baring to Shelburne, 27 January 1797.

[57] BHA, Box 97, John Smith to Shelburne, 15 June 1785.

[58] BA, DEP 193.40, entries for 1783–8; BA, NP1.B7.3; BL, vol. 61, Leslie Grove bond, 27 August 1782.

[59] BA, NP1.B6, 2nd Lord Lansdowne to Baring, 12 November 1805 and 20 December 1805.

[60] BA, NP1.B6, 2nd Lord Lansdowne to Baring, 20 September 1805.

can send to the City for a thousand pounds in what money you may want at the shortest notice.'[61] The contents of Bowood and Lansdowne House went under the hammer on Baring's instructions, right down to the aristocratic escutcheons, but he interceded on the family's behalf to hold back pictures, jewels, and sculpture. 'I cannot conclude this letter', wrote the new Lord Lansdowne to Francis Baring, 'without expressing my sense of obligation which my family should feel to you'.[62]

VI

In Baring, Shelburne gained a personal friend who served him with an integrity, devotion, and duty that did not diminish with the years. It was a friendship born in the political arena. He provided and interpreted information on three of the five areas that were closest to Shelburne's heart. While Baring steered clear of Ireland and electoral reform, Shelburne benefited greatly from his huge knowledge of public finance, America and the East India Company. On many of these issues Baring thought as Shelburne thought; he therefore validated Shelburne's views. The tragedy for Shelburne is that Baring came on to the scene so late, for the most part when his political career was over. With the exception of the victualling contract and its triumph of commission over fixed-price, Baring's effect on moulding Shelburne's policies was probably modest. But the potential had been there. At Westminster, Baring filled the gap left by Ashburton's death and Barré's blindness; he was Shelburne's trusted eyes and ears and reliable purveyor of political gossip. Against this backcloth, Baring can be seen as a significant financier of Shelburne for a short but probably critical period. But for the most part he managed to remain unentangled and his commitment, while very substantial for himself, was modest relative to others.

Francis Baring was, however, probably the real winner. With Ashburton's help, Shelburne plucked him from relative obscurity and added immensely to his prestige and credibility as a financier. Cobbett's ranting said it for some when, forty years later, he reckoned Baring to be 'a merchant's clerk at the close of the American rebel-war (1783) ... (who) owed his rise to his having became [sic] a handy city-man to the father of the present Marquess of Lansdowne'.[63] Certainly Baring would not have been slow to exploit the opportunities, introduced to him by Shelburne, through a presence at the heart of the political establishment. Surely they held him in good stead as he rose through the ranks of the East India Company to become its chairman in the early 1790s, as he made United States the motor of his

[61] BA, NP1.B6, Baring to Lord Henry Petty, 7 May 1805.
[62] BA, NP1.B6, 2nd Lord Lansdowne to Baring, 21 July 1805.
[63] Cobbett's Weekly Register, 17 July 1824, p. 132.

business after 1790, and as he emerged as a leading issuer of British govern-ment bonds after 1793? By his death in 1810 he was reckoned probably the most powerful merchant in Europe. He was as rich as Shelburne had ended up poor. Had not Shelburne, perhaps more than any one else, been the making of Francis Baring? Good reason for Baring to have commissioned that 1787 portrait from Reynolds.

The Shelburne-Baring connection is a microcosm of the meeting of poli-tics and finance with all the advantages and conflicts that come with it. Baring's commercial intelligence was better than anything an ambassador or secret service could provide, his expert knowledge of trade and finance far better than that of the most senior Treasury clerk. Both were of mate-rial assistance to Shelburne's ministry. But such associations – in a wholly unregulated environment – bring with them the potential for conflict of interest. There is good evidence for Baring's involvement in such conflict during Shelburne's ministry.

And the association carried down the years. Some 125 years later a future Lord Lansdowne wrote to a future senior partner of Barings. 'My dear John', Lansdowne began, 'I have rec'd the PM's reply. He thinks, as I do, that there can be no objection so far as we are concerned.'[64] And so the government gave its approval for Baring Brothers' finance of Japan covertly in the Russo-Japanese War; another meeting of politics and finance, another potential conflict of interest. Here is a seam untapped by the historian.

---

[64] BA, 200187.

Part Two

Politics

5

Shelburne: A Chathamite in Opposition and in Government 1760–82?

Frank O'Gorman

The political career of William, Earl of Shelburne has for two centuries been as much of an enigma to historians as it was to contemporaries. Indeed, Shelburne remains a controversial character and he is remarkably difficult to place. No agreed and coherent interpretation of his political career exists, perhaps because it is by no means easy to integrate the different elements in Shelburne's background into a consistent interpretation of his political life: his Irish origins, his early military career, his fascination with the law, his Christianity, his free trade principles, his Whiggish elitism, and not least, his ambition.[1] Furthermore, it was not so much Shelburne's unprepossessing personal attributes – his yearning to be liked, his need to be admired and respected, his unctuous flattery, his propensity to bully and domineer – which caused him to be mistrusted but the fact that he appeared to lack consistent political direction and singleness of purpose, or as Edmund Burke noted, he appeared to lack 'a uniform rule and scheme of life'.[2] His liberalism has interested recent historians but relating his career to a nineteenth-century paradigm of political change may be less helpful than to locate him within one which he, and his contemporaries, would have recognized.[3] Probably the most important of the central threads of Shelburne's political career in these years was his attachment to the ideas and attitudes of the Elder Pitt. What these ideas and attitudes were, and how far they may be treated as the cornerstones of Shelburne's political career, we shall consider in this chapter. Such a purpose may be rewarding but it ought not to violate Shel-

---

[1] And, indeed, his education. As Shelburne himself admitted: 'I had no great chance of a very liberal education … no great example before me; no information in my way … my education was neglected to the greatest degree.' Fitzmaurice, *Shelburne*, I, 7, 9.

[2] Sir Philip Magnus, *Edmund Burke. A Life* (London, 1939), 317. See also the comments of Jeremy Bentham in Sir John Bowring, ed., *The Works of Jeremy Bentham*, 11 vols (Edinburgh, 1838–43), X, 116; John Norris, *Shelburne and Reform* (London, 1963), 5.

[3] Norris, for example, offers an engagingly modern version of the eighteenth-century statesman as a liberal reformer.

burne's own warning: 'It suits the pedantry of the historians, who are for ever making everything into a system, and it saves others the great trouble of combining and thinking. But no great river arises from one source, but on examination will be found to come from the accidental junction of a number of small streams.'[4]

The political career of Shelburne has its origin in the politics of the early days of the reign of George III when he emerged as an important friend and ally of the Earl of Bute. After serving in the naval expeditions to the French coast in 1757 and 1758 he saw action under Prince Ferdinand of Brunswick and Lord Granby in Germany, where his conduct at Minden in August 1759 and Kloster Kampen in October 1760 drew favourable attention. He was rewarded with a colonelcy and the post of *aide-de-camp* to the new king. Shelburne was thus early identified as an ally of Lord Bute and as a potential enemy by the Duke of Newcastle and his friends.[5] In fact, Shelburne had already established a relationship with Bute even before the new reign began and on his return to England he is to be found giving advice to the favourite, pressing on Bute, for example, the case for an early general election in 1761.[6] He became the link between Bute and Henry Fox, a man of considerable political ability whom Bute badly needed to support his own insecure position.[7] In particular, he needed Fox to force the Peace Preliminaries through Parliament in 1762–3.

Shelburne's curious ability to offend and alarm many of his contemporaries was soon in evidence. After the Peace Preliminaries had passed through the Commons in December 1762, Henry Fox declared his wish to retire to the House of Lords while retaining his office of Paymaster General. Shelburne should have made it clear to Fox that he ought to have surrendered his profitable office when he took his peerage and his failure to warn him earned him the abiding hostility of Henry Fox and, conceivably, later, of his son, Charles James Fox. Interestingly, he confessed: 'I know it; I know the constructions put upon my conduct; few, very few, judge of me as I am.'[8] In spite of this, Bute used Shelburne as his intermediary in the negotiations which led to the establishment of the administration of George Grenville in 1763. Bute tried to press on Grenville Shelburne's claim to a Secretaryship but Grenville refused, pointing out Shelburne's youth and lack of experi-

---

4   Fitzmaurice, *Shelburne*, I, 79.
5   Ibid., 82. It is worth noting here that Shelburne was returned for the family borough of Chipping Wycombe in June 1760 without opposition and again at the General Election of 1761. In the same month, his father died. Shelburne gave up the seat and took his seat in the House of Lords in November 1761.
6   L.B. Namier, *England in the Age of the American Revolution*, 2nd edn (London, 1966), 144.
7   L.B. Namier and J. Brooke, *The House of Commons, 1754–90*, 3 vols (London, 1964), III, 272.
8   Fitzmaurice, *Shelburne*, I, 127, 167–75.

ence and the likelihood of his promotion offending senior claimants, who might be driven into opposition. Shelburne was ready to settle for the Presidency of the Board of Trade in the new ministry but any credit he may have obtained from his willingness to accept a lesser office was dashed when he attempted to make his acceptance of the post conditional upon the promise of access to the king. Such a promise was both unnecessary and unprecedented and Bute refused.[9] Shelburne's situation as a friend and protégé of Lord Bute was already likely to draw critical attention to himself. His persistence in pressing his own political claims threatened to make him a figure of even greater political controversy.[10]

In the months that followed, Shelburne's rising ambition unquestionably weakened his attachment to the Grenville ministry. He continued to seek further advancement even though he was dissatisfied with the government's emerging colonial policy. The death of the Secretary of State for the Southern Department, Lord Egremont, in August 1763 precipitated anxious negotiations with the Elder Pitt for the strengthening of the administration. Pitt responded by seeking far-reaching ministerial changes which were unacceptable to the king. Now in a stronger position than ever, George Grenville demanded the elimination, once and for all, of Lord Bute's continuing influence over the king 'behind the curtain'. In the first sign of his later attachment to the Great Commoner, Shelburne, sensing the favourite's coming demise, and bitter and angry that Bute and the king had not advanced his interests, began to woo Pitt. On 20 August 1763 he wrote to Pitt, a token of the attachment that was to last for many years.[11] At the same time, and of more immediate moment, he resigned his office of President of the Board of Trade.[12] Bute and the king interpreted the timing of his resignation as little more than Shelburne's abandonment of the cause of George III's monarchy.[13] Shelburne's connection to Bute, however, was not to be finally extinguished until he joined Pitt in his attack on the Grenville administration over the government's prosecution of John Wilkes in the winter of 1763–4. To prepare their tactics on the issue of seditious libels,

[9] P.D.G. Thomas, *British Politics and the Stamp Act Crisis* (Oxford, 1975), 25.

[10] Henry Fox had initially recommended to Bute that Shelburne be placed at the Board of Trade so that his interest in economic matters may be used in the attempts to settle the problems of colonial America (Fitzmaurice, *Shelburne*, I, 146–7).

[11] Horace Walpole, at least, believed that many reasons for Shelburne's behaviour were given 'but the only one that people choose to take is that thinking Pitt must be Minister soon'. Horace Walpole to Sir Horace Mann, 13 September 1763, in W.S. Lewis, Warren Hunting Smith, and George L. Lam, ed., *Horace Walpole's Correspondence with Sir Horace Mann* [*The Yale Edition of Horace Walpole's Correspondence*, vols 17–19], 3 vols (New Haven, CT, 1954) III, 113.

[12] W.S. Taylor and J.H. Pringle, ed., *Correspondence of William Pitt Earl of Chatham*, 4 vols (London, 1838–40), II, 241–3.

[13] See the letters between Shelburne and Bute of 19 and 20 September 1763; Fitzmaurice, *Shelburne*, I, 208–10.

Pitt summoned Shelburne to an interview on 18 November and attended the important debate on Lord North's motion on 24 November, that seditious libel was not covered by parliamentary privilege and, by implication, that Parliament could proceed to expel Wilkes from the House. Although Pitt was on the losing side in the division by 258–133 he was joined in the minority by Members under Shelburne's influence, Fitzmaurice, Barré, and Calcraft. Shelburne himself spoke out against the government in the Lords on 29 November but found himself in a minority of 35 against 114.[14] For their defiance Barré lost his minor offices and Shelburne was dismissed from his office as *aide-de-camp*.[15]

Shelburne had now burned his boats with Bute and the king and had begun the lengthy and somewhat tortuous process by which he eventually attached himself to the star of the Elder Pitt. Yet there was little inevitability about Shelburne's ultimate attachment to the Great Commoner. He possessed his own small, but talented, grouping in Parliament and as early as 1762 he had been building his own personal following within the East India Company.[16] By 1763, however, the war was over and most of the grounds of disagreement between them – not least Pitt's wartime alliance with Newcastle – were things of the past. Yet although Pitt may not have been the magnificent figure that he had been in the previous decade, he was still by far the greatest man of the age, a natural magnet for the likes of Shelburne. Even in these later years, Pitt remained a compelling character, sustained by his fearsome reputation as a great imperial and patriotic statesman. Shelburne's connection to Pitt took some time to manifest itself but it eventually amounted to the strongest and most long-lasting political attachment in his career in active politics. Between 1763 and the death of Pitt in 1778, Shelburne made no serious attempt to strike out an independent line for himself and accepted the broad lines of policy and strategy that Pitt marked out.[17] It is most significant that the small band of public men who voluntarily surrounded Pitt appear to have chosen Shelburne as his successor when, as Lord Chatham, he died in 1778.[18]

To what political doctrines, then, was Shelburne, in effect, committing himself? Pitt's fundamental political beliefs embraced a lifelong commitment to a powerful patriotism, an identifiable and coherent notion of the national interest which right-thinking politicians, led of course by a patriot leader, acting in the interests of national unity, could both ascertain and act upon. To Pitt this pursuit of the national interest usually meant a hostile attitude towards the Catholic Bourbon powers, the maintenance of Protestant alli-

[14] For details of these debates, see my *Rise of Party in England: The Rockingham Whigs, 1760–82* (London, 1975), 79–80.
[15] Fitzmaurice, *Shelburne*, I, 210–15.
[16] Norris, *Shelburne and Reform*, 22.
[17] Ibid., 20–1.
[18] I.R. Christie, *The End of North's Ministry, 1780–82* (London, 1958), 223–4.

ances in Europe and a vigorous prosecution of British imperial objectives. This may not have been the entirety of Shelburne's political philosophy, in some respects more 'enlightened' than Pitt's, but there was nothing here from which Shelburne could dissent.

In this crusade, Pitt believed that the crown should throw its preroga-tives and its influence at the disposal of a patriot minister. As John Norris explained: 'For years he had a vision of the monarchy and the minister acting in partnership to unite the nation and bury the divisive heritage of Jacobitism.'[19] Although Pitt made much of his horror of corruption and his distaste for secret influence, he well understood the need for the support of the crown in the disposal of ministerial patronage.[20] In spite of his earlier relationship with Lord Bute, Shelburne readily adopted Pitt's rhetoric on the urgency of attacking secret influence and was frequently to be found denouncing it. 'Secret influence, are measures adopted by a set of men, who, on his Majesty's accession, listed under the banners of the Earl of Bute, who impudently called themselves King's friends ... who have acted without principle, with every administration, sometimes supporting them, sometimes betraying them, according as it served their views of interest.'[21]

What was needed was a Patriot minister to pursue the national interest, untrammelled by political compromises and party interests. Idealizing the role of the individual in politics, Pitt refused to cultivate men, preferring to await the call of patriotic duty from the king to form an administra-tion.[22] Indeed, Pitt's hatred of party may have had its origins in the divisions and disunion which they had inflicted on the country in his earlier days – Pitt had been born in 1708. He repeated this disapprobation constantly throughout his political career.[23] As Shelburne wrote of Pitt later in life: 'He did not cultivate men because he felt it an incumbrance, and thought that he could act to more advantage without the incumbrance of party.'[24] Shelburne clearly admired the heroic element in Pitt, his detestation of the compromises and considerations of political parties for Shelburne was no instinctive team player and came to share Pitt's horror of parties, preferring governments based on individual talent and service to the nation rather

---

[19] Ibid., 25.
[20] Fitzmaurice, *Shelburne*, I, 69–70.
[21] May 1770, *Parliamentary History*, XVI, 972–4.
[22] Norris, *Shelburne and Reform*, 19–20. This was in direct contradistinction to the Rockingham Whig idea that political virtue might be sought in conflict and in diver-gence, and, in particular, in the balance between government and a party aristocracy. D. Jarrett, *The Begetters of Revolution: English Involvement with France, 1759–89* (London, 1973), 85–6.
[23] See the wise words of Marie Peters, 'The Myth of William Pitt, Earl of Chatham: Great Imperialist, Part II', *Journal of Imperial and Commonwealth History*, 22 (1994), 393–431, esp. 417.
[24] Fitzmaurice, *Shelburne*, I, 59.

than to a partial cause.[25] Nevertheless, as Shelburne later realized, it was one thing to profess patriot principles, quite another to enact them: 'The real difficulty remains in getting people to apply the principles which they have admitted, and of which they are now so fully convinced. Then springs the mine composed of private interests and personal animosity.'[26]

The establishment of Shelburne's connection with Pitt did not effect any immediate change in the pattern of Shelburne's political conduct. Indeed, he went into temporary political retirement in 1764. At the same time, there are signs that Shelburne had not entirely abandoned his political independence. Evidence of this came on his speech on the Regency Bill of 1765, which argued for the need for parliamentary accountability in the event of a regency, a tactic not necessarily designed to win Pitt's approval.[27] Nevertheless, he appears to have shared Pitt's general disapproval of George Grenville's harsh policy towards the American colonists and in 1765 he appears to have been in fairly regular letter-writing contact with him.[28] Indeed, he followed Pitt's example and refused to enter the new Rockingham administration, declining an offer of the Board of Trade.[29] Acting as Pitt's mouthpiece,[30] he made it clear to Rockingham that he would work only with Pitt. 'No system could be formed, durable and respectable, if Mr. Pitt could not be prevailed on to direct and head it.' And he added, almost as a declaration of war against Rockingham: 'As to my future conduct your Lordship will pardon me if I say that "measures not men" shall be the rule of it.'[31] Shelburne was quite unwilling to be swallowed up in the Rockingham group and continued to keep his distance from them, a tactic that impressed Pitt.[32] As he told him: 'Tis you, Sir, alone, in everybody's opinion, can put an end to this anarchy, if anything can.'[33]

Shelburne was on the whole content to allow Pitt to shape his American

---

[25] Marie Peters, *Pitt and Popularity: The Patriot Minister and London Opinion during the Seven Years War* (Oxford, 1980), 42, 45, 63, 69, 78–9,109, 179, 216–17, 264; J. Black, *Pitt the Elder* (Cambridge, 1992), 72–102, passim; see also Lord Rosebery, *Chatham: His Early Life and Connections* (London, 1910), 328, for Pitt's admiration of Bolingbroke.

[26] Fitzmaurice, *Shelburne*, I, 18.

[27] A tactic argued by Lord Lyttleton, who was closer to Pitt than Shelburne was. See Norris, *Shelburne and Reform*, p. 22. There is a useful account of the Regency Issue as it affected Shelburne in Fitzmaurice, *Shelburne*, I, 226–8.

[28] Ibid., I, 225.

[29] Ibid,. I, 229–32.

[30] Ibid., I, 252; Shelburne to Pitt, 21 December 1765, *Chatham Correspondence*, II, 353–8.

[31] Shelburne to Rockingham, 11 July 1765, Fitzmaurice, *Shelburne*, I, 232; *Autobiography and Political Correspondence of the Third Duke of Grafton*, ed. Sir W.R. Anson (London, 1898), 55–9.

[32] Fitzmaurice, *Shelburne*, I, 229.

[33] Shelburne to Pitt, December 1765, Fitzmaurice, *Shelburne*, I, 253–4.

thinking during the Rockingham administration of 1765–6. For example, he was with Pitt during the hours before he delivered his famous speech to the Commons on 14 January 1766.[34] In that speech Pitt announced his opposition to the Declaratory Act and encouraged the government to repeal the Stamp Act. But this marked his recognition that the Stamp Act could not be enforced rather than any repudiation of the principle of external taxation, a position to which Shelburne undoubtedly subscribed. Furthermore, Shelburne assisted Pitt in drawing up the stiff conditions for closer cooperation with the government which Pitt outlined to Rockingham on 20 January 1766: not only the Repeal of the Stamp Act but the abandonment of the (then projected) Declaratory Act. Not surprisingly, these, and further overtures with the court in February 1766 came to nothing.[35] Nevertheless, there can be little doubt that Shelburne's decision to oppose the Declaratory Act was his own and, as we shall see later, had its origin in his own conception of imperial relationships. On colonial issues, at least, Shelburne's opinions merged with those of Pitt. They were not completely dictated by him.[36]

However, when the Rockingham ministry collapsed it was unquestionably Pitt – now Earl of Chatham – who took the lead, and Shelburne who accepted the role of follower in the negotiations that led to the formation of the Chatham administration in July 1766.[37] Despite the hostility of the king,[38] Shelburne became Secretary of State for the Southern Department. He believed that the cement that would bind members of the administration into a loyal and patriotic grouping would be Chatham's own personality and reputation, because, 'nothing but his compass and extent of mind can save this country from some great confusion.'[39] But Chatham's measures were ill thought out and impractical and the Cabinet was, in fact, seriously divided on them. For example, he wished to reform the administration of India by bringing the East India Company under government control but he had not worked out how this might have been accomplished and simply expected his ministers to do as they were told. On the whole, Shelburne followed his master's line, asserting that Indian territory must be brought under the sovereignty of the crown. He contested the right of the Company to territorial revenue, granting to it merely a share of those revenues. Charles Townshend, the Chancellor of the Exchequer, together with other members of the Cabinet, disliked such extravagant claims to sovereignty, preferring a

---

[34] There is clear evidence that he had had a meeting with Pitt before he delivered his speech. Ibid., I, 25.

[35] Pitt to Shelburne, 21 January 1766, ibid., I, 259 (incorrectly given there as February 1766). For the February overtures, see ibid., I, 260–4.

[36] O'Gorman, *Rise of Party*, 143–5. For a more considered view of the evolution of Shelburne's imperial policy and ideas, see below.

[37] See Fitzmaurice, *Shelburne*, I, 278–82.

[38] Ibid., I, 280.

[39] Ibid., I, 330.

pragmatic agreement between Parliament and company. Unable to compose these disagreements, Chatham retired to Bath.

The government was no more united on its stance on American policy. Shelburne, as Southern Secretary was closely involved and he was determined to stamp his own mark on colonial affairs. He was at once anxious to indicate that his own policy towards the colonists should be differentiated from that of Rockingham. Consequently, he was anxious to appear to be conciliatory towards the colonists and at once made a number of friendly gestures as preliminaries to a more general settlement of the whole of the territory between the older colonies and the Mississippi.[40] However, the coming to power of the Chatham administration had done nothing to quell the rising force of protest in the colonies against the Mutiny Bill and even against the Navigation Acts. In these circumstances it was difficult to persevere with a conciliatory policy and, in practice, Shelburne was not noticeably 'liberal' in his attitude towards the colonies at this time. Chatham's defence of the Americans during the debates on the Repeal of the Stamp Act had always been conditional upon their continuing obedience to Great Britain. Shelburne, in fact, was perfectly prepared to enforce the billeting of troops on private houses to enforce the Quartering Act.[41] Indeed, as I have argued elsewhere, neither Chatham nor Shelburne did much to persuade Charles Townshend against bringing forward his 'duties', nor to contesting the latter's underlying belief that the colonists ought to pay the cost of their own defence.[42] There is some evidence that Shelburne not only expressed some interest in such a policy but that he even sympathized with the idea of raising a revenue to fund the Civil List in each colony.[43]

Shelburne's failure to prevent the emergence of a harsher policy weakened him in the eyes of the colonists and his position deteriorated further with the entry of the Bedford Whigs into the cabinet in November 1767. They received three cabinet posts, one of which, a third Secretaryship of State, was carved out of Shelburne's department. Although the Bedfords had wished to remove Shelburne, he managed to cling on to his truncated post. The Bedfords had been among the strongest supporters of the Stamp Act and had opposed its repeal with great energy. Harsh and authoritarian measures towards the colonists were now all but certain. As late as the spring of 1767 Shelburne could still cooperate with Chathamites like Camden and Grafton but he became increasingly isolated and had little sympathy with the Cabinet's policy towards the Americans and towards

---

[40] Ibid., I, 300–1, 304–6.
[41] R.J. Chaffin, 'The Townshend Acts of 1767', *William and Mary Quarterly*, 3rd series, 27 (1970), 103–4.
[42] O'Gorman, *Rise of Party*, 201–2.
[43] Fitzmaurice, *Shelburne*, I, 299–307.

Wilkes.[44] Furthermore, on the issue of Corsica, Shelburne, the Southern Secretary, stood alone in the Cabinet, regarding French annexation of the island as a threat to British naval security in the Mediterranean. His counterpart as Northern Secretary, the Bedfordite Lord Weymouth, advocated peace at almost any price, making possible an important French gain in the Mediterranean without the firing of a single shot. Shelburne protested but, lacking Chatham's active support, and even the king's, his position became impossible. In October 1768 Shelburne was dismissed. Within a few days Chatham also resigned and the Chatham administration was at an end.

Significantly, Chatham did not call upon any of his followers to resign. Over the next few years he refused to do anything to organize what remained of his (potentially sizeable and significant) parliamentary following and showed little interest in the many schemes for a 'united opposition'. Although Shelburne tried to remain respectful to Chatham and to keep him informed of events in London, he received little thanks for it.[45] Occasionally Chatham stirred himself, for example, denouncing the Royal Marriages Act of 1772 which, he claimed, gave George III near-tyrannical powers, but such interventions were rarely sustained.[46] He almost took pleasure in offending other sections of the opposition over, for example, the Irish Absentee Land Tax in 1773. However, he managed to win Shelburne, if not Rockingham, round to supporting the tax, claiming that it had implications for the American issue.[47] For much of the time, however, he simply ignored Shelburne, especially on Indian matters in the early 1770s. Chatham was content merely to rage at the torrent of corruption which he believed the Indian patronage would provoke, but left Isaac Barré and Shelburne to devise more constructive proposals.[48] Chatham, in truth, was not much interested in the constant routine of opposition which might have helped him to maintain his own political influence.

Why did Shelburne not make more of an effort to breathe some life into the Chathamite connection? Perhaps Shelburne remained in awe of the great man, reluctant to take such an initiative. Derek Jarrett wrote that in the mid-1770s Shelburne 'was intelligent enough to see that there was no future in the steadily narrowing horizons of Chathamism but he had

---

44 O'Gorman, *Rise of Party*, 234–5.

45 The death of George Grenville in 1771 removed one of Shelburne's rivals for Chatham's support. As Peter Brown remarked (*The Chathamites: A Study in the Relationship between Personalities and Ideas in the Second Half of the Eighteenth Century* [London, 1967], p. 56), Chatham regarded himself as fundamentally more united in family connection with Grenville and Temple, his brothers-in-law, rather than with Shelburne at this time. Grenville's defence of the rights of electors in 1768 pleased Chatham and it went some way towards reducing his anger at Grenville's authorship of the Stamp Act.

46 Peters, *The Elder Pitt*, 214.

47 Ibid.

48 Chatham to Shelburne, 14 April 1773, 17 June 1773, *Chatham Correspondence*, IV, 258, 278; Peters, *The Elder Pitt*, 215–16.

not the confidence to launch out and create a party of his own'.[49] In fact, Shelburne's position after his resignation in 1768 was not a strong one. George III had only appointed him in order to please Chatham and was not unhappy to see him go. The Rockinghams were suspicious of him because of his lionizing of Chatham and his somewhat inconsistent conduct on America. At the same time, the Grenvilles and Bedfords disliked him for his posturing as one of the friends of America while his 'overstrained affectation of extreme courtesy, and a habit of using unnecessary compliments in conversation' impressed nobody.[50] He lacked the personal and diplomatic arts that might have transformed the Chathamite connection into an effective political grouping, even though he had the intellectual resource to have done so and enjoyed the support of those whom Derek Jarrett called 'intellectuals and dissenters and hardware merchants'.[51] Furthermore, the death of his wife in January 1770 was a serious personal setback and led him to undertake a twelve-month tour of Europe, thus removing him temporarily from domestic politics.[52]

There is no indication that Chatham ever asked Shelburne to make greater political exertions on his behalf and no evidence that he expressed any gratitude for Shelburne's loyalty towards him. Indeed, there is no reason to believe that Shelburne and Chatham enjoyed any degree of personal intimacy. Pitt, for example, refused Shelburne's request for a British earldom to designate his Wiltshire and Buckinghamshire properties, although in the early 1770s Shelburne had attempted to find a suitable military career for Lord Chatham's heir and might have expected something in return.[53] The warmth of their relationship should not be exaggerated. 'I was in the most intimate political habits with him for ten years ... and necessarily was with him at all hours in town and country, without drinking a glass of water in his house or company, or five minutes conversation out of the way of business.' Later things became a little better 'where I fell into more familiar habits with him' but the two were never close.[54] Only rarely, when he needed political support, did Chatham display any sort of warmth towards Shelburne.[55] The two men did not see a lot of each other. In 1769, for example they met on only a very few occasions.[56] Shelburne, nevertheless, continued to revere the person and ideals of the great man. 'My sincere and only wish is to do what is agreeable to Lord Chatham, not so much from a motive of

---

49 Jarrett, *The Begetters of Revolution*, 134.
50 Fitzmaurice, *Shelburne*, I, 390.
51 Jarrett, *The Begetters of Revolution*, 135.
52 Brown, *The Chathamites*, 24.
53 Fitzmaurice, *Shelburne*, I, 424 ff.
54 Ibid., I, 50.
55 See, for example, the glutinous letter of September 1770 printed in ibid., I, 413–14.
56 Peters, *Pitt and Popularity*, 203, n. 92

private regard, as a thorough conviction that nothing but his compass and extent of mind can save this country from some great confusion.'[57] Were such statements designed to procure Chatham's gratitude? It is impossible to be sure. However, we can certainly agree with Shelburne's biographer that 'Their correspondence nearly always shows Shelburne addressing his chief like some doubtful worshipper at the shrine of a God.'[58]

After 1773 Chatham rarely attended Parliament. Without much enthusiasm, and certainly without any encouragement from Chatham, Shelburne became, in effect, the leader of the Chathamites. Party man he might not be but he nevertheless became one of the leaders of the opposition to Lord North. The necessities of life in opposition thus drove Shelburne into the role of party leader. As John Norris wrote '… he was the most capable debater among the Opposition lords, and certainly the best informed, and on a wide variety of topics'.[59] Indeed, the extent of Shelburne's social and political ambition was impressive. His ability to maintain a vast network of written and other contacts was the foundation of a remarkable command of European and British politics. Certainly, his knowledge of what was happening inside the governments of France and America impressed his contemporaries while he made much of his visit to France in 1776. Yet he was none too well suited to the role of party leader. Neither Chatham nor Shelburne believed in the concept of party as a uniquely legitimating force in politics. On the one hand, Shelburne brought into the constituencies in which he had a preponderant interest – Calne, Chipping Wycombe, West Looe and, on occasion, Arundel – independent men such as Isaac Barré, John Dunning, and Lord Mahon. Not for Shelburne the idea of treating Members of Parliament as political lobby fodder. On the other hand, he showed little or no interest in building up his own little connection into a party. At the General Election of 1768 his connection numbered no more than five or six.[60] By the time of that of 1780 the numbers had swelled to around ten but it declined thereafter.[61] And any idea that he might have had an interest in building up a 'Chathamite' party is belied by the significant fact that Shelburne did not inherit a single MP from Chatham either before or after he died.[62] Nevertheless, with a party of less than a dozen in the Commons and little more than a handful in the Lords it was, in fact, easier for him than it was for Rockingham to harass the ministry effectively during the American War. Indeed, annoyance with the inactivity of the

---

[57] Fitzmaurice, *Shelburne*, I, 330.
[58] Ibid., II, 25.
[59] Norris, *Shelburne and Reform*, 95.
[60] John Brooke, *The Chatham Administration 1766–1768* (London, 1956), 250–1.
[61] I. Christie, *The End of North's Ministry, 1780–1782* (London, 1958), 224.
[62] Brooke, *Chatham Administration*, 255.

Rockinghams lay behind his willingness to cooperate with Charles James Fox between 1776 and 1778.[63]

A further reason for Shelburne's rising political reputation in the 1770s was his generous, and occasionally courageous – if intermittent – embrace of progressive and libertarian causes, a feature that perhaps lends a singular uniqueness to his career. In the view of recent writers, the inspiration for Shelburne's reformism was less the seventeenth-century tradition of Whig reform than the newer influences generated by what used to be called the continental Enlightenment. The influence of various figures upon him – of Morellet, Beccaria, and Bernis – and his experiences in the salons of Paris – have been discussed in some detail by John Norris and Derek Jarrett.[64] However, and rather more importantly, the practical translation of these ideas into action in the 1770s owed much to Protestant Dissenters, both in London and in the provinces, such as David Williams, Capell Lofft, Thomas Brand Hollis, James Burgh and, most of all, Richard Price and Joseph Priestley. The influence of Jeremy Bentham came a little later.[65] We have constantly to remember that during this period Shelburne was a practical politician more concerned with tactical than with ideological niceties. His opinions on reform more widely were vague and rarely the subject of systematic treatment. Although he professed intellectual motives for his reformism, he was also motivated by the opposition's obsession with secret influence and he was opportunistically inclined to take advantage of political circumstances whenever he could. His earliest involvement with reform, for example, had little to do with the Elder Pitt but owed more to the outcry associated with the person of John Wilkes, who initially stirred up the climate of anti-government resentment in which reformist ideas could eventually take root. As early as 1763, when he was at the Board of Trade, he had great reservations about the government's attacks upon the person of John Wilkes but was persuaded to suppress his worries.[66] Persuaded a little later by the example of Pitt, Shelburne in the Lords and his followers in the Commons proceeded to vote against the government in November 1763 on the issue of whether parliamentary privilege extended to seditious libels.[67]

Later in the decade, Shelburne continued in the same vein of reactive

---

[63] Shelburne married into the Fox connection in 1779 when he married his second wife, Lady Louisa Fitzpatrick, the sister of Richard Fitzpatrick, a close colleague and friend of Fox. By then, however, their friendship was in decline and the marriage was without effective political consequence at this time.

[64] Norris, *Shelburne and Reform*, 82ff; Jarrett, *The Begetters of Revolution*, 127–35.

[65] Although Norris claims that Shelburne made the intellectual journey from customary justifications for political conduct towards the emergence of utilitarian ones at this time such a transition is much less apparent in the 1760s than it appears later. Norris, *Shelburne and Reform*, 57.

[66] Fitzmaurice, *Shelburne*, I, 195–7.

[67] Ibid., I, 211–13.

reformism by endorsing selective issues thrown up by the career of John Wilkes. In 1768–70, for example, he was anxious, like Chatham, to oppose the expulsion of John Wilkes from the House of Commons and to resist the seating of Henry Luttrell following the Middlesex Election of 1768. The two played their part in the 'united opposition' and in the Petitioning Movement of 1769. Although Chatham was the driving force, Shelburne supplied the detail and the organizational planning which were essential to the campaign to rouse the freeholders of the counties. Chatham and Shelburne displayed further energy in 1770–1 in supporting the rights of juries to be the judges of intention in matters of libel and in defending the rights of printers to print parliamentary debates.[68] Although there was never any prospect of success, Chatham and Shelburne backed a number of motions by radical MPs on a broad programme of economical reform, including place and pension bills, a bribery bill, and parliamentary control of the civil list. Neither was this all. In 1771 Alderman Sawbridge brought in a bill to shorten the duration of parliaments. Chatham gave his support in the Lords, a view with which Shelburne was quick to identify himself. The relationship between Chatham and Shelburne could not be better described than in a letter which Shelburne wrote to his great mentor: 'I have mentioned the shortening of the durations of Parliament to your Lordship more than once, but I have scrupled telling you how very much I have been pressed upon it, until I saw it coincided with your Lordship's general views for the public.'[69] This was good for Shelburne's standing in the city and out of doors although it created considerable tensions with other elements in the 'united opposition' of these years, notably with the Rockingham Whigs.[70] In the spring of 1771, indeed, Chatham and Shelburne not only pledged themselves to shorter parliaments but dabbled with the idea of increasing the number of county members in the House of Commons. 'I never heard a reflecting man doubt on the county representation being the greatest restorative possible of the constitution.[71] By the end of 1771, the reform initiative had stalled, but Chatham and Shelburne had enhanced their public reputation as reformers and critics of the government, especially in the City of London which Shelburne wished to rescue from Wilkite influence.

When issues of reform surfaced again at the end of the 1770s, Shelburne believed that the nation faced such a combination of crises at home and abroad as to call for great men such as himself to undertake reforms that

---

68 As Norris states: 'Between 1768 and 1780 Shelburne became a reformer and he began by kicking a few pretty open goals on the subject of the rights of the Middlesex Freeholders in 1768 and 1769.' See also Fitzmaurice, *Shelburne*, I, 421–3.

69 Shelburne to Chatham, 9 April 1774, ibid., 1, 423.

70 Norris, *Shelburne and Reform*, 74–6; Veitch, *The Genesis of Parliamentary Reform* (London, 1913), 35–6. Shelburne to Chatham, 9 April 1771, in *Chatham Correspondence*, IV, 146–8.

71 Shelburne to Chatham, 25 February 1771, Fitzmaurice, *Shelburne*, I, 423.

were now manifestly seen to be necessary. The regular discussion of colonial constitutional issues together with Shelburne's growing realization that the unrepresentative nature of the British electoral system enabled ministers to ignore public opinion drove him in the direction of a more thoroughgoing and systematic version of parliamentary reform. Furthermore, the death of Chatham in 1778, Shelburne's patronage of Price, Priestley, and others, and the emergence of a 'Bowood Circle' inclined him still further towards a determined acceptance of the theoretical case for reform.[72] Even now, however, the trigger for his involvement in reform agitation was his political recognition that the political system needed to be stripped of the corruption that was weakening and destroying it. As we have seen, throughout this period Shelburne is to be found deploring the influence of the crown in terms that would have done credit to any Rockingham Whig.[73] In the crisis brought about by the American War it was urgent that secret influence should be destroyed. Indeed, it was more urgent to set about trimming and reforming that influence than to be striving all the time to embarrass the North administration.[74] His speech to the Lords on 1 June 1780 reiterated his fear of the dangers from secret influence in England 'where the immediate object of the Ministers was, he said, to increase the influence of the Crown and the power of the sovereign'. To this danger the only effective defence was to be 'a perfect representation of the people'.[75] Political leaders now had to lead and drive public opinion, not meekly follow it: 'People talk of public opinion; and what creates or constituted public opinion. Numbers certainly do not.'[76]

These were fine words but on this occasion, as on others, he was jumping on to someone else's bandwagon. For Shelburne had not initiated the campaign for economical reform of 1779–80 which had been under way for some months before he took any part in it.[77] Following Burke and the Rockinghams' example, Shelburne advocated a sweeping reform of the Civil List, a reduction in fees and a reallocation of offices as well as an overhaul of accounting methods.[78] Furthermore, it was not he who stirred the Yorkshire Movement into life at the end of 1779. Yet it was Shelburne's political – and largely opportunistic – involvement in the Yorkshire Movement which

---

[72] Robert E. Toohey, *Liberty and Empire: British Radical Solutions to the American Problem, 1774–76* (Lexington, KY, 1978), 120; J. Norris, *Shelburne and Reform*, 84–5; Jarrett, *The Begetters of Revolution*, 127–35; Brown, *The Chathamites*, 83–7.

[73] Fitzmaurice, *Shelburne*, I, 410–14.

[74] Norris, *Shelburne and Reform*, 89.

[75] 1 June 1780, *Parliamentary History*, XXI, 629.

[76] Fitzmaurice, *Shelburne*, I, 24.

[77] O'Gorman, *Rise of Party*, 401–9.

[78] Many of his ideas are to be found in his 'Scheme for a Commission of Public Accounts', introduced to the House of Lords on 6 February 1780. Christie, *The End of North's Ministry*, 17.

in the end led him to articulate a position on the reform of Parliament which was much more radical than the Rockingham Whigs found acceptable.[79] Without a party whose unity might have to be taken into consideration, Shelburne was able reach his own decisions on parliamentary reform. His reform would have involved the abolition of some rotten boroughs, the redistribution of these and other seats, shorter parliaments and a more equal representation.[80] In the end, such an ambitious programme proved to be far in advance of opinion both within Parliament and without, and it had to be sacrificed in the interests of the campaign for economical reform.[81] And Shelburne knew that the Rockinghams would never agree to his scheme of political reform. Furthermore, the Gordon Riots in early June 1780 caused yet further divisions between them. Shelburne strongly dissented from the government's harsh punishment of the rioters and resented the support which the Rockingham Whigs now gave to North's ministry. Seizing his opportunity, North opened negotiations with the Rockingham party with a view to establishing a coalition government.

This was not the first occasion on which the possibility of some sort of coalition between the North government and sections of the opposition had been discussed. Indeed, the case for a 'united opposition' against successive governments of George III had always been the need for good men to coalesce against the evils of secret influence.[82] Between 1776 and 1782 there occurred a number of negotiations for strengthening the North administration. On none of these occasions was there any serious prospect of negotiating a general arrangement which included both the Rockinghams, on the one hand, and Chatham and Shelburne, on the other. While the Rockingham Whigs tended towards the demand for a total change of men and measures, Chatham and Shelburne were much less willing to force the king's hand, recognizing that the dignity of the monarch must be respected and that a more partial arrangement might be negotiable.[83] As Lord North told the king: 'Lord Chatham would certainly be more reasonable than Lord Rockingham's party.'[84] Furthermore, because the Rockinghams and the

---

[79] O'Gorman, *Rise of Party*, 415. The Wiltshire Committee refused to endorse his reform proposals and decided against joining the Association and sending delegates to London.
[80] Fitzmaurice, *Shelburne*, II, 80–1, 85; *Parliamentary History*, XXII, 1003.
[81] Veitch, *Genesis of Parliamentary Reform*, p. 65.
[82] W.M. Elofson, *The Rockingham Connection and the Second Founding of the Whig Party, 1768–1773* (Montreal and London, 1996), 37.
[83] I.R. Christie, *Wars and Revolutions, Britain 1760–1815* (London, 1982), 21–2. In March 1778 when the Rockingham Whigs began to move motions in Parliament for a change of administration, the Chathamites were lukewarm. It was one thing to criticize the policies of the North ministry, quite another to dictate to the King who his ministers should be. On such motions they did not like to attend either House. See O'Gorman, *The Rise of Party*, 369.
[84] Lord North to George III, 15 March 1778, J.W. Fortescue, ed., *The Correspondence of King George III from 1760 to December 1783*, 6 vols (London, 1927–8), IV, 5, 6–7.

Chathamites disagreed on so many important issues, the prospect of their ever working smoothly together in office was always problematic. Consequently, some conversations in 1776 had perfectly predictable outcomes. Shelburne insisted that Chatham must be paramount in any new arrangement and that on most issues he was to be above criticism. The Rockinghams were appalled at Shelburne's presumption.[85] Later in 1776 a wave of rumours swept over London that Shelburne was to be taken into the North ministry. The rumours were entirely without foundation but the Rockinghams seized on them and found in them justification for their habitual suspicion of Shelburne.[86]

Nevertheless, proposals for a coalition between government and opposition occasionally surfaced during the American War of Independence, especially at times of political and military crisis. In early 1778, on hearing of the treaty between the American colonies and France, Lord North persuaded the king to open conversations with the Opposition with a view to strengthening his administration. North had his eye on Chatham, who would be provided with an honorific place, possibly with a cabinet seat, Shelburne and Sir Joseph Yorke would become Secretaries of State, Dunning would become Attorney General and places would be found, among others, for Fox. On hearing of these proposals, Shelburne declared: 'Lord Chatham must be the dictator.'[87] In fact, Lord North agreed with him, advising the king about the same time that Chatham should become First Lord of the Treasury.[88] The reaction of the opposition dashed any faint hopes that there may have been for a successful outcome. In any case, Chatham, now ill and apathetic, was not interested.[89] As for the king, he was alarmed at North's generosity. He wished only to strengthen the existing administration, not to replace most of its leading members. Nevertheless, the king's stated preference for the Chathamites over the Rockingham Whigs was to be of high historical importance.

Further discussions took place in December 1779. North and other ministers, encouraged by Shelburne's repugnance at the notion of American independence, were anxious to sound him out. The king was persuaded to direct Thurlow to talk to him, excluding from consideration for the moment

---

[85] G.H. Guttridge, *English Whiggism and the American Revolution* (Berkeley and Los Angeles, 1966), 86.

[86] Burke was particularly suspicious of Shelburne ('He is suspicious and whimsical', Burke to Garrett Nagle, 2 August 1776, in T.W. Copeland, ed., *The Correspondence of Edmund Burke*, III [Chicago, IL, 1961], 283–5). At the time, rumours that Shelburne was about to desert the opposition were receiving wide currency. See O'Gorman, *Rise of Party*, 356.

[87] Fitzmaurice, *Shelburne*, II, 17.

[88] North to the king, 14 March 1777, Fortescue, *Correspondence of George III*, IV, 68.

[89] Lord J. Russell, ed., *Memorials and Correspondence of Charles James Fox*, 4 vols (1853–7), I, 186–7; Fitzmaurice, *Shelburne*, II, 18.

the Rockinghams on account of their demand for American independence. Significantly Shelburne returned a conciliatory response, requesting further details of what was being offered and reaffirming his opposition to American independence. Rockingham, when he became involved in these discussions, was much less amenable. He required freedom to negotiate peace and, if necessary, American independence, the passage of Economical Reform legislation and a change of ministers so extensive as to amount to a new administration. Such terms were totally unacceptable to George III and the negotiation came to nothing. Nevertheless, the king cannot have been displeased with Shelburne's apparent willingness to be of service to the monarch. On America, in particular, he was prepared to respect the king's sensitivities.[90] In fact, these approaches impressed the king and probably mark the moment when the king and Shelburne began that rapprochement which was to become such an important political reality in 1782.[91]

In June 1780 further negotiations were attempted. The North ministry was now more confident, following upon a significant improvement in military fortunes in America and in its public reputation in the immediate aftermath of the Gordon Riots. A General Election, furthermore, was imminent and if the opposition could be brought into the government the elections would prove much less contentious than might otherwise have been the case. The Rockinghams laid down the same stringent conditions of some months earlier: the end of the war, recognition of American independence, extensive measures of Economical Reform and substantial changes in the Cabinet (Sandwich's resignation was the only one specifically demanded, and Fox and Richmond the only new ministers specified). In effect, and as before, this would have amounted to a substantially new administration pursuing new policies. (Interestingly, Rockingham did not go as far as publicly to nominate himself to the Treasury.) These stiff conditions yet again were enough to make a successful outcome to the negotiations impossible. The king was willing to make one or two Cabinet posts, and perhaps a few other offices available to the Rockinghams, but little else. What is most remarkable about the negotiations of 1780, however, is the fact that Rockingham failed to include Shelburne in these discussions, a damaging and, in the last analysis, disastrous mistake and one which anticipated the divisions between Fox and Shelburne in 1782. Surely, in ignoring him in this way Rockingham was causing considerable public offence to the nobleman, leaving Shelburne no alternative but to assume that Rockingham was not to be trusted and that in any future administration he, Shelburne, must look to his own devices.[92] The Duke of Richmond was right to warn Rockingham:

> If You was drawn in to talk of Persons and Measures and did not say You must consult with Lord Shelburne the Duke of Grafton and Lord Camden, it was evident You had broke with them. This point they have ascertained and You may be sure they will take Care to let Lord Shelburne and the others know You have negotiated without naming them.

That was fair criticism but Richmond was also ignoring Rockingham's failure on this occasion to insist on the first place for himself.[93] It may have been likeable modesty on Rockingham's part – as Ian Christie comments, had he done so 'such a defiance of the royal prerogative of choosing ministers was wholly revolting to George III'[94] – but his failure to do so was no doubt remembered by George III two years later. The monarch's ability to forget Shelburne's public statements on the evils of secret influence reflects his desperate need to defend himself against the Rockinghams.

In the same way, the monarch cannot have been unaware that Shelburne's stance on the vexed issue of American independence was much more acceptable to him than the stance of the Rockingham Whigs. Shelburne's theories of empire were most clearly articulated in the debates on American independence in 1782–3[95] but Shelburne had from the earliest days professed his own ideas on the government of the colonies and these in their origin owed little to Chatham. Accepting the doctrine that a viable British empire in North America demanded the westward expansion of colonial trade and settlement, Shelburne insisted that such an expansion would directly benefit British commerce. Shelburne's imperial ideas may perhaps be traced to Adam Smith, whom he had known since 1758 but, more directly to Dean Josiah Tucker, who had sought to influence Shelburne while he was trying to push the Treaty of Paris through Parliament in 1762–3.[96]

From the earliest days of his political career he had been suspicious of a restrictive policy of military and financial control in the colonies, preferring to permit the colonists to finance their own expansion into the western

[92] George III to Thurlow, 6 February 1780; Fortescue, *Correspondence of George III*, V, 2–5; Robinson to Jenkinson, 16 April 1780, ibid., V, 44–5.
[93] Richmond to Rockingham, 9 July 1782, R1–1906, Wentworth Woodhouse MSS., Sheffield City Archives.
[94] Christie, *Wars and Revolutions*, 351. For Rockingham's paranoia at this time about secret influence, see O'Gorman, *The Rise of Party*, 425. See also Christie, *End of North's Ministry*, 44–5, citing Rockingham's letter to Portland of 1 September 1780 where he attributes the dissolution of Parliament to the ministers' fear 'that delay might risk the *influence of the Crown* getting out of their hands'.
[95] See John Cannon's chapter in this volume.
[96] Toohey, *Liberty and Empire*, 117–19.

wilderness. Chatham's imperial ideas were not markedly different, although he remained more of a mercantilist than Shelburne. Like Shelburne, he wished to move beyond the unhappy disputes over taxation which bedevilled the relations between the colonists and the mother country in the first decade and a half of the reign of George III in order to seek some recognition of their fundamental common interests. They both believed that American and British liberties were intertwined; that if one were damaged then the other would also be affected. Shelburne's conception of the empire in North America was perhaps more grandiose and more ambitious than Chatham's and, as such, less capable of translating into reality.

Indeed, imperial doctrines, however ambitious and well-meaning, perhaps inevitably failed to square with the realities and problems of power. In the 1760s Shelburne may have believed that uncontrolled westward expansion might make the colonists easier to control but there was no convincing evidence to support his contention. The colonists on the eastern seaboard were difficult enough to govern without enlarging their geographical base. All of Shelburne's hopes for the colonies rested on the maintenance of law and order. For example, how was the government to reassert British rule in the aftermath of the Stamp Act disorders? Indeed, the repeal of the Stamp Act did little to conciliate opinion in the colonies. During his tenure of office during the Chatham administration Shelburne hoped that well intentioned negotiations could secure agreement with the colonists on the vexed issue of sovereignty.[97] It is some measure of the harsh realities to which an enlightened politician such as Shelburne might be driven that he is to be found advocating the billeting of troops in private houses in New York.[98] Even worse, his reaction to colonial defiance of the Mutiny Act led to him to threaten the rioters with high treason, deportation and trial in England.[99] In the early months of the Chatham administration Shelburne remained keenly in favour of the military enforcement of the Declaratory Act and agreed with the policy of raising revenue to fund the Civil List in each colony.[100] Fortunately, the ministry rejected Shelburne's plan for a military governorship and for billeting troops in private houses. Even after his resignation he remained almost as anxious as the Bedford Whigs to punish those guilty of disorder in the colonies.[101]

It is in Shelburne's reaction to colonial events in the 1770s that his broader imperial ideas were presented more consistently to the British public. Once again, it would be misleading to portray Shelburne simply

[97] Norris, *Shelburne and Reform*, 32.
[98] For a further discussion of Shelburne's willingness to billet troops on the homes of the colonists, see my *Rise of Party*, 556 n. 52.
[99] John W. Derry, *English Politics and the American Revolution* (London, 1976), 152–3.
[100] There is evidence that at this time Shelburne's authoritarian attitude to the colonists antedated Chatham's. O'Gorman, *Rise of Party*, 557 n. 56.
[101] Elofson, *The Rockingham Connection*, 51.

as a mouthpiece for Chatham. Shelburne was quicker than most to spot the likely future significance of the Boston Tea Party and the likely consequences of the ministry's attempt to punish Massachusetts. Shelburne was less alarmist than Chatham, to judge from the latter's angry reaction to the Boston Tea Party.[102] In the crucial months before the outbreak of war, in fact, there is little to suggest that Chatham and Shelburne were cooperating very closely on colonial matters. Just to show, however, that he was not for ever running to Chatham, Shelburne made a great show of welcoming Rockingham's speech of 31 October 1776, a speech that signalled the first signs of Rockingham's ultimate retreat from the Declaratory Act.[103] When Chatham came to deliver his great speech on conciliation in 1775, there is evidence that it surprised Shelburne and that he did not agree with all of its contents.[104] Whereas Chatham's Plan for Conciliation would have the Americans decide how to tax themselves, Shelburne realized that by now they could never be persuaded to do so and that the best that could be hoped for was a joint Sinking Fund which might pay off American debts to the mother country. However, Shelburne, like Chatham, believed that conciliation was only possible if Britain respected the constitutional rights of the colonists and made liberal concessions that might persuade them to lay down their arms. What that meant in practice was that ministers must abandon their coercive legislation, recognize America's right to self-government, and regulate their commerce only with colonial approval. Like most British commentators, Shelburne seriously underestimated the desire of the Americans for complete independence once the war had begun. But he was arguably more aware than Chatham was that war in America would lead not only to war against France but also against other European powers. When American independence came to be a reality, Shelburne tried to argue that political independence need not necessarily lead to a total breakdown in the old relationship between mother country and colonies. His speeches in 1775–6,[105] 'marked his position as the destined successor in the lead of the section of the party which recognized Chatham as their chief'.[106] He continued for some years to hope that the colonists might accept some recognition of their former relationship with the mother country. Shelburne was prepared to abandon the Navigation Laws and other manifestations of British power but he ultimately aspired to a system in which England and the colonies might in the future cooperate to their mutual advantage.[107]

---

[102] Peters, *The Elder Pitt*, 217–18.

[103] O'Gorman, *Rise of Party*, 350–1.

[104] Keppel to Rockingham, 5 January 1776, R1–1651, Wentworth Woodhouse MSS, Sheffield City Archives, cited in Black, *Chatham*, 295.

[105] *Parliamentary History*, XVIII, 922, 1220.

[106] Fitzmaurice, *Shelburne*, I, 486.

[107] H.T. Dickinson, *Liberty and Property: Political Ideology in Eighteenth-Century Britain* (London and New York, 1977 and 1979), 111; Fitzmaurice, *Shelburne*, II, 19.

During the early years of the war, Shelburne at times adopted a near-apocalyptic tone in his analysis of the North American empire. He believed that it was not too late to modify the old imperial system to resolve American dissatisfaction. More ambitiously, Shelburne was then dreaming of a voluntary Atlantic co-prosperity sphere, even a loose federation, whose global ambitions would frustrate Bourbon imperialism.[108] In early 1778 he spelled out his hopes to Chatham. He yearned for the restoration of peace and the adoption of some kind of federal union in which both Britain and America would share the same allies, the same enemies, the same purse, and wield one sword. Surely, two nations with a common heritage, a common language, common institutions, and mutual interests could find some grounds for compromise and settlement. 'The moment that the Independence of America is agreed to by our Government, the sun of Great Britain is set, and we shall no longer be a respectable people.'[109] If independence were to be conceded, Britain, not America, would be the greater loser. It followed, then, that to both Chatham and Shelburne the idea of American independence was totally unacceptable. To the very end Chatham opposed independence: 'I will as soon subscribe to Transubstantiation as to Sovereignty by Right in the Colonies', he wrote to Shelburne in December 1777.[110] Shelburne was in total agreement. 'I am as entirely of your Lordship's opinion as to not subscribing to the Independence of the Colonies.'[111] Although Chatham's death 1778 liberated Shelburne from his tutelage to the great man and, ultimately, enabled him to establish his own ideological directions, it was still some years before he accepted the reality of American independence. Down to 1782 there was no such recognition on his part. On 7 December 1778 Shelburne was still claiming that American independence would fatally weaken Britain: 'the mother country could not exist as an independent state; its splendor and glories would be no more, and she would be but a power of the second order in Europe'.[112] As Dr Peters makes clear, Shelburne's position has much to be said for it. 'Shelburne was advocating ... a defensive holding operation in America combined with generous offers of conciliation – by no means an unviable policy'.[113] Whether such a policy could ever have overcome potential opposition in court, parliament and country is another matter.

It certainly could not survive military realities in America. The entry of France in the war in 1778 determined the Rockingham Whigs to abandon the Declaratory Act and to accept the impending reality of American inde-

---

[108] Norris, *Shelburne and Reform*, 32–3.
[109] Toohey, *Liberty and Empire*, 119.
[110] Bowood House Archives, S13 ff122–27, cited in Peters, *Pitt and Popularity*, 224. See also Fitzmaurice, *Shelburne*, II, 9–10.
[111] Shelburne to Chatham, 23 December 1777, ibid., II, 13. See also 17, 20–1.
[112] 7 December 1778, *Parliamentary History*, XX, 1–43.
[113] Peters, *Pitt and Popularity*, 225.

pendence. With the widening of the American War into a near global conflict, Shelburne began to see new dangers. Rather the reality of American independence, he told Parliament on 1 June 1780, than for Great Britain and its parliament to be subdued by its own armies and its constitution destroyed. Better a smaller, free nation than a empire held by force of arms: 'He would be much better pleased to see America forever severed from Great Britain, than restored to our possession by force of arms, or conquest.'[114] For some time, he professed to believe that it was only in alliance with the Rockingham Whigs that the war might be brought to an end and new systems prevail:

> He had united with those with whom he had the honour to act for several years; their principles were the same; their future role of conduct was to be correspondent; whatever different opinions they might have held they no longer interfered with their general plan; they were confidentially and fully united in the great leading principle, of new men and new measures; if the salvation of the country was to be effected, it was only by those means; or if the country was to be saved from the ruins which threatened us on every side, it was only by a change of system.[115]

After the defeat at Yorktown in 1781 American independence became inevitable. Shelburne could only hope that the coming peace treaty would preserve something of the common Anglo-American interests which he had for some years been advocating. As Lord North's ministry tottered to its destruction in the winter of 1781–2 and as the prospect of its replacement by the Rockingham Whigs and Shelburne's tiny connection became more likely, Shelburne may well have wondered about his own role in the coming peace negotiations. The following two years were to reveal what that role was to be. And if the attainment of Shelburne's political objectives depended upon the defeat of British armies in America and the achievement of the independence of the North American colonies, it was to be in the end the passage of American independence which was to overwhelm and eventually destroy him.

One thing, at least, was certain by 1782. Shelburne had emerged as one of the leaders of the opposition and in a position to rival that of the Marquess of Rockingham. And this had occurred in spite of a number of serious political disadvantages: the suspicion of George III, the rivalry of the Rockingham Whigs, the vexatious position of Chatham, the political weakness which arose from his opposition to a popular war, and, not least, Shelburne's own personal unpopularity within and without parliament. However, it was not merely his inherited wealth and position which had enabled Shelburne

---

[114] *Parliamentary History*, XXI, 1023–43, cited in Fitzmaurice, *Shelburne*, II, 81; Toohey, *Liberty and Empire*, 120.
[115] 1 December 1779, *Parliamentary History*, XX, 1165.

to attain the political prominence which he had by 1782. Mistrusted he may have been but no one could doubt either his intellectual gifts or his political disinterestedness. Still, it remains true that the heir of Chatham owed much to the memory of the great imperial statesman. Yet although his alliance with Chatham was Shelburne's most important political lodestar between 1763 and 1782 it was never a completely dominating consideration. Shelburne had been Chatham's associate, he had become his political heir and he had certainly been Chatham's inferior. But he had never been Chatham's servant. The essential paradigm within which Shelburne's career should be assessed is that of the enlightened, independent Whig in politics, struggling to assert himself in a world dominated by the king and his ministers, the party grouping of the Marquess of Rockingham and, not least, the person and influence of Chatham himself.

6

Shelburne and Ireland:
Politician, Patriot, Absentee

Martyn J. Powell

In April 1784 the *Hibernian Journal* announced to its patriotic readership:

> we are now unequivocally convinced, that whether the arch-corrupter, North;
> the insinuating insidious Pitt; the profligate gambling Fox, or the apostate
> Renegade Shelburne, rules the Helm, the systematic Government of Ireland is
> Tyranny, Oppression, and an Iron Rod![1]

Such hyperbole was unwarranted, but the core of the newspaper's comment
was correct. Few British politicians – including those of the longstanding
opposition to Lord North during the American War – would put Irish interests before those of the empire. That said, there were subtle – and some
not-so subtle – differences between the Irish policies adopted by Britain's
political groupings and their leaders. I have written elsewhere of Fox's determination to balance the interests of the British parliament and empire with
the interests of the Irish subject.[2] But in many ways, despite his blasted
political reputation – and it is difficult to talk up the achievement of a politician who makes so many enemies that his career is over, despite persistent
rumours of a comeback, at the age of forty-six – Shelburne is a much more
credible figure than Fox as an advocate of Irish interests within the British
empire.

During the course of this chapter I intend to argue that in his approach
to Irish issues – including policy-making – Shelburne adopted a stance that
was influenced by two dominant considerations. The first is his commitment
to a broadly Chathamite political world-view, and the second, his first-hand
experience of Ireland through his landholdings. In terms of the former, he
was certainly aware of the need to improve Britain's mode of governing
Ireland, and indeed India and the United States; but unlike the king, Lord

---

[1]   *Hibernian Journal*, 7–9 April 1784.
[2]   Martyn J. Powell, 'Charles James Fox and Ireland', *Irish Historical Studies*, 33 (2002),
169–90.

North, the Bedfordites, and indeed many of his colleagues in opposition during the American War, he was invariably reluctant to do this at the expense of Irish liberties, and, indeed, public opinion. This latter point leads directly to the importance of his first-hand Irish experience. An awareness of how one's policies played inside and outside the parliament on College Green, Dublin, was always going to be more pressing for a politician who was both Irish-born, and the owner of such extensive estates in his native land. Of course, Irish absentees were not famed for their concern for land or tenants – many rarely travelling to Ireland. But Shelburne was a notable exception. He drafted many improving schemes for Irish land and society, and went on fact-finding missions. In this sense the term 'patriot' in the title is not the misnomer that some might think. As we shall see, Shelburne may have agreed to legislative independence and the renunciation act[3] reluctantly, but his concerns over the state of Ireland were genuine, and would occupy his thoughts long after his political career in Britain had ended. For this reason it is of vital importance in considering Shelburne and Ireland to look beyond his career as a policy-maker. His role as absentee landlord was of fundamental importance, and meant that his public life was played out on at least two stages.

II

Shelburne was born in Dublin, and had impressive Irish antecedents, not only through aristocratic lineage, the County Kerry Fitzmaurices, but also his great-grandfather, the pioneering political economist Sir William Petty. Shelburne had his first schooling in Dublin, but much of the credit for early learning, and indeed family affection, went to his aunt, Lady Arbella Denny, the notable Dublin philanthropist and founder of the first Magdalen asylum. After university and a sojourn in the army he was returned for the County Kerry seat in the Irish parliament. His father's death in 1761 ensured that Shelburne did not take this up, and he was elevated to the Lords. At the same time he inherited the family's extensive Irish estates including the family's patrimony in County Kerry and extensive lands in Queen's County.

His early political career was influenced by Henry Fox and a figure much disliked in Irish circles, John Stuart, 3rd Earl of Bute, although Shelburne usually exhibited a distaste for the Scots typical of Irish whiggery, describing them as 'the most selfish and narrow minded people existing'.[4] Both of

---

[3]   This act, coming shortly after legislative independence, was an additional concession forced upon the British government by Irish patriotic opinion. The need to shore up the settlement was, at least in part, a result of Lord Mansfield's willingness to pronounce upon an Irish legal matter whilst the repeal of the Declaratory Act – removing the British Lords' role as Ireland's final judicial court-– was pending.

[4]   BL, Bowood MS, B63A, f40, Irish Travel Journal, 29 September 1772. He also opined:

these men would play a role behind the scenes in Irish politics in the years following the Money Bill dispute of the 1750s, which focused upon the Irish parliament's exclusive right to dispose of a surplus in the Irish treasury. This crisis ensured that a court-country split began to metamorphose into a kind of party politics in Ireland. Thanks to his Irish connections Shelburne had a clear grasp of such developments. He knew some of the key players on both government and opposition sides, including Primate George Stone and the Kildare family. Shelburne was also on good terms with higher ranking figures amongst his tenantry, such as Dean Coote in Queen's County, but his main conduit for political gossip was Sir James Caldwell, an Irish printer and peerage-hunter.[5] Shelburne stayed with Caldwell on his estate when in Ireland and the two met for dinner, coffee, and the playhouse in Dublin. But we should also recognize that this was something of a friendship of convenience. Caldwell saw the Shelburnes as a ticket to lordly advancement, while Shelburne was sufficiently embarrassed by Caldwell to withdraw an invitation to share a cabin with him on the crossing back to Britain.[6]

Though Shelburne was *au fait* from a relatively early stage with attempts to improve British governance of Ireland, his personal involvement in Irish policy-making did not begin until his appointment as a senior minister in Chatham's cabinet in 1766. From the moment of its inception it is clear that the Chatham ministry had ambitious plans for imperial reform. Chatham had become particularly interested in India, or rather Indian revenue, and he was equally determined that Ireland should start to pay its way. In Chatham's opinion the main obstacle to reform in Ireland, and by extension the implementation of government policy, was the domination of the Irish administration by the so-called undertakers, the local power-brokers who ensured a smooth ride for government measures in parliament; that is, if they were minded to be of assistance. The obvious flaws in this system led Chatham to support the introduction of a septennial bill, which was expected to gain the new viceroy, Lord Bristol,[7] popular support, and contribute to the erosion of the undertakers' power base through the imposition of a constantly resident viceroy. Shelburne, however, appeared to have little impact upon this process. Despite his ministerial responsibility for

'I can scarce conceive a Scotchman capable of liberality, and capable of impartiality'; Fitzmaurice, *Shelburne*, II, 308, and fought a duel against a Scottish MP.

[5] JRL, MS B3/14, f121, Sir James Caldwell to Shelburne, April 1755; JRL, MS B3/20, f247, P. Magran to Sir James Caldwell, 18 August 1770. For more on Caldwell's aspirations, see Toby Barnard, 'The Artistic and Cultural Activities of the Caldwells of Castle Caldwell, 1750–83', *Irish Architectural and Decorative Studies*, 10 (2007), 90–111.

[6] JRL, MS B3/29, f24, Sir James Caldwell to Lady Caldwell, 29 April 1766; JRL, MS B3/29, f33, Sir James Caldwell to Lady Caldwell, 22 October 1772; JRL, MS B3/29, f33, Sir James Caldwell to Lady Caldwell, 3 November 1772; JRL, MS B3/29, f44, Sir James Caldwell to Lady Caldwell, 10 December 1772.

[7] Bristol served as viceroy 1766–7.

Ireland, almost all of the nitty-gritty detail on the new ministry's Irish policy was ironed out between Chatham and Bristol.[8] Indeed Shelburne became isolated in the ministry, distrusted due to his inconstant party loyalty – a constant refrain in his career.

After Chatham fell ill, the responsibility for formulating and implementing colonial policy was transferred to Shelburne. However, Shelburne was never in the vanguard of an aggressive imperial policy, and he was certainly more circumspect than Charles Townshend, the Chancellor of the Exchequer. They may have shared some notions on the raising of American revenue. For example, Shelburne saw the reaffirmation of the American Declaratory Act in return for a general pardon as a way out of the Massachusetts crisis in 1767, which had started with the boycott of goods subject to Townshend's new colonial duties.[9] But in more general terms he regarded difficult constitutional issues as best avoided if the security of the empire was at stake.[10] Perhaps conscious of the need for stability in Ireland, he was governed by pragmatism, and an awareness of the realpolitik of landlord control. Charles Townshend's death in September 1767, removed one adversary, but his elder brother George, 4th Viscount Townshend, had been appointed Irish viceroy, and had a similar reformist's zeal. When he arrived in Ireland, set to shake up the Irish political system, his political reputation was complicated. As a supporter of a British militia bill and now a Chathamite recruit he was feted, but his connections with Bute were held against him. To many Irish politicians Shelburne was similarly Janus-faced, unfairly perhaps as in reality the Irish policies favoured by the Chathamites in 1766 and 1767 were more assertive than those put forward by Bute.

Townshend's administration began in confusion, and Shelburne clashed with the viceroy over constitutional reform. The Octennial Act limiting the duration of Irish parliaments to eight years was the key to popularity – at least in terms of patriot public opinion and independent-minded MPs – and the reform of government, but Townshend referred to a judges' tenure bill, allowing the same security of tenure during good behaviour as their English counterparts, in the king's speech. The ministry feared that minor constitutional concessions might 'draw in question the nature of the connection between Great Britain and Ireland, which it has been always thought sound policy to avoid'.[11] Shelburne duly delivered the required rebuke, taking no pains to temper the language he used with Townshend – diplomacy was never his strong point – even though they were friends after seeing military

---

[8] See Martyn J. Powell, *Britain and Ireland in the Eighteenth-Century Crisis of Empire* (Basingstoke, 2003), 88–92.

[9] See also Lewis Namier, *Charles Townshend* (London, 1964), 172–7.

[10] A.L. Humphreys, 'Lord Shelburne and British Colonial Policy, 1766–1768', *English Historical Review*, 50 (1935), 258, 270, 276.

[11] CHOP, ii, 199, Townshend to Shelburne, 5 November 1767; ibid., 212–13, Shelburne to Townshend, 18 November 1767.

action together.[12] Yet the cabinet had erred by not mentioning the Octennial Act directly and its insistence on amending the judges bill through Poynings Law, which allowed Privy Council scrutiny in Westminster of Dublin legislation, riled the Irish Commons.[13] Moreover, the eight year bill made a general election imminent, which had the consequence of endangering a plan to augment the Irish army.[14] These were cabinet decisions – the latter was insisted upon by Lord Mansfield and the lawyers – but Shelburne had chapter and verse on the dangers of the augmentation proposal from Irish contacts like Sir James Caldwell.[15] Shelburne was also culpable in allowing Townshend to remain ignorant over the identity of the new Lord Chancellor, whilst somehow the information that it was to be the Englishman, Lord Lifford, found its way into polite Dublin circles.[16]

Shelburne was therefore a rather unwilling ally in the Townshend revolution, and at times a major obstacle. A letter in reply to Caldwell, who was advocating Townshend's continuance as viceroy, was far from effusive in its praise.[17] But some of his reflections suggested long-term views on the subject that were not necessarily at odds with those held by Townshend. During discussions over constant vice-regal residency Shelburne made it clear that 'there must be a final period to Lords Justices', and although he noted that this policy-change had 'been long in contemplation here', he had personal views on the matter.[18] Shelburne thought uninterrupted residency would make the Irish country gentlemen secure against undertaker bullying,[19] which was indicative of his dissatisfaction with the role of the boroughmongers in Irish politics. His Queen's County tenants, members of the Ossory Club, a patriotic political society, were convinced – most likely due to his connections with the ever-popular Chatham – that Shelburne was a suitable person to appeal to against the 'schemes of an ambitious and tyrannical Aristocracy'.[20] He would later refer to Lord Shannon, one of the most influential peers in Ireland, as a 'disciple of the old school', effectively

---

[12] Henry Lansdowne, *Glanerought and the Petty Fitzmaurices* (Oxford, 1937), 59.

[13] *CHOP*, ii, 195, Townshend to Shelburne, 27 October 1767; ibid., 205, 13 November 1767.

[14] *CHOP*, ii, 307, 16 February 1768; ibid., 313, Townshend to Shelburne, 5 March 1768; DCRO, D3155/WH3473, Waite to Wilmot, 22 March 1768; *CHOP*, ii, 315, Shelburne to Townshend, 14 March 1768.

[15] JRL, MS B3/10, xi, ff293–8, Sir James Caldwell, to Shelburne, 3 February 1768.

[16] HMC, *Twelfth Report, Appendix, Part V. The Manuscripts of his Grace the Duke of Rutland, K.G., Preserved at Belvoir Castle. vol. ii* (1889), 299, Townshend to [Granby], 6 January 1768.

[17] JRL, MS B3/14, f128, Shelburne to Sir James Caldwell, [n.d].

[18] Ibid.

[19] Quoted in Bartlett, 'The Townshend Viceroyalty' (Queen's University Belfast PhD, 1976), p. 91, Townshend for Lord Frederick Campbell; ibid., 43; Fitzmaurice, *Shelburne*, I, 357.

[20] BL, Bowood MS, B72, f3, Ossory Club Address to Shelburne, 3 January 1772.

a barrier against much needed parliamentary and religious reform.[21] Even so, Shelburne would always appear as a voice of generosity and moderation on Irish and imperial matters when compared to his cabinet colleagues. Shelburne and the Bedford connection found it particularly difficult to reconcile differences, and he left government after it became evident that the king, the Duke of Grafton and Camden shared their misgivings.

III

Shelburne had timed his departure well, and he joined the British opposition in condemning government on its handling of John Wilkes. In Ireland, Townshend appeared to have lost control. A privy council Money Bill – a constitutional point insisted on by Shelburne before he left government – was rejected on the grounds that it had not been drawn up in the Irish parliament, and, on the advice of another Chathamite, Lord Camden, the Irish parliament was censured and prorogued, an act that caused popular outrage.[22] Irish patriotism, a somewhat fickle creed, eventually forgave Townshend and Camden, and in contrast to Shelburne both became crowd and club heroes. Shelburne did not seem to have the knack of making friends, and keeping them, in quite the same fashion. Shelburne's consistent support for British parliamentary supremacy over Ireland needs to be recognized. But it was married with other, more whiggish and oppositional, concerns. For example, it is unlikely that Shelburne would have supported Townshend's methods of building a Dublin Castle party. Like many British politicians he was a fierce critic of Irish jobbery.[23] Whilst Townshend was dividing the Irish revenue board to increase the patronage available to government, Shelburne argued against 'the unlimited Power assum'd by the Crown of granting Pensions on your Revenue'. He told the Ossory Club that 'the creation of new unnecessary offices appears to me an evil of still greater extent'.[24]

Firmly ensconced as lieutenant in the Chathamite wing of the opposition, Shelburne harried the Grafton and North ministries on their treatment of Wilkes, together with American and Irish policies, though he confirmed his principled approach to imperial policy by backing North's India bill.[25] As one of the wealthiest Irish absentee landlords in Britain, Shelburne might have been expected to play a key role in the multi-party spoiling campaign

---

[21] Ibid., B63A, f77, Memorandum of a Tour of Ireland, 1794.

[22] Thomas Bartlett, 'The Irish House of Commons' Rejection of the "Privy Council" Money Bill in 1769. A Re-Assessment', *Studia Hibernica*, 19 (1979), 70–1.

[23] BL, Bowood MS, B63A, f2, Memorandum relative to my estates in Ireland, July and August 1770.

[24] Ibid., B72, f6, Shelburne to the Ossory Club (draft), 10 March 1772.

[25] There were limits however, and he argued against further parliamentary interference in Indian affairs in 1786; Fitzmaurice, *Shelburne*, 369–70.

led by Rockingham against an absentee tax in 1773.[26] But although he was said to have advocated impeachment for any minister who advised that the bill should be accepted and returned to Ireland,[27] he followed Chatham's more principled lead, and opted not to take on a full-blooded role. When the tax failed, Shelburne's response revealed general dissatisfaction with kow-towing to patriot opinion, and the new modes, which he predicted 'would uphold "Poynings" Act, and all the old doctrine of the dependence of Ireland upon England, in all cases whatsoever'.[28]

The British opposition fastened upon the Dublin Castle government and Irish policy as a potentially weak link in North's ministry. But the speeches of opposition MPs were more likely to be defending the rights of the British parliament than expressing sympathy with Irish patriotism. On 10 November 1775 Shelburne attacked the North ministry for taxing America while Ireland was allowed to contribute such a meagre sum to the defence of the empire. He also criticized the Dublin Castle administration for gaining an address on the American War that referred to the king's rights, but not to the rights of the British parliament.[29] Harrying the government was obviously paramount, and like other opposition leaders his motives were often less than noble, but Shelburne had never wavered on the issue of Britain retaining a superintending power over the colonies.[30]

The drift into war with the American colonies and the resulting growth of the defensive paramilitary bodies known as the Volunteers threatened Shelburne's political world view. Rockingham described the growth of the 'illegal' independent companies as 'a matter truly alarming', but Shelburne went a step further and rashly referred to the armed Irish populace as 'an enraged mob'. His comments were made in response to Rockingham's motion calling for action on Ireland, and to a degree, were taken out of context. Shelburne emphasized the loyalty of the Irish men in arms, 'of whom there was not a man but would defend his country against the common enemy,

---

[26] The income from his lands is reckoned to have been worth c. £50,000 p.a. by the end of Shelburne's life; John Cannon, 'Petty, William, Second Earl of Shelburne and First Marquess of Lansdowne', ODNB.

[27] *The Harcourt Papers*, ed. E.W. Harcourt, 15 vols (Oxford, 1880–1905), ix, North to Harcourt, 29 October 1773.

[28] T.F. Moriarty, 'The Irish Absentee Tax Controversy of 1773: A Study in Anglo-Imperial Politics on the Eve of the American Revolution', *Proceedings of the American Philosophical Society*, 118 (1974), 400; *The Correspondence of William Pitt Earl of Chatham*, ed. W.S Taylor and J.H. Pringle, 4 vols (London, 1838–9), iv, 319, Shelburne to Chatham, 8 January 1774; ibid., 320, Chatham to Shelburne, 10 January 1774.

[29] *Parliamentary History of England from … 1066 to … 1803*, 36 vols (London, 1806–20), xviii, 921–7; *London Evening Post*, 9–10 November 1775.

[30] Frank O'Gorman, *The Rise of Party in England: The Rockingham Whigs 1760–82* (London, 1975), 368.

should any attempt be made on it'.[31] In fact, during the Seven Years War Shelburne's father had offered to raise an independent regiment, and was ticked off by Pitt for being more concerned with 'whimsical peculiarity of dress' than practical matters. He was told that it would be far wiser to have his men dressed in the regimentals of your country, and thus 'appear like firm and determined soldiers, not like scampering Hussars'.[32]

Shelburne senior's eagerness to put couture before capability would have made him well-suited to the lively Volunteer culture of the late 1770s. Yet his son had badly underestimated their support among the public. He referred to their illegality in the British Lords, and for his pains he was abused in the Irish Commons.[33] He also misjudged the longevity of the movement, incorrectly predicting that the Volunteers would disarm once commercial relief had been promised.[34] In fact, the armed associations remained a central component of Irish political life for nearly ten years. Indeed, almost all of Ireland's senior politicians took up arms. Shelburne had made a monumental gaffe; one that would prevent him from enjoying any credit for future interventions in Irish affairs. For example, despite his sympathy for the campaign for the removal of restrictions upon Irish trade, chiming as it did with his own economic views, he was criticized in the *Limerick Chronicle* for refusing to contemplate any direct negotiation on the matter by the Irish parliament.[35] A more serious sin in patriotic Irish eyes was his willingness to discuss the possibility of an Anglo-Irish Union. His public comment on the matter, predicting that English manufacturers would acquiesce to Irish commercial concessions, 'as soon as it was understood that the common interests of both countries was to be united in the regulation of their trade and intercourse', in the British Lords in May 1779, most probably influenced by Adam Smith, would have gone down rather badly in a country that twenty years earlier, in a more peaceful phase, had witnessed a major anti-Union riot.[36] He would misjudge Irish opinion again when in office in 1782, as home secretary. Sir George Yonge was made an Irish vice treasurer, probably at Shelburne's behest, in spite of the fact that he was English, and according to one Irish sceptic 'opposed our trade bills and talked of overhauling them on some future day of power'. Not only that,

---

[31] *Parl. Hist.*, xx, 643–9; Conor Cruise O'Brien, *The Great Melody: A Thematic Biography and Commented Anthology of Edmund Burke* (London, 1992), 189; *Limerick Chronicle*, 20 May 1779.

[32] JRL, MS B3/14, f125, Sir James Caldwell to Shelburne, 29 November 1759.

[33] *Parl. Hist.*, xx, 1157–69; *The Last Journals of Horace Walpole, during the Reign of George III from 1771–1783*, ed. A.F. Stewart, 2 vols (London, 1910), ii, 356.

[34] *Limerick Chronicle*, 20 May 1779.

[35] Ibid., 21 June 1779.

[36] *Parl. Hist.*, xx, 650, 11 May 1779.

he was also 'prompt and forward with his foolish opinion of the supremacy of this country over Ireland in all cases'.[37]

IV

Shelburne's comments in 1779, unlike those by some members of the government, were not borne out of panic, but rather a more considered desire to see Ireland's Free Trade demands absorbed into a wider reform package. Indeed he had formulated a scheme for a federal union – and had discussed it with the agricultural expert Arthur Young – which would see Ireland give up the hereditary revenue, a fund in possession of the crown typically used to finance the military establishment and pensions, in return for free trade.[38] The fall of the North ministry in 1782 finally enabled Shelburne to put some of his plans into action. As the link between the king and his hated new Rockingham ministers, Shelburne, the home secretary, was extremely influential. But for the second time in his career he was hampered by poor relations with the current viceroy, the 3rd Duke of Portland, another man keen to cause upheaval in Dublin Castle. As with America, Shelburne's Irish policy was to vacillate and concede as little as possible. Distrusted in Ireland, his name was on a list drawn up by Edmund Malone, Irish-born editor of Shakespeare's works, of politicians considered hostile towards Irish patriotism.[39] Perhaps wisely then his outward countenance was positive. A speech by Shelburne on 11 April in the British Lords provided further fuel for Irish speculation that constitutional independence would be granted immediately. Richard Fitzpatrick, Shelburne's brother-in-law, observed slyly to his cousin Charles James Fox that Shelburne's speech 'gives great satisfaction here, and probably if there had been any chance of soothing this country into moderation, would have done infinite mischief'.[40] The relationship between Shelburne and his Rockinghamite partners was less than cordial. Most of the Rockinghamites distrusted the 'Jesuitical' Shelburne; Richard Brinsley Sheridan commented on the 'reserve and a

---

[37] HMC, *Fourteenth Report, Appendix, Part IX. The Manuscripts of the Earl of Buckinghamshire, the Earl of Lindsey, the Earl of Onslow, Lord Emly, Theodore J. Hare, Esq., and James Round, Esq. M.P.* (London, 1895), 164, Lucan to Pery, 3 April 1782.

[38] Earlier schemes for a federal union, put forward by the likes of Malachy Postethwayt and William Knox, also focused on allowing Ireland an unrestricted free trade in return for some kind of revenue contribution. See Douglas Kanter, *The Making of British Unionism 1740–1848: Politics, Government and the Anglo-Irish Constitutional Relationship* (Dublin, 2009), 40–4.

[39] HMC, *Twelfth Report. Appendix, Part X. The Manuscripts and Correspondence of James, first Earl of Charlemont, vol. i, 1745–1783* (London, 1891), i, 400, Malone to Charlemont, 9 April 1782.

[40] *Parl. Hist.*, xxii, 1260; *Memorials and Correspondence of Charles James Fox*, ed. Lord John Russell, 4 vols (London, 1853–7), i, 399, 17 April 1782.

disingenuous management' that was evident in Shelburne's dispatches to Portland. He also accused Shelburne of planning to make Portland 'answerable for the consequences' of concessions.[41] Portland, however, was equally guilty of double-dealing. Portland informed Shelburne on 6 May that all of Ireland's demands had to be conceded immediately, yet only days earlier he had written a secret letter to Fox holding out the possibility of retaining the Declaratory Act, which allowed the British parliament to legislate directly for Ireland. He admitted that he had decided not to pass this information on to Shelburne as it would encourage the home secretary to delay.[42]

Given the king's inflexible views on Ireland it was only to be expected that Shelburne would attempt to avoid constitutional concessions for as long as possible. But this should not really have been a sticking-point as Fox's views on Ireland were close to those of Shelburne. Domestic security, and the need to concede as little as possible to the Irish patriots in the long term, were Fox's priorities.[43] When legislative independence was conceded, both Shelburne and the Rockinghams thought in terms of a 'final adjustment'. For Shelburne it was of vital importance that Ireland recognized Britain's superintending power in matters of state and commerce that were of 'common concern'.[44] Shelburne's role here was central, as, influenced by the Abbé Morellet, Adam Smith, and Josiah Tucker, he had a strong theoretical grasp of a final adjustment, particularly its economic and imperial implications.[45] Although Shelburne was invariably pragmatic – he was critical of Portland's attempts to construct an Irish Whig party, reminding him of the necessity of zeal for governmental service and Britain's prerogative, and was moved to censure the viceroy in the Lords[46] – this latter period in Shelburne's career was influenced by a progressive, ambitious, and to a certain extent, unworkable strategy. His final adjustment was a federal or commercial Union, a scheme to which he would return in 1785 and 1799.

The ministerial crisis triggered by the death of Rockingham on 1 July 1782 could not fail to have an impact upon Anglo-Irish relations. The news that Shelburne was to be the next Prime Minister was welcomed in Ireland by the traditional supporters of government, such as John Beresford the chief revenue commissioner, and John Scott, who had been dismissed

[41] *The Letters of Richard Brinsley Sheridan*, ed. C. Price, 3 vols (Oxford, 1966), i, 144, Sheridan to Fitzpatrick, 20 May 1782.
[42] TNA, HO100/1/144–5, 29 April 1782; *Corr. of Charles James Fox*, i, 414–16, 28 April 1782; TNA, HO100/1/178–180, Portland to Shelburne, 6 May 1782.
[43] BL, Add. MS 47580, f93, 28 April 1782.
[44] TNA, HO100/1/216–8, Shelburne to Portland, 18 May 1782; *Parl. Hist.*, xxiii, 26; *Memoirs of the Life and Times of the Rt. Hon. Henry Grattan by his son Henry Grattan Esq. MP*, 5 vols (London, 1839–46), ii, 270, Grattan to Fox, 6 May 1782; *Life and Times of Henry Grattan*, ii, 354–5.
[45] James Kelly, *Prelude to Union: Anglo-Irish Politics in the 1780s* (Cork, 1992), ix, 44–5.
[46] TNA, HO100/2/7–12, Shelburne to Portland, 8 June 1782; National Library of Ireland, MS 51/A/3, Portland to Thomas Townshend, 31 July 1782.

from his post as attorney general; although their situation under Rockingham and Portland had been so bleak that it is probable that they would have welcomed almost any change. Shelburne supposedly favoured an older method whereby 'every man is to act not on the supposition of a system, but to consider himself as dependent on the viceroy of the day'.[47] As a former secretary of state for the south and home secretary, Shelburne had considerable experience of handling Irish affairs. Moreover, he was seen as a 'safe pair of hands' on the Irish issue. He was sympathetic both to aspects of Irish patriotism (those that did not threaten the Anglo-Irish connection) and to the traditional supporters of government. A rather resentful Portland attempted to contradict the view that Shelburne was popular in Ireland, claiming that the Irish were 'apprehensive of his love of power'. Moreover, the sniping against the Volunteers was not forgotten, as when it was announced that Shelburne was to be the new Prime Minister the Volunteers declared against the withdrawal of 5000 troops from Ireland for use by the British navy.[48] As the minister who eventually conceded the renunciation act, albeit reluctantly, there was potential for a comeback – at least in terms of Irish public opinion. But this was less a case of backing the right horse, and more one of letting his viceroy, Lord Temple, get on with it. Shelburne was reluctant to speak to the chief secretary, William Wyndham Grenville, despite his determination to dominate all areas of policy-making. Shelburne's tack was to instruct Temple that if a renunciation was made it was not to include external legislation, and to delay until better news arrived from the Paris negotiations.[49] Temple threatened to resign, got his way, delivered the Renunciation Act and took the plaudits.[50] The reality of the situation was that Shelburne had been sidelined by his fellow ministers, William Pitt the Younger and Thomas Townshend. William Grenville declared his amazement at 'this, which has been done entirely without the concurrence or even knowledge of Lord Shelburne'.[51] The Prime Minister was known to be inflexible on the issue of Ireland's independence, and for

---

[47] BL, Add. MS 34418, f511, Cooke to Eden, 22 July 1782.

[48] Corr. of Charles James Fox, i, 464–6, Fitzpatrick to Ossory, 15 July 1782; NLI, MS 51/A/1, Portland to Thomas Townshend, 16 July 1782.

[49] TNA, HO100/3/354, Townshend to Temple, 21 December 1782.

[50] In fact, the measure was a 'Recognition' rather than a 'Renunciation' Act – there was no retrospective element. As Grenville put it, recognition was about establishing and explaining the constitutional settlement of 1782, 'whereas by a renunciation parliament confesses that something further really was necessary', NLI, 51/E/2a, memorandum by W.W. Grenville on reasons for renunciation, 19 December 1782; TNA, HO100/8/59–60, Temple to Thomas Townshend, 13 January 1783; HMC, Thirteenth Report, Appendix, Part III. The Manuscripts of J. B. Fortescue, Esq., preserved at Dropmore, vol. i (London, 1892), 181, Temple to W.W. Grenville, 15 January 1783.

[51] Quoted in Peter Jupp, 'Earl Temple's Viceroyalty and the Renunciation Question, 1782–3', Irish Historical Studies, 68 (1971), 514.

this reason, rather than the urgency of imperial and domestic affairs, he was deliberately kept in the dark by his fellow ministers.

After the collapse of his ministry over the peace treaties ending the American War, Shelburne remained on the sidelines of British – and also Irish – politics for the rest of his life; his career tainted by personal unpopularity. There were, however, near comebacks, and periods of more serious interest, some of which involved Ireland. He was a supporter of parliamentary reform, and his first-hand experience of Irish electoral corruption was doubtless influential. He did not shy away from 'Tests' set by electors for parliamentary candidates, suggesting this course of action – in this case an insistence on an MP's opposition to the distribution of pensions and offices by the Castle government – to Queen's County's Ossory Club as early as 1772.[52] During the Rutland viceroyalty (1784–7) most Irish newspapers were convinced that Shelburne was able to exercise influence through Rutland's chief secretary, Thomas Orde – 'Shelburne's man, Orde'[53] as one put it – who had held posts in the Rockingham and Shelburne ministries. The *Dublin Morning Post* claimed that Shelburne was 'constantly consulted on the affairs of Ireland' and the hostile *Hibernian Journal* referred to the 'weak, temporizing, humbugging system that Lord Shelburne instructed Orde to adopt for the Government of Ireland'.[54] The *Belfast News-Letter* was convinced that Shelburne's planned return to this kingdom 'is to act as a coadjutor to the Duke of Rutland and Mr Orde'.[55]

Shelburne clearly did have friends in the Irish government after the fall of his ministry. The Dublin Castle-sponsored *Volunteer Evening Post* adopted a strikingly pro-Shelburne tone in its opening issue. Thomas Orde and Shelburne kept up their correspondence and Rutland recommended that Shelburne be offered a step in the peerage.[56] Instrumental in its early stages, Shelburne also remained active in support of the Genevan exile Francois d'Ivernois's plans to set up a community, a New Geneva, near Waterford.[57] Shelburne backed Free Trade once again during Pitt's commercial propositions of 1785, possibly exercising some influence over Orde, who was piloting it through the Dublin parliament.[58] Shelburne's line was certainly more measured than that of Pitt, as, taking into account Ireland's economic weakness, he did not see it fit to request a contribution from its coffers at this stage.[59]

---

[52] BL, Bowood MS, B72, f6, Shelburne to the Ossory Club (draft), 10 March 1772.
[53] *Hibernian Journal*, 5 May 1784.
[54] *Dublin Morning Post*, 23 October 1784; *Hibernian Journal*, 21 May 1784.
[55] *Belfast News-Letter*, 20–4 August 1784.
[56] *Volunteer Evening Post*, 27–9 November 1783; John Norris, *Shelburne and Reform* (London, 1963), 275–6.
[57] Norris, *Shelburne and Reform*, 279.
[58] Lansdowne, *Glanerought*, 94–5.
[59] Fitzmaurice, *Shelburne*, II, 295–6.

Although the French Revolution could not help but influence Shelburne's attitude towards Ireland and Irishmen – his sympathy resulted in a rupture with his ever-loyal Irish lieutenant Colonel Isaac Barré[60] – in terms of the Anglo-Irish connection it was trade that dominated Shelburne's thoughts – and speeches – during the latter years of his career. During the Union debates Shelburne initially supported the Anglo-Irish Union as a commercial treaty, condemning the parochialism of the British wool lobby. He had expressed similar views on the selfishness of American merchants who put the pursuit of profit before the welfare of the country's indigenous inhabitants.[61] Shelburne was convinced that 'Ireland cannot be governed as it is, or as it has been heretofore', and saw 'no arrangement possible but an Union'.[62] What kind of Union this would be was a conundrum that Shelburne would spend some time mulling over. He initially disliked a parliamentary Union, but had doubts over the wisdom of the commercial or federal alternative that had been part of his hoped-for final adjustment of 1782. This would be 'giving it up to the Catholics on account of their numbers'.[63] Indeed, rather presciently he considered the possibility of separate executives in Ulster and the south, based on property rather than numbers.[64] Inaction was not a possibility, and it is clear that he had no fondness for Grattan's 'Patriot' parliament, describing its acts as 'base, servile, barbarous, inhuman and unprincipled'.[65] He referred to 'the severity publicly and privately recommended by the part of the Irish government which originated all the ill'.[66]

V

Given Shelburne's imperial grand view, whether chiefly commercial or pragmatic, 'patriot' does not always appear to be the most suitable appellation. Yet he was a certain kind of Irish patriot. He was not a parliamentary patriot, but the patriot found in the Dublin Society, concerned with the vices undermining Irish society, and determined to put forward an improving vision. In this, he was undoubtedly influenced by his admiration for the economic

---

[60] Ibid., 399.

[61] G.C. Bolton, *The Passing of the Irish Act of Union: A Study in Parliamentary Politics* (Oxford, 1966), 373; Humphreys, 'British Colonial Policy', 261.

[62] BL, Bowood MS, B72, f116, Notes of Lord Landsdowne's reply to Lord Fitzwilliam in the Debate on the Irish Union which may serve to correct the Papers.

[63] Quoted in W.B. Willcox, 'Lord Lansdowne, the French Revolution and the Irish Rebellion', *Journal of Modern History*, 17 (1945), 36, Shelburne to Coutts, 19 December 1798.

[64] Willcox, 'Lord Lansdowne, the French Revolution', 36n.

[65] *Life of Shelburne*, II, 422.

[66] Willcox, 'Lord Lansdowne, the French Revolution', 35, Shelburne to Coutts, 15 July 1798.

patriotism of his aunt, Lady Arbella Denny.[67] The social and economic structure of Ireland would absorb a measure of his interest throughout his life. In
comparison with other Anglo-Irish politicians, Shelburne was well-informed
on Irish affairs,[68] and he was alive to public opinion as well as high political
wrangling. He socialized with the great Dublin printer George Faulkner and
advised Caldwell to write a pro-government pamphlet on the augmentation
issue.[69] Shelburne's knowledge of the socio-economic state of the country
was first-rate, and the letters that he received on Irish matters were supplemented by a number of tours and visits. He visited Ireland and took his seat
in the House of Lords in 1764, recorded travel journals in 1770, 1772, and
1775, the latter for the benefit of his circle at Bowood, and even attended
the Irish Lords in 1769 whilst secretary of state. As a tourist he was no less
acerbic than the hated Richard Twiss, and, indeed, his 1775 tour took place
at exactly the same time as Twiss's *Tour in Ireland*. Like Twiss he found the
Irish rather tardy in joining the consumer boom: 'the Inns very bad, and
a great scarcity of Post Horses'.[70] Hospitality at Tralee was out of proportion with income.[71] County Cork was 'grossly backward'.[72] The people in
the mountains around Nedeen, County Kerry, were 'timid and lying as well
as crafty and lazy'.[73] Elsewhere he demonstrated a tendency for moralizing,
criticizing Lord John Cavendish's lottery scheme of 1783 as 'dangerous' and
'offensive' because it 'corrupted the manners of the people'.[74] He argued for
the suppression of ale-houses, reserving them for travellers; support for clubs
and friendly societies would better serve the locals.[75] He clearly had doubts
over the merits of cultivating an Irish tourist trade: 'I observe nobody gets
rich in water drinking places – whoever brings money brings that example
of idleness and dissipation, which shortly carries it away again.'[76]

But unlike Twiss, Shelburne was approaching Ireland with a generosity
of spirit – he praised the many examples of improvement he found,[77] – and

---

[67] See Chapter 2.

[68] A situation that was probably enhanced by his marriage to the younger-sister of the
Anglo-Irish peer, the 2nd Lord Upper-Ossory.

[69] JRL, MS B3/14, f128, Shelburne to Sir James Caldwell, [n.d]; JRL, MS B3/29, f36, Sir
James Caldwell to Lady Caldwell, 9 November 1772.

[70] BL, Bowood MS, B63A, f24, Irish Travel Journal, 30 August 1772.

[71] Ibid., MS B63A, f39, Irish Travel Journal, 27 September 1772.

[72] Ibid., f41, 2 October 1772.

[73] Ibid., f59,, 18 August 1775.

[74] Fitzmaurice, *Shelburne*, II, 265.

[75] Ibid., 305. He gave the Clothworkers Club in Calne a club room and donated twenty
pounds to their funds, but they had to remove themselves from the White Hart Inn, and
their yearly feast cancelled; *Life of Shelburne*, II, 306n.

[76] BL, Bowood MS, B63A, f37, Irish Travel Journal, 21 September 1772.

[77] Including the estates owned by Lord Clanbrasil, Lord Kenmare and Lord Hillsborough,
whose politics he disliked, BL, Bowood MS, B63A, ff19–20, Irish Travel Journal, 30
August 1772; ibid., f37, Irish Travel Journal, 21 September 1772.

he had a reformer's agenda. Inspired by the likes of Josiah Tucker, Shelburne drew up ambitious plans for economic and social reform in Ireland; producing several such documents between 1779 and 1793. Ireland's two religions offered two different targets, with different problems. He wanted an end to the Penal Laws, and, during the Union debates, favoured Catholic Emancipation, on the grounds that property qualifications would ensure continued Protestant rule.[78] On a personal level he was on good terms with certain Irish Catholics; he stayed with Lord Kenmare, a leading campaigner for Catholic relief, albeit from the conservative wing of Ireland's Catholic Committee.[79] But like many Irish improvers of this period, he retained his views on the retarding qualities of the Catholic religion. As he put it: 'I was bred up in abhorrence of Popery – and rejoice to see the day arrive which ought to convince the most bigotted of the fallacy of that idolatrous mode of worship.'[80] He also may have had doubts about the wisdom of Catholic relief, as in 1794 he commented on the way 'power is lavished on the bulk of the people'.[81] In 1798 he derided the prospect of an independent Ireland: 'The mass of the nation is incapable of it; you may as well give independence to the slaves on a Jamaica estate.'[82] In this light his campaign – with lengthy documents on the subject[83] – for the establishment of more Protestant schools becomes understandable.

For Shelburne, the Anglican Church was no better friend to Ireland. Resentment against tithes resulted in outbreaks of agricultural violence by the Whiteboys and cattle houghers, and they were active on Shelburne's Kerry estates.[84] As early as 1772 he was exhibiting fears that his property in Ireland was becoming 'precarious';[85] he had already asked Townshend for troops to be quartered in Kenmare to aid in law enforcement.[86] Shelburne had no doubt of the real causes 'of the general spirit of outrage, which is acknowledged on all hands to gain ground through the kingdom'.[87] While he was staying in Belfast in 1772 he seemed sympathetic to the Steelboys' complaints against the clergy and Lord Donegall.[88] He referred to 'the non-

[78] BL, Bowood MS, B72, f118, Notes of Lord Lansdowne's reply to Lord Fitzwilliam in the Debate on the Irish Union which may serve to correct the Papers.

[79] Ibid., B63A, f37, Irish Travel Journal, 21 September 1772.

[80] Ibid., B72, f80, Draft letter on the Irish Church, c. 1792–3.

[81] Willcox, 'Lord Lansdowne, the French Revolution', 30, Shelburne to Coutts, 14 January 1794.

[82] Ibid., Shelburne to Coutts, 1 August 1798.

[83] BL, Bowood MS, B72, ff34–6, Lord Shelburne's Memorandum on Education; ibid., ff38–68, Shelburne's notes on the Educational scheme for Ireland introduced by Thomas Orde to Rutland, 1787.

[84] Ibid., 74.

[85] Ibid., f7, Shelburne to the Ossory Club (draft), 10 March 1772.

[86] Lansdowne, *Glanerought*, 59.

[87] BL, Bowood MS, B72, f80, Draft letter on the Irish Church, c. 1792–3.

[88] Ibid., B63A, f18, Irish Travel Journal, 30 August 1772.

residence of most of the clergy, the numberless sinecures, and pluralities, their general manners',[89] and had personal experience of such abuses in the form of Mr Lake Godfrey, who took a very casual attitude towards residence at his living in Glanerought.[90] Shelburne fulminated that 'the lands, which I give to the poor for nothing, will be oblig'd to pay enormously to the Parson'.[91] His solution was the enforced residency of the Church of Ireland clergy.

On estates too, Shelburne was clear-sighted on the evils of absenteeism: 'that the absence of the rich proprietors retards civilization, the progress of manners, and many liberal improvements'.[92] Like many of his contemporaries he railed at mercenary land agents, having problems with his agent in Kenmare, and saw a type of public election as a possible solution, along with letting directly to under-tenants.[93] Shelburne, however, was not simply indulging in the usual propaganda peddled about Irish agriculture. He had concrete proposals, such as the shortening of leases to encourage improvement and for an Agricultural Society in every county (he personally designed its winners' medals in 1792).[94] Most impressively Shelburne took practical steps to improve his own lands and help tenants. He divided farms, built new farmhouses, made it a maxim that leases should not exceed twenty-one years, gave land rent free for periods dependent on improvement, and allowed bog and rock to be kept in common; a system remarked upon by Arthur Young when he visited Kerry.[95] He also planted trees and built roads.[96] Young praised Shelburne's appointment of an improving manager at his farm in Rathan, Queen's County, and when his lands near Stradbally were offered to let, the 'Improvements on the Lands' were trumpeted in the advertisement.[97] In the revolutionary 1790s Shelburne insisted that improvement was the way forward, and that other landlords had a duty to follow his lead.[98] However, such sentiment did not appear to interfere with his business decisions, and in the early 1800s he was at odds with his

[89] Ibid., B72, f96, Draft letter on the Irish Church, c. 1792–3.

[90] Ibid., B63A, f34, Irish Travel Journal, 13 September 1772.

[91] Ibid., f65, 25 August 1775.

[92] Lansdowne, *Glanerought*, 106–7.

[93] BL, Bowood MS, B63A, f59, Irish Travel Journal, 18 August 1775; ibid., f21, 30 August 1772.

[94] Ibid., B72, f24, Proposal and Notes on the Government of Ireland, c. 1779; ibid., ff34–6, Lord Shelburne's Memorandum on Education; ibid., Marquess of Lansdowne – ideas for striking 3 Gold Medals for his Agriculture Society in Ireland, 12 July 1792.

[95] Ibid., B63A, f56, Irish Travel Journal, 14 August 1775; ibid., f60, 25 August 1775.

[96] Lansdowne, *Glanerought*, 98–105.

[97] Arthur Young, *Tour in Ireland: With General Observations on the Present State of That Kingdom*, 2 vols (Dublin, 1780), i, 76–8; *Finn's Leinster Journal*, 9–13 January 1779.

[98] Lansdowne, *Glanerought*, 86; Wycombe to John Cross, 21 November 1801, BHA S. 113, f146.

son over the sale of Irish lands; Lord Wycombe was counselling the sale of their English property.[99]

Despite activity that can be seen as broadly patriotic Shelburne was never fêted in the manner enjoyed by other senior opposition leaders of the 1760s and 1770s, such as Pitt the Elder, Camden, Charles James Fox, or even Isaac Barré. He had friends and connections amongst the Irish elite, not only neighbours in rural Ireland, but also ties forged in urban Dublin (he had a house on St Stephen's Green). Those whom he suggested as suitable hosts for his son Lord Wycombe's tour in 1794 included Lord Kenmare, Lord Bective, Lord Belvedere, the Duke of Leinster, the La Touche family, Sir Laurence Parsons, Lord Shannon, and the Perry family.[100] Yet he also lamented, in 1794, that he had 'no political connection with Ireland'.[101] For their part the Irish seemed unwilling to avow a close relationship with the one-time Prime Minister. Ireland had its Pitt and Keppel Clubs, but no Shelburne equivalent. His staunch supporter Colonel Barré, was far more popular, and was given the freedom of the Corporation of Galway in October 1768 and the Dublin Joiners' Guild and Cork's corporation of Chandlers in July 1776.[102] The Free Citizens drank bumpers to Barré, along with Camden, Chatham, Burke, and Sir George Savile.[103] Admittedly, there were some minor honours. Shelburne was awarded honorary membership of the Cork Committee of Merchants in 1772,[104] and he was toasted at a dinner for Lord Camden in Belfast in 1776.[105] One London commentator noted that he was 'as much Esteemed by his constituents as he was in Ireland';[106] though matters on his estates were clearly not always smooth as John Fortescue MP represented members of the public in a minor legal battle with Shelburne in 1767.[107]

Indeed these few plaudits were offered before his unfortunate remarks on the Volunteers, which, when added to a general aura of untrustworthiness fostered by his British political career, meant that he became *persona non grata* in Ireland's patriotic literary public sphere. Newspapers circulated spiteful invective, and the phrase 'unruly' or 'enraged' mob made regular appearances.[108] According to the *Hibernian Journal* whilst dining with

99   Wycombe to John Cross, 21 November 1801, BHA, S. 113, f146.
100 BL, Bowood MS, B63A, ff75–77, Memorandum of a Tour of Ireland, 1794.
101 Willcox, 'Lord Lansdowne, the French Revolution', 32, Shelburne to Coutts, 5 November 1794.
102 *Faulkner's Dublin Journal*, 8–11 October 1768; *Hibernian Journal*, 24–6 July 1776; *Hibernian Chronicle*, 15–18 July 1776.
103 *Hibernian Journal*, 15–17 July 1776
104 BL, Bowood MS, B72, f13, John Thompson to Shelburne, 11 September 1772.
105 *Londonderry Journal*, 6 September 1776.
106 JRL, B3/10, vii, f57, Col. Philip Skene to Sir James Caldwell, 10 October 1774.
107 JRL, MS B3/16, f88, James Fortescue to Sir James Caldwell, 14 July 1763.
108 *Volunteers Journal*, 16 August 1784.

a Genevese gentleman in Dublin, Shelburne reacted to his Irish Brigade Volunteers uniform by remarking: 'Did I invite any foreign Officer to dine with me this Day?'[109] The same newspaper claimed that Thomas Orde owed his early career break to being employed by the necessitous Shelburne to liaise with London's money lenders.[110] Elsewhere, hearing of Shelburne's intended three-month visit in late 1784, the *Belfast News-Letter* referred to 'this island, which he has so often wished sunk in the sea, so his property was out of it'.[111] The *Volunteers Journal* termed a plan to foment idle distinctions between Irishmen to be 'in the true Shelburne style'.[112]

VI

Shelburne would not have thanked Richard Price, a member of the Bowood circle, for his encouragements to the Irish on the renunication issue: 'as you won all you have obtained by your military spirit, you must crown the good work under the auspices of the same bright handmade!'[113] The issue of Volunteering was a sore point, and must have blighted Shelburne's relationship with Ireland, at least until Volunteering became politically more divisive in 1784. But his testiness on this issue was symptomatic of his views on Ireland. He was more than happy to make a contribution towards its socio-economic progress, and this could be done at a local level, or through the relaxation of British trade barriers. Anything that threatened the security of the empire, and the tranquillity of Ireland, had to be opposed; and this applied to Grattanite patriots, the Volunteers and even rapacious agents and clergymen. His Chathamite views on issues like parliamentary reform, the freedom of the press, and the American War should have made him as popular as his mentor, Camden, or even Barré. But Shelburne betrayed the same characteristics in dealing with Ireland as he did with his one-time cabinet colleagues, many of whom revelled in sniping at this arriviste – at least in terms of Westminster politics – Irishman.[114] Too many sardonic remarks would characterize his ministerial days, just as they would undermine his reputation as a patriot. Yet Shelburne should be recognized not only for personal ambition, but also for a much broader improving vision; one that certainly went beyond many resident members of the Protestant

---

[109] *Hibernian Journal*, 30 January–2 February 1784.
[110] Ibid., 16–19 April 1784.
[111] *Belfast News-Letter*, 20–4 Aug 1784.
[112] *Volunteers Journal*, 10 May 1784.
[113] *Freeman's Journal*, 10–12 October 1782.
[114] *The Grenville Papers: being the correspondence of Richard Grenville, Earl Temple, K.G., and the Right Honourable George Grenville, their friends and contemporaries*, ed. W.J. Smith, 4 vols (1852–3; repr. New York, 1970), ii, 35.

Ascendancy. His enlightened – a term used by D.L. Mackay in relation to his solutions to the American problem[115] – reformist agenda within the framework of the British empire would, if enacted, have done much to calm unruly mobs.

[115] D.L. Mackay, 'Direction and Purpose in British Imperial Policy, 1783–1801', *Historical Journal*, 3 (1974), 498.

7

Lord Shelburne's Ministry, 1782–3:
'A Very Good List'

JOHN CANNON

I

Among the rather select band of Lord Shelburne's admirers, the young Benjamin Disraeli, author of *Coningsby* and *Sybil*, stands out for his enthusiasm, verging on hyperbole. Shelburne, he declared, was one of the suppressed characters of English history, his administration had been brief but not inglorious, and Shelburne himself had been 'the ablest and most accomplished minister of the eighteenth century'. It was, wrote Disraeli, a mystery that his ministry had failed, and a matter for sad speculation what great things it might have achieved. Shelburne's administrative ability had been conspicuous and his performance in Parliament second only to that of Edmund Burke.[1]

In this somewhat strained panegyric, there are grains of truth. Certainly the portents for Shelburne's ministry when formed in July 1782 after the unexpected death of Lord Rockingham were far from hopeless. Shelburne, though still only forty-five, had been an active member of the House of Lords since his early twenties and had twice held office, the second time as Secretary of State: he had however shown himself to be an uncomfortable colleague, prone to quarrelling, and given to threats of resignation. His parliamentary following, though small, was distinguished, and included Isaac Barré, John Dunning, and James Townsend, capable and experienced debaters. Shelburne was himself a good parliamentary speaker – certainly by comparison with his predecessor, Lord Rockingham, or his successor, the Duke of Portland, though with a tendency to instruct rather than delight, and a liking for vituperation. Though he deplored his defective education (which had included Christ Church, Oxford), he had improved it by wide reading and was one of the best-informed politicians of the day. Through

---

[1]   Benjamin Disraeli, *Sybil* (Harmondsworth, 1980), chap. iii.

the celebrated Bowood Circle, he was in regular communication with many of the most advanced thinkers in Britain, America, France, and Geneva.

Not least of his advantages in July 1782 was that he had the support of George III – not indeed on personal grounds, for in his youth the king had detested him – 'a worthless man' – but because they needed each other for protection against Charles Fox and the Rockinghams. The king and Shelburne had insisted from the beginning of the Rockingham ministry that Shelburne should have equal standing with Rockingham, that his recommendations must carry equal weight, and that the negotiation should be carried on through him. Shelburne had consolidated his position by close attention to the king's wishes, particularly on economical reform, which might otherwise have been a bone of contention. The issue of economical reform was, he assured the king in April 1782, 'who should contribute most to Your Majesty's dignity, comfort and splendour', to which George replied, artlessly, 'nothing could be more proper than Lord Shelburne's language'. On 19 April the king gave Shelburne the Garter as a gesture of support – a distinction that Horace Walpole thought 'unprecedented'.[2]

But with these advantages went undeniable reservations. Shelburne had acquired, rightly or wrongly, a reputation for insincerity and hypocrisy unsurpassed in a not unduly high-minded period. In his early days he was regarded as an unusually pushy and ambitious Irish outsider.[3] The reputation was not redeemed by an ingratiating and uneasy manner, even, or perhaps particularly, when he was trying to be agreeable. Henry Dundas, a forthright Scot, whom Shelburne approached in the summer of 1782 for support, remarked on 'the civility and courtship rather a little overdone on so slight an acquaintance'.[4] An open and honest manner is by no means a necessity in politics, but in a crisis it may be of value, as the careers of Sir Robert Walpole and Lord North might have suggested to Shelburne.

In addition, Lord Shelburne had long formed the opinion that party allegiance was a divisive factor and should be avoided – a view which he shared with his mentor, the earl of Chatham, and which suited the personalities of both men. But it led Shelburne to an unbalanced belief in the power and influence of the monarchy. It was to be a disadvantage that, though he had been elected to the House of Commons at twenty-four, he had never taken his seat there, being rapidly elevated to the Lords by the death of his father. He adopted towards the lower house a lofty and somewhat disdainful attitude, which was strangely outmoded and warped his

[2] Fortescue, vol. 5, nos 3665, 3666; *Walpole Correspondence*, 25, 273, H. Walpole correspondence to Mann, 5 May 1782.

[3] *Walpole Correspondence*, 9, 329. H. Walpole correspondence to Montagu, 11 December 1760; P. Toynbee and L. Whibley, ed., *The Correspondence of Thomas Gray*, 3 vols (Oxford, 1935), 2, 716, Thomas Gray to Mason, 10 December 1760.

[4] Henry to Robert Dundas, 18 April 1782, Dundas of Arniston MSS., National Archives of Scotland.

judgment. The think-tank with which he surrounded himself at Bowood, though it has impressed many historians, was no substitute for the cut-and-thrust of Commons life. Walpole had needed no think-tank at Houghton, nor Lord North a think-tank at Bushy Park.

There were two items on the agenda which the new first minister could not avoid in the summer of 1782. The first, which in opposition Shelburne had strongly urged, was economical reform. There were two evident dangers. The first was that though popular in the country at the end of a protracted and expensive war, it was bound to lose Shelburne friends among the victims, who might be of some consequence should the fate of the ministry become a close-run thing. The second was that it was extremely complex and might become to the minister a distraction from even more important matters. The other item was the pressing need to conclude peace on the best terms that could be obtained. Recent developments had given hope that it need not involve abject humiliation. After Yorktown, almost everyone accepted that the thirteen colonies were lost and there were many, like the king, who were willingly inclined to bid the Americans farewell as ungrateful and persistently malcontent subjects. Yet both Canada and the British hold on India had been preserved, and at the battle of the Saintes in April 1782 Rodney had won an unexpected naval victory, capturing the French commander, de Grasse. The Spanish onslaught on Gibraltar had been beaten off with heavy losses to the enemy. Britain's bargaining position was not hopeless.

II

As soon as Shelburne's appointment as first minister was confirmed, Charles Fox tendered his resignation, and was accompanied by Lord John Cavendish, Rockingham's Chancellor of the Exchequer, and a number of junior ministers. But the remaining members of the Cabinet, some of whom had close links with the Rockinghams, stayed with Shelburne. Initial reaction was that the resignations were far from mortal to the ministry and that Fox had been unwise. But a misunderstanding, largely of Shelburne's making, got his administration off to a bad start in the few weeks before Parliament was prorogued. The Rockingham cabinet had been split on the question whether independence for America was unconditional, or dependent upon a general settlement. The issue was less important than it seemed to be because it was more likely to be decided by the victorious Americans than by Downing Street, but it involved the views of the monarch. Shelburne had long since committed himself to the opinion that independence must be conditional, and this had been a factor in engaging George III's confidence. Even before Rockingham's death, Fox had declared that he must resign on the question, since he believed that an unconditional recognition of independence would enable Britain to deal more effectively with France and Spain, America's allies. In answer to the insinuation that his resignation was based upon pique rather than policy, Fox pointed out that he had previously brought the question before the cabinet. Shelburne's response in the Lords – if truly reported – was awkward and contorted: 'he had certainly said that "in his opinion" that was the cause, but he had not asserted it as a fact'.[5] It was a minor skirmish, but it helped Fox to recover lost ground, and it returned to trouble the first minister when Parliament reassembled in December after the recess.[6]

Shelburne's summer and autumn were extremely busy. To Grafton he complained about Economical Reform: 'it is impossible to describe to you how provokingly my time is taken up with the nonsense of Mr. Burke's bill. It was both framed and carried through without the least regard to "facts"'.[7] Shelburne made some progress towards cutting costs, but lavish new pensions to two of Shelburne's closest supporters – one of £4000 p.a. to Dunning (now Lord Ashburton) and another of £3200 to Barré – suggested that his zeal for Economical Reform had waned.[8] Parliamentary reform was another issue which could prove embarrassing. It might well lead to difficulties with the king, since it could hardly be separated from Catholic Emancipation, to which George was strongly opposed, and it would make negotiations with the Northites extremely awkward. But Shelburne was strongly committed to parliamentary reform, having endorsed Chatham's proposals during the years of opposition. Christopher Wyvill and the advocates of reform in the Association movement were greatly heartened when Shelburne took the Treasury. In the end, Shelburne side-stepped the problem with some aplomb. In August 1782 he wrote to Wyvill that he would 'act nobly' towards the Association. But when Wyvill began to pass this splendid news to his followers, Shelburne explained that the message was 'a contribution to him personally' and no guarantee of government intention. Once again Shelburne's sincerity was called into question and the cause of parliamentary reform was left for his new lieutenant, William Pitt, to pursue.[9]

During the rest of the recess, Shelburne's attention was focused on the complex peace negotiations, in which the plight of the loyalists caused considerable delay. Shelburne retained Richard Oswald as his representa-

5   *Parliamentary History*, 23 (1782–3), 200–1.
6   J.E. Norton, ed., *Letters of Edward Gibbon*, 3 vols (London, 1956), 2, 311, Gibbon to Lord Sheffield, 14 October 1782.
7   W.R. Anson, ed., *Autobiography and Political Correspondence of Augustus Henry, Third Duke of Grafton* (London, 1898), 338.
8   The matter was raised in the Commons as soon as Shelburne took office with some cutting remarks from T.W. Coke and Bamber Gascoyne. Frederick Montagu replied that the pensions had been approved by Rockingham. The issue was raised once more by Thomas Powys after Shelburne's retirement in the debate of 6 March 1783. *Parl. Hist.*, 23 (1782–3), 152–88, 584–602.
9   C. Wyvill, *Political Papers … to effect a reformation of the parliament of Great-Britain*, 4 vols (York, 1794–1802), 3, 333–62.

tive in Paris, despite the fact that Oswald had a fatuous trust in Benjamin Franklin's 'deep regard for old England', which Franklin repaid by disseminating fake atrocity propaganda to enflame American opinion. The issue of unconditional recognition reignited as soon as Parliament met. In the Commons, Pitt asserted that recognition was unconditional, while in the Lords Shelburne stated the reverse, and then took refuge in a pitiful refusal to answer questions.[10] Fox and his allies greatly enjoyed exploiting the government's disarray, but when he pressed the matter to a division, the Foxites received a sharp rebuff, losing by 46 votes to 219. Lord North, in a long and considered speech, led his troops to vote with the government on the grounds that Parliament should not intervene while diplomatic discussions were still continuing. Once again, the debating honours were equal, but the episode damaged Shelburne's position in three important ways. First, it created tension with Pitt, on whose inexperience the king blamed the disaster. Pitt refused to recant and did not forget.[11] Second, George III did not fail to notice that Shelburne's performance has been anything but 'neat', and wrote ominously to the first minister that these things would not happen 'if there were any energy or discipline in government'.[12] Third, and most important of all, Shelburne may have taken North's intervention as an assurance that he would support the government when the time came. Lord Carmarthen, for one, could not comprehend the first minister's confidence that the opposition to the peace would not number more than sixty. Shelburne appeared to be under the impression that Fox would command no more than a Rockingham rump.

III

While negotiations continued at Paris, in London there were private conversations and discreet dinner parties. Lord Shelburne was very dependent upon the support of his Cabinet colleagues, who gave credibility to his ministry, but he scarcely seemed to acknowledge that, one by one, they were abandoning him. At the very outset of his ministry he had confided to Lord Carmarthen, with whom he was on close terms, that he 'could not bear the idea of a "round-robin" administration, where the whole cabinet must be consulted for the disposal of the most trifling employments'.[13] From the beginning Cabinet meetings proved difficult and parliamentary perfor-

---

[10] *Parl. Hist.*, 23, (1782–3), pp. 265, 308–9.

[11] Fortescue, vol. 6, no. 4015, 8 December 1782; *Parl. Hist.*, xxiii, 283. 'The explanation he had given of the provisional agreement he had given on mature consideration, and he persisted in it.'

[12] Fortescue, vol. 6, no.4012, 6 December 1782; ibid., no. 4015, 8 December 1782.

[13] O. Browning, ed., *The Political Memoranda of Francis, Fifth Duke of Leeds*, Camden New Series, 35 (London, 1884), 70.

mances erratic. Keppel and Richmond in the Lords, and General Conway in the Commons, had all intervened to confirm Fox's interpretation of the resignation question.[14] The same members had expressed concern at the conduct of negotiations by Oswald, and particularly at any suggestion that Gibraltar might be exchanged for some West Indian island. Lord Temple, in Dublin as Lord Lieutenant, was very unhappy at the lack of communication with Shelburne in London, and began to contemplate resignation. Lord Grantham, brought in as foreign secretary to replace Fox, complained that he was the last to know what was happening.[15] Lord Carlisle, Lord Steward of the Household, was increasingly uneasy that more was not being done to assist the loyalists. By the time the peace treaty was laid before Parliament in January 1783, Keppel, Carlisle, and Grafton had all resigned, and Richmond, though retaining his post as Master of the Ordnance, ceased to attend the cabinet. Shelburne reinforced the garrison as best he could, bringing in the young Duke of Rutland to replace Carlisle, and Lord Howe to succeed Keppel at the Admiralty. He did not seem unduly perturbed: of the defections of Keppel and Richmond, he assured Grafton 'I shall see it with indifference ... yet I must bear it.'[16]

Born and bred in County Kerry and a large landowner in Ireland, Shelburne could be expected to take a great interest in Irish affairs. During the American War, the Irish could scarcely be prevented from arming to defend themselves, but as the power of the Volunteer movement increased, it became to some doubtful which side it was on. First it demanded commercial concessions, which Lord North conceded in December 1779. Next it insisted on Ireland's legislative independence from England, which the Rockingham administration acknowledged in June 1782. Shelburne, in 1779, had moved for an examination of Irish grievances, observing darkly that the American War 'had commenced on less provocation than this country had given Ireland', and on taking office as Home Secretary in 1782 he had declared, grandly, that 'the voice of a people ought to be attended to'.[17] In private, he was a good deal more circumspect. To Richard Fitzpatrick, Portland's Irish secretary and by chance Shelburne's own brother-in-law (though no admirer), he wrote, on 19 April 1782, that 'the only thing I fear of you is giving way too easily'.[18] Not surprisingly, Fitzpatrick thought that Shelburne spoke with forked tongue.

14 *Parl. Hist.*, 23 (1782–3), 201, 166.
15 V. Harlow, *The Founding of the Second British Empire, 1763–93*, 2 vols (London, 1952), 1, 336; Lord John Russell, ed., *Memorials and Correspondence of Charles James Fox*, 4 vols (London, 1853), 2, 9, Fitzpatrick to Ossory, 2 December 1782.
16 Anson, ed., *Grafton*, 350.
17 *Parl. Hist.*, 20, 666; 22, 1268.
18 Shelburne to Fitzpatrick, 19 April 1782, in Fitzmaurice, *Shelburne*, 1875–6, 3, 142. See also J.A. Cannon, *The Fox–North Coalition: Crisis of the Constitution* (Cambridge, 1969), 11–13, and 12, n2.

To the king, Shelburne confessed that he was perplexed at 'a subject through which I do not see some sort of way' – which was more candid than helpful. It was, however, he added, 'never off my mind'.[19] No sooner had legislative independence been granted than a fresh agitation in Ireland declared that there were reservations to the concessions.[20] By this time Shelburne was first minister and deep in the peace negotiations. Lord Temple, who had replaced Portland as Lord Lieutenant, became anxious and sent his secretary (younger brother and future Prime Minister) W.W. Grenville, to inform and consult in London. The consultations did not go well – indeed, they hardly began. First Shelburne explained that he could only give Grenville five minutes of his time and at length walked out while Grenville was still talking. Admittedly, brevity was not a Grenville weakness. For good measure, Shelburne brushed aside Temple's fears: 'he was "inclined to think", not that he thought, your government would go on more easily than you expected', reported Grenville.[21] With this gnomic assurance, Temple had to be content. Preparations for an Irish Judicature bill, which would remove the anomaly, were put in hand, to be placed on the statute book after the Coalition had taken office in 1783.

IV

To the king, a few days after taking office, Shelburne admitted his total ignorance of the House of Commons.[22] He did however take steps to strengthen his position there. The acquisition as Chancellor of the Exchequer of young Pitt, who had refused a minor post in the Rockingham administration, was of great importance. Thomas Townshend, the Secretary of State, was not a front-rank politician and it was understood that Pitt would take the lead.[23] During the remaining six months of 1782 Pitt greatly strengthened his position with a number of remarkable speeches: whether he had equally strengthened Shelburne's is another matter. Next, Shelburne had turned his attention to Henry Dundas, the Lord Advocate of Scotland, a more than useful debater, and fugleman of the Scottish members. Dundas's price was high – the office of Keeper of the Signet[s] for life – and though the king

---

19 Fortescue, vol. 6, no 3743, 14 May 1782.
20 For Temple's relations with Shelburne, see P. Jupp, *Lord Grenville, 1759–1834* (Oxford,1985), and for further discussion of the constitutional disagreements see the same author's 'Earl Temple's Vice-Royalty and the Renunciation Question, 1782–3', *Irish Historical Studies*, 17 (1971), 499–520.
21 Buckingham and Chandos, Richard Plantagenet Temple Nugent Brydges, Duke of, *Memoirs of the Court and Cabinets of George the Third* (London, 1853), 1, W.W. Grenville to Temple, 7 and 15 December 1782.
22 Fortescue, vol. 6, no. 3837, 9 July 1782.
23 Ibid., no. 3838, 9 July 1782.

had a rooted dislike of life appointments, by 11 July he had conceded and urged Shelburne to settle while he had the chance.[24] Shelburne's next move was to recruit two of North's most trusted lieutenants, Charles Jenkinson and John Robinson, who had nursed Lord North through many dark days during the dying months of his ministry. With the help of a direct approach from the king, Jenkinson was secured: 'the mask is now certainly cast off', wrote George, 'it is no less than a struggle whether I am to be dictated to by Mr Fox ... Lord Shelburne certainly must and shall have my fullest support'.[25]

Robinson was careful to obtain North's approval before agreeing in August 1782 to supply Shelburne with a detailed list of the House of Commons, together with some estimate of their probable allegiance. The king's acknowledgement to Robinson was enthusiastic.[26] The preamble to Robinson's list pointed out how fluid the situation was and how tentative his guesses: nevertheless, on the assumption that North would in the end lead his troops to Shelburne's rescue, he concluded that the government of the day would command an overwhelming majority.[27] This, perhaps hastily read, became the basis for Shelburne's extraordinary over-confidence. To Lord Carmarthen he confided in November that he had the support of nearly all the property of the country and that his opponents would scarcely muster sixty votes.[28] To Fitzpatrick a little later he remarked airily that he knew nothing of the House of Commons but that they showed him 'a very good list'.[29] One does not know whether the arrogance or the simplicity was the more remarkable. W.W. Grenville in December was frankly nonplussed when Shelburne assured him that victory was 'a moral certainty'. To his brother in Dublin, Grenville reported:[30]

> I never heard any man in the whole course of my life affirm any one thing more distinctly, positively and unequivocally than he did when he told me that the government was upon a sure foundation here.... Either Lord Shelburne is the most abandoned and direct liar upon the face of the earth, or he is deceived himself, too grossly to be imagined.

[24] Ibid., no. 3841, 11 February 1782. Dundas had been sole Keeper of the Signet since 1779 but wanted it for life.

[25] Ibid., no. 3847, 13 July 1782.

[26] Ibid., no. 3871, 7 August 1782.

[27] One copy of the list is in the Bowood MSS and another in the Melville MSS. The first part of the list is printed in W.T. Laprade, ed., *Parliamentary Papers of John Robinson, 1774–1784*, Camden Society, 3rd Series, 33 (London, 1922), 42–8.

[28] Browning, ed., *Leeds*, 76.

[29] Russell, ed., *Memorials of Charles James Fox*, 2, 10, Fitzpatrick to Lord Ossory, 2 December 1782.

[30] Buckingham, *Memoirs*, 1, 89, 15 December 1782, both quotes.

On the charge of lying, Shelburne must surely be acquitted: he was a skater who had no idea how thin was the ice.

The position when Parliament reassembled was, indeed, hard to predict since it depended to a great extent on the terms of the peace treaty. One estimate, as good as many others, was that Lord Shelburne and the court could expect 140 votes, North would retain some 120, and Fox's followers were about 90.[31] Clearly some understanding, if not a formal coalition, was necessary if a stable administration was to be formed. Nevertheless, there would remain some two hundred members of Parliament, country gentleman for the most part, whose views would be decisive. During the recess, Lord North had reserved his position, partly no doubt for tactical reasons, partly because he genuinely did not know what the country gentlemen, scattered to their estates, would think. A direct approach to North by the king received a cautious reply, which George found displeasing.[32]

In the closing months of 1782, Shelburne's timetable became very tight. The provisional peace with the Americans was signed on 20 November, but negotiations with France and Spain continued over the Christmas period and were not concluded until 20 January. As late as 28 December, Shelburne made a fresh concession, offering the island of Tobago to the French and, characteristically, not telling his Cabinet colleagues about it. At the same time he was still trying to get the question of recognition sorted out. The meeting of Parliament on 3 December had produced preliminary skirmishing but nothing decisive and the formal debate on the peace terms was fixed for 17 February. On 1 February, Pitt, who would have to carry the burden of debate, warned the first minister that time for political negotiations was running out. Once again, the ministry was at odds. Pitt had a rooted objection to discussions with Lord North, at whose hands he had suffered some sharp sarcasm in the preliminary debates.[33] Shelburne was equally opposed to approaching Fox and his friends. The first minister solved the dilemma in his usual way by not telling Pitt that an approach to North had already been made.[34]

One of the men engaged to sound out Lord North was John Robinson, the strength of whose commitment to assisting Shelburne seems not to have

---

[31] Norton, ed., *Letters of Gibbon*, 2, 31, Gibbon to Lord Sheffield, 14 October 1782. In *HMC, 15th Report, Appendix, Part VI, The Manuscripts of the Earl of Carlisle*, 1887, 633–4. George Selwyn suggested Shelburne 130, North 120, Fox 80.

[32] Fortescue, vol. 6, no. 3872, 7 August 1782; no. 3873, 10 August 1782. Lord North was still smarting from the king's refusal to pay off the outstanding election debt. For the king's reaction, see *HMC, 15th Report, Appendix, Part VI. The Manuscripts of the Marquess of Abergavenny*, 1887, pp. 54–5, Jenkinson to Robinson, 16 & 22 September 1782.

[33] Russell, ed., *Memorials of Charles James Fox*, 2, 30; Cannon, *The Fox–North Coalition*, 44, n5.

[34] W.W. Grenville to Temple, 6 February 1783, Buckingham, i, 143.

been realized by his former chief. It had been universally accepted before North resigned, Robinson argued, that the American colonies were irre-trievably lost:[35]

> Does your Lordship think that the objections to the articles of Peace
> are such as would justify you to say that we should go on with the war?
> … Are you sure of your following? May it not happen that Mr Fox may
> approve of those very articles of the Peace to which you would object?

But North and Dundas met only to quarrel and William Eden wrote to North that to offer approval of the articles would be dishonourable. A meeting of Pitt and Fox on 10 February was brief and decisive: 'I did not come here to betray Lord Shelburne', said the former, before stalking out.[36] Fox and North then reached an understanding to collaborate in the debate, and when Richard Rigby approached North once more on behalf of Shel-burne, he was told 'It is too late'.[37]

The long-awaited debate took place in both Houses simultaneously on 17 February. Even at this late stage the ministry suffered another embar-rassing mishap. When the articles were laid before Parliament on 27 January, Pitt had strongly opposed a proposal to publish them, only to be told that his colleagues in the Lords had already agreed to do so. It was of little conse-quence, but it caused a laugh at Pitt's expense and suggested an unfortunate lack of communication between the ministers.[38]

The debate in the Lords was a curious affair, with two former ministers – Richmond and Keppel – attacking the terms of the settlement. As expected, the abandonment of the loyalists was for many peers the sticking point. Grafton, despite his discontents, supported the ministry, assuring the Lords that the peace was 'as favourable as this country has any right to expect'. Keppel, his former colleague, disagreed: 'we ought to have had a better peace: our situation entitled us to it'. Richmond could not accept the terms but would not vote on the question. Lord Stormont, a previous Secretary of State in Lord North's government, launched a powerful attack upon the 'most blameable ignorance' of the British negotiators, singling out 'that very extraordinary geographer, Mr Richard Oswald'. The surrender of Tobago had been quite unnecessary. Why had the Channel not been referred to as 'the British seas', as it always had been? The question called up Lord Grantham to admit that the last had been 'a most unaccountable and unhappy mistake of his own'. Shelburne reserved himself for a late reply, clearly intended as a *tour de force*. He began on a note of self-congratulation: 'he had stepped

---

[35] HMC *Abergavenny MSS*, Robinson to North, 1 February 1783, 57; Buckingham, *Memoirs*, 1, 148–9. W.W. Grenville to Temple, 11 February 1783.

[36] Ibid., 148–9, W.W. Grenville to Temple, 11 February 1783.

[37] Russell, ed., *Memorials of Charles James Fox*, 2, 39.

[38] *Parl. Hist.*, 23, 359–61.

forward to the service of his country when even brave men shrank from the danger'. Though we had given up a considerable share of the trade of Canada, the House should remember that monopolies were 'always unwise'. 'It was not true that our allies, the Indian nations, had been abandoned to their enemies ... they were remitted to the care of neighbours'. As for the loyalists, his heart had bled, but 'if better terms could be had, think you that I would not have embraced them?' The treaties were approved by 72 votes to 59 – 'undoubtedly the smallest majority I ever remember in so full a House', minuted the king.[39]

The debate in the Commons was even longer and the vote was not taken until 7.30 next morning. The main interest was the speech of Lord North, who had agreed with Fox that it would be more appropriate if he moved a resolution deploring the treatment of the loyalists. North was at his best and was assisted by the unexpected intervention of a stray dog, which allowed him to demonstrate his relaxed and pleasant command of the chamber. Lord Mulgrave, a distinguished naval officer, called the treatment of the loyalists 'a national disgrace'. Fox defended his new alliance with North in lofty terms – perhaps too lofty: 'my friendships are perpetual, my enmities are not so'. Pitt was less charitable: the coalition was 'among the wonders of the age ... it stretched to a point of political apostasy which confounded the most veteran observers of the human heart'. But he marred the impression by an unnecessary sneer at Sheridan's background in the theatre, laying himself open to one of the classic rejoinders of all time:

> The propriety, the taste, the gentlemanly point of it must have been obvious to the House . . . Flattered and encouraged by the Rt. Hon. gentleman's panegyric on my talents, if ever I engage again in the compositions he alluded to, I may be tempted to attempt an improvement on one of Ben Jonson's best characters – the Angry Boy in the *Alchemist*.[40]

Townshend and Dundas were effective. The former thought that Lord North, of all people, had no right to criticize the terms of peace when all the unpleasant circumstances had arisen from his own maladministration. But the government went down to defeat by 205 votes to 224.[41]

There was some consolation for the ministers in the voting of the county members, regarded as a barometer of independent rectitude: thirty-eight voted with them, twenty-two against, with twenty absent or abstaining. The stage was set for an heroic rearguard action. In the spring of 1780 North had been in a minority of eighteen on Dunning's motion, carried much against his will, but had rallied to a majority of eighty-two by November. In 1784, William Pitt, successor to the coalition ministry, found himself in a

[39] Ibid., 373–435; Fortescue, vol. 6, no. 4122.
[40] *Parl.Hist.*, 23, 436–93.
[41] Ibid., 491.

minority of thirty-nine in January but a majority of 168 by May. Honours, particularly peerages, and a dissolution of Parliament could work wonders. Lord Temple later claimed that the king blamed Shelburne for abandoning a situation that was tenable.[42] But Shelburne, exhausted and bewildered, was in no shape for the fight. Lord Carmarthen, who dined with him two days after, found him 'totally devoid of spirit and inconsistent with the opinion I have entertained of his Lordship's activity of mind'.[43] Worse still, few of his supporters had any enthusiasm for continuing. Lord Camden, who undertook the thankless task of candid friend, explained to Shelburne that 'unfortunately it appears plainly that the personal dislike was too strong for him to attempt to stem'.[44] On 23 February, the Duke of Rutland had the experience, perhaps uniquely, of attending his first Cabinet only to find that the government he was joining was no more.

Few of the civil servants who worked under Lord Shelburne shared Disraeli's enthusiasm for his administrative ability. Sir Richard Sutton, under-secretary in the 1760s, thought that 'of all ministers [he] was the most difficult to please. He was never satisfied with what anyone did, or even with what he did himself.' William Knox, under-secretary in the 1770s, concurred: 'those who had served him in office abhorred him as a principal'. George Rose, secretary to the Treasury in Shelburne's government, left him determined 'never to be in a room with him again while in existence'.[45]

V

Where does responsibility for this catastrophe rest? The least plausible answer is that provided by Lord Shelburne himself, who concluded that he had been betrayed by the king. This is curiously reminiscent of the explanation put forward in 1770 by his model, Lord Chatham, for the failure of his ministry. There was no truth in Chatham's assertion that he had been undermined by secret influence and very little in Shelburne's thirteen years later. The widespread dislike of Shelburne was scarcely secret. The most that might be surmised is that, as events unfolded, the king began to realize some of Shelburne's limitations. Of course, the fact that some place holders were absent from the crucial debate, or even voted against the peace, helped to feed speculation that royal hints had been dropped. But the abandonment of the loyalists, coupled with anxiety over Shelburne's plans for Economical Reform, was quite enough to explain many of these votes. Suspicions may

[42] Buckingham, i, 303.
[43] Leeds, 82.
[44] Fitzmaurice, *Shelburne*, 1875–6, 2, 359.
[45] HMC, *Report on the Manuscripts in Various Collections*, VI, 1909, 284; L.V. Harcourt, ed., *The Diaries and Correspondence of the Rt. Hon. George Rose*, 2 vols (London, 1860), 1, 25–8.

well have been encouraged by a misleading statement of the division list issued by the *Morning Post* on 27 February. Under the heading 'Court, place-holders and serving officers', it named twenty-seven members who had voted with Lord North and against the peace. This was sensational, but untrue. Scarcely any of the members named were courtiers or place-holders, though a number of them had been until North resigned in March 1782. They had stayed with their old leader. There was nothing sinister about the list except the *Morning Post*'s headline.[46]

Two pieces of evidence often brought forward to support Shelburne's assertions are not very convincing. Thomas Orde, Shelburne's man-of-business, reported to him the opinion of John Hatsell, Clerk to the House of Commons, that 'the stability or downfall of your administration depends solely (as Your Lordship has always said) upon the Highest. It is his will.'[47] Shelburne is said to have been greatly 'struck' by this unremarkable opinion – though why he should have been if he had always thought so is not apparent. Nor is it clear why the information gathered by a House of Commons clerk, who had probably never conversed with the king, should be superior to that of the first minister of the crown, in daily contact. The second piece of evidence is even more melodramatic. Shelburne is reported to have said subsequently of the king:[48]

> He obtained your confidence, procured from you your opinion of different public characters, and then availed himself of this knowledge to sow dissension.

But this evidence was first published in John Nicholls, *Recollections and Reflections, personal and political*, a rag-bag of gossip and reminiscence, printed some forty years after the event. That Shelburne was bitter and felt deserted is not in doubt. George, too, felt deserted, as he had done when Grafton resigned in 1770 and North in 1782. But in support of Shelburne in 1782 the king had written to North, Jenkinson, and Robinson in the most forthright terms, and he had seen North a number of times to beg his assistance in person. Nor was George, by nature, much of a dissembler. It was not easy in a court to conceal royal opinions. The king had been brought to the verge of madness and abdication by the loss of the American colonies and was singularly unlikely to be able to keep his views to himself. Nor was there any need to build dissension into Shelburne's ministry: it was there in abundance from the very beginning. Shelburne was the king's refuge against the hated Fox: why should George blow up his own redoubt?

One other aspect of the vote raised eyebrows. The forty-five Scottish members could usually be relied upon to support the government of the day.

---

[46] The *Morning Post* list is reprinted as an appendix in J. Norris, *Shelburne and Reform* (London, 1963).
[47] Fitzmaurice, *Shelburne*, 1875–6, 2, 361. Thomas Orde to Shelburne, 21 February 1783.
[48] Ibid., 3, 441.

On this occasion, those present divided eighteen to eighteen. This is not surprising. Shelburne's dislike of the Scots was well known. He had fought a duel in 1780 with William Fullarton, a Scottish Member of Parliament. Shelburne's biographer and great-grandson, Lord Fitzmaurice, felt obliged to apologize for the vehemence of Shelburne's contempt for the Scots.[49] They owed him few favours.

The role of William Pitt, Chancellor of the Exchequer and heir-apparent, is not easy to trace. He does not seem to have been close to the first minister and there is little correspondence. There is no reason to suggest double-dealing, but Pitt was ambitious and able. His remark that he would never accept a subordinate post was considered by many unbecoming in a man of twenty-two. His period in office had not been without embarrassments, such as the rough handling in debate by jocose Lord North, and the repeated misunderstandings about American recognition, which the king and Shelburne were agreed in putting down to his youthful inexperience.[50] His total refusal to consider working with North, followed by his abrupt termination of the meeting with Fox, posed the question who would take the lead were Shelburne to retire. In the debate of 24 February, Pitt made the most handsome – even fulsome – tribute to his stricken chief: posterity would do justice to his many virtues. But Pitt added:[51]

> Notwithstanding a sincere predilection for this nobleman, I am far from wishing him retained in power against the public approbation.... If his removal can be innocently effected, I am persuaded he will retire, firm in the dignity of his own mind.

It was less a vote of confidence than a political obituary. Even after he had accepted the first ministership in December 1783, Pitt's relations with Shelburne remained tense. There was no question of bringing him back into government: 'it would be like bringing back Lord Bute', remarked Townshend.[52] When Pitt wrote in 1784 to offer a marquessate, Shelburne momentarily wondered if he was to be invited to return. Barré was instructed to start negotiations and sound out the ground. But Barré, old and ill, was more in touch than Shelburne and did not go. When Orde reproached Pitt for not consulting Shelburne, Pitt confessed that he had been remiss, but he had found the situation so awkward that he had burned all his drafts.[53]

In the last analysis, Shelburne's failure was all his own. He had no concept of man management, either in theory or in practice. He remained in many

---

[49] Ibid., 441: 'a sad set of innate cold-hearted impudent rogues'.
[50] Russell, ii, 30; Fortescue, vol. 6, 175, George III to Shelburne, 8 December 1782.
[51] *Parl. Hist.*, 23, 550–2.
[52] Fitzmaurice, *Shelburne*, 1875–6, 3, 412. Townshend was promoted to the peerage as Baron Sydney in March 1783 and to viscount in 1789.
[53] Ibid., 402.

ways a strange visitor to the Westminster Parliament. He was at his best at Bowood, patron and host, his rule unchallenged and unchallengeable. He believed, like Chatham, that it was better to sail alone, without crew. But Chatham was a national hero: Shelburne was not. It is significant that the most perceptive criticisms came, not from his political opponents, but from his allies. In the summer of 1782 he succeeded in alienating both Lord Camden, whom he had inherited from Chatham, and the Duke of Grafton, perhaps his closest confidant. Grafton, conscious of his dignity as a former Prime Minister, complained to Camden that all he got from Shelburne was 'a great civility' and the 'appearance of communication'. Camden, in return, urged Grafton to soldier on, but conceded that Shelburne had been distant 'as if when his administration was settled, he had no further occasion for those, to whom he was endebted for the credit of his administration'.[54] Lord Temple, back from Ireland, summed it up simply to Lord Carmarthen:[55]

> He joined with me in amazement at Lord Shelburne's imprudent conduct with regard both to making and preserving friends: he said his head seemed to have been turned by his high situation, that he did not sufficiently communicate his ideas to his brother ministers, but assumed a dictatorial tone too frequently.

Shelburne was not the luckiest of men. A government transport ship was named *The Lord Shelburne*. It was a leaky vessel and in 1787 sank in a gale off the Azores with fifteen feet of water in the hold.[56]

[54] Anson, ed., *Grafton*, 333; Grafton to Camden, 28 July 1782; Camden to Grafton, 1 August 1782.
[55] Ibid., 333, Grafton to Camden, 28 July 1782; Camden to Grafton, 1 August 1782.
[56] HMC, *Reports on the Manuscripts of Reginald Rawdon Hastings Esq.*, III, ed. F. Bickley (1934), 201–5.

8

Shelburne, the European Powers, and the Peace of 1783

ANDREW STOCKLEY

Writing to Charles Jenkinson on 13 November 1782, Lord Shelburne noted that:

> Parliament and the Peace make Government a perfect Pandora's box.... It is impossible for me to say whether I can conduct our Barque without losing some masts and endangering others.... But I will do my best.[1]

For making peace was complicated. At the start of 1782 Britain was still caught up in attempting to suppress the revolt of her American colonies. She was also at war with France, Spain, and the Netherlands. The War of American Independence involved armed conflict in the Channel, the Mediterranean, and the Atlantic, in Africa, India, America, and the Caribbean. The peace of 1783 had to deal with lands and territory in all four quarters of the world.

Until almost the end of the war, the British government had been unwilling to contemplate American independence. A series of military reverses and defeat at the battle of Yorktown spurred the House of Commons into renouncing offensive warfare in America in February 1782. Lord North, the minister who had presided over one of Britain's least successful wars, resigned before he was censured. The War of American Independence was not so much won by America as abandoned by Britain. The challenge for North's successors was to find an acceptable peace.

George III was forced to admit the opposition to power and the Marquess of Rockingham became first minister at the beginning of April 1782. The Rockingham ministry was, from its inception, an uneasy alliance of what had previously been the two major opposition groupings. Charles James Fox

---

[1] BL, Add. MSS 38192, fol. 105; quoted at p. 1 in Andrew Stockley, *Britain and France at the Birth of America: The European Powers and the Peace Negotiations* (Exeter, 2001), which this chapter draws upon. Jenkinson had been Lord North's Secretary at War and supported Shelburne's ministry in the House of Commons.

became foreign secretary and the Earl of Shelburne took responsibility for home and colonial affairs. Fox sent Thomas Grenville to negotiate peace terms with France and Shelburne sent Richard Oswald to negotiate with America's representatives in Paris. Both sets of negotiations made little headway. Fox and Shelburne disagreed over the conditions for recognizing American independence. Neither trusted France. Fox resumed the search for a continental alliance and offered concessions to America and the Netherlands with a view to separating them from France and lowering the latter's peace terms. Britain and France each suspected the other of seeking delay, on the one hand to detach French allies, on the other while awaiting the results of military operations in the East Indies and off Gibraltar.

Everything changed with the death of Rockingham in July 1782, followed as this was by Shelburne's elevation to the treasury and Fox's consequent resignation from government. The peace of 1783 was, in all essential respects, framed during the Shelburne ministry. Shelburne was himself heavily involved in the negotiations, assisted by his foreign and home secretaries, Lord Grantham and Thomas Townshend. Alleyne Fitzherbert replaced Grenville in Paris and Henry Strachey was sent to bolster Oswald in negotiations with the American envoys. Preliminary peace treaties were signed with America on 30 November 1782, and with France and Spain on 20 January 1783. Britain and France also agreed terms for an Anglo-Dutch settlement at this time.

Richard Morris, in his book *The Peacemakers*,[2] portrays the negotiations as having resulted in a one-sided victory for the American envoys. Morris assumes that American independence was the most important issue on the table and, as such, decidedly neglects the European negotiations in favour of the American settlement.

The American peace preliminaries were novel in that they recognized the birth of America as a free and independent nation, but they were, at the same time, highly traditional in the way in which they were framed in accordance with national self-interest and with consideration to the European balance of power. France had pursued American independence as a means of striking at British power and prestige. Shelburne offered substantial concessions in order to detach America from the Bourbon alliance.

American independence had become inevitable and it was now imperative that Britain separate America from France as soon as possible. Independence was bad enough, constituting a heavy blow to Britain's reputation and prestige, but were America to move permanently into France's orbit, Britain's traditional enemy would be strengthened unacceptably, both politically and in terms of trade. Benjamin Vaughan, friendly with both Shelburne and Benjamin Franklin, one of the American envoys, was later to

---

[2] Richard Morris, *The Peacemakers: The Great Powers and American Independence*, reprint edn of 1965 edn (Boston, MA, 1983).

note: 'It was a race at the moment; whether we should have America, or France should have her.' Britain's objective must be 'to break asunder the combination of our enemies' and, in particular, to 'take a growing power at some expence out of the hands of an enemy'.[3]

Shortly after becoming first minister in July 1782, Shelburne told the Lords that while he considered American independence 'a dreadful blow to the greatness of this country ... now the fatal necessity of seeing it fall upon us appeared in full view', he was forced to give way. Writing to Oswald in Paris, he noted that although he had hoped for reunion between Britain and her colonies, since America would settle for nothing less than independence, 'if it is given up, ... it shall be done *decidedly*, so as to avoid all future Risque of Enmity, and lay the Foundation of a new Connection better adapted to the present Temper and Instincts of both Countries ...'[4]

The United States obtained extensive boundaries allowing considerable room for expansion, her fishermen retained fishing rights in British America, and Shelburne accepted minimal guarantees for the loyalists (the Americans who had continued to support Britain during the war). Shelburne hoped that a generous settlement would avoid any resentment or ill-feeling which might otherwise jeopardize Britain and America continuing trading on much the same basis as before the war. America would remain an expanding market for British manufactures and re-exports, and would continue to be an important source of raw materials. British rather than French trade would benefit.

If European considerations were important in determining the terms of the American settlement, they were critical for the Anglo-French negotiations. For contemporaries, these were of much greater significance. Britain and France were two of the great powers of Europe and therefore of the world. They were traditional enemies, at war with each other during the course of the long eighteenth century as often as they were at peace. As the War of American Independence wound down in 1782, there was widespread feeling in Britain that the American colonies may well have to be relinquished, but that revenge should then be exacted against France.

Historians who have examined the European negotiations in detail have often tended to portray them in terms of a struggle for advantage: a diplomatic battle between Shelburne on the one hand, and the French foreign minister, the comte de Vergennes on the other, each seeking to outwit his opponent, and to gain as much as possible with respect to the lands, territories, and commerce which were available. The argument has often been in terms of who succeeded – who came out best from this particular struggle. Henri Doniol plumps for Vergennes, arguing that he humbled Britain by

---

[3] Vaughan, Memorandum, February 1783, Shelburne Papers, Clements Library, University of Michigan, CL (S) 87/2, fols 212 and 210.
[4] Shelburne to Oswald, 27 July 1782, in Fitzmaurice, *Shelburne*, 1875–6, III, 246.

compelling American independence and recovering France's standing in Europe.[5] Vincent Harlow takes the side of Shelburne, measuring diplomatic success in terms of imperial possessions. Shelburne did best because he had an eye to the future: he pursued trade rather than dominion, and sought a new empire in the east to replace the colonies lost in the west. Britain under Shelburne turned from an empire based around America to one centred upon Asia and India.[6]

An imperial yardstick is no more appropriate for evaluating the peace negotiations than an American one. Both represent an attempt to read subsequent developments back into the negotiations: to say, this is what later happened, therefore the negotiators must have intended it. Following the negotiations step by step, dispatch by dispatch, private letter by private letter, reveals quite a different pattern, not so much one of a struggle for advantage, but of a willingness to compromise, not so much one of a battle over imperial and worldwide holdings, but of a desire for future co-operation in Europe.

The start of negotiations was not auspicious. Throughout the Rockingham administration Vergennes had been pursuing a policy of delay. Spain was expecting military success from her siege of Gibraltar and wanted to postpone negotiations until after this occurred; Vergennes was hoping for equally good news from a taskforce sent to India. French defeat at the battle of the Saints (in the West Indies) in April 1782 meant that Vergennes needed to recapture the initiative. No country could afford to appear militarily vulnerable at a time of impending peace negotiations. Shelburne's accession to power had, if anything, only reinforced Vergennes's policy of 'wait and see'. Vergennes was highly suspicious of Shelburne's intentions; he was the lieutenant of Chatham and was remembered as a francophobe from his militant attitude towards France's acquisition of Corsica in 1768.[7]

On 17 August Vergennes wrote: 'je doute bien fort que le Lord Shelburne désiroit sincèrement la paix' ['I very much doubt that Lord Shelburne sincerely desires peace']. On 18 August, but one day later, he praised Shelburne for displaying 'cet ardent amour pour la paix' ['a fervent desire for peace'].[8] Vergennes's turnaround can be traced to Admiral de Grasse, who at this point reported a conversation with Shelburne in which the latter

[5]   Henri Doniol, *Histoire de la participation de la France á l'établissement des États-Unis de l'Amérique*, 5 vols and supp. (Paris, 1886–92), V, iv and V Supp., 388.
[6]   Vincent Harlow, *The Founding of the Second British Empire 1763–1793*, 2 vols (London, 1952–64), I, 406.
[7]   See H.M. Scott, *British Foreign Policy in the Age of the American Revolution* (Oxford, 1990), 115–22, on Shelburne's hostility to France when Southern Secretary in 1768.
[8]   Vergennes to Montmorin, 17 and 18 August 1782, Correspondence Politique (Espagne), Archives du Ministère des Affaires Etrangères, Paris, CP (E) 608, fols 203 and 210. Quotations from Vergennes and Rayneval have been translated into English.

offered generous concessions to the European belligerents across all areas. Vergennes noted: 'tout cela me paroit si singulier ... que si l'opinion de l'honnêteté et de la verité de M. le Cte de grasse étoit moins bien établie, je serois assez tenté de regarder ce projet comme un roman fait à plaisir' ['all this seems so remarkable, that if the honesty and truthfulness of the Comte de Grasse was less well established, I would be tempted to consider this proposal a fantasy'].[9] Shelburne, by offering what appeared to be almost unbelievably generous terms, brought an end to the foot shuffling and delay which had characterized the negotiations to date. Vergennes sent his under-secretary, Gérard de Rayneval, to England to investigate. Rayneval first met with Shelburne in early September. By the end of October, most of the Anglo-French peace terms had been agreed, and negotiations were concluded extremely quickly by eighteenth-century standards.

The change in pace and in attitude was dramatic and can be attributed to three major causes. The first of these is that by August 1782, both Shelburne and Vergennes, for different reasons, desired a quick end to the war; the second is the relationship of trust and confidence which was established between the two men; and the third relates to their personalities and belief systems, namely Shelburne's idealism and Vergennes's concern to redress but not overturn the balance of power. All three factors helped transform what at first sight might have seemed a struggle for advantage into a very real willingness to compromise over a range of areas.

Time and again Shelburne emphasized his belief that he must obtain peace before Parliament returns. At the very least he must reach a point of ultimatum so that, if France refuses all reasonable terms and peace is not possible, he will have clear grounds for urging Parliament to continue the war. Shelburne had been appointed by the favour of the king and, with Fox's resignation from the ministry, lacked a natural majority in the House of Commons. He had been somewhat fortunate that Rockingham died only a few days before the summer recess. George III prorogued Parliament on 11 July, thereby granting a reprieve of several months until Shelburne would be forced to meet the Lords and Commons.

Shelburne was determined to use the intervening period to his advantage. Once Parliament resumed, he would lose a considerable amount of flexibility. Any proposed or rumoured concessions would be attacked (as indeed occurred over Gibraltar in December 1782), and he would face a barrage of speakers pleading for various special interests. As he noted to Fitzherbert: 'it is Our Determination that it shall be either War or Peace, before we meet the Parliament, for I need not tell you that we shall be then to meet so many opinions and passions supported by party and different

---

[9] Vergennes to Montmorin, 18 August 1782, ibid., fol. 210.

mercantile interests, that no negotiation can advance with credit to those employ'd or any reasonable prospect for the Publick'.[10]

Lacking a firm basis of support in the Commons, Shelburne was particularly vulnerable to attack and criticism. If he failed to make peace and proved unable to present a *fait accompli* when Parliament returned, opposition factions would make much of his lack of a decided line. He would, on the one hand, be attacked on the basis of rumoured concessions and a supposed willingness to sacrifice British interests and, on the other, for showing no real disposition towards peace but in fact wanting to revive the war. Shelburne believed that, for his ministry to survive, he needed to wrap up negotiations before Parliament returned at the end of the year.

Parliament was originally prorogued until 3 September. This was extended until 10 October then until 26 November. Parliament was then again prorogued until 5 December. William Eden, in opposition to Shelburne, commented 'that the Ministers are moving Heaven and Earth … [in seeking] a Pacification before the meeting of Parl[iamen]t'.[11] Having been able to announce that Anglo-American preliminaries had been signed, Shelburne survived the few sitting days remaining for 1782, then took advantage of the Christmas recess to try to rush the European negotiations to a final conclusion. Fitzherbert was instructed to write immediately peace had been signed, being told 'it is very material indeed, that if humanly possible, this important news may arrive here before the 21st [January]',[12] when Parliament was to resume sitting.

Shelburne's concern to obtain a quick settlement was reinforced by his belief that the country was exhausted in military and financial terms. There was a discernible feeling of war weariness. There had been a substantial increase in Britain's debt, taxes were relatively high, and the war had caused an appreciable amount of economic hardship. In early 1783 there were riots in Newcastle on account of the high price of corn, disturbances in Liverpool, and mutinies among the fleet and several regiments.[13]

Shelburne's concern for a quick settlement meant that he needed to overcome Vergennes's suspicion of him if he was to have any chance of invigorating the European negotiations. Shelburne took the initiative and gave de Grasse a false impression of the concessions he would make. De Grasse's account of his meeting with Shelburne differs markedly from Shelburne's report to George III. It seems somewhat unlikely that de Grasse should have completely misunderstood Shelburne, fabricated a series of peace proposals,

---

[10] Shelburne to Fitzherbert, 21 October 1782, in Fitzmaurice, *Shelburne*, 1875–6, III, 286.

[11] Eden to Loughborough, 5 October 1782, British Library, Add. MSS 34419, fol. 56.

[12] Grantham to Fitzherbert, 14 January 1783, PRO, FO 27/5, fol. 189.

[13] See e.g. Townshend to George III, 28 January 1783, 13 and 15 March 1783; Conway to George III, 1 February, 1 March and 25 March 1783, in Fortescue, VI, 226, 275, 278, 227, 255, 312.

and relayed these to Vergennes – all with the happy consequence that the latter was then moved to send an emissary to England. The much more probable explanation is that Shelburne was unwilling to inform the king of what he had done – that he had deceived de Grasse and offered substantial concessions in order to lure Vergennes into serious negotiations. Shelburne disowned de Grasse's report once Rayneval arrived in England, but by then the bait had been taken and he had to hand a means of direct communication with Vergennes as desired.

The generous terms offered may have been enough to cause Vergennes to send Rayneval to England – but by August Vergennes was also predisposed to desire peace sooner rather than later. Vergennes appreciated the danger of a separate peace and the need to increase the pace of the European negotiations. The military situation had worsened. Spain was unlikely to take Gibraltar, there was no news from India, and Vergennes was increasingly worried by the condition of the French and Spanish navies. A ballooning national debt meant that France had exhausted her credit, whereas Britain boasted a much more modern financial system and was better able to finance the war. Vergennes was also concerned by a rebellion in the Crimea, fearing this would be used by Russia and Austria as a pretext to attack Turkey. One of the keys to Vergennes's thinking was his unwavering belief in the concept of the balance of power. This meant preserving the territorial status quo in Europe and preventing any of the great powers expanding at the expense of the smaller states. Vergennes believed that an attack on the Ottoman empire would endanger the European equilibrium but needed to be free of war to exert any influence.

At a series of conferences in London and at Bowood, Rayneval came to believe that Shelburne was sincere in desiring peace. He was impressed by Shelburne's charm, his apparent candour and confidence, and the seeming moderation of the terms he proposed. Shelburne led, as he had done in August, and proposed that Britain and France should seek not just peace but reconciliation and future co-operation.

On 18 September he told Rayneval:[14]

je désire non seulement de contribuer au rétablissement de la paix entre nos deux Souverains, mais aussi à les amener à une cordialité qui fera leur bonheur réciproque. Non seulement ils ne sont pas des ennemis naturels, ainsi qu'on l'a pensé jusqu'à présent; mais ils ont des intérêts communs qui doivent les raprocher. Autrefois on n'osoit pas tirer un coup de canon dans l'Europe sans le consentement de la France et de l'Angleterre. Et aujourd'hui les Puissances du Nord veulent être quelque-chose par Elles-mêmes: ... réunissons-nous, soyons bien

---

[14] Rayneval memorandum on his September 1782 conferences in England, 13 September 1782, Correspondence Politique (Angleterre), Archives du Ministère des Affaires Etrangères, Paris, CP (A) 538, fols 179–80.

d'accord, et nous ferons la loi au reste de l'Europe.... Si nous sommes d'accord nous reprendrons notre ancienne place et nous arrêterons toutes les révolutions en Europe ...

[I not only wish to contribute to the re-establishment of peace between our two sovereigns, but also to bring about a cordiality which will be to their reciprocal advantage. Not only are they not natural enemies, as people have thought until now, but they have common interests which should draw them closer. Once no one dared fire a canon in Europe without the consent of France and England. Today the northern powers wish to make something of themselves. If we join together and are truly in agreement, we can lay down the law to the rest of Europe. If we are in agreement, we can resume our former place and stop all revolutions in Europe.]

Rayneval's reports to Vergennes were glowing. Referring to Shelburne as '*ce ministre du caractère et des principes*' ['this minister of character and principles'],[15] Rayneval was persuaded that Shelburne genuinely sought peace. He informed Shelburne that he agreed with his comments on political and economic co-operation, that he believed Versailles also desired '*un rapprochement sincère et permanent*' ['a sincere and permanent rapprochement'], and that their two countries could become '*les arbitres de la tranquilité de l'Europe*' ['the arbiters of peace in Europe'].[16]

Rayneval was to prove the vital link between Shelburne and Vergennes. Conducting the most important negotiations in England during September and December 1782 ran contrary to normal British practice but suited both Shelburne (giving him direct control over British diplomacy) and Vergennes (who trusted Rayneval implicitly). Rayneval was convinced that Shelburne's proposals would not only prove acceptable to but would be positively welcomed by Vergennes. He presumed correctly. Vergennes responded warmly, both to the apparent moderation of the peace terms offered and to the prospect of Anglo-French co-operation which he envisaged might deter aggression in the Crimea.

From the time of Rayneval's visit, the European negotiations were conducted and concluded with extraordinary dispatch. The contrast with the delay and the foot-shuffling which had marked the beginning of negotiations is truly remarkable. Shelburne might, at first, have been tailoring his message to his audience, speaking, as was his wont, vaguely and in terms of generalizations, talking of co-operation in order to draw France in and to get serious negotiations underway and resolved before Parliament met. But when Vergennes picked up his ideas and ran with them, Shelburne soon came to believe in his own oratory. The idea of co-operation soon took on a synergy of its own. The two parties agreed to bypass Austria and Russia, who had been granted official roles as mediators. Vergennes argued for a durable

---

[15] Rayneval to Vergennes, 18 September 1782, ibid., fol. 203.
[16] Rayneval memorandum, fol. 182.

settlement, and both parties agreed that the base of the negotiation would be to separate, as much as possible, British and French interests in different parts of the world so as to avoid dissension and quarrels.

This is not to imply that all was plain sailing. There were obvious limits upon the extent to which mutual trust and confidence could engender co-operation and the compromise of claims. Shelburne was restricted by what the king, Cabinet, and Parliament were likely to allow him to concede. British attachment to Gibraltar and India was particularly strong. Military success, in the form of the battle of the Saints and the relief of Gibraltar, coupled with the conclusion of American preliminaries, only served to increase domestic opposition and to inhibit him from offering too many concessions to France. Vergennes, like Shelburne, faced a significant war party. Castries, the Minister of Marine, believed France was entitled to substantial gains, particularly in India. When Britain amended and raised her terms in late November 1782, Vergennes, exasperated, noted that French and Spanish ministers were no less bound to consider and act upon public opinion.[17]

But despite domestic opposition and military constraints, Shelburne and Vergennes reached a relatively rapid peace settlement. Mutual trust and confidence was of critical importance. This did not mean that either was indifferent to his country's interests; nothing could be further from the truth. Both continued to look to their national interests. But trust and confidence meant each sought to advance those interests within a framework of co-operation and compromise. The Anglo-French peace terms are remarkable not for who won what where, but for the manner in which they were concluded. They represent a willingness to compromise rival claims, a desire to separate the two parties, and a determination to provide the basis for future co-operation.

British losses were comparatively minor. There was no great alteration to the balance of power as had occurred in 1713 or 1763. With only a few small adjustments, Shelburne maintained Britain's pre-war position in India and the West Indies. France gained a district around Pondichery and Karikal with an annual revenue of around £30,000. Britain ceded Tobago. Shelburne obtained Negapatam from the Dutch, together with a British right to free navigation in the Dutch East Indies. The British East India Company commented favourably on the peace in view of the precarious position of British forces in the region.[18]

British concessions elsewhere were not that significant. France obtained the least used portion of the Newfoundland fishery. Articles dealing with Dunkirk and fortifications in India and Newfoundland touched matters of

---

[17] Vergennes to Rayneval, 25 November 1782, CP (A) 539, fol. 39.
[18] *The Parliamentary History of England from the Earliest Period to the Year 1803*, 36 vols (London, 1806–20), 23, cols 474–7 (17 February 1783).

honour not substance. In Africa Britain ceded the Senegal River and its dependencies but was guaranteed the Gambia River and Fort James and a share in the lucrative gum trade. Such concessions were to be expected given Britain's failure at war. By striking out for co-operation, Shelburne lost little. He gained a faster peace and persuaded France to pressure her allies into settling more quickly and more reasonably.

Vergennes could also be satisfied. French territorial gains in India were modest but French arms had had little success and Vergennes was unlikely to win substantial concessions as British victories at the battle of the Saints and in the relief of Gibraltar began to shift the military momentum in her favour. Vergennes nevertheless ensured that Britain disgorged the vital port of Trincomali in the East Indies, he obtained the restitution of Senegal and the island of Gorée, and secured the removal of previous restrictions on Dunkirk, fortifying St Pierre and Miquelon, and building a ditch around Chandernagore, which although largely symbolic, had been seen as humiliating for France. The exclusivity of the French fishing zone off Newfoundland was made considerably more explicit (a point of major concern to Vergennes in view of disputes that had arisen since 1763).

Considered against France's war aims, Vergennes obtained much of what he sought. The 1763 settlement ending the Seven Years War was not overturned, but this was never Vergennes's objective nor was it achievable in the military circumstances of 1782. Vergennes's primary war aim was the winning of American independence and the weakening of British power and prestige which would ensue. An independent United States, dependent upon and grateful for French military assistance, could only benefit France's international standing and her commercial success. While some direct gains for France were necessary, Vergennes's aim was to redress the balance, not to overturn it in the other direction, nor to sow the seeds of a future war by being too greedy.

When Spain and the Netherlands proved difficult allies, holding out for unreasonable terms, Vergennes played an important part in pressing them to make concessions in order to advance the peace. While Spain failed to gain Gibraltar, she made advantageous acquisitions elsewhere. Britain ceded Minorca and the two Floridas and agreed to restrict the area available for British subjects to cut logwood in Spanish Central America. France ended up having to restore Dominica to Britain in return for Tobago in order to ensure the Spanish settlement. The Dutch recovered virtually all their colonies despite a disastrous war effort and proving thoroughly obstreperous. At the end of the war all of the Dutch major overseas holdings were in the hands of either Britain or France and the Netherlands did well to retain Trincomali.

If Vergennes made some concessions, he did so appreciating what could realistically be expected and what was impossible to obtain without prolonging the war by at least another campaign. Working with Shelburne, he ensured an early exit from what had become a militarily and financially draining war, and increased his freedom of action for dealing with the impending crisis in the east. Rayneval's belief that Shelburne genuinely desired peace and was to be preferred to any alternative first minister led him to defend Shelburne's conduct and to urge Vergennes to reach accommodation on each occasion that a serious difficulty arose.

Vergennes was convinced. When urging Spain to reduce her terms, he continually emphasizes the need to make peace with Shelburne. He believed, he wrote, 'que le ministère Anglois désire sincèrement la paix, et ... qu'elle soit prompte.... Si nous voulons la paix, il faut que la base en soit posée avant ... la rentrée du parlement d'Ang[leterre]. Si nous manquons cette époque, le ministère anglois ne sera plus le maître de ses résolutions, et Dieu sait quand la négociation pourra être renouée' ['that the English ministry sincerely desires peace, and that it be made promptly. If we want peace, the basis must be laid before the English Parliament returns. If we do not meet this deadline, the English ministry will no longer determine what is resolved, and God knows when the negotiation can be renewed'].[19] Whereas other leaders might well continue the war with vigour, Shelburne held out the prospect of future co-operation. For Vergennes, Shelburne and peace had become intertwined.

Even after Shelburne lost office, Vergennes continued to hope that he and Grantham might retain influence. Vergennes repeatedly testified to Shelburne's candour, frankness, and sincerity, and expressed delight at the prospect of Pitt becoming first minister. The latter had worked closely with Shelburne and 'il y a lieu de croire qu'il conservera au moins une influence secrète sur les délibérations du Cabinet' ['there is reason to believe he will have at least a secret influence on Cabinet deliberations'].[20]

The peace of 1783 is not to be measured by the nineteenth- or twentieth-century yardsticks of American or imperial interests. For Britain and France these were subordinate to the European balance of power. The West Indies, Africa, and India were all tokens in a European game. Their value was what they could add to the prestige and power of one of the European combatants. Different exchanges and equivalents were debated, bartered, and altered down to the very last moment. In return for Dominica, France could either take more land in India or she could have Tobago. For Shelburne it was not important whether it was territory in the east or in the west: either offer meant that France would gain and Britain would lose to the same amount. What was important was the relative and comparative strength of the two powers and the consequence this would have upon the European balance. What was truly striking about the peace of 1783 was not

---

[19] Vergennes to Montmorin, 27 October 1782, Correspondence Politique (Espagne), Archives du Ministère des Affaires Etrangères, Paris, CP (E) 609, fol. 144.
[20] Vergennes to Moustier, 2 April 1783, CP (A) 541, fol. 319.

the counters which were exchanged nor the terms which were agreed, but the atmosphere in which these were settled.

Britain was highly fortunate that in 1782 Vergennes's concern for the balance of power led him to moderation in the terms he demanded, and caused him to accept Shelburne's offers of goodwill, hoping that this might result in co-operation against the eastern powers and that continued rapprochement might ultimately inhibit Anglo-French conflict.

France was equally fortunate in the personality and beliefs of the Earl of Shelburne. It is not necessary to assume that Shelburne meant everything he said about Anglo-French rapprochement. While he must be credited with sufficient idealism for breaking through the barriers of traditional prejudice against France, Shelburne's convictions were never entirely consistent. He began by trying to win over the French without necessarily believing all he said about co-operation and amity but, paradoxically, ended as a convert to the echo of his own words.

As mentioned, Shelburne gave de Grasse a false impression of the concessions he would make. When Rayneval arrived in England and he was forced to depreciate the French admiral's recollections, Shelburne attempted to cover himself by emphasizing the sincerity of his desire for peace and by claiming to favour Anglo-French reconciliation and future co-operation. Shelburne often had a tendency to say what he believed his listeners would like to hear – one of the reasons he was widely distrusted by other British politicians. Finding that Rayneval warmed to his talk of rapprochement and keeping the eastern powers in check, Shelburne, desperate to provide some momentum to the peace negotiations, played up this message for all it was worth. It was only over the course of the next few months, as his trust and confidence in Rayneval and Vergennes developed, as they demonstrated a willingness to make concessions and to buttress him against an ever-widening circle of domestic enemies, that Shelburne himself came to fully believe in what he was saying. 'Rapprochement' and 'co-operation' became ideals and slogans, to be repeated in much the same way as 'free trade' throughout his later years.[21] Shelburne was flattered by the attention he received from Rayneval and Vergennes. During the course of 1782–3 he underwent a sea change in his attitudes. Previously seen as a fierce opponent of France in the mould of Chatham, he was for the remainder of his life to be labelled a francophile. Shelburne supported the Anglo-French commercial treaty of 1786 and was branded a radical for his pro-French attitude during the French revolutionary wars. Shelburne's last speech to the House of Lords on 23 May 1803 urged a policy of reconciliation towards France.

---

[21] Shelburne advocated greater freedom of commerce between Britain and France, suggesting that political and economic cooperation would complement each other. See e.g. Rayneval memorandum, fol. 180.

Shelburne has been described as an 'intellectual magpie';[22] he would pick up and run with new ideas but often failed to understand their full ramifications. Shelburne was certainly sincere when he informed Vergennes in May 1783 that he rejected 'l'Idée injuste d'une inimitié naturelle entre les deux Nations' ['the unjust idea of a natural enmity between our two nations'] and wished to substitute 'la certitude d'une amitié solide' ['the certainty of a solid friendship'],[23] but as with his beliefs on free trade, he lacked any developed or coherent plan for giving effect to such feelings. His idealism was considerable and the sweep of his vision quite remarkable. But as an advocate of free trade, parliamentary reform, and reconciliation with France, he was seriously out of step with his time. The originality of Shelburne's ideas and his willingness to depart from tradition only contributed to the suspicion in which he was held.

Shelburne was in many ways visionary but he was, at the same time, vague as to details and imprecise in his thinking. France benefited from the fact that, carried away by his own idealism, Shelburne was willing to make concessions – even if Vergennes's confidence was somewhat misplaced when he believed that Shelburne's expressions of goodwill might be translated into a future *démarche* against the eastern powers. With Shelburne, what you got was never quite what you saw.

Hopes for Anglo-French reconciliation were to prove ephemeral. The British Parliament, while pledging to uphold the peace settlement, censured the terms which had been agreed. Shelburne lost office in February 1783 and Charles Fox, returning as foreign secretary, immediately reversed his policies and reverted to the much more traditional anti-Bourbon standpoint. Vergennes continued to suggest joint action over the Crimea, but Fox's only response was to reveal Vergennes's overtures to Russia and to pursue the mirage of a Russo-Prussian continental alliance. Yet it was Fox not Shelburne who was the more representative of British political opinion. Shelburne's ideas of Anglo-French rapprochement were radical to the point of being almost unworkable. Hostility towards France was axiomatic in the late eighteenth century and had, certainly since the 1740s, provided the mainstay to British foreign policy. France's proximity and larger population, together with her commercial and colonial power, made her Britain's most dangerous rival.

Public prejudices were as intense as those of the politicians. War weariness was an important moderating factor towards the end of 1782, but even those who advocated a comprehensive peace were likely to resist any terms which could be portrayed as unwarranted concessions to the Bourbons. An anonymous correspondent recommended to Shelburne 'to push Vigorously

---

[22] Scott, *British Foreign Policy*, 324.
[23] Shelburne to Vergennes, 19 May 1783, CP (A) 542, fol. 265.

against France, in order while the Sword is drawn, effectually to Chastize that perfidious, that offending Nation, the Natural and everlasting Enemies of England. Every attempt to Distress them is Just, and I wou'd Strip them of all their foreign Possessions and destroy their Navy never to sail again. They richly deserve this treatment.'[24]

Writing two years later, one British ambassador declared: 'If we ever cease to suspect France of being our enemy, if ever we suffer it (when it is in our power to prevent it), to increase its riches, its influence and strength, and if we ever omit an opportunity for sinking, distressing, and keeping it under, we shall be guilty of the highest political folly, and the minister who advises such measures will deserve something more than dismission.'[25] Hostility to France was so entrenched, engrained, and widespread that any prospect of Anglo-French rapprochement must, in retrospect, appear to have been somewhat dubious.

Admittedly, Shelburne was able to persuade those he worked most closely with towards his way of thinking. George III and Grantham both came to share, at least in part, his view of the benefits of rapprochement with France. The king had given Shelburne his full political confidence and, while at first extremely wary of the French, he came to believe in their sincerity. In January he told Rayneval 'que la france et l'Ang[leterre] étaient faites pour être amies; que leur union convenoit parfaitement à leurs intérêts ...; qu'elle préviendra la guerre non seulement entre les deux puissances mais aussi entre les autres souverains de l'Europe ...' ['that France and England were made to be friends; that their union perfectly suited their interests; that it would prevent not only war between the two powers, but also between the other sovereigns of Europe']. 'Nous avons eu ... un premier partage de la Pologne, il n'en faut pas un second' ['we have had ... the first partition of Poland; there need not be a second'].[26]

Unremitting in his hostility to the Fox–North coalition, George III continued privately to favour some measure of co-operation with France throughout 1783. The king maintained a frosty silence as Fox laboured without effect to gain improvements in the definitive treaties and thereby validate his opposition to the preliminaries. He noted only: 'as I did not object to the Preliminary Articles I have no reason to complain of such advantages as might be gained in the Definitive Treaty not being equal to the Sanguine hopes of some persons'.[27] For the king's own belief was that 'all would certainly have been finished not only more speedily, but with more

---

[24] Anon. to Shelburne, undated, CL (S) 72, Vaughan Memorandum, fol. 213.
[25] Harris, 17 January 1786, quoted in Jeremy Black, 'The Papers of British Diplomats, 1689–1793', *Archives*, XX:88 (1992), 225–53, at 243.
[26] Rayneval to Vergennes, 24 and 28 January 1783, in Doniol, *Histoire de la participation*, V, 279 and 285.
[27] George III to Fox, 7 May 1783, in Fortescue, VI, 377.

credit and dignity, if Lord S[helburne] and his friends had been allowed to complete what they had so happily begun'.[28]

Like the king, the foreign secretary, Lord Grantham had not been informed of the full content of Shelburne's overtures to de Grasse but was brought on board relatively quickly in September. During November, December, and January, Grantham held lengthy conferences with Rayneval and was responsible for much of the precise detail of the negotiations. Grantham and Shelburne exchanged a lengthy correspondence and were often in conference. Shelburne's confidence in his foreign secretary was considerable. Shelburne's opinion may have guided and been decisive in the negotiations but he did not act alone.[29]

Rayneval and Vergennes came to rely upon Grantham's sincerity and goodwill towards France – Shelburne was not the only hinge upon which they sought to establish an Anglo-French relationship. Rayneval repeatedly testifies to Grantham's goodwill and 'tout ce qu'il a fait pour acheminer la paix au risque de son existence ministérielle' ['all that he did to facilitate the peace at the risk of his ministerial career'].[30]

Shelburne succeeded in bringing Grantham and the king on side. But aware of anti-French feeling, instinctively secretive and non-collegial, Shelburne failed to confide in most of his Cabinet and kept them away from the detail of the negotiations. He assisted this by conducting some of the most important negotiations in secret with Rayneval (contrary to British practice in previous peace negotiations). Shelburne's Cabinet met frequently and discussed the various peace terms at length. But wary of the fact that its members did not share the generosity of his vision towards America or France, Shelburne provided them with little understanding of his motivations or the reasoning behind the various concessions being offered, hoping to stave off protest and dissent. By February 1783 many of his Cabinet colleagues openly distrusted him and were highly critical of the concessions he had granted.

Shelburne had significant personal charm which he used to effect with both the king and Rayneval. A generous patron and a systematic correspondent, he developed a circle of intellectuals, radicals, and reformers among whom he was both liked and respected. He had some abilities as a politician, building up support across a range of MPs. He was, however, widely distrusted by his contemporaries. One noted that 'His adversaries

---

[28] Orde to Shelburne, 28 August 1783, Lansdowne Manuscripts, Bod. Lib., Bod. 27, fol. 29.
[29] Grantham's importance has been underestimated. See Stockley, *Britain and France at the Birth*, 147–50.
[30] Rayneval to Vergennes, 9 January 1783, CP (A) 540, fol. 123.

accused him of systematic duplicity and insincerity.'[31] He certainly had a tendency to adapt his message to his audience, telling the king that Parliament was to be blamed for any peace, telling the Lords that he had been forced to conclude preliminaries due to the poor state of Britain's navy and finances, while all the time claiming to favour Anglo-French co-operation when talking to Rayneval. Shelburne's personality appeared quite contradictory. On the one hand, he was somewhat unfairly condemned by Fox and his associates as a creature of the king. On the other hand, he attracted the opprobrium of North's followers for his radical friends and his advocacy of parliamentary and fiscal reform. To many, Shelburne appeared something of an opportunist – the opposition leader who had declared that American independence would represent the setting of the British sun but was now prepared to preside at what seemed to be an extraordinarily generous peace settlement.

Shelburne was not helped by a tendency towards unnatural and exaggerated mannerisms, particularly when ill at ease. His descendant and biographer, Lord Fitzmaurice, notes 'an overstrained affectation of extreme courtesy, and a habit of using unnecessary compliments in conversation'.[32] One MP described Shelburne as 'a palaverer beyond description. He palavers everybody and has no sincerity.'[33] Many of Shelburne's more successful relationships were with social inferiors. Suspicious of others and seeming insincere, he was unable to inspire confidence among his social equals and found it difficult to work with the political leaders of the Whig aristocracy.

Shelburne inspired trust – and distrust. His peace was praised – and excoriated. The novelty of his foreign policy meant that he failed to confide fully in his Cabinet colleagues and ultimately hid his true beliefs from Parliament. But his reputation also ran before him; even although only partly justified, many of his peers in both Cabinet and Parliament were ready to believe the worst of him. His home secretary, Townshend, was correct to lament 'the effect and absolute influence of Prejudice'.[34] Shelburne was, at least outwardly, more stoical, telling his wife: 'It's a moment of great anxiety and a very deep game. However I am in no way Flurry'd and I think possess myself, as much as if I was playing cribbage with you. I will do what I think right, and will take my chance for approbation or support.'[35]

When explaining the peace terms to the House of Lords, Shelburne focused upon financial and military problems, arguing that these had forced

---

[31] Sir Nathaniel Wraxall, *Historical Memoirs of My Own Time (1772–1784)*, 2 vols (London, 1815), II, 60.

[32] Fitzmaurice, *Shelburne*, 1875–6, II, 168.

[33] David Hartley, quoted in George H. Guttridge, *David Hartley MP: An Advocate of Conciliation 1774–1783* (Berkeley, CA, 1926), 298.

[34] Orde to Shelburne, 28 December 1783, in Fitzmaurice, *Shelburne*, 1875–6, III, 411–12, reporting a conversation with Townshend.

[35] Shelburne to Lady Shelburne, [1782], Bod. 4, fol. 50.

him to make concessions. Shelburne was a skilled debater and used his speech to try to rebut the major criticisms of the peace which had been levelled. He began by using a free trade justification, arguing that concessions to the Americans would promote rivalry and greater trade. Doubtless catching the mood of the house, he quickly changed tack and reverted to the more forceful argument that British military and financial exhaustion had required peace and that he had obtained the best terms that were possible.[36] Shelburne's own awareness that Anglo-French rapprochement was unlikely to sell well, that open talk of economic or political co-operation would have to be deferred for some time into the future, was of itself an implicit admission that, even had his policy not been immediately overturned by Fox, it was hardly likely to succeed on its own merits.

Shelburne was able to present a relatively comprehensive peace to Parliament soon after it returned. But he had committed a serious error of judgment in believing that a peace settlement might help sustain his ministry. What he said in the Lords was by and large irrelevant. The peace was censured in the Commons on what were essentially party political grounds. Had he failed to make peace, he would doubtless have been censured for prolonging the war.

No settlement was likely to be overwhelmingly popular in the wake of a failed war. The peace of 1783 was one which arose out of defeat, a condition which Britain was unaccustomed to, and which made it somewhat improbable that Shelburne would gain much credit, whatever the terms he negotiated. The Duke of Grafton had warned Shelburne when both were still in opposition in 1781: 'Peace must be bought, I grant, but Such is the Temper of the Times, that ... the Nation ... will now send the Odium of the Terms of the Peace against those who make it, instead of those who had brought on the different Wars, [and] had conducted [them] ... in so shameful a manner.'[37]

Vergennes's handling of the peace negotiations was also challenged but, possessed of strong support from the French king, he was able to weather criticism of the peace terms and survive in office. The peace of 1783 enabled Vergennes to turn his attention to the east but, lacking any prospect of support from Fox, France had to accept Russia's annexation of the Crimea. Free of war, France was however able to warn Austria against intervening and forced Russia to trim her objectives. For the remainder of his ministry Vergennes continued to pursue Anglo-French rapprochement, able to regard continental alignments in a much more flexible and mechanistic manner than could any British minister. Diplomatic *renversements* were not uncommon. Vergennes's miscalculation lay in failing to appreciate

---

[36] *Parliamentary History*, 23, cols 407, 411, 417–19 in particular.
[37] Grafton to Shelburne, 14 November 1781, CL (S) 72, Vaughan Memorandum, fols 7–8.

the power of political prejudice in England. The British would not quickly forgive France her role in the war or in the achievement of American independence.

When negotiating the European definitive treaties, Fox attempted to re-open a number of the key articles agreed at the time of the preliminaries, seeking to make gains which might justify his criticism of Shelburne. The result was a stymied negotiation. Britain and France, mutually distrustful, were each unwilling to make concessions that might allow the other to claim she had won an advantage. The contrast with the preliminary negotiations could not have been greater. Fox ended up agreeing to definitive treaties virtually identical to the terms Shelburne had concluded.

Shelburne had sketched a peace which was founded upon compromise and co-operation. But the moment was fleeting, and the distrust and stalemate which marred the definitive negotiations proved more indicative of the course of Anglo-French relations for some time to come.

Part Three

The Bowood Circle Revisited

9

'Opening the Door to Truth and Liberty': Bowood's French Connection

Robin Eagles

When Lord Shelburne[1] underwent his 'conversion' to France, he did so with unfettered enthusiasm. As Derek Jarrett suggested, Englishmen encountering Paris and Parisians in the eighteenth century tended either to be excited or irritated by their experience. After his character-reforming visit of 1771, 'Shelburne was one of the excited ones; and the importance of his excitement lay in the fact that most of those upon whom the traditional patriot movement had been built were among the irritated ones.'[2] Throughout the eighteenth century Paris and London vied with each other to be acknowledged the first cities of Europe, much as France and Britain competed for supremacy, whether on the field of battle or in the realms of artistic patronage and the development of imperial trading monopolies. Fear and suspicion of the continent was seen by many Englishmen, then, as something to be cultivated as a way of improving their patriotic credentials.[3] In an oration preached to the lord mayor of London in 1713 on the death of Henry Compton, the notorious warrior-bishop of London, Thomas Gooch (later himself raised to the episcopate, first as bishop of Bristol) asserted that Compton's own foreign travels had served to underpin his sense of national identity: 'He observ'd and examin'd the Civil and Ecclesiastical Polities

Acknowledgements: I am grateful to Kathleen Doig, Dorothy Medlin, and Arlene Shy for allowing me access to the text of 'Enlightened Exchange: The Correspondence of Andre Morellet and Lord Shelburne', in advance of publication, since published in *British–French Exchanges in the Eighteenth Century*, ed. Kathleen Doig and Dorothy Medlin (Newcastle upon Tyne, 2007).

[1]   In 1784 Shelburne was advanced in the peerage to Marquess of Lansdowne. For the sake of simplicity I have referred to him throughout this piece as Earl of Shelburne.
[2]   Derek Jarrett, *The Begetters of Revolution: England's Involvement with France, 1759–1789* (London, 1973), 128.
[3]   Linda Colley, *Britons: Forging the Nation 1707–1837* (New Haven, CT, 1992); Gerald Newman, *The Rise of English Nationalism: A Cultural History 1740–1830* (London, 1987); Stuart Semmel, *Napoleon and the British* (New Haven, CT, 2004).

abroad; he made them his Study but not his rule. The more he stayed in France and Italy the more English-Man he was.'[4] In similar vein, Hester Thrale concluded the journal of her two-month sojourn in France in the autumn of 1775 with the telling summary: 'I have at last brought my Niggey [one of her younger daughters] safe home again to England – which I shall now love on more rational Grounds than ever I did yet – I see now that it is better than France.'[5]

Lord Shelburne's response to his continental travels could not have been more different from those of the bishop and the Bluestocking. As such he formed part of a controversial tradition within English politics and, given the elements that unite them, it is ironic that he regarded another great Augustan figure, Henry St John, Viscount Bolingbroke, secretary of state in the final years of Queen Anne's reign, someone with whom he had so much in common, with such unqualified dislike. To Shelburne, Bolingbroke was 'both a political and personal coward'.[6] Publication of Bolingbroke's letters served only to cement Shelburne's dismissive opinion of his predecessor, as they showed (according to him) 'how little real knowledge he had under that imposing style, and what Alderman Beckford used to call that diarrhoea of words'.[7] To say the very least, Shelburne would certainly not have taken kindly to being compared with Bolingbroke. And yet, it seems difficult to avoid the comparison. Both men's careers failed to live up to their early promise. Both were difficult to get on with. Both were notorious for their affection for France.[8]

And in this last sense, as a true cosmopolitan the Augustan towered over the Georgian. Bolingbroke's command of the French language was legendary. Indeed according to James MacPherson, the 'discoverer' of Ossian, it was only his mastery of French that explained Bolingbroke's survival in office at a time when Oxford and many others were seeking to be rid of him.[9] His fluency impressed Voltaire, who was used to dealing with Englishmen who at best struggled with the international language of diplomacy. 'I have found in this illustrious Englishman', he declared, 'all the learning of his country and all the politeness of ours. I have never heard our language spoken with more

---

[4]   Cited in Edward Carpenter, *The Protestant Bishop: Being the Life of Henry Compton, 1632–1713 Bishop of London* (London, 1956), 11.

[5]   *The French Journals of Mrs Thrale and Doctor Johnson*, ed. Moses Tyson and Henry Guppy (Manchester, 1932), 165.

[6]   Fitzmaurice, *Shelburne*, I, 22.

[7]   Fitzmaurice, *Shelburne*, I, 25.

[8]   Shortly after the death of Queen Anne, Bolingbroke fled to France, where he lived for the following eight years before negotiating a return to England, but he remained closely in contact with a number of eminent Frenchmen of his day and was well-known for his fluency as a French speaker.

[9]   James MacPherson, *Original Papers; containing the secret history of Great Britain, from the restoration to the accession of the House of Hanover*, 2 vols (London, 1775), ii, 530.

energy and correctness.'[10] Having flirted too openly with the Jacobite court in exile in the dying days of the reign of Queen Anne, Bolingbroke was forced to seek sanctuary in France at the time of the Hanoverian succession, where he served briefly as a minister in the Pretender's court. Following his return from exile, accompanied by his former mistress by then second wife, the widowed Marie-Claire de Marcilly, marquise de Villette, Bolingbroke continued to remain in close contact with certain French acquaintances and when he died several of the few bequests he was able to make from his depleted funds were made to Frenchmen.[11]

By comparison, Shelburne was something of a francophile minnow in the great cosmopolitan pond. He came to France relatively late in life, and although he peppered his autobiography with the occasional choice *bon mot* he was not at all adept at its language. His correspondence with his continental acquaintance was generally conducted in English[12] and he was at times hampered by his naturally curious mind, which alighted on many things but it might be said mastered few of them. It was an aspect of his character captured early on, though in a different context, by Charles Price, when reporting his resignation from government in September 1763. Shelburne, Price related, 'resigned last Friday; like a monkey in a china shop; he was captivated at first with the brilliancy of the scene, and after having thrown down all the pots vases etc in his way has now leap'd out of the window'.[13] Although on this occasion it was not long before Shelburne was called back to government (1766–8), after his own short-lived administration in 1783, and once it was clear that the Younger Pitt had no place for him in his cabinet, he retreated into relative obscurity to pursue his private enthusiasms. At his death, the few sparse reports that filtered their way into the newspapers made no obvious mention of France in the life of the former great minister of state. The *Hull Packet* noted that, 'He had filled a large space in society as a statesman, an orator, an accomplished gentleman, a most excellent landlord, a liberal patron on the arts, and a most amiable man in private life',[14] while the *Caledonian Mercury* acknowledged his 'share in the dangers and honours of the seven years war' and that as a minister he was 'neither idle nor undistinguished', but said nothing of Bowood, of Shelburne (later Lansdowne) House or the circle that Shelburne gathered around him there.[15]

Similarly, if one were to rely on Shelburne's will for an estimation of the nature of his acquaintance, his likes and dislikes, one might be forgiven for

[10] Quoted in Sheila Biddle, *Bolingbroke and Harley* (London, 1975), 81–2.
[11] TNA, PROB 11/793, fol. 255.
[12] This is certainly true of his correspondence with André Morellet.
[13] University of Nottingham Library, Portland mss, Pw F 7908, Charles Price to 3rd Duke of Portland, 6 September 1763.
[14] *The Hull Packet*, 14 May 1805.
[15] *Caledonian Mercury*, 11 May 1805.

concluding that France meant nothing to him at all. There is no mention of the place or any of its people in the document and as for his desires about his funeral, he specified only that he wished 'to be buried wherever I may happen to drop without any kind of pomp'.[16] In this fashion, the will mirrors neatly Shelburne's earliest years. Nothing in his upbringing suggested that he would one day be reckoned among the most enthusiastic of the British francophile elite. Born in Ireland into an Anglo-Irish family based in Buckinghamshire and Kerry, Shelburne's early education was over-seen by his tyrannical grandfather[17] and later in life he regretted openly that he had not paid greater attention to his (Huguenot) French tutor. To the young Shelburne this unfortunate tutor, Pélissier, was but 'a narrow-minded clergyman ... with no great parts and no great learning' and the one indication that there may have been more to him than Shelburne then appreciated was his possession of 'a dash of that pertness of character which commonly belongs to the French'.[18] His first experience of the country itself was the less than auspicious one of that of a young soldier participating in the assault on Rochefort.[19] Indeed, for the first thirty years of his life, there is nothing in Shelburne's experience that points to him as a francophile, or as someone remotely interested in affairs beyond the Channel. Yet, within twenty years his loyalties and enthusiasms had been transformed by contact with the philosophes and in Bowood they found a centre for enlightenment thought second only to the great salons of Paris. How this *volte-face* came about and just how extensive, lasting and significant was Bowood's 'French connection' is the subject of this chapter.

Although Shelburne's will makes no specific mention of France or things French, a cursory look through its provisions does hint at the extent of the man's cultural interests. To his eldest son and heir, Lord Wycombe, he left (among other things) his pictures, statues, books, manuscripts, maps, prints, drawings, and plate. To his second surviving son, Lord Henry Petty, he left the contents of his private library at Lansdowne House as well as the Bowood library of Henry's mother, Shelburne's second wife, Lady Louisa Fitzpatrick.[20] It is, moreover, to some extent, unfair to make too much of the fact that Shelburne was slow to acquire experience of France. Having outgrown his private tutor, Shelburne completed his education at Westmin-ster and Christ Church, Oxford (where he again found himself under the restraining influence of a 'narrow-minded tutor').[21] Shelburne's recollections of his time at Oxford were almost universally negative, but at Christ Church

---

16 TNA, PROB 11/1428, fols 323–8.
17 John Cannon, 'William Fitzmaurice Petty, 2nd Earl of Shelburne and 1st Marquess of Lansdowne', ODNB.
18 Fitzmaurice, *Shelburne*, I, 9–10.
19 Fitzmaurice, *Shelburne*, I, 72–3, 82.
20 TNA, PROB 11/1428, fols 323–8.
21 Fitzmaurice, *Shelburne*, I, 13.

it seems possible he may have rubbed shoulders with at least some for whom France was significant, Christ Church later acquiring a relatively cosmopolitan reputation.[22] Having finished with Oxford, and as the family coffers would not stretch to a tour of the continent, Shelburne was forced instead to look for meaningful employment in the army. At twenty, he was involved in the first military operation of his career and that particular conflict (the Seven Years War) endured until he was almost twenty-six. Election to the House of Commons for Chipping Wycombe (on the family interest) occurred while he was still abroad[23] (though he seems never to have taken his seat) and shortly after, his succession to his father's peerage and admission to the House of Lords initiated a political career that absorbed him more or less completely until his early thirties.[24] Foreign interests when they came appear to have directed his gaze initially towards America rather than Europe. As President of the Board of Trade in 1763 relations with the American colonies were central to his concerns and twenty years later America would again be to the fore for his considerations in his efforts to negotiate an acceptable peace treaty.[25]

Shelburne's first contact with peacetime France in 1771, then, could be said to have been the first occasion when he could reasonably have been expected to indulge an interest in travel on the continent, though it might be thought peculiar that the Duke of Richmond, with whom he was initially on very good terms, sharing as they did, 'an unsociably abstemious life, a military background, and ability in parliamentary speaking', did nothing to introduce him to France earlier.[26] As a French landowner and peer in his own right as seigneur d'Aubigny, Richmond was a frequent visitor. Indeed, in 1776, tiring of Britain and British politics, the duke resolved to retire to his French estates permanently, 'preparing a retreat for himself against the day when despotism should have made England intolerable and when America would not be open to the exile'.[27]

While he may not have travelled there socially, Shelburne's prominence in two administrations in the 1760s, first as one of the lords of trade in 1763 and then as secretary of state for the southern department in 1766, meant that he was not unknown in France. In November 1766, the British

[22] Bod. Lib. MS Bland Burges, 18, Richard Perryn to Sir James Bland Burges, 1773.

[23] Sir Lewis Namier and John Brooke, ed., *History of Parliament: The Commons 1754–90*, 2 vols (London, 1985), iii, 272.

[24] The earldom of Shelburne was an Irish peerage. Shelburne sat in the British House of Lords by virtue of his British barony of Wycombe until 1784 when he was promoted Marquess of Lansdowne.

[25] R.A. Humphreys, 'Lord Shelburne and a Projected Recall of Colonial Governors in 1767', *American Historical Review*, 37:2 (1932), 269.

[26] Alison Olson, *The Radical Duke: Career and Correspondence of Charles Lennox Third Duke of Richmond* (Oxford, 1961), 46.

[27] G.H. Guttridge, *English Whiggism and the American Revolution* (1963), 90.

ambassador at Paris, William Henry Nassau de Zuylestein, Earl of Rochford, communicated to Shelburne a conversation he had had with the French minister, Choiseul, in which Choiseul had 'expressed the greatest personal regard for your character, that he had great hopes from your lordship's frankness and fair method of proceeding, that all little difficultys [sic] between the two courts would be easily adjusted'.[28] The following year Rochford recommended the Baron de Longuevil to Shelburne at the desire of 'some principal people and persons of distinction'. Longuevil was eager to disencumber himself of his Canadian estates and hoped that Shelburne would provide him with an introduction to the governor to facilitate the sale.[29]

Ultimately, though, it was the Irish Huguenot, Isaac Barré, rather than the Anglo-French peer Richmond or the diplomat Rochford, who was to be Shelburne's first guide in France. The occasion of their tour was not a happy one, being in part an attempt for Shelburne to recover from the loss of his young first wife, Lady Sophia Carteret, earlier that year, and the journal he compiled of their wanderings in France and Italy provides little insight into the society they encountered. The *London Evening Post* noted Shelburne's departure from London on 11 May,[30] and he and Barré set out from Dover the following day. Having endured a crossing of six hours, they arrived in Calais, where the two companions passed their first night on French soil. Two days later, Barré and Shelburne set out for Paris, arriving there on 16 May. En route, Shelburne noted the 'excellent agriculture . . . better than I ever saw in England', 'not a weed' was to be seen and he was intrigued by the fact that the 'work [was] mostly done by women'. From this cursory inspection of French agricultural methods, he concluded that, 'I am persuaded it would answer to any Englishman to spend one harvest here to see their method.' Following a short stay in Paris, Shelburne and Barré struck out for Lyons and from thence onwards into Italy.[31]

Thus far, although Shelburne's journal hinted at his approval of what he had seen, there is little indication of any particularly dramatic conversion being undergone and the brief journal entries emphasize that their immediate goal was Italy and there was little time to linger in France on the way south. It was, thus, the return trip that was to prove genuinely life changing for him. For even if the journal remains coy on the point, during their second sojourn in Paris Shelburne was admitted to the hallowed groves of the salonières and to acquaintance with a number of the philosophes, chief of whom (for Shelburne) was to be the abbé Morellet (though it must be admitted that among the philosophes Morellet himself was far from

[28] Bod. Lib. ms film 2009, fol. 118. Microfilm copies of the Bowood manuscripts are deposited at the Bodleian Library. I have used the microfilm references throughout the piece.

[29] Bod. Lib. ms film 2009, fol. 126.

[30] *London Evening Post*, Saturday 11 May 1771.

[31] Bod. Lib. ms film 2019.

chief). Thus, as Jarrett summarized, 'it was in Paris that his horizons were really widened and his ideas "liberalized", as he himself put it'.[32] Shelburne was admitted to an audience with the king and encountered a variety of figures central to the Parisian scene. Curiously, contrary to what Fitzmaurice suggests, he seems not to have made his way to the salon of Madame du Deffand, her letters to Horace Walpole in November and December making reference to his movements, but noting that she had not seen him.[33] It was not until Shelburne's return to France that he was able to add du Deffand to his fast growing list of Parisian acquaintance.[34] But he certainly encountered many others: Madame Geoffrin, Madame de Boufflers, and Mademoiselle de l'Espinasse.[35] He was admitted to the salon of Madame Helvétius, and that of the cartographer and chemist Trudaine de Montigny, who introduced him to the statesman Turgot.[36] It was also during this visit that he became one of the regular guests at d'Holbach's Café de l'Europe.[37] Indeed, Shelburne appears to have come close to sensory overload in this his first experience of Paris, a reaction neatly reflected in his response to encountering Monsieur de Malesherbes:

> I have seen what I had previously considered could not possibly exist, a man, absolutely free from fear and hope alike, yet full of life and warmth ... have never been so profoundly struck by any one in the course of my travels, and I feel sure that if I ever accomplish anything great in what remains of my life, I shall do so encouraged by my recollection of M. de Malesherbes.[38]

Although Shelburne undoubtedly interested Parisian society quite as much as Parisian society fascinated him, Barré's influence during this visit should not be underestimated. The Irish son of Huguenot refugees, Barré had first met Shelburne during the Rochefort campaign. A follower of Wolfe, Barré had gone on to serve as one of Wolfe's staff officers at Quebec, where he lost both his patron and an eye. He returned to a stormy falling-out with Pitt the Elder, and took up with his young protégé from the siege of Rochefort, who, having found him safe seats in the family boroughs of Chipping Wycombe and Calne ironically led him eventually back into service in Pitt's association.[39] The two finally fell out over the French Revolution, but from the 1760s until about 1790 Barré's was the guiding hand first in Shelburne's interaction with America and later with the salons of Paris. Barré also points

---

[32] Derek Jarrett, *The Begetters of Revolution*, 128.
[33] *Walpole Correspondence with Deffand*, v, 144–5, 153.
[34] *Walpole Correspondence with Deffand*, vi, 100.
[35] Fitzmaurice, *Shelburne*, I, 425.
[36] Fitzmaurice, *Shelburne*, I, 426.
[37] Fitzmaurice, *Shelburne*, I, 428.
[38] Idem.
[39] Namier and Brooke, ed., *The Commons 1754-90*, ii, 50–4.

to another aspect of Shelburne that it is necessary to remember. For, it is important to bear in mind that for all his elite background – Westminster, cabinet office, an earldom – Shelburne was at heart an outsider happiest in the company of men of lesser rank. This, it seems reasonable to conclude, coloured his attitude towards France and his conception of free trade and a world citizenry. It might also be suggested that this encouraged his association with Morellet, a man of relatively humble beginnings, by no means the foremost thinker in France, and a man who struggled with his English quite as much (if not more so) than Shelburne floundered in French.[40]

If 1771 was a turning point for Shelburne, 1772 consolidated his new interest with the arrival of Morellet in England. Of all his new-found Parisian acquaintance, Morellet appears to have emerged as the one with whom Shelburne was most in sympathy, and while one should not be too naïve about this burgeoning friendship, for after all Morellet's fare was paid for by Trudaine de Montigny as part of a fact-gathering reconnaissance of England, one should not be too cynical either. Shelburne later hoped that Morellet would collaborate with Jeremy Bentham and Richard Price in setting up a new journal to be entitled *the Neutralist*.[41] There seems little doubt that there was genuine affection on the part of both and Shelburne certainly attempted to exert his influence in France on Morellet's behalf to ease his rocky financial situation.[42] Not that Morellet was the only Frenchman to benefit from Shelburne's munificence, the abbé Rayneval enjoying similar hospitality.[43] Indeed Shelburne was the subject of severe criticism at the height of the American War for continuing to welcome Rayneval to his table,[44] and he was lambasted for his failure always to demonstrate the like hospitality to his own countrymen. The struggling poet, George Crabbe, was shown the door on more than one occasion in 1780, treatment that no doubt added to Shelburne's dubious reputation as someone willing to sell his own compatriots in return for foreign favours.[45]

In 1772, though, Morellet was Shelburne's principal discovery. On his arrival in London, Morellet found Shelburne absent, but a welcome arranged for him by Shelburne's brother, Hon. Thomas Fitzmaurice, a friend of Dr Johnson.[46] Morellet was hampered by his poor grasp of English, but relieved

---

[40] André Morellet was the son of a paper merchant from Lyons. His precocious intellect gained him a place at the Sorbonne alongside Turgot and he was later invited to contribute articles to Diderot's *Encyclopédie*. See Dorothy Medlin and Arlene Shy, 'Enlightened Exchange: The Correspondence of André Morellet and Lord Shelburne'.

[41] Stephen Conway, 'Bentham versus Pitt: Jeremy Bentham and British Foreign Policy 1789', *Historical Journal*, 30:4 (1987), 794.

[42] J. Merrick and D. Medlin, ed., *André Morellet (1727–1819) in the Republic of Letters and the French Revolution* (New York, 1995), 17.

[43] *Middlesex Journal and Evening Advertiser*, 13 July 1776.

[44] *London Courant and Westminster Chronicle*, 7 August 1780.

[45] Edward Walford, *Old and New London* (London, 1878), iv, 326–38.

[46] Namier and Brooke, ed., *The Commons 1754–90*, ii, 430–1.

to find that most of his new acquaintance spoke some French. After London, the first leg of Morellet's tour was Wycombe, where they were joined by Dr Hawksworth, editor of Cook's voyages, and David Garrick (who were both friends of Fitzmaurice), Barré, and Benjamin Franklin.[47] On Shelburne's return Morellet was spirited back to London to wonder at the Pantheon, the opera, and the theatres of Garrick and Samuel Foote.[48] Other members of Shelburne's set were introduced to Morellet's acquaintance: Richmond, John Montagu, 4th Earl of Sandwich, and Lord Chief Justice Mansfield to name but a few. After six weeks in London, Morellet was shown the delights of Blenheim, Windsor Castle, Pope's house at Twickenham and Hagley Hall, before finally being transported to Bowood:

> Une grande et belle maison, un beau jardin, une riche bibliothèque, des voitures et des chevaux.... C'est la surtout que j'ai trouvé un excellent usage, celui d'être etabli toute la journée dans une bibliothèque qui servait de salon, et qui fournissait continuellement ou des sujets à la conversation, ou des secours pour verifier les points debattus.

> [A large and beautiful house, a lovely garden, a well-stocked library, carriages and horses.... It is there above all that I found an excellent custom, of passing the entire day in a library that served as a salon, and which continually furnished either subjects for conversation, or help in verifying points in debate.][49]

The success of Morellet's visit to Bowood was mirrored by Shelburne's continuing delight in immersing himself in France, whence he returned at regular intervals following his first foray, and the opinions of those he met there had progressively greater and greater influence on the direction of political thinking. At the heart of this was the concept of international co-operation, which Shelburne believed could be developed admirably through reform of the mint to cure corruption and end once and for all the need to resort to armed conflict. One such scheme proposed that:

> we should propose to France that our standard should be always sent to Paris to be assay'd there, and you might send yours to London, and both to be sent afterwards to Amsterdam to put the coin of both kingdoms out of reach of all suspicion or abuse. It has often struck me that countrys might be made a check upon each other, and that this principle might be variously applied if we could once get rid of old prejudices, or thinking war can ever prove a remedye for any thing.[50]

Not that everything about France was political or economic. In his domestic

---

[47] Fitzmaurice, *Shelburne*, ii, 457.
[48] Fitzmaurice, *Shelburne*, ii, 458.
[49] Fitzmaurice, *Shelburne*, ii, 459–60.
[50] Bod. Lib. ms film 1996, fols 119–21.

arrangements too, Shelburne was eager to ensure that everything was à la mode, thus in December 1774, the quest for a new cook found Shelburne commissioning Barré and Morellet to scour Paris for a suitable candidate,[51] and Shelburne also appears to have been the draw for the architect, François-Joseph Belanger, making a tour of England at about the same time.[52] Shelburne employed his contacts to acquire books otherwise difficult to come by in Britain, such as the memoir of Count Cagliostro, 'a famous adventurer, who furnishes conversation at this time to all Paris', a copy of which he despatched to the Duke of Rutland,[53] and made use of his interest to smooth the way for those of his acquaintance seeking patronage or an easy passage. In August 1784 he recommended Monsieur Bombelles, formerly French envoy to the Holy Roman Empire at Ratisbon, to Rutland, Bombelles then being about to travel through Scotland and Ireland,[54] and the following year also provided President Virly [sic] with a letter of recommendation to the duke.[55]

Unsurprisingly, Shelburne's increasing prominence in British political life, coupled with his association with France and patronage of French men of letters at Bowood, soon attracted opprobrious comments from some quarters. One anonymous publication of 1776, A letter to the Rt Hon the earl of Shelburne, on the motives of his political conduct, made plain its opinion that Shelburne's rise was the result of desperation in a country devoid of true talent and of a complex political sleight of hand:

> My Lord, I do not address your lordship from any regard to your private virtues; they may be extensive, for what I know: nor to your talents as a man of taste, the patron of genius, the protector of patriotic orators, political pamphleteers, and experimental philosophers.
>
> By a series of industrious chicane, which is never the effect of real genius, you have risen to a degree of consequence in this country. Nature designed you for some of those middling employments, where great industry, much artifice, void of real principle, an apparent ardour for religion, would have gradually led to the fortune of Jew.

At the root of the deception, that had enabled a man of mediocre talents to rise to the forefront of political life, was the artifice of France and the treacherous duplicity of the order with whom the Jesuit of Berkeley Square was to be so firmly associated:

---

[51] Bod. Lib. ms film 969, fol. 24.

[52] Kenneth Woodbridge, 'Bélanger en Angleterre: Son Carnet de Voyage', *Architectural History*, 25 (1982), 10.

[53] *HMC Rutland*, iii, 287.

[54] Ibid., 133.

[55] Ibid., 232. This is possibly a misreading of Francois Viry, a diplomat in service with the king of Savoy.

At this time you had the most motley political appearance that was possible: you placed yourself in the rank of the English patriots; but having in vain, for a long time, strove in France to attain the French accent, you had associated yourself with Jesuits: a resemblance in talent and disposition infallibly bring on a connection, you determined to chuse your counsellors from among them; the Jesuits were in possession of all the genius and learning in the world; and nothing but a radical want of sincerity, and a regard to your interest in England, prevented you from becoming one of the Society of Loyola.

It was a droll and ridiculous situation; an English patriot in appearance, and a French Jesuit in heart ...[56]

Shelburne's return to government between 1782 and 1783, first as one of the secretaries of state in the Rockingham administration and then as Prime Minister, proved short-lived and all his acquaintance in France could not ameliorate the confusion created by the British system for allocating to one secretary of state primacy in negotiating with the Americans in Paris while the other sought to make peace with the French. Shelburne's rivalry with his fellow secretary, and cousin through his second marriage, Charles James Fox, and his controversial efforts to proceed further than many in the government thought prudent (once more inviting comparison with Bolingbroke and his activities in negotiating the Treaty of Utrecht) made him again the subject of brutal personal sleights, such as the scatalogical cartoon depicting *L-d Shel-, begging monsieur to make piss or p-e* (J. Barrow, 1783).[57] But Shelburne's personal connection with France undoubtedly enabled him to cultivate a warm relationship with the French minister of foreign affairs, Charles Gravier de Vergennes, which in turn helped to drive through a rapid and broadly positive peace settlement, much of which was hammered out at conferences hosted by Shelburne at Bowood and his London home.[58] Despite this, when the Younger Pitt came in following the collapse of the Fox–North coalition, which had ousted Shelburne's administration in the spring of 1783, Shelburne himself was left in the cold. Thomas Orde believed Shelburne's exclusion to be a deliberate ploy to facilitate Pitt's fledgling administration:

I plainly perceive the awkwardness of his situation, while it can be thought, and indeed is said without contradiction, that he who laid the foundation nobly and

---

[56] Anon., *A letter to the Right Honourable the Earl of Shelburne, on the motives of his political conduct, and the principles which have actuated the opposition to the measures of administration in respect to America* (London, 1776).

[57] British Museum Department of Prints and Drawings, BM 6168.

[58] Andrew Stockley, *Britain and France at the Birth of America* (Exeter, 2001), 98, 102, 129–30.

honourably for the present ministerial establishment is made the only sacrifice for the security of its success.[59]

In place of ministerial office, Shelburne was forced to be satisfied with a marquessate, which he saw very much as a reward acquired for him through Rutland's interest, who had formerly served in Shelburne's cabinet and had been appointed Lord Privy Seal by Pitt, esteeming it 'a singular piece of good fortune to owe this where I have already so many hereditary obligations'.[60] The reward could well be seen as reciprocal, as two years previously Shelburne had been instrumental in securing a garter for Rutland.[61]

Yet, despite being consigned to the wilderness, the early years of Pitt's ministry, and 1786 in particular, should perhaps be seen as the highpoint of Shelburne's interaction with France as it saw the ripening of both Shelburne and Morellet's plans with the commercial treaty between France and Britain. The direct result of one of the clauses negotiated by Shelburne and Vergennes in 1783,[62] it was a subject in which Shelburne assured Morellet 'no Frenchman can be more interested than I am' and which as Shelburne pointed out in a letter to Morellet of 11 October, 'though it may not go so far as you or I may wish at present, it will lay the foundation of all by opening the door to truth and liberty....'[63] The commercial treaty offered Shelburne a mild sop to his pride, which was otherwise sorely bruised by his marginality within the British political scene. Congratulating Morellet once more in November, he went on to bemoan his own poor fortune:

> It happens to few great men to see the seeds they have sown grown to trees in their own time. However this will be your case if this treaty comes to be formally perfected. I am very proud to give it all the support possible in both town and country – tho no body can be worse us'd than I am by the ministry who have concluded it on our side.[64]

Whatever his opinions about his usage at the hands of British political society, Shelburne made use of the passage of the Eden Treaty to give one of his most noteworthy speeches in the Lords, in which he took the opportunity of publicly rebutting the notion that France and Britain were 'natural and necessary enemies'. On the contrary, under Elizabeth I 'a model of wisdom', under Cromwell 'no Frenchman surely' and again under Walpole, Britain

---

[59] *HMC Rutland*, iii, 120–1.
[60] Ibid., 154.
[61] G.E.C. Cockayne, *Complete Peerage*, xi, 269–70.
[62] J. Holland Rose, 'The Franco-British Commercial Treaty of 1786', *English Historical Review*, 23:92 (1908), 710.
[63] Bod. Lib. ms film 1996, f. 110.
[64] Bod. Lib. ms film 1996, fol. 117.

and France had been close and natural allies. William III had taken England in a different direction, but Shelburne had his views on that as well:

> as there may be spots even in the sun, with all possible admiration of king William, it must also be allowed that his foreign politics did not make the brightest part of his character as an English king.[65]

According to Shelburne, 'England had no natural enemy' and as he was keen to emphasize, 'whoever has travelled in France, knows that its public opinion (which happily governs at present in all enlightened countries) is totally changed'. Shelburne was happy to point out that the treaty was imperfect and that he could undoubtedly have done better himself, but despite such reservations, having kept his audience in suspense for at least two hours, he offered it his support. It is a speech that sums up neatly his creed: idealistic, enthusiastic, at times bombastic and impractical, and not particularly sophisticated for all the trappings of economic theory and the musing of the philosophes. Yet for all that, Shelburne remained of fundamental importance in shaping the thought of others away from the intrinsic gallophobia that had informed so much previous cultural and economic theory by virtue of his position as a patron of men of real talent. Certainly, his attitude could not have been more different from that of Charles Montagu, Lord Halifax, the godfather of the Bank of England in the reigns of William III and Queen Anne, who had happily reported to a colleague how he had bustled about in the city early one morning, 'to push the American project ... my brains do so crow with our great success, that I cannot help drawing schemes for destroying the French....'[66]

Alongside his performance in the House and his extensive circle of acquaintance, the strength of Bowood's French connection is perhaps most clearly illustrated by Shelburne's heir, Lord Wycombe's first major foray into French society under the guiding hand of the inevitable Morellet in the latter part of 1787. Wycombe had been thoroughly prepared for the initiation and had, in fact, already travelled in France under the watchful eye of Vergennes in 1784 and a year before Wycombe's second trip, Shelburne had written proudly to Morellet boasting how, 'our little boy goes on very well, and speaks your language as well as his own tolerably fluently'.[67] He should, then, have been admirably equipped for his tour through France the following summer. Certainly he seems to have managed rather better than some of his compatriots abroad (in Geneva):

> I am sorry to find that some English amongst whom Lord Paget's name is mentioned, have got into difficulties at Geneva, where they have been impris-

65 *Parliamentary History*, xxvi, 558.
66 British Library, Additional mss. 61118, fol. 106.
67 Bod. Lib. ms film 1996, fol. 106.

oned, I believe for demanding in a riotous manner the keys of the town when the usual hour of going in and out was past....[68]

For Wycombe there were to be no such embarrassments. Writing from Lyons, he had been able to assure his father that he was, according to instructions, cultivating the archbishop of Bordeaux and the bishop of Blois. He had been among Morellet's relations ('very pleasant and unaffected people')[69] and from Bordeaux a fortnight afterwards he was able to report dinner parties with Madame Dillon, Monsieur de Brienne, and (most importantly) that he was being shown particular attention by the duc de la Rochefoucauld, prominent member of the Academy of Science and vigorous supporter of American independence, who enquired 'very particularly' after Shelburne.[70] Wycombe discovered at first hand just how far his father's reputation reached in France, for he was struck by the way in which the de Briennes offered him their notice, despite having had no introduction. Their attention, he concluded, was owing to:

> the good offices of Madame de Martinville, and of the archbishop [Bordeaux] whose nephew talks of coming to England; he took great pains to be civil to me, and I ventured to assure him you would be glad to make his acquaintance, as you was anxious to have an opportunity of proving the respect you entertained for his uncle.[71]

Wycombe's tour was filled with similar examples of cordiality, during which conversation ranged from an appreciation of the latest opera by Beaumarchais,[72] the author of the scandalous *Marriage of Figaro*, to the merits of the commercial treaty.[73] He breakfasted with the Prince de Nassau,[74] undertook commissions on behalf of his father with the duc de Polignac, favourite of Marie Antoinette, Rayneval and (of course) Morellet,[75] and was called on by Madame de la Valière and Madame de Boufflers.[76] The former minister

---

[68] Bod. Lib. ms film 2029, fol. 72.

[69] Bod. Lib. ms film 2029, fol. 71.

[70] Louis-Alexandre, duc de la Rochefoucauld was later assassinated at Gisors in 1792. Bod. Lib. ms film 2029, fols 76–7.

[71] Bod. Lib. ms film 2029, fols 81–2.

[72] The opera was probably *Tarare*, by Antonio Salieri, which premiered in Paris in June 1787. Salieri later reworked it with Da Ponte and it was produced in Vienna the following year under the title *Axur, Re d'Ormur*.

[73] Bod. Lib. ms film 2029, fols 21, 76, 91.

[74] Karl Christian, Prince of Nassau, was married to Princess Carolina of Orange-Nassau, a daughter of William IV, Prince of Orange and George III's daughter, Anne, the Princess Royal. Bod. Lib. ms film 2029, fol. 86.

[75] Bod. Lib. ms film 2029, fol. 91.

[76] Bod. Lib. ms film 2029, fol. 125.

of finance, Jacques Necker, spoke of Shelburne 'with the utmost respect'[77] and the recent ambassador to Britain, the comte d'Adhémar, 'always held the handsomest language with respect to you'. In return Wycombe recommended to his father's attention Comte Amande de Custine,[78] who was eager to make Shelburne's acquaintance, explaining that, 'as there are few families to whose kindnesses I am under greater obligations than that with which he is connected, I thought I might without presuming too far, satisfy his wish'.[79]

One should, of course, not be too much swayed by so much *politesse*, though it does appear that beyond the courtesies, Shelburne was held in genuine affection and esteem by a number of the foremost of French society. But in the midst of all the compliments, Wycombe detected something that his father, awash with enthusiasm for France and the prospects of commercial union, could not:

> it particularly becomes me to thank you for the freedom with which you communicate to me your opinion on the present very important topics of political discussion; I have the most implicit confidence in the justice of your doctrine respecting war, but I have already presumed to say, that from what I see and hear, I cannot bring myself to have the same reliance that you seem to have in the wisdom or even the liberality of administration here, although it seems sufficiently inclined to peace.[80]

Wycombe's doubts were to prove prescient and for Shelburne, as for so many in the Whig elite, the outbreak of the French Revolution in 1789 was to prove a year of cruelly disappointed aspirations, which rather than hailing the opening of a new and more open relationship between the two powers resulted in more than a dozen years of bitter and protracted conflict. Even so, as William B. Willcox noted, Shelburne's 'affection for France ... colored [sic] his attitude toward the Revolution and blinded him to the danger inherent in French conquests'.[81] Ironically, the revolution would both lead to his reconciliation with one of his oldest foes, Charles James Fox, who for all his anti-French *gasconades* was as natural a friend of France as of England, and see the ending of one of his most important friendships: that with Isaac

[77] Bod. Lib. ms film 2029, fol. 93.

[78] Amand-Louis-Philippe-Francois, comte de Custine (1768–94) was the son of General Adam-Philippe, comte de Custine. The general was one of the Revolution's early supporters, but he fell foul of the politicians and was arrested in July 1793 following a series of military reverses. Amand de Custine rallied to father's defence for which he was also arrested. The general was sent to the guillotine in August 1793, his son followed him there in January 1794.

[79] Bod. Lib. ms film 2029, fol. 147.

[80] Bod. Lib. ms film 2029, fols 95–6.

[81] William B. Willcox, 'Lord Lansdowne on the French Revolution and the Irish Rebellion', *Journal of Modern History*, 17:1 (March 1945), 29–30.

Barré.[82] Perhaps less importantly for Shelburne, in the long term it would end all hopes of a political comeback. When he wrote to Morellet in July, Shelburne was full of hope that the changed circumstances in France would prove for the French their very own glorious revolution, and without at least some of the concomitant suffering undergone by the British:

> I am oblig'd to you for your sentiments about the interesting state of your publick affairs. It appears to me that things are going their natural progress, the same which one observes in various historys and particularly our own. It's not to be suppos'd that the road can be a smooth one, or the birth void of labour. It's happy for you that you have not an obstinate king like our race of Stuarts or a violent minister like Lord Strafford – By this means you'll avoid the ceremony of a civil war ... but some inconveniencys as well as some wrong things you must put up with.[83]

Shelburne may have wished that the revolution would prove a happy occasion for France – and in so doing he was hardly alone – but it rapidly proved not only to be something quite other than he and his circle had desired, but proved the occasion of the destruction of significant numbers of those who had graced Bowood or provided Shelburne and his coterie with hospitality in France. The murder of the duc de la Rochefoucauld in 1792 and the execution of dozens of Shelburne's acquaintance in Paris, many of whom he had welcomed at Bowood devastated his circle, but almost more difficult to bear was the blame directed against those, like Morellet, believed responsible for precipitating the chaos. In November 1789, Shelburne conveyed to Morellet how he was 'torn to pieces by your aristocrats here on your account – I defend you the best I can, but Madame de Boufflers says that it's all your doing'.[84] Thus, Bowood, which had done so much to encourage change in France, was itself forced to undergo a change in its role as a haven for cosmopolitanism. Shelburne used his interest to assist Talleyrand's escape to America, while Lord Wycombe, playing the role of Scarlet Pimpernel, helped spirit Madame de Flahault out of Paris along with her young son and the manuscript of her novel *Adele* (he was unable to prevent the execution of her husband).[85] In 1791 a disconsolate Shelburne could do little but complain to Morellet:

---

[82] Fitzmaurice, *Shelburne*, ii, 399.
[83] Bod. Lib. ms film 1996, fol. 150.
[84] Bod. Lib. ms film 1996, fols 158–9.
[85] Fitzmaurice, *Shelburne*, ii, 394. Mme de Flahault's son, Charles, was generally held to be the result of her liaison with Talleyrand. A Napoleonic General, he eventually settled in England and married Margaret Mercer Elphinstone, daughter of Admiral George Elphinstone. Their daughter Emily Mercer de Flahault would later marry the 4th Marquess as his second wife. Their son Edmond is the biographer of Lord Shelburne.

Your Revolution my dear Abbé is excessively hard upon individuals but the effect it must have upon the whole world exceeds all power of imagination – we must contrive to meet once more before we die to talk over such great events and their consequences.[86]

The Revolution, undoubtedly, altered irremediably the nature of Bowood's connection with France. In 1789 Shelburne was still able to toy with fanciful enquiries from the continent concerning obscure items of cosmopolitan genealogy – were the dukes of Liubourg and the seigneurs de Fanquemont vassals of the crown of England?[87] – but the Terror put an end to such innocent diversions.[88] Shelburne's response to it may have been blinded rather than aided by too close a knowledge of those involved, but he was undoubtedly in sympathy with the sentiments of his young nephew by marriage, Henry Fox, 3rd Lord Holland, who wrote to him from Berlin lamenting the actions of the Jacobins and 'that so glorious a cause as the enfranchisement of such a country as France is supported by people and individuals, whose conduct upon several occasions not only does not claim respect but excites both horror and contempt'.[89] Despite this, in 1794 Shelburne was still able to convince himself (and to attempt to convince others) that peace was for the having, if only both sides were willing to negotiate. In a letter to Thomas Coutts, Shelburne insisted, 'As to the French refusing to negotiate with Pitt, I hold it nonsense. Things may not go quite so smooth, or in regard to lesser points so well, but the great point of peace or war can never turn upon men.'[90] By 1797 such optimism had faded and even he was sanguine on the question of an imminent invasion of Britain by France.[91] By December of the following year, tired of hearing of 'nothing but war from London and from abroad', pessimism had given way to mawkish resignation, leading him to grumble to Coutts, 'I assure you I never wish to hear or think about public affairs.'[92]

Despite this, Shelburne's fundamental enthusiasm for France and its people remained. The prospects for peace in 1801 found Shelburne intent upon seeing 'the *bonne ville* de Paris once more' and he turned to the redoubtable Morellet:

---

[86] Bod. Lib. ms film 1996, fol. 169.
[87] Bod. Lib. ms Eng. lett. c. 144, fol. 202.
[88] Dorothy Medlin and Arlene P. Shy, 'Enlightened Exchange: The Correspondence of Andréw Morellet and Lord Shelburne', in *British–French Exchanges*, ed. Doig and Medlin, 61.
[89] Fitzmaurice, *Shelburne*, ii, 391.
[90] Willcox, 'Lord Lansdowne on the French Revolution and the Irish Rebellion', 32.
[91] Bod. Lib. ms. Eng. lett. c. 144, fols 210, 212.
[92] Willcox, 36.

to make a plan for me how *I can see and not be seen*, insisting that his aim was not to make connections, much less to intrigue, or to be active in any pursuit, but my curiosity will be insatiable, as long as it can be gratified in a quiet way.[93]

It was an aspiration never to be realized, but Shelburne's last speech in parliament neatly summarized his continuing belief in the need for 'conciliation' urging that 'discretion and prudence be not sacrificed to false glory'.[94] His death, two years later, barely noticed in the press, was left to be communicated to Bentham by their mutual friend, the Genevan Etienne Dumont.[95] Bowood's French connexion had undoubtedly been damaged by the experience of war, but its spirit, however tarnished and fragmented, endured.

[93] Fitzmaurice, *Shelburne*, II, 430.
[94] Ibid., 432.
[95] Ibid., 435.

10

Lord Shelburne's Constitutional Views in 1782–3

EDMOND DZIEMBOWSKI

As suggested by the title of John Norris's study, the name of Shelburne conjures up the idea of reform.[1] But what reform is it all about exactly? During his ministry from July 1782 to February 1783, Shelburne implemented a programme which combined the liberalization of trade with the reform of the tax system and the modernization of the administration. In Norris's opinion, parliamentary reform and, to a larger degree, reform of the executive and legislative bodies, did not represent a priority in Shelburne's ministerial agenda. Yet, a memoir written in 1783 by one of Shelburne's best friends, the French abbé Morellet, presents a vast programme which hinged on an ambitious institutional reform.[2] According to Morellet, Shelburne wanted to reconsider the foundations of the British political system. His aim was to reach a new institutional balance in which the executive power would have been considerably strengthened.

Before approaching Morellet's account, it is first advisable to go back over Shelburne's ministry and over the problems raised by his management of affairs. The constitutional views which are set forth in Morellet's memoir invite us, in the second place, to wonder about the ideological dimension of Shelburne's plan. Finally, one must put Shelburne's constitutional views in a wider context, which, at first sight, seem anachronistic according to a Whig interpretation of History, emphasizing the growing importance of representative institutions. The European political context of the 1770s and 1780s challenges this view and throws some light on this fascinating political episode.

Acknowledgements: I would like to thank Clarissa Campbell Orr for her valuable remarks on the draft of this chapter.

[1]   John Norris, *Shelburne and Reform* (London, 1963).
[2]   'Tableau de l'administration de Mylord Shelburne et exposition de ses principales vues sur l'économie intérieure et la politique extérieure, par l'abbé Morellet', Archives du ministère des Affaires étrangères (A.E.), Mémoires et Documents (M.D.), Angleterre, 6, fols 191–210.

The Enigma of Shelburne's Ministry

When the Shelburne ministry was formed in July 1782, not many observers were ready to bet on its longevity. An informer for the French ministry echoed this opinion: 'A profound speculator told me yesterday that Mylord Shelburne had no more than nine months' ministry in his womb.'[3] The obstetrical metaphor proved to be true. Lord Shelburne resigned on 24 February 1783, slightly more than eight months after taking office. The fate of his administration seems to confirm Hamish Scott's assertion according to which Shelburne was 'the greatest enigma in eighteenth-century politics'.[4] The eight months of his ministry are in many ways paradoxical. They show indeed an intelligent politician promoting an innovative and ambitious programme and, at the same time, repeating the errors, which had already proved fatal in 1766 to his mentor, William Pitt the Elder, Earl of Chatham.

Shelburne entered politics in 1761 as a friend of Lord Bute's before joining forces with Pitt in 1763. With the exception of a short stay in government between 1766 and 1768, he spent the first twenty years of his career in the ranks of the opposition. It was in March 1782, with Lord North's resignation, that his rapid political ascent started, first as Secretary of State in the Marqus of Rockingham's ministry, then, after the death of the latter on 1 July 1782, as First Lord of the Treasury.

The man who was coming to power was longing to reform his country. It is not an overstatement to say that with Shelburne, the Enlightenment and the *Lumières* entered Whitehall. Shelburne was gradually initiated into the ideas of the Enlightenment by two prestigious thinkers: Richard Price and Joseph Priestley. Utilitarianism and faith in progress which can be discerned in his political programme owe a great deal to Priestley's ideas. Shelburne's concern for a rational reform of the state structures in 1782 must have originated in Price's works on political arithmetic and finance which he had been reading for a decade.[5]

In 1771, not long after his first meeting with Price, Shelburne left for a tour in France and Italy. In Paris, he met the man who was going to be his friend and his initiator in the field of economics: André Morellet (1727–1819). The next year, Morellet was invited to stay at Bowood.[6] That is when, apparently, the Frenchman's ideas started to make an impression on Shelburne. Contributor to the *Encyclopédie*, translator of the works of

[3]   A.E., Correspondance politique (C.P.), Angleterre, 537, fol. 346r, Lerchenberg to Vergennes, London, 16 July 1782.
[4]   H.M. Scott, *British Foreign Policy in the Age of the American Revolution* (Oxford, 1990), 323.
[5]   Norris, *Shelburne and Reform*, 84–6.
[6]   *Mémoires de l'abbé Morellet, de l'Académie française, sur le dix-huitième siècle et sur la Révolution* (Paris, 2000), 201–13.

Beccaria, sworn enemy of the anti-*philosophes*, the *abbé Mords-lès*, as Voltaire used to call him, was then a figurehead of the enlightened circles in Paris. This friend of Turgot's and this disciple of Vincent Gournay's was also one of the most prominent economic theorists in France. When he met Morellet, Shelburne had hardly departed from the mercantilist ideas valued by the politicians of his time.[7] By his own reckoning, the man who made him consider political economy in a new light was his French friend. At the end of his ministry, he wrote to Morellet: 'your conversation and information had essentially contributed to liberalize my ideas' ['que j'avois contribué à libéraliser vos idées'].[8]

Breaking clearly with the spirit of a century which John Cannon regards as 'the most conservative in British history',[9] this enlightened statesman was at the same time the heir to a political movement which thrust its ideological roots deep into the seventeenth century: Chathamism.[10] Being Lord Chatham's Lieutenant-General for fifteen years or so marked Shelburne in two essential areas: his views on party and his ideas on the authority devolved to the First Lord of the Treasury. On 9 July 1782, before the House of the Lords, Shelburne claimed to be the faithful heir to the Earl of Chatham, 'who had always declared "that this country ought not to be governed by any party or faction, and that if it was to be so governed, the Constitution must necessarily expire"'.[11] During his whole career Chatham positioned himself on the fringe of the Whig oligarchy. Besides his formidable eloquence, this 'political outsider'[12] had a trump card available: his popularity, which allowed him to circumvent the obstacle of party by addressing extra-parliamentary opinion. In 1766, when he was back in power, Chatham formed a totally atypical ministry composed of personalities chosen for their abilities and not

---

7   According to John Norris, Shelburne was an early disciple of Adam Smith and Josiah Tucker (Norris, *Shelburne and Reform*, 31–2). The fact seems doubtful. As Hamish Scott has shown, Shelburne was still a 'relatively orthodox mercantilist' during the Chatham ministry (Scott, *British Foreign Policy*, 323), but Richard Whatmore (Chapter 12) reasserts the importance of Smith.

8   *Lettres d'André Morellet*, ed. D. Medlin, J.-C. David, and P. Leclerc (Oxford, 1991), I, 484, Shelburne to Morellet, 23 March 1783. See also I, 560, Morellet to the Marquess of Lansdowne, late June–9 July 1785: Morellet proudly reminds his friend the words he wrote to him in 1783 ('*que j'avois contribué à libéraliser vos idées*'). See also I, 568, excerpt from the speech of the Marquis de Chastellux during the ceremony of reception of Morellet at the *Académie française* in which Chastellux asserts that the verb 'liberalize' used by Shelburne contributed to create a neologism in the French language: the verb '*libéraliser*' (ibid., I, 568).

9   John Cannon, *Parliamentary Reform 1640–1832* (Cambridge, 1973), 24.

10 On the influence of republicanism upon Pitt the Elder, see Caroline Robbins, *The Eighteenth Century Commonwealthman* (Cambridge, MA, 1959), 274–6, and Edmond Dziembowski, *Les Pitt. L'Angleterre face à la France 1708–1806* (Paris, 2006), 52–67, 233–9.

11 Fitzmaurice, *Shelburne*, 1875–6, III, 238.

12 Jeremy Black, *Pitt the Elder* (Cambridge, 1992), 1–30.

for the number of MPs they controlled in both Houses.[13] It was this political experience which Shelburne evoked before the Lords. Like his mentor, he had made the maxim 'measures not men' his own. He intended to govern by winning over politicians of all backgrounds. However, the example of the Chatham ministry was not suitable to be set up as a model. Formed in July 1766, the administration was soon given a rough handling in Parliament. As early as the end of 1766, the determination to govern in a radically different way, proudly exhibited by Chatham a few months before, had met with the harsh realities of public affairs. In 1782–3, Shelburne met with the same realities. Defeated on the preliminary peace talks debate, he tendered his resignation on 24 February 1783. His downfall seems to prove that the views on party in which he believed were totally unsuited to the political context of his time.[14]

When he was in power, Shelburne put in practice a style of government totally at odds with the emerging conventions of the time. By writing directly to the British diplomats negotiating the peace in France and by seeing the French envoy Gérard de Rayneval, he was encroaching on the field of the Secretary of State for Foreign Affairs (see Chapter 6). As he did not trust the collegial tradition of government work, he preferred to convoke a few ministers in a select group to settle the matters in hand as quickly as possible.[15] This view on the authority of the first minister has only one precedent: that of Chatham, who, in 1766, regarded the members of his administration not as his colleagues but as underlings who just had to carry out his policy. As in 1766, so in 1782, this authoritarian way of governing upset established custom and annoyed the political world. William Grenville's reaction attested to this when he commented sarcastically on Shelburne's method: 'You will certainly think the mode of keeping a cabinet unanimous by never meeting them at all an excellent one.'[16] The Duke of Grafton's indignant reaction is another example of the uneasiness of the politicians. Grafton 'would never consider his lordship [Shelburne] but as holding the principal office in the Cabinet'. He blamed Shelburne for the fact he wanted to become '*Prime* Minister'.[17]

---

[13] John Brooke, *The Chatham Administration 1766–1768* (London, 1956), 1–19.

[14] At the end of his ministry, Shelburne realized that the Chathamite conception of party was leading his ministry to disaster. As the opposition began to strengthen, he adopted a more realistic view and tried to convince the Northites to enter into a ministerial coalition. Unfortunately, his efforts were vain: Lord North, at the same time, was negotiating an alliance with Charles James Fox and his Whig followers (John Cannon, *The Fox–North Coalition. Crisis of the Constitution 1782–4* [Cambridge, 1969], 44–9).

[15] Norris, *Shelburne and Reform*, 242.

[16] Quoted by John Cannon, *The Fox–North Coalition*, 37.

[17] *Autobiography and Political Correspondence of Augustus Henry Third Duke of Grafton K. G.* (London, 1898), 361.

In his manuscript, Grafton underlined the first term, and the stroke of his pen is far from being insignificant. When he wrote those lines, the way the political world looked at the office of First Lord of the Treasury had hardly changed since Walpole's time, whereas the tasks which were ahead of the First Lord were much heavier than those which Sir Robert had once had to shoulder. Even if the ministers blamed their colleague for encroaching upon their sphere, the reforming ambition which Shelburne made obvious resulted in considerable additional work. In fact, the spirit of reform, because it extended the field of ministerial interference, contributed to the gradual transformation of First Minister into Prime Minister. But this mutation, whose highlight was the Pitt administration (1783–1801), happened almost imperceptibly. In 1802, William Pitt was toasted by his partisans as 'the Pilot that weathered the storm'. In 1782, Shelburne would have liked to be regarded as 'the Pilot' of the ministerial ship. His mistake was to underestimate the weight of tradition and to take his colleagues' recriminations in a high and mighty way. In the eyes of the political world his tactlessness made him a candidate for authoritarian power.

We are, indeed, faced with an enigma. If Shelburne behaved in an offhand manner towards the political world, how could he convince politicians of the validity of his reforms? If we left the analysis at this point, the man would seem to be devoid of all realism. But it is on this point that Morellet's memoir throws an invaluable light on Shelburne's attitude.

Anatomy of Shelburne's Project by Morellet

After the fall of his ministry, Shelburne left England to spend the summer at Spa in the Low Countries. In this town he met his friend Morellet, with whom he had several talks. These constitute the substance of the memoir written by Morellet for the French Secretary of State for Foreign Affairs, the comte de Vergennes. This report, entitled 'Survey of the administration of Mylord Shelburne and exposition of his main views on domestic and foreign policy', is all the more invaluable since Shelburne's confidences, which constitute the substance of it, were shared only a few weeks after his ministry, while he still had his behaviour at the head of affairs fresh in his mind. The 'Survey of the administration of Mylord Shelburne' provides remarkable clarifications on the ex-minister's achievements and ideas. In the final analysis, this document can be read as the assessment of an uncompleted work.

Let us start our study of Morellet's report with a simple observation: parliamentary reform, a subject which had been a burning issue over the previous months, is hardly ever mentioned.[18] In 1779–80, Shelburne supported the

---

[18] Morellet briefly mentions parliamentary reform as he evokes Shelburne's opinion on Ireland. Ireland, he writes, 'is now busy establishing a good representation and seems to

campaign of the Yorkshire association. He then reminded the electorate of Wiltshire (the county where Bowood was situated) of his commitment to the fight led by 'our late great countryman Lord Chatham' in favour of the increase of the county representation.[19] However, after forming his ministry, Shelburne distanced himself from the Yorkshire movement.[20] According to Norris, he still felt attached to a moderate reform of parliamentary representation, but, mainly for political reasons, he had to give up this aspect of his programme. Shelburne was then wooing the Northites, a political group which was predominantly hostile to the modification of the electoral system.[21]

As Charles James Fox's attitude tends to show, the historian's hypothesis seems satisfactory. After becoming Lord North's political ally, Fox gave up in his turn his reformism for tactical reasons.[22] Nevertheless Morellet offers a different interpretation of Shelburne's behaviour. His report clearly shows that parliamentary reform was no longer a priority in the hierarchy of the measures Shelburne had planned to take. His political project could even suit an unreformed House of Commons. This is at this stage of our exposition that we have to look at the Shelburnian system as it appears from Morellet's memoir.

The most well known element of the system, trade liberalization, is developed at length in the report. As Morellet reverently points out, Shelburne considered 'the general system of trade freedom and communication between nations on a large scale'.[23] Shelburne, who dreamt of the liberalization of trade between the European powers, was convinced that the measure would have extremely positive effects on international relations. Free trade was to tighten the links with France and ease the sources of tension, which, for decades, had essentially been due to maritime and colonial rivalries. Shelburne seems to have understood that the rivalry between Great Britain and France in the second half of the eighteenth century had left the powers eager for territorial expansion (Russia, Prussia, and Austria) entirely free

take very wise measures to succeed in this project. England, for her part, does not want to or cannot take the same measures' (A.E., M.D., Angleterre, 6, fol. 204v). These words tend to show that Shelburne did not believe in the success of parliamentary reform in Britain.

[19] Norris, *Shelburne and Reform*, 126–8.

[20] John Norris refers to a meeting held in Bowood in January 1782 attended by Isaac Barré, John Dunning, and William Pitt the Younger. During this meeting, Shelburne and his political allies 'had prepared a parliamentary motion embodying the demands for shorter parliaments, addition to county representation and the abolition of rotten boroughs' (ibid., 162). Shelburne did not move this motion in the House of Lords.

[21] Ibid., 254–5.

[22] Ian R. Christie, *Wilkes, Wyvill and Reform. The Parliamentary Reform Movement in British Politics 1760–1785* (London, 1962), 176–9.

[23] A.E., M.D., Angleterre, 6, fol. 203v.

to act as they wished in Central and Eastern Europe.[24] He suggested an updated version of the Franco-British accord signed by Dubois and Stanhope in 1716–17. An alliance between the two countries would make them the arbitrators of Europe and guarantee the European balance of power. Shelburne's foreign policy was taking the exact opposite of Pitt the Elder's:

> According to Lord Shelburne, France and England are not, as it is often said, natural enemies, they should rather help each other to establish their domination throughout the world not so much by force, but by the influence given by enlightenment and the progress of arts and sciences, and if jealous sovereigns disturbed the peace in Europe by attacking one of these two nations, he would not be surprised to see English army troops allied to France to protect Flanders or Alsace from an invasion.[25]

Well aware of the difficulties besetting his path, he told Morellet that his economic measures would have been met with strong resistance:

> the English, and especially the current administration,[26] are unaware of the true principles of free trade. Unfortunately, in England, trade jealousy is not only a mistake made by the current administrators, and more generally speaking by any administration. It is a truly national, popular and universal error. And in the state of quasi-anarchy in which the country is immersed, the people's opinion cannot be challenged.

> [les Anglais, et surtout l'administration actuelle [...] méconnaissent les vrais principes de la liberté du commerce [...] Malheureusement, en Angleterre, la jalousie de commerce n'est pas seulement l'erreur des administrateurs actuels, et plus généralement parlant de l'administration. C'est une erreur vraiment nationale, populaire, universelle. Et, dans l'état de presque anarchie où se trouve aujourd'hui ce pays, on ne peut pas, comme en d'autres, braver l'opinion du peuple.][27]

The reformer's project would thus have been hindered by prejudice. Yet a weapon still remained at the minister's disposal: his political and institutional programme, the keystone of his system of reforms:

---

[24] Scott, *British Foreign Policy*, 330–1.

[25] A.E., M.D., Angleterre, 6, fols 206r–206v. Although Morellet was a devoted admirer of Shelburne's work, he was reluctant to sympathize with an opinion so contrary to the rules of the sacrosanct diplomacy. He warned Vergennes: 'the subject I am going to discuss is more sensitive [...] I have to point out that Lord Shelburne's opinion on this issue is not entirely fixed' ['le sujet auquel je vais parler est plus délicat [...] je dois faire observer que les opinions du Lord Shelburne sur cette matière ne sont peut-être pas entièrement arrêtées']. This remark shows that Morellet quoted accurately his friend's words, even when he did not agree with him.

[26] The 'current administration' was the Portland ministry formed on the basis of the Fox–North coalition.

[27] A.E., M.D., Angleterre, 6, fols 198v–199r.

Nobody knew this obstacle as well as Mylord Shelburne, but he was determined to overcome it thanks to two powerful means: firmness and skill. I have already talked of the former by mentioning his projects for a better police force and for the authority granted to the king by the Constitution. [...] This system would have exempted the ministry from having to be popular at the expense of the nation's good. While repressing the people's first violence, he would have had enough time to convince them of where their true interests lay. It is obvious that rage, or let's say, the need to be popular have been one of the principles of unwise steps and errors on the administration's part for a long time.

[Personne n'a mieux connu cet obstacle que Mylord Shelburne, mais il était résolu d'employer à le vaincre deux puissants moyens : la fermeté et l'adresse. J'ai déjà parlé du premier en indiquant ses vues pour l'établissement d'une meilleure police et de la partie d'autorité que la Constitution donne au roi [...] Ce système aurait dispensé le ministère d'être populaire au préjudice du bien de la nation. Il eût eu le temps de faire entendre au peuple ses véritables intérêts en réprimant sa première violence, et il est visible que la rage ou, si l'on veut, le besoin d'être populaire sont depuis longtemps en Angleterre un des principes des fausses démarches et des erreurs de l'administration.][28]

Shelburne adopted Chatham's anti-oligarchic programme based on the principle of double support to the king and the country. Morellet points out that his friend 'had agreed to be minister' ['voulait bien être [...] ministre'] of George III, but that 'he also wanted to be the minister of the nation' ['voulait en même temps être celui de la nation'].[29] This seems to be in keeping with the purest Chathamite doctrine. Yet appearances can be deceptive, since for Shelburne, the expression 'minister of the nation' is the opposite of his former leader's conception. As Morellet wrote, Shelburne rather haughtily rejected popularity acquired 'at the expense of the nation's good' ['au préjudice du bien de la nation']. He denounced the 'rage' [rage] and 'the need to be popular' ['besoin d'être populaire']. The end of the report is even more explicit. Morellet reports that Shelburne does not hesitate to criticize Chatham, described as a 'glib tongue' ['beau parleur'].[30]

If the disciple distanced himself from his mentor, it was mainly because, contrary to Chatham, Shelburne was never popular. Well-known from the start of his political career for his hypocrisy, Shelburne was still regarded with suspicion in 1782–3. Quoting public opinion, an agent from the

---

[28] Ibid., fol. 199v.

[29] Ibid., fols 192v–193r.

[30] Ibid., fol. 209v: Shelburne criticizes the 'glib tongues who are absolutely incapable to take a decision on a question on which they will talk wonderfully all day long' ['les beaux parleurs absolument incapables de prendre un bon parti sur une affaire dont ils parleront admirablement tout un jour']. Three politicians known for their supreme talent in the art of eloquence are depicted by Shelburne as 'glib tongues': Charles James Fox, Edmund Burke, and Chatham.

French ministry described him as a 'combination of apparent candour and real duplicity' ['un composé de candeur apparente et de réelle duplicité'].[31]

If Shelburne wanted to be the minister of the nation, he was by no means blind to the difficulties awaiting him. Given his notoriety, both his personality and his actions would arouse suspicion and would even trigger resistance in the country. In addition to this first handicap, Morellet pointed out an aggravating circumstance: Shelburne lived in a country in which 'the mob can peacefully tear down the house of a Lord or a commoner who has fought popular opinion' ['la populace peut démolir paisiblement la maison d'un Lord ou d'un commoner qui a combattu une opinion populaire'].[32] The recent example of the Gordon Riots was a vivid reminder for all the politicians of the time. Eventually, the reaction of Parliament was likely to be hostile to the Minister's reformist programme.

Morellet is definite about the fact that Shelburne wanted to answer these dangers by 'firmness' ['la fermeté']. First, firmness towards the people was needed, with the establishment in London and in the big cities of the kingdom of a police force in charge of efficiently controlling popular feeling.[33] Second, would come firmness towards the members of Parliament, with a drastic reduction of the House of Commons' prerogatives. According to Morellet, Shelburne thought that the efficiency of the institutions had been progressively corrupted by an abnormal growth of the powers of the House of Commons which had 'against the spirit of the constitution, the scrutiny of actions which were not its responsibility, such as appointments to places, war operations, peace conditions, etc, which are essential rights of the royal prerogative' ['contre l'esprit de la Constitution, la connaissance d'objets qui ne lui appartenaient pas, tels que la nomination aux emplois, les plans des opérations de guerre, les conditions de la paix, etc, qui sont autant de droits essentiels de la prérogative royale'].[34] The Minister's project followed on from this comment:

> In Mylord Shelburne's plan, the House of Commons would have been reduced to its true rights by recovering all the prerogatives granted by the Constitution. It would have dealt with finances alone, which is fair since it represents the nation which provides money. Lord Shelburne did not want anything to limit the House's power on this point, nor anything to be hidden. But he also did not want it to acquire any additional prerogative. All the doors to the Treasury had to be opened for it at all times while all the others had to be closed. This plan was, as we can see, in favour of the king's authority, yet without increasing it further than what it should be in the spirit of the constitution.

---

[31] A.E., C.P., Angleterre, 537, fol. 357v, Lerchenberg to Vergennes, London, 23 July 1782.

[32] A.E., M.D., Angleterre, 6, fol. 193v.

[33] Ibid., fols 193v–195v.

[34] Ibid., fols 191v–192r.

[Dans le plan de Mylord Shelburne, la Chambre des Communes aurait été réduite à ses véritables droits, en recouvrant tous ceux que lui attribue la Constitution. Elle aurait eu seule dans ses mains toute l'affaire de la finance, ce qui est juste puisqu'elle représente seule la nation qui fournit l'argent. Lord Shelburne ne voulait pas que, sur ce point, rien bornât le pouvoir de la Chambre, ni, surtout, que rien lui fût caché. Mais il ne voulait pas qu'elle pût faire un pas par delà. Toutes les portes de la trésorerie devaient sans cesse lui être ouvertes en même temps que celle des autres bureaux qui lui seraient fermées. Ce plan était, comme on voit, très favorable à l'autorité du roi, sans l'accroître pourtant au-delà de ce qu'elle doit être dans l'esprit de la Constitution.][35]

It should be kept in mind that the French *philosophe* was an expert in the British political system. He was thus fully aware of the revolutionary – taken in its primary meaning – dimension of his friend's comments. By depriving the House of Commons of most of its prerogatives that it had gradually acquired for a century, Lord Shelburne's project logically led to questioning the legacy of 1689. Some anecdotes about Shelburne's ministry seem to confirm Morellet's report. In December 1782, when the opposition in the House of Lords urged Lord Shelburne to give details on the peace talks, he fiercely defended the royal prerogative in the diplomatic sphere.[36] We have already alluded to Shelburne's authoritarianism when he was at the head of affairs. His cavalier manner of treating his colleagues, and the fact that he was anxious to deal with matters assigned to departments beyond his responsibility, show his undeniable propensity to authoritarianism. Even if Shelburne is unlikely to have managed to carry out a project so clearly opposed to the institutional evolution of his country, it is still the case that his intention of balancing the political system in favour of the executive was perfectly logical. Determined to apply a consistent programme of measures when he came to power, Shelburne considered the various spheres of action to be interdependent. The First Lord of the Treasury was the conductor leading his musicians through a piece he would have composed beforehand. For his policy to be a success, this conductor also had to obtain the support of the nation as well as the political world's recognition. And this was precisely the issue. The unpopularity of the man who was nicknamed 'the Jesuit of Berkeley Square' would not allow him to become the new Pitt the Elder, that is to say a 'Minister of the people' whose main strength would lie in the support of the nation at large. In the Commons, the tiny

---

[35] Ibid., fol. 192r.
[36] Fitzmaurice, *Shelburne*, 1875–6, III, 310: 'The great advantage of Monarchy in the English Constitution was that it trusted to the Crown the secrets which must necessarily attend all negotiations with foreign powers [...] while the Crown did remain a part of our Constitution, and those negotiations were trusted to the prerogative, he could have no conception of their calling for the secrets of any negotiation which the King might be carrying on for the purpose of peace.'

group of Shelburnites was by no means in a position to tip the scale in his favour. Despising the means of corruption that he was fighting by carrying on the economical measures initiated by the Rockingham administration, Shelburne had no other solution than increasing the executive power at the expense of the legislative body.

This project raises one last question: had the Prime Minister worked out this plan as soon as he came to power or had he developed it after having thought about the causes of his failure? At first sight the second assumption seems the most likely. In the prerogatives of the House of Commons that Shelburne considered as excessive, the 'peace conditions' were one of the most important. These words seem to echo back the parliamentary rebuff of February 1783. Convinced that an innovating policy had hardly any chance of meeting the support of the political world, Shelburne would have, from then on, intensified the authoritarian aspect of his programme. However, his public statements on the royal prerogative and his project of a police force could imply that he planned, when he took office, to show more firmness towards the people and Parliament. Shelburne wanted to succeed in establishing as soon as possible a police force based on the French model. He approached some of the French living in London to ask for their help.[37] Intending to create a police force was a nearly as risky as the project involving the House of Commons, as such an institution represented, for Britons, the embodiment of the most despicable despotism.[38]

Shelburne intended to impose reforms he believed to be good for his country, but which, unfortunately, were not popular at all. As he was aware that formidable obstacles blocked his way, he had come to look at British institutions suspiciously. Due to the excessive freedom they offered to the people and the excessive power they gave to the Commons, these institu-

---

[37] Shelburne asked the French adventurer Charles Théveneau de Morande, whose pamphlets had challenged Louis XV's authority, to conceive a plan for the police in the English capital. On this collaboration, see Louis Pierre Manuel, *La Police de Paris dévoilée* (Paris, 1790), I, 244. After Shelburne's resignation, Pitt the Younger took an interest in Morande's project. The French ambassador told Vergennes about 'Mr Pitt's desire to be shown the book on the Police which he had heard was highly praised' ['le désir de M. Pitt, qui m'a fait prier de lui faire connoitre un ouvrage sur la Police dont il avoit entendu dire du bien'] (A.E., C.P., Angleterre, 542, fols 33v–34r, Moustier to Vergennes, London, 15 April 1783). Shelburne is seen here more than ever as someone who does not share a lot with his colleagues. It seems that it was only after Shelburne's downfall that Pitt has been informed of Morande's plan.

[38] In the beginning of the nineteenth century, a lot of Britons were, more than ever, opposed to the creation of a police force. As was the case in the eighteenth century, the comparison was made with France, now under Napoleonic rule. In 1812, the Earl of Dudley wrote: 'I had rather half a dozen people's throats should be cut in Radcliffe Highway every three or four years than be subject to domiciliary visits, spies, and all the rest of Fouché's contrivances' (quoted in Clive Emsley, *The English Police. A Political and Social History* [London, 1996], 22).

tions were preventing the fundamental reforms needed by his compatriots. For Shelburne, a modern constitution was a constitution in which the weight of the executive power had to be reinforced.

Ideological Dimension: Shelburnism and Toryism

In 1845, in his novel, *Sybil, or the Two Nations*, Benjamin Disraeli described in glowing terms 'one of the suppressed characters of English history [...] brave and firm' who possessed 'unrivalled knowledge and dexterity'.[39] Disraeli, who was then in favour of the conservatism tinged with social reforms of the Young England movement, had found a tutelary figure: Shelburne, whose action, after Bolingbroke's, which he also praised, had been a important moment in the history of Toryism:

> Lord Shelburne adopted from the first the Bolingbroke system; a real royalty, in lieu of the chief magistracy; a permanent alliance with France, instead of the Whig scheme of viewing in that power the natural enemy of England, and, above all, a plan of commercial freedom, the germ of which may be found in the long-maligned negotiations of Utrecht, but which in the instance of Lord Shelburne were soon in time matured by all the economical science of Europe, in which he was proficient.[40]

It is striking to note how this brief description of Shelburne's achievements at the ministry echoes back the detailed account of his administration, written sixty years before by Morellet. But can we follow Disraeli when he identifies Shelburne as one of the vital links in the evolution of Toryism? At first sight it seems difficult to rank among Tories a man who started his political career under the influence of Pitt the Elder, a politician who kept insisting on his commitment to the sources of Whiggism. Besides, Shelburne's ideological path after his ministry seems to rule out any affiliation to Toryism. During the French Revolution, Shelburne, who had then been created Marquess of Lansdowne, opposed the governmental measures against radical societies and established an alliance with the leader of the Whig opposition, Charles James Fox. Lansdowne ended his political career defending the same principles he had stood up for at Chatham's side. His loyalty to the principles of Whiggism thus seems unquestionable. Yet Shelburne would not be the first politician to change sides: Fox, whom we have just talked about, started his political career by standing up for Tory ideas. Second, Pitt the Elder's ideological corpus had some common points with Toryism: the role assigned to the monarch, which was the cornerstone of Chathamism since 1766, as well as the claim to speak on behalf of the nation, are close to the ideological

---

[39] Benjamin Disraeli, *Sybil, or the Two Nations* (Leipzig, 1845), 17–19.
[40] Ibid., 17.

arsenal of the Tories. Finally, one can raise the question of the singularity of Shelburne's institutional project, which goes against the largely shared idea in the eighteenth century describing the Commons as 'the Grand Inquest of the Nation'.[41] This project can seem surprising coming from a man who possessed enlightened political views. It appears to be fundamentally retrograde, not to say reactionary. By mentioning the 'spirit of the Constitution', Shelburne went back to 1689, when royal authority was still exclusively master of diplomacy and of appointments to ministerial departments. Shelburne thus refers to one of the characteristics of the primitive Tory ideology: preventing any infringement of the royal prerogative by the Parliament.

Such a return to the origins is all the more puzzling as the Tory party, in 1782, seemed to have died peacefully. If, as Linda Colley pointed out, the party had kept many supporters during the first half of the eighteenth century,[42] it underwent radical transformation during the Seven Years War. Some Tories, such as William Beckford, became allies of Pitt the Elder and sometimes evolved towards radical positions which were hardly related to ideological foundations of Toryism.[43] After George III's accession to the throne, in October 1760, what remained of the Tory party was absorbed in the ruling oligarchy. At the end of the decade, the bipolar ideological landscape which prevailed at the time of Walpole had ceased to exist. New issues were at stake that divided the political nation: Wilkes and liberty, parliamentary reform, rebellion in America. The Revolution Settlement then seemed to be part of the common heritage.

Yet the political trend linked to Toryism had not totally disappeared from the ideological landscape. The case of David Hume is the most familiar. Far from denouncing the rising influence of the Crown, the philosopher bewailed the decline of the royal prerogative since 1760.[44] Oliver Goldsmith went even further. In the preface of his *History of England* (1771), he claimed he was highly in favour of the strengthening of royal authority.[45] This opinion was shared by politicians. On 25 May 1778, an incident

---

[41] Peter D.G. Thomas, *The House of Commons in the Eighteenth Century* (Oxford, 1971), 14.

[42] Linda Colley, *In Defiance of Oligarchy: The Tory Party, 1714–60* (Cambridge, 1982).

[43] Marie Peters, 'The "Monitor" on the Constitution, 1755–1755: New Light on the Ideological Origins of English Radicalism', *English Historical Review*, LXXXVI, 341 (1971), 706–27.

[44] James J. Sack, *From Jacobite to Conservative. Reaction and Orthodoxy in Britain, c. 1760–1832* (Cambridge, 1993), 122.

[45] 'It is not yet decided in politics, whether the diminution of kingly power in England tends to increase the happiness, or the freedom of the people. For my own part, from seeing the bad effects of the tyranny of the great in those republican states that pretend to be free, I cannot help wishing that our monarchs may still be allowed to enjoy the power of controlling the encroachments of the great at home. A king may easily be restrained from doing wrong, as he is but one man; but if a number of the great are permitted to divide all authority, who can punish them if they abuse it? Upon this principle, therefore,

attracted a lot of attention in the House of Commons. The treasurer of the Navy, Welbore Ellis, transfixed the audience by starting an analysis of the Constitution which seemed to come straight from a Tory pamphlet published during the Exclusion Crisis: 'He did not think the House of Commons an assembly calculated for the discussion of state affairs; it was the business of Parliament to raise supplies, not debate on the measures of government. The one was the proper object of legislation, the other of executive power.'[46] This declaration, which, verbally, erased a century of institutional mutations, unleashed a storm of protests.

Morellet's memoir seems to suggest that Shelburne belonged to this political trend. The politician at the beginning of his career was close to Lord Bute, who, as George III's favourite, intended to restore royal authority.[47] It is interesting to note that the beginning of the respective careers of Welbore Ellis and Shelburne offer a striking similarity. Both men turned to Lord Bute at the accession of George III.[48] Admittedly, in 1763, Shelburne broke away from this background by becoming Pitt the Elder's political ally. But his volte-face did not appear to be sincere, hence the not very flattering nickname of 'the Jesuit of Berkeley Square'.[49] Besides, his alliance with Pitt did not necessarily imply a renunciation of his former convictions. Pitt's project of governing by uniting the parties was likely to win over the politicians who kept an inclination for Toryism.

and not from any empty notion of divine or hereditary right, some may think I have leaned towards monarchy', Oliver Goldsmith, preface of the *History of England* (1771) in *Collected Works of Oliver Goldsmith*, ed. Arthur Friedman (Oxford, 1966), V, 339–40.

[46] Quoted in Thomas, *The House of Commons*, 15.

[47] According to John Brooke, Lord Bute's ideas were very close to the Whig orthodoxy (*King George III* [London, 1972], 55–9). In his recent biography of George III, Jeremy Black insists on the influence of Bolingbroke's idea of a patriot king on Bute's programme: *George III. America's Last King* (New Haven, CT and London, 2006), 10–14. Bute's project of restoring the royal prerogative was by no means the sign of despotic thoughts. This restoration, nevertheless, erased a century of institutional transformations which was an important part of the Whig patrimony.

[48] Sir Lewis Namier and John Brooke, ed., *The History of Parliament. The House of Commons 1754–1790* (London, 1964), II, 397–400.

[49] In October 1765 Bute sold to Shelburne his unfinished mansion of Berkeley Square (Peter D. Brown, 'Bute in Retirement', in *Lord Bute. Essays in Re-interpretation*, ed. Karl W. Schweizer [Leicester, 1988], 249). As we see, the presence of Shelburne's House in the infamous nickname is not fortuitous. Its function is to remind the public that Shelburne, after having concluded a political alliance with Pitt, remained in excellent terms with Bute, which was the most obvious proof of his Jesuitical character!

Shelburne's Ideas in European Context

According to Morellet's own summary:

It is a very wrong and, alas, still a very common idea that the strength of a good police force in big States and, most of all, in big cities, proves to be contrary to the liberty of the citizen. Civil liberty consists in two things: to be able to do everything that is not offensive to a third person and to be protected from any offense from a third person. This liberty of action and this assurance of being protected from offenses constitute the liberty of the citizen. [...]

Although these notions are somewhat theoretical, the truths they convey are sensible. It is clear, for example, that in countries where we cannot travel without being soon victim of robbery, where the mob can peacefully tear down the house of a Lord or a commoner who has fought a popular opinion, that in such a country, I say, liberty is not as great as it ought to be. Yet, some persons who pretend to be in favour of English liberty assert that these views are necessary inconveniences of the constitution, as they belong to the national liberty, that they cannot be corrected without being detrimental to this liberty, and if they do not believe in this paradox, at least they assert it to become popular and to give more strength to the party they have joined.

We must thank a minister for having challenged such prejudices in order to reform such horrible abuses, and that was the task that Mylord Shelburne undertook.

[C'est une idée bien fausse et malheureusement encore bien commune que la vigueur d'une bonne police dans un grand Etat et surtout dans les grandes villes est contraire à la liberté du citoyen. La liberté civile consiste en deux choses : pouvoir faire tout ce qui ne nuit pas à un tiers et être à l'abri de la part d'un tiers de tout ce qui peut nuire. C'est de cette liberté d'agir soi-même et de cette assurance de n'être pas exposé à une action nuisible de la part d'un autre que se compose la liberté du citoyen. [...]

Quoique ces notions soient un peu abstraites, les vérités qu'elles présentent sont sensibles. Il est clair, par exemple, que dans un pays où l'on ne peut voyager sans avoir la bourse du voleur toute prête, où la populace peut démolir paisiblement la maison d'un Lord ou d'un commoner qui a combattu dans le parlement une opinion populaire, que dans un pareil pays, dis-je, la liberté n'est pas aussi grande qu'elle devroit l'être. Cependant, de prétendus partisans de la liberté angloise soutiennent que ces vues sont des inconvéniens nécessaires de la constitution, puisqu'ils font partie de la liberté nationale, qu'on ne peut les corriger sans donner atteinte à cette liberté, et qu'ils ne croient pas de bonne foi à ce paradoxe, au moins le soutiennent-ils pour être populaires et pour donner de la force au parti qu'ils ont épousé.

On doit savoir gré sans doute à un ministre d'avoir bravé ces préjugés pour réformer de si horribles abus, et c'est l'ouvrage qu'avoit commencé Mylord Shelburne.][50]

---

[50] A.E., M.D., Angleterre, 6, fols 193v–194r.

Morellet's report gives us interesting insights on the reception of the British political model in eighteenth-century France. Far from being Britain's institutional future, the limited monarchy depicted in the document has become an old-fashioned form of government belonging to the most appalling gothic times. Morellet did not adhere to the liberal interpretation of the English constitution popularized by Montesquieu. He deplored the 'abuses' ['abus'] of the English political system and he denounced the 'prejudices' ['préjugés'] of the political nation. In a certain way, Morellet looked at the 'necessary inconveniences of the constitution' ['inconvéniens nécessaires de la constitution'] of Great Britain with the eyes of a French *Contrôleur général des Finances*, frightened by the hotchpotch of old *libertés* and *privilèges* hindering the good management of state affairs.

As Derek Jarrett has brilliantly shown, comparative history helps us to understand the wave of reformism of the later decades of the eighteenth century.[51] If we put the Shelburne ministerial experience in the European political context of the 1770s and 1780s, it not only loses its insularity, but it becomes much less bizarre. Many historians have pointed out the fact that Shelburne was not made to become a British statesman: 'He might have made a great Minister of an enlightened despot, a Pombal, a Turgot, a Floridablanca', remarked John Ehrman, suggesting that Shelburne was born on the wrong side of the Channel. He had the misfortune to live in the country which was maybe the most alien (politically speaking) to his character and to his ideas.[52] And, indeed, his ministerial behaviour had undeniable common points with the work of the enlightened reformers of the continent.

If we stop considering the eighteenth century with teleological spectacles focused on the irresistible march towards liberty, parliamentarism, and democracy, we uncover the era's second face. If, as the Necker experience shows, a liberal policy was sometimes undertaken in continental Europe, the dominant feature of the 1770s and the 1780s was nevertheless the strengthening of central authority dedicated to fundamental reforms. In France, the two decades before the Revolution saw three notable attempts to increase the powers of the monarch: in 1771, when the Maupeou revolution crushed the opposition of the *Parlements* and gave Louis XV and his ministers a freedom of action totally new in the annals of the French monarchy; in 1781, after the dismissal of Necker, when Vergennes tried to restore the foundations of absolute monarchy; and lastly, in 1788, when the Brienne–Lamoignon ministry launched a vigorous attack against the *Parlements* in order to implement important administrative and financial reforms.[53]

---

[51] Derek Jarrett, *The Begetters of Revolution. England's Involvement with France, 1759–1789* (London, 1973).

[52] John Ehrman, *The Younger Pitt, I, The Years of Acclaim* (London, 1969), 86.

[53] Jean Egret, *Louis XV et l'opposition parlementaire, 1715–1774* (Paris, 1970); Munro

Outside France, we notice the same will to curb or to suppress any form of resistance to enlightened reforms. In 1772, by restoring the powers of the king of Sweden, Gustavus III's coup put a stop to that nightmarish version of the British political system, the so-called 'Age of Liberty' (1718–72), marked by the supremacy of the Swedish representative body, the Riksdag, the reign of corruption and the impotence of the executive.[54] In the Austrian Habsburg monarchy after Maria Theresa's death in 1780, Emperor Joseph II launched a highly ambitious reformist policy. The success of his economical, social, religious, and administrative measures was closely linked to the strengthening of his authority. As was the case in France during the Maupeou revolution, and in Sweden after Gustavus III's coup, Joseph II tried to diminish the powers of the institutions standing in the way of his enlightened policy (the Diets in Central Europe, the Provincial Estates and the States-General in the Low Countries).[55] In Poland, after the shock of the first partition in 1772, King Stanislas Augustus Poniatowski implemented an important programme of reform in the sphere of education with the help of the enlightened nobility, and, at the same time, tried to extricate himself from the miserable state of Merovingian kingship in which the monarchy of Poland had fallen since the end of the seventeenth century. His aim was not to become an absolute king. More modestly, Stanislas would have contented himself with the powers of a limited monarch similar to those of the king of Great Britain.[56] Shelburne himself had long been in contact with the Poniatowski family and their relatives among the Czaytoryski family, some of whom had visited Bowood in 1768, and Shelburne sent his son John (the future 2nd Marquess) to Poland to visit in 1786. For his part, King Stanislas admired Shelburne for his cosmopolitan outlook.[57]

In Versailles, Stockholm, Vienna, Warsaw, and in London during Shelburne's ministry, the ambitious aims of enlightened reformism seemed to call for the increase of executive power. Lord Shelburne's brief ministry tried to put in practice an ideological mixed bag related to enlightened reformism, to Chathamism and to some aspects of Toryism. Far from being an aberration, the project described at length in Morellet's report was the logical outcome of Shelburne's reflections on the outlook of Chathamism. Could this political movement outlive its eponymous hero? Apparently, the answer

Price, *Preserving the Monarchy. The comte de Vergennes, 1774–1787* (Cambridge, 1995); Jean Egret, *La pré-révolution française (1787–1788)* (Paris, 1962).

[54] Michael Roberts, *The Age of Liberty: Sweden 1719–1772* (Cambridge, 1986); Claude J. Nordmann, *Gustave III. Un démocrate couronné* (Lille, 1986).

[55] Derek Beales, *Joseph II, Vol. I: In the Shadow of Maria Theresa 1741–1780* (Cambridge, 1987); *II: Against the World, 1780–1790* (Cambridge, 2009); Jean Bérenger, *Joseph II. Serviteur de l'Etat* (Paris, 2007).

[56] Jean Fabre, *Stanislas-Auguste Poniatowski et l'Europe des Lumières* (Paris, 1952); Adam Zamoyski, *The Last King of Poland* (London, 1992).

[57] Richard Butterwick, *Poland's Last King and English Culture* (Oxford, 1998).

could only be negative. It is a truism to say that the Great Commoner had embodied the Chathamite project. It was then logical that Chathamism would follow its creator in the grave. After Chatham's death, Shelburne found himself at the head of the group of politicians who wanted to continue the crusade initiated by the great man against the factions and the oligarchic nature of the regime. Surrounded by a very small group of supporters in Parliament, he could not hope to impose his views to the political world. Besides, he knew that he would never possess the national notoriety of the hero of the Seven Years War. The prospect of an appeal to the nation, one of the main features of Pitt the Elder's career,[58] seemed totally unrealistic for a politician known as the 'Jesuit of Berkeley Square'. Aware of these two political weaknesses, he was then inexorably led to build a project which would consolidate his ministerial position. The example of the enlightened reformism in Europe seemed to confirm the validity of his analysis. In the beginning of the 1780s, political modernity seemed closely linked with a strong executive power. Ultimately, Lord Shelburne's ministerial experience must be seen as an attempt to transfer the Chathamite political legacy to politicians who did not have the chance to bear the name of William Pitt. Yet Shelburne feigned to ignore William Pitt the Younger's precocious and irresistible rise to the political firmament,[59] a rise that would prove to be catastrophic for Shelburnism. This avatar of Chathamism was condemned to remain for posterity a brief interlude in the history of the two Pitts.

[58] Dziembowski, *Les Pitt*, 96–100, 128–40.
[59] Morellet's memoir is almost silent on Pitt the Younger. The Chancellor of the Exchequer in Shelburne ministry is only mentioned once, and in an evasive way, among two other Shelburnites, Ashburton and Barré (A.E., M.D., Angleterre, 6, fol. 192v).

11

Jeremy Bentham at Bowood

EMMANUELLE DE CHAMPS

Lord Shelburne (after 1785, Lord Lansdowne) has often been presented as Bentham's 'mentor',[1] or 'patron', while Derek Jarrett, with a note of irony, called the utilitarian philosopher 'another of [Lord Shelburne's] tame intellectuals'.[2] In the later part of his life, Bentham was keen to repeat a flattering comparison Shelburne had made between their relationship and that of Bacon and Buckingham.[3] These comparisons and simplifications do not do justice, however, to the relationship between Jeremy Bentham and Lord Shelburne.

By focusing on the links between Bentham and Shelburne, this chapter will clarify the meaning of the phrase 'the Bowood Circle', when used in connection with Bentham. As first used by Charles Milner Atkinson in 1905, it referred in a generic way to the people Bentham had met during his stays at Bowood, Shelburne's Wiltshire residence in the 1780s.[4] It was taken up by Jarrett in his 1955 thesis entitled 'The Bowood Circle, 1780–1793. Its Ideas and its Influence'.[5] Jarrett narrowed down the definition of that circle to Bentham, Etienne Dumont and Samuel Romilly, who were all close to Lord Lansdowne in the years 1788 to 1793. More recently, the phrase has

---

Acknowledgements: I would like to thank James H. Burns, Catherine Fuller, Catherine Pease-Watkin, and Clarissa Campbell Orr for their helpful comments at various stages of the writing of this text.

[1]   Mary Mack, *Jeremy Bentham: an Odyssey of Ideas 1748–1792* (London, 1962), 370ff.
[2]   Derek Jarrett, *The Begetters of Revolution. England's Involvement with France, 1759–1789* (London, 1973), 131.
[3]   See *The Correspondence of Jeremy Bentham, Vol. 4, 1788–1793*, ed. A.T. Milne (London, 1981), 182, and for a later reminiscence, *The Correspondence of Jeremy Bentham, Vol. 12, 1824–1828*, ed. Catherine Fuller and Luke O'Sullivan (Oxford, 2006), 432–33. Shelburne himself also presented their friendship in this light, jestingly referring to Rousseau and the Maréchal de Luxembourg; see *Correspondence of J. Bentham, Vol. 4*, 116, 242.
[4]   Charles Milner Atkinson, *Jeremy Bentham, His Life and Work* (London, 1905), 77.
[5]   Derek Jarrett, 'The Bowood Circle, 1780–1793. Its Ideas and its Influence' (Unpublished B.Litt., Oxford, 1955).

been used by scholars to refer in a broader sense to Shelburne's entourage at the time of the French Revolution, ranging from Price and Priestley to Fox and Sheridan, and also including Dumont and Romilly.[6] Leaving politicians and aristocrats such as Fox and Sheridan aside, this chapter focuses on the relationships between Lansdowne and some of his protégés during the 1780s in order to put Bentham's relationship with the aristocrat in context. It then presents Bentham's relationship with Lansdowne in more detail and explains the philosopher's ambiguous feelings towards aristocratic patronage. Lastly, it casts light on the reasons why contacts between Lansdowne and Bentham all but stopped after 1793.

Patron–Client Relationships at Bowood and Berkeley Square

Shelburne's support of numerous writers and scientists was a well-known public fact. The forms it took bear witness to the number of avenues open for patronage in eighteenth-century Britain, and must be looked at in detail in order to assess the specificity of Shelburne's relationship with Bentham. It is not possible to draw up a list of the writers and scientists patronized by Shelburne here,[7] but a few examples may illustrate the various forms it took and the subtle economy of duties and services entailed, in which the private and the political were closely intertwined. The notion of 'friendship' – a word used by patrons and dependents alike – inscribed patronage within the social codes of eighteenth-century polite society.[8] This assertion went together with claims of 'independence' on the part of the client, or protégé.[9] The notions of 'friendship' and 'independence' must, however, be set against the highly hierarchical structure of British society and the true financial dependency of many clients. First-hand experience of patronage also had

[6] For a different interpretation of the phrases 'Bowood writers' or 'the Bowood Circle' as referring to Dumont, Sheridan, Fox, Romilly, and Bentham, see Richard Whatmore, 'Etienne Dumont, the British Constitution and the French Revolution', *The Historical Journal*, 50(2007), 23–47. As R. Whatmore points out in this volume, the phrase 'the Bowood Circle' best refers to the people 'belonging to Lord Shelburne', 'without reference to a party programme'. See Chapter 12 in this volume.

[7] Shelburne has recently been described as 'the patron of what might be called the radical Enlightenment in England' by Edward G. Andrew, *Patrons of Enlightenment* (Toronto, 2006), 9. For an overview of the artists and philosophers patronized by Shelburne, see 170.

[8] On the numerous uses of 'friendship' in eighteenth-century England, see Naomi Tadmor, *Family and Friends in Eighteenth-century England: Household, Kinship, and Patronage* (Cambridge, 2001), 167–236.

[9] On the value contemporaries set to 'independence' and the implications of the word, see Matthew McCormack, *The Independent Man. Citizenship and Gender Politics in Georgian England* (Manchester, 2005), 1–11 and 104–39.

a direct impact on the ways in which the thinkers studied here understood political and social relationships at a more theoretical level.

In practice, 'patronage' had a variety of meanings. It could not mean the same thing for men of independent means or expectations, such as Richard Price and Jeremy Bentham, and for those who were directly dependent on the financial support of the aristocrat, like Joseph Priestley and Etienne Dumont. The attitudes of these intellectuals – to use an anachronistic notion for lack of a better word – towards the social subordination implied by the patron–protégé relationship show the complexity of this relation. This casts light on the range of possibilities that were open to each of them, and on the extent of their 'independence'.

Much of Priestley's hesitation before accepting Shelburne's offer of a position as a librarian and companion hinged precisely on the issue of independence. Shelburne's biographer, his descendant Edmond Fitzmaurice, describes his hesitation as 'rhetorical' and suggests it was a way to improve the financial terms on which he was hired.[10] However, Priestley's friends feared 'that the state [he] should be brought into would be too dependent and humiliating, and not leave [him] sufficiently master of [his] own conduct'.[11] In his Memoirs, Priestley insisted that Shelburne did not interfere with any of his philosophical, scientific, or political pursuits. Referring to the controversial publication of his Disquisitions Relating to Matter and Spirit in 1777 – following which he was widely branded as an atheist – he wrote that some of Shelburne's friends had tried to dissuade him from publishing the book, in order not to 'brin[g] odium on [his] patron', but he was careful to stress that Shelburne had made no such demands in person.[12] Though Priestley stressed that the disgrace into which he fell the following year was not related to Shelburne's opinion on his religious stand, the controversy probably played a part in their separation in 1780, which was widely noted in literary and polite circles.[13] Priestley's unease towards his position as a paid companion to an aristocrat can be felt in his disparaging comments on the aristocratic character, and his praise of the middling ranks of life, as embodiments of

[10] The terms of the contract were far from insignificant: Priestley received a salary of £250 per annum, lodgings, and the promise of a life-long pension should the engagement be broken off. Fitzmaurice, Shelburne, 1875–6, II, 243.

[11] Priestley to Price, 27 September 1772, in W. Bernard Peach and D.O. Thomas, ed., The Correspondence of Richard Price (Durham, NC, 1983), I, 136–7.

[12] Priestley later recalled: 'It being probable that this publication would be unpopular, and might be a means of bringing odium on my patron, several attempts were made by his friends, though none by himself, to dissuade me from persisting in it. But being, as I thought, engaged in the cause of important truth, I proceeded without regard to any consequences, assuring them that this publication should not be injurious to his lordship.' Memoirs of Dr. Joseph Priestley to the Year 1795, in Autobiography of Joseph Priestley, ed. Jack Lindsay (Bath, 1970), 114.

[13] See J. Lindsay's introduction to Autobiography of J. Priestley, 24.

moral and political independence.[14] However, in his *Memoirs*, Priestley was eager to exempt Shelburne from the flaws of other aristocrats, and to stress his exemplary moral character.[15]

In the same way, a few years later, the Genevan Etienne Dumont felt the economic and emotional dependency in which his situation placed him, as the following episode illustrates. He had been employed in 1786 to supervise the studies of Shelburne's younger sons by his second marriage. He remained lodged, and certainly paid, by Lansdowne until he was awarded a sinecure (also through Lansdowne) in 1791.[16] Even afterwards, he remained closely dependent on the aristocrat's support, as a letter to Romilly in November 1793 testifies. He recalled a long conversation with Lansdowne, and reported the latter's encouragements for the translation of Bentham he had undertaken. He wrote that Lansdowne had promised him a position if he ever came back into office, and recalled the Marquess' 'interest and benevolence' towards him. But a few hours later, probably after a discussion with Lansdowne, he picked up his pen to add a very different postscript, writing that he understood he was not welcome in the house any longer, was considered as a stranger and had been made to feel 'like a useless weight in the household'.[17] The tone of the letter reveals Dumont's sensitivity, but also the sense of purpose that Lansdowne's patronage had given him. Despite this episode, their relations remained good, and Dumont's attitude to the Lansdowne family, even after the death of the first Marquess, remained markedly deferential.

The situations of Richard Price and Jeremy Bentham were different. Price, Priestley's contemporary and close friend, was, like him, a well-known dissenting minister, but he had been made rich by marriage. He was a frequent guest of Shelburne from the 1770s until his death in 1791. There is no evidence that he received from him more than customary gifts and occasional hospitality. He self-consciously used his connection with the politician to put forward his views on the economy, and domestic and

---

[14] See for instance: 'Persons who are born to a moderate fortune, are, indeed, generally better educated, have, consequently, more enlarged minds, and are, in all respects, truly *independent*, than those who are born to a great opulence.' J. Priestley, *Essay on the First Principles of Government*, ed. Peter Miller (Cambridge, 1993), 15.

[15] Priestley stressed Shelburne's steadiness of character in opposition to the inflammatory aristocratic temper. *Autobiography of J. Priestley*, 115.

[16] Richard Whatmore, 'Etienne Dumont, the British Constitution and the French Revolution', 35n. This episode, as Jarrett has noted, was in direct opposition to Shelburne's public stance against sinecures during his ministry. See Derek Jarrett, *Three Faces of Revolution: Paris, London and New York in 1789* (London, 1989), 76 and John Norris, *Shelburne and Reform* (London, 1963), 199–215.

[17] Etienne Dumont to Samuel Romilly, 29 November 1793, Dumont MS, Bibliothèque Universitaire de Genève, box 17.

colonial policy.[18] His letters to Shelburne reveal the friendly terms on which they remained, despite occasional disagreements on the question of American independence or political reform. From 1782, during Shelburne's ministry, his letters became more frequent. Price forwarded pleas addressed through him to Shelburne, and acted as an advisor on economic matters.[19] Within the deferential framework of eighteenth-century conventions, there was space for such direct contact, though Price had no illusions about the concrete influence his more daring opinions might have on the minister's decisions. For instance, on the formation of the new ministry in 1782, he repeated to Shelburne the necessity of 'the acknowledgement of the independence of America' and that 'something should by all means be done to purify the fountain of legislation among us, and to reform the representation of the kingdom'. He then apologized in these words: 'On reviewing [this letter] I feel pain lest I should be thought to act impertinently, but the attention and friendship by which your Lordship has always done me great honour encourages me to resolve to send it.'[20] He was aware of limitation of his 'influence' and did not conceal it to his hopeful radical friends. Despite his advocacy of true republican independence of character, he cultivated his friendship with the aristocrat and self-consciously made use of their friendship for political purposes.

Common dependency, varied as it might be, on Lord Shelburne did not necessarily imply close personal links or political agreement between these thinkers. Priestley and Price had been acquainted long before Price recommended him to Shelburne. Dumont and Bentham met in February 1788 at Lansdowne's, and though their friendship was first very much linked to the Marquess, it soon took on its own pace, culminating in Dumont's editorship of Bentham's manuscripts. Chronologically, Bentham's relationship with Shelburne did not allow him to develop close personal contacts with Priestley or Price. Priestley had left Shelburne's employment in 1780 and never met Bentham through him (though they corresponded on scientific issues in the 1770s). By the start of the French Revolution, Price – though still close to Lansdowne – was a respected patriarch, and though he and Bentham did meet twice at Lansdowne House, there is no further evidence for their connection during that period.

---

[18] See D.O. Thomas, *The Honest Mind. The Thought and Work of Richard Price* (Oxford, 1977), 145–8.

[19] For letters to Shelburne during his ministry, see *The Correspondence of Richard Price*, II, 115–83.

[20] *The Correspondence of Richard Price*, II, 117. Except in economic matters, where he was confident his views could be adopted, he represented to his correspondents the uncertainty that Shelburne would respond favourably to their demands. See letter his letter to Cartwright, ibid., I, 245.

Bentham and Shelburne: The Ambiguities of Patronage

These selected examples cast an indirect light on the relationship between Bentham and Shelburne, which has so far been mostly documented by Bentham's own testimonies. Towards the end of his life, the philosopher wrote about the relationship three times: first in a draft preface to the second edition of the *Fragment on Government*, written in 1822;[21] second in a letter written in 1828 containing a 'History of the intercourse, of Jeremy Bentham with the Lansdowne family: addressed by himself to the [third] Marquess of Lansdowne',[22] and lastly in the recollections published by John Bowring as the 'Memoirs of J. Bentham' in the last volume of the *Complete Works*.[23] Their friendship from 1788 to 1792 is confirmed by Lansdowne's letters to Morellet,[24] but otherwise the sources are mostly from Bentham's side.

The philosopher recalled that Shelburne knocked at his door at Lincoln's Inn in the summer of 1781, having discovered that he was the author of the *Fragment on Government* which had been published anonymously in 1776, an anecdote taken up by Shelburne's biographer, but disproved by subsequent research.[25] The conditions in which they met must be clarified. They reveal much about the philosopher's and the politician's mutual expectations. In his later years, Bentham recalled that Shelburne had 'raised [him] from the bottomless pit of humiliation' and 'made [him] feel [he] was something'.[26] Scholars have stressed the philosopher's search for recognition in the 1770s.[27] During that decade Bentham self-consciously tried to find a place for himself in the 'Republic of letters' at a time when the '*métier d'homme de*

---

[21] Jeremy Bentham, 'Preface Intended for the Second Edition of the *Fragment on Government*', *A Comment on the Commentaries and A Fragment on Government*, ed. J.H. Burns and H.L.A. Hart (London, 1977), 502–51.

[22] *The Correspondence of J. Bentham*, Vol. 12, 436–43.

[23] *The Works of Jeremy Bentham*, ed. John Bowring, 11 vols (Edinburgh, 1843), X, 88–123. The chronology of events is faulty, and the correspondence provides a much more reliable source.

[24] '[Y]ou already know the high Esteem I have for Mr. Bentham and the affection which our whole Family, Men women and Children bear him.' *Lettres d'André Morellet*, ed. Dorothy Medlin, Jean-Claude David, and Paul Leclerc (Oxford, 1991–6), II, 125. For other testimonies, see letters between Jeremiah Bentham and Lord Shelburne, BL Add Mss, 33540, f. 256, 303, 306; 33541, f. 85–6, 286, 289.

[25] Bentham's account is to be found in his reminiscences to J. Bowring in *Works of J. Bentham*, X, 88. See also Fitzmaurice, *Shelburne*, 1875, III, 449. Fitzmaurice also erroneously claimed that 'Bentham became an almost constant inmate of Bowood' from July 1780 (III, 449) and that the *Theory of Morals and Legislation* [presumably the *Introduction to the Principles of Morals and Legislation*] was written there. For a refutation of these assertions see Elie Halévy, *La formation du radicalisme philosophique* [1904] (Paris, 1995), I, 275n.

[26] *Works of J. Bentham*, X, 115.

[27] Mack, *Odyssey of Ideas*, 335ff. See also *Works of J. Bentham*, X, 78, 84.

lettres' became structured around intellectual and social pursuits.[28] Bentham used most of the existing channels available to a hopeful philosopher willing to contribute to public debate at home and abroad: he tried to enter into correspondence with leading French *philosophes* of the time and thought of submitting an essay for an international competition on penal law organized by the Berne Academy.[29] In a pattern he pursued throughout his life, he worked simultaneously on a large-scale plan of legal reform and on more topical issues, hoping to trigger political change.

Unlike the grim picture of that decade given in the later *Memoirs*, in which Bentham described to John Bowring his dejection at the lack of recognition he experienced, his correspondence of the late 1770s reveals his enthusiasm for forming new connections and securing introductions. He hoped to make a name in public life by his publications, but he also tried more personal channels to recognition by sending his works to selected influential writers and politicians. Bentham's eagerness is not to be explained only in psychological terms, but as the search for status in the complex social networks of the Enlightenment. Together with the esteem of established philosophers, the tribute of the aristocracy was an indispensable requirement for a literary career. In France, the salons offered a space for public recognition and opened up various means of financial support on the part of the aristocracy.[30] In England, aristocratic patronage took different forms, as we have seen, but was a central feature of intellectual life.[31]

The Bentham family was of independent means. Jeremy received an education which was typical of the aspiring urban bourgeoisie, attending Westminster School and Oxford University – following in the footsteps of many young aristocrats, including Shelburne himself. As an elder son, he had significant financial expectations, but they were not realized until his father's death in 1792. He studied law at Lincoln's Inn, but after his refusal to take cases, his father was reluctant to provide him with more than a basic allowance, which put him in what he much later described 'a state of penury', while he 'kept up the appearance of a gentleman'.[32] To supplement

---

[28] Michel Delon, 'Les secondes Lumières en France', in W. Schneiders, *The Enlightenment in Europe. Unity and Diversity* (Berlin, 2003), 13–19.

[29] For this period of Bentham's life and his contacts with the French Enlightenment, see J.H. Burns, 'Bentham, Brissot et la science du bonheur', and S. Audidière, 'La correspondance sans suite de Bentham et Chastellux: la thèse de la félicité publique, du "revenu net" au calcul "félicitaire"', in *Bentham et la France*, ed. E. de Champs and J.-P. Cléro, Studies on Voltaire and the Enlightenment (Oxford, 2009), 3–19 and 21–34.

[30] Antoine Lilti, *Le monde des salons. Sociabilité et mondanité à Paris au XVIIIe siècle* (Paris, 2005), esp. 168–216.

[31] Edward Andrew, 'The Senecan Moment: Patronage and Philosophy in the Eighteenth Century', *Journal of the History of Ideas*, 65 (2004), 277–99.

[32] *Correspondence of J. Bentham, Vol. 12*, 436. He received about £100 a year throughout the 1770s, which was insufficient to cover his London expenses; see John R. Dinwiddy, *Bentham* (Oxford, 1989), 4.

his income, he chose a path open to many of the Enlightenment literati, that of translation.[33]

Bentham's approach to Lord Shelburne must be understood in this broader social context. In 1778, he made several attempts to be noticed by influential politicians or aristocrats. He volunteered to replace Adam Ferguson, the Scottish moralist, as a companion to Governor Johnstone – then a Commissioner to the American Congress – 'for the sake of company and advice'.[34] In the same year, he approached the 4th Earl of Sandwich, first Lord of the Admiralty, with intelligence from his brother, Samuel, a naval engineer.[35] Early in 1779, Samuel suggested asking Shelburne for introductions.[36] Though Bentham's interest in Lord Shelburne as a patron of the arts and sciences and a powerful politician can be easily explained,[37] it remains surprising from a political point of view. Since 1773, Bentham had been close to John Lind, one of Lord North's protégés, whereas Shelburne had been one of the leaders of the Opposition throughout his ministry. However, Shelburne was not a party-man and Bentham consistently rejected all political allegiance, which might have made it easier to make contact with him.

Due to his father's wealth, Bentham's position towards Shelburne did not hinge predominantly on financial issues. Before they met, the philosopher self-consciously intended to set the terms upon which he would be introduced. Being solicited by the Bentham brothers, Shelburne had asked Samuel to call at Shelburne House in May 1779, an invitation which was declined, and then repeated to Jeremy in July 1780 – and also declined.[38] Explaining to Samuel why he had refused Shelburne's invitations twice, Bentham explained that they should 'meet upon a much better footing in November than now', hoping that by then Shelburne would have read the book which he was to publish as *An Introduction to the Principles of Morals and Legislation*. He also remarked: 'I did not want him to fancy that his acquaintance was a thing I [was] disposed to jump at.'[39] In April 1781, Bentham offered Shelburne a series of tracts,[40] which could be the reason why the politician visited him in Lincoln's Inn in June or early July 1781.

---

[33] *Correspondence of J. Bentham*, Vol. 2, 185. He translated Voltaire's *Le taureau blanc* and embarked on a translation of Marmontel's *Les Incas* which seems to have remained unpublished. Ibid., 370.

[34] *Correspondence of J. Bentham*, Vol. 2, 94, 104.

[35] *Correspondence of J. Bentham*, Vol. 2, 259–63.

[36] 'The scheme of Ld. Shelburne delights me of all things. [. . .] It is possible that by Blanquet's means you might get mention made of the Fragment and the H. Lab. Bill to Ld. Shelburne.' *Correspondence of J. Bentham*, Vol. 2, 221–3.

[37] In March 1779, Bentham introduced Ingenhousz to his brother Samuel in these words: 'He is on good terms with Banks, Priestl[e]y, Ld. Shelburne, etc. in short all the literati and amateurs.' *Correspondence of J. Bentham*, Vol. 2, 246.

[38] *Correspondence of J. Bentham*, Vol. 2, 257–8, 470.

[39] *Correspondence of J. Bentham*, Vol. 2, 471

[40] *Correspondence of J. Bentham*, Vol. 3, 16–17.

Shelburne immediately invited him to spend some time at Bowood, where the philosopher stayed in the late summer of that year.

Bentham had high hopes that Shelburne would launch his career as a legal reformer. In a manuscript fragment, probably written during, or shortly after his first stay at Bowood, he parodied the style of the Book of Revelation, and dreamt he was 'the founder [. . .] of the sect of the *utilitarians*'. He then described how an angel 'flew at [his] window' and gave him a book entitled 'Principles of Legislation'. 'One day as I was musing over this book there came unto me a great man named L[d S.] ... and he said unto me what shall I do to [. . .] save the nation? I said unto him – take up my book, & follow me.' In the remaining part of the dream, they meet 'a man named George', whom they cure by making him swallow a page of the book by force, and a woman called Britannia, who is brought to life again in the same way.[41]

The French Revolution

Bentham and Shelburne had remained in touch when Bentham departed for Russia to visit his brother, who was in Prince Potemkin's service, in August 1785. On his return in February 1788, Bentham was a frequent guest at Lansdowne House in London. The early years of the French Revolution were those during which Bentham and Lansdowne were the closest. Through him, Bentham met Samuel Romilly and Etienne Dumont, who were to become close friends.[42] In the summer of 1789, Bentham was one of the few people external to the family allowed in Lady Lansdowne's room during her illness. His second extensive stay at Bowood took place from late August to the end of October 1789. After Lady Lansdowne's death, he accompanied her former companions, Miss Fox and Miss Vernon, with Lord Lansdowne, on a tour to Warwick. Throughout 1790, he was a frequent guest of Lansdowne House and, though he led a solitary life in his Hendon house, he maintained an extensive correspondence with the family, but also with Dumont, Romilly and – to a lesser extent Benjamin Vaughan.

In those years, sociability was reinforced by heightened political and intellectual links between Lansdowne, Romilly, Bentham, and Dumont. Bentham's enthusiasm for the early days of the French revolution closely followed Lansdowne's optimistic stance towards French affairs. Though many people in his circle – including many of his aristocratic French

---

[41] For a full transcript of the 'dream', see James E. Crimmins, *Secular Utilitarianism. Social Science and the Critique of Religion in the Thought of Jeremy Bentham* (Oxford, 1990), 314.

[42] For a detailed account of how Bentham and Dumont met, see Charles Blount, 'Bentham, Dumont and Mirabeau, an Historical Revision', *University of Birmingham Historical Journal*, 3 (1952), 53–167.

correspondents – watched the state of the country with growing dismay, Lansdowne himself encouraged his son Lord Wycombe, as well as Dumont and Romilly, to travel to France and take an active part in the unfolding events. This atmosphere accounts for Bentham's attempts to contribute to intellectual debate in France: from the autumn of 1788, he drafted several pamphlets in French, which were corrected by Dumont, marking the start of a fruitful intellectual collaboration.[43] Through Lansdowne, Bentham had access to numerous sources on French institutions, history, and current affairs. Lansdowne's contacts in France opened up new channels for his writings to be sent to France, such as Morellet, and – via Dumont – Mirabeau.[44]

That Lansdowne himself was informed of Bentham's work during that period, and that he encouraged him, is beyond doubt. In January 1789, answering a request from the philosopher to use his library, he wrote:

> My Dear Bentham,
> As long as you honour me with your Friendship, you may treat the House to which I belong with every Freedom you think proper. [. . .] I am very glad to hear that you intend taking up the cause of the people in France. Nothing can contribute so much to general Humanity and Civilization, as for the Individuals of one country to be interested for the prosperity of another; I have long thought that the people have but one cause throughout the World.[45]

In retrospect, however, Bentham might have had a tendency to romanticize Landowne's personal role in his activities at the time. In an account written in 1831, the philosopher recalled the circumstances in which his *Draught of a Plan for the Judicial Establishment in France* was composed. The similarity of this episode to the 'dream' written down fifty years before is striking and should warn us against taking it as a trustworthy description of the collaboration between Lansdowne and Bentham in those years:

> To the whole impression the last hand was put in the attic of Lansdowne House, in which residence & in that part of it I had taken up my abode for the facility of communication with my friend & subsequent translator & Editor Etienne

---

[43] Dumont went on to edit in French a significant part of Bentham's manuscripts: *Traités de législation civile et pénale* (Geneva, 1802), *Théorie des peines et des récompenses* (London, 1811), *Tactique des Assemblées législatives* (Geneva, 1816), *Traité des preuves judiciaires* (Paris, 1823), *De l'organisation judiciaire et de la codification* (Paris, 1828).

[44] *Lettres d'André Morellet*, 125. On the practical impetus provided by Lansdowne, see *Correspondence of J. Bentham*, Vol. 3, 621.

[45] *The Correspondence of J. Bentham*, Vol. 4, 21. More generally, on Bentham's involvement with Lansdowne, Dumont and Romilly in 1789–91, see James H. Burns, 'Bentham and the French Revolution', *Transactions of the Royal Historical Society*, 5th series, 16 (1966), 95–114 and Philip Schofield, *Utility and Democracy. The Political Thought of J. Bentham* (Oxford, 2006), 78–108. Bentham's relationship with Dumont is extensively covered in Cyprian Blamires, *The French Revolution and the Creation of Benthamism* (Basingstoke, 2008), 181–99.

Dumont whose chamber was contiguous to the one then occupied by me. Anxiously attentive to the work throughout its progress was my Noble Host. At length the glad tidings reached him that the impression in its several parts had reached his garret: up he came, put together a hundred copies & down he went with them on his shoulders. Barthélémy, the French Minister, was then sitting in one of the rooms of the ground floor. Into the room went Lord Lansdowne & threw down his burden at the feet of the Diplomatist. 'Take charge of these books' said he, '& send them to the Duc de la Rochefoucaul[d]'.[46]

The collaboration between Lansdowne and Bentham also extended to British politics in at least one instance. From 15 June to 23 July 1789, the *Public Advertiser* carried four letters signed 'Anti-Machiavel' and written by Bentham. They attacked Pitt's foreign policy regarding Russia and Sweden. As Bentham wrote to the Marquess before the debate took place, 'Your prisoner has broke ground, and now is the time for you to bring up your battering cannon.'[47] Indeed, as Conway recalls, Lansdowne had asked Bentham to prepare public opinion for an attack against Pitt in Parliament, but Bentham's willingness to embrace the cause, and the way he did so, were not solely dictated by Lansdowne, but echoed his long-standing interest in political relations and his pro-Russian sentiments. This is, however, the only known instance in which Bentham agreed to contribute explicitly to Lansdowne's political aims.[48]

Bentham's disillusionment with the turn taken by the French Revolution also followed that of his Bowood friends. Whereas Lord Lansdowne continued to welcome French *émigrés* in his houses, the September massacres and the subsequent events of 1793 led Dumont and Romilly to break with the democratic ideals they had once entertained.[49] Bentham's opinions followed a similar trend, leading him eventually to submit, on Romilly's urging, a refutation of the Declaration of the Rights of Man to the *Anti-Jacobin Review* in 1801.[50]

---

[46] BL Add MSS, 33 550 ff. 397–8. François Barthélémy was a French diplomat, Louis Alexandre de la Rochefoucauld d'Enville was a member of the Assemblée constituante until his resignation in August 1792.

[47] *Correspondence of J. Bentham*, Vol. 4, 73.

[48] For a detailed analysis of this episode, see Stephen Conway, 'Bentham versus Pitt: Jeremy Bentham and British Foreign Policy, 1789', *Historical Journal*, 30:4 (1987), 791–809.

[49] In September 1792, Romilly wrote to Dumont: 'je me promène la moitié du jour dans une agitation extrême, et par l'impossibilité de rester en place, en pensant à tous les événements malheureux qui découlent d'une source d'où nous nous sommes flattés de voir sortir le bonheur du genre humain'. *Life of Samuel Romilly*, II, 6. In the following months, this feeling had left place to deep disillusionment. See C. Blamires, *The Creation of Benthamism*, 219–21.

[50] The pamphlet, 'Nonsense Upon Stilts' had been written several years earlier. See *Rights, Representation and Reform*, 317–75.

The Break with Lansdowne

In the description of his 'intercourse with the Lansdowne family' addressed to the second Marquess, Bentham spelled out his disinterest: 'To a man in a governing situation, not often does it happen, to have a more faithful or affectionate friend, than *your father* had in *me*: not the less so, for being a *so* disinterested one.'[51] However, issues of patronage and reciprocal services constantly underlay the relationship between Bentham and Shelburne. Towards the end of Bentham's first stay, Shelburne offered to provide for Samuel Bentham in some way or other, though in private Bentham expressed his 'doubts as to the sincerity of [this proposal]'.[52] When Jeremy set out to join his brother in Russia, Lansdowne furnished him with introductions to circles in Paris, Lyons, Marseilles, and Florence.[53] On his part, Bentham wrote with pieces of intelligence he could gather on his journey and sent a number of gifts (including two angora goats).[54] When both his sons were in Kritchev,[55] Jeremiah Bentham continued to forward their letters to Lansdowne and later presented him with the portrait of Bentham as a thirteen-year-old Oxford student. In 1788, when Bentham renewed his acquaintance with him in London, Lansdowne asked him for advice during the trial of Warren Hastings[56] and as their friendship grew, came to ask for more direct services from him. The issue of political patronage came up again at Lansdowne's initiative in 1788. He stressed that he would do something for Bentham if ever he came back into office.[57] A memorandum in Bentham's hand, dated 27 June 1789, indicates that Lansdowne might

---

[51] *The Correspondence of J. Bentham*, Vol. 12, 437. See also the following anecdote which Bentham repeated at least in three different places: 'Lord Shelburne used frequently to say "Tell me what is right and proper – tell me what a man of virtue would do in this matter". I told him that Balaak, the son of Zippoi, wanted Balaam to prophesy, who answered "that which the Lord puts into my mouth will I prophesy"; and that was the answer I made'; *Fragment on Government*, 524 and *Works*, X, 116, and slightly differently in *Correspondence of J. Bentham*, Vol. 12, 437.

[52] *Correspondence of J. Bentham*, Vol. 3, 147 and intro, xxii.

[53] Ibid., 340.

[54] Ibid., 407–8, 576.

[55] BL Add Mss. 33540, ff. 256, 306.

[56] *Correspondence of J. Bentham*, Vol. 3, 617.

[57] 'He has accused himself repeatedly, and *sans ménagement*, for not offering me a place when he was in; and commissioned me to consider what would suit me in the case of his coming in again. He supposes I should prefer a place at one of the Boards, to engaging in what is called politics, viz. coming into Parliament with a precarious place. Whether he meant all this, or whether the use of it was to make me contribute to make people think he was to come in, I cannot take upon me to say. Perhaps partly one and partly th'other, but my notion is, he will never come in, in any efficient place. As for me, my real thoughts being upon that, as upon all other occasions, as you know, the easiest for me to give, I gave him, viz. that I was not fit for a place, and that if I were, I should not

again have made more overt proposals, when he seemed to have prospects of returning to government.[58]

In that context, one can understand Bentham's disappointment when he heard that one of Lansdowne's parliamentary seats for Chipping Wycombe, had been offered to Sir John Jervis. In a famously long letter, he appealed to the principles of 'justice' and friendship, and accused the Marquess of choosing 'insignificant' men rather than independent and principled ones such as himself.[59] Lansdowne tactfully denied having made such an offer, but he did admit that he had always believed Bentham's character to be unsuited to a parliamentary career (which Bentham himself had recognized earlier). Lansdowne had in fact offered one of his seats to Samuel Romilly, who turned it down for political reasons, showing that this type of patronage was not unattainable for some of Bentham's close friends, even from a less genteel background.[60] This episode illustrates the deep ambiguity at the heart of the patron–client relationship, while revealing Bentham's inadequate mastery of the codes of polite society.

On a more personal level, too, Bentham seems to have been deluded as to the extent of his intimacy with the family. In his 1828 recollections, he asserted that 'Ladies – more in *number* than there are fingers on the hand that writes this – Ladies, connected with him, most of them by the ties of consanguinity, were at different times offered by [Lord Lansdowne] to me in marriage.'[61] He then named the widowed Lady Ashburton (Dunning's widow), though no evidence for that proposal has survived. The 'Ladies of Bowood', that is to say Caroline and Elizabeth Vernon and the younger Caroline Fox, were the companions of Shelburne's second wife, Louisa, Lady Lansdowne, and remained the guests of the Marquess after her death in

---

wish to have one – that I hoped always to be happy enough to preserve his good opinion, and so forth, and that was enough for me.' *Correspondence of J. Bentham, Vol. 3*, 617.

[58] *Correspondence of J. Bentham, Vol. 4*, 145n.

[59] *Correspondence of J. Bentham, Vol. 4*, 145–70.

[60] 'Lord Lansdowne did offer me a seat in Parliament, and strongly pressed me to accept it, with an assurance that I was to be at perfect liberty to vote and act as I should think proper. This was at a time when I had got a tolerable share of business at the bar, when I seemed certain of gaining a competence in my profession, and when, in point of fortune, I should have risked very little by going into Parliament. It was that which, above all things, I should have rejoiced in, if I could have gone into the House of Commons perfectly independent, and not with the consciousness that I was placed there by an individual whose opinions might, on some important subjects, be very different from my own. [...] I had the good sense and the honesty to decline it.' *Life of Samuel Romilly*, 87–8.

[61] *Correspondence of J. Bentham, Vol. 12*, 441. One should also remember that Samuel Romilly also met his wife, Ann Garbett, through Lansdowne – though the match between a successful lawyer, be he of low birth and the daughter of a businessman was certainly acceptable socially. Despite Bentham's inherited wealth, his lack of a professional career made a marriage into the high aristocracy unlikely.

the summer of 1789. Bentham's friendship with the family also extended to them, as Bowring stressed in his 'Memoirs of Jeremy Bentham'. However, there seems to be evidence that Bowring left aside some aspects of this relationship, though the loss of many original letters makes it difficult to document.

Bowring stresses Bentham's intimacy with 'the Ladies' and insists on the playfulness of their correspondence. The surviving letters or draft letters clearly indicate that Bentham greatly enjoyed their company, and was particularly fond of Caroline Fox. Bentham might, however, have been more serious than Bowring allows, and might even have considered a marriage proposal, though only indirect evidence survives. In November 1790 he sent the three 'ladies of Bowood' a pamphlet published in France (which he presented as his own) on the creation of 'Marriage Houses' intended to remedy the 'evils of celibacy', by making details of young persons' expectations available to suitable bachelors.[62] The letter was written in the hand of Lansdowne's personal secretary under Bentham's dictation – whether the Marquess endorsed the prank is not known. The ladies were shocked, and forwarded the letter and the pamphlet to Lansdowne immediately. There is evidence that, from then on, they insisted on seeing Bentham only when larger parties were assembled, and not privately as before.[63] This could substantiate Atkinson's intriguing hint that 'Bentham [...] had made advances to Caroline Fox such as proved unacceptable to that lady and rendered habits of close intimacy in some sort embarrassing.'[64] Bentham indeed proposed to Caroline Fox, but not before 1805, on the death of the first Marquess, but his offer was kindly turned down.[65]

In these two anecdotes, the political and the personal are blended. Despite the remaining shadow that hangs over these episodes, they reveal how much Bentham expected from his relationship with Lansdowne, on a political and social level and certainly account for the cooling of their relationship from 1791. After 1792, his name disappears from the Lansdowne

---

[62] Unpublished letter from Elizabeth Vernon to Lord Lansdowne, 11 November 1790. BL, Bowood Papers, Box 49, f. 146.

[63] See especially Bentham's letter as reproduced from Bowring in *Correspondence*, Vol. 4, 355–9. The tone of the letter, in which Bentham laments that he has been banned from the ladies' company for too long, is difficult to reconcile with Bowring's claim that '[t]he letter which follows, in which a little disappointment and annoyance is obviously united with the pleasantry and irony of its style, was addressed to the ladies of the Bowood family, on occasion of their having denied themselves to Bentham when he called'. Bowring, X, 271.

[64] C.M. Atkinson, *Jeremy Bentham*, 123. Atkinson suggests that this proposal might have occurred after Jeremiah Bentham's death in 1791, which left Jeremy with a substantial income.

[65] See 'Outline of Jeremy Bentham's life, January 1802 to December 1805', *The Correspondence of Jeremy Bentham*, Vol. 7, 23 and Caroline Fox's reply, 332–4.

House Dinner Books.[66] Bentham attributed their estrangement to the fact that his Panopticon schemes had brought him closer to Pitt, Lansdowne's political enemy, but there are good reasons to believe that it was also partly due to his disappointment on these two counts.

There is no denying that Lansdowne was a formative influence in Bentham's life and played a key role in his political and personal development. As in all patron–protégé relationships, the private and the political were closely intertwined. This accounts for the number of avenues Lansdowne's patronage opened for the aspiring philosopher in the 1780s, but also for the later cooling of their relationship in later years. Having seen how Bentham – like Price, Priestley, Dumont, and Romilly – grappled with the issues of dependence and affiliation makes it difficult to endorse the idea that Lansdowne was at any point Bentham's 'mentor', when the philosopher himself seems to have gone out of his way to prove that he was no 'tame intellectual'. At a broader level, their relationship also testifies to the changes which occurred in polite society from the 1790s onwards, and to the waning of the system of aristocratic patronage for intellectuals in Britain.

Lastly, the phrase 'the Bowood Circle', ought to be reserved – following Jarrett's insight – for the close network consisting of Romilly, Dumont, and Bentham, who shared ideals and expectations in the early years of the French Revolution, and remained close in the decades that followed. As we have seen, each entertained distinctive links with Lansdowne and benefited from the acquaintance in markedly different ways. For all three of them, however, their involvement with the Marquess in the years 1789–92 had long-lasting consequences.

[66] From January 1789 to December 1792, the Lansdowne House Dinner Books record 33 occurrences of Bentham's name. The period also includes his extensive stay at Bowood in the summer of 1789. These figures are quoted with permission of The Trustees of the Bowood Collection.

12

Shelburne and Perpetual Peace: Small States, Commerce, and International Relations within the Bowood Circle

RICHARD WHATMORE

I

Providing an intellectual identity for William Petty, 2nd Earl of Shelburne and his Bowood Circle, has become something of a parlour game for interested historians.[1] The first problem is Shelburne's character.[2] How could someone with such an antagonizing personality sustain a coherent group of any kind? Edmund Burke's comments about Shelburne's character in public and in private were vitriolic, but widely seconded by many who came into contact with him.[3] Shelburne was likened to Gabriel Malagrida, the plot-

Acknowledgements: I would like to thank Clarissa Campbell Orr, Knud Haakonssen and Rachel Hammersley for commenting on this chapter.

[1]   Derek Jarrett, 'The Bowood Circle, 1780–1793. Its Ideas and its Influence' (Unpublished B.Litt., Oxford, 1955); John Norris, *Shelburne and Reform* (London, 1963), 82–98; Derek Jarrett, *The Begetters of Revolution: England's Involvement with France, 1759–1789* (London, 1973); Albert Goodwin, *The Friends of Liberty: The English Democratic Movement in the Age of the French Revolution* (London, 1979), 101–5; Andrew Hamilton, 'Atlantic Cosmopolitanism and Nationalism: Benjamin Vaughan and the Limits of Free Trade in the Eighteenth Century' (Unpublished PhD, University of Wisconsin-Madison, 2004); Edward G. Andrew, *Patrons of Enlightenment* (Toronto, 2006), 170–81.

[2]   The bitterness Shelburne generated is clear from Anon., *A letter to the Right Honourable the earl of Shelburne, on the motives of his political conduct: and the principles which have actuated the opposition to the measures of administration in respect to America* (London, 1776), 1–2: 'Nature designed you for some of those middling employments, where great industry, much artifice, void of real principle, an apparent ardour for religion, would have gradually led to the fortune of a Jew.' See also Anon., *The Cabinet Conference; or, tears of ministry* (London, 1779).

[3]   Edmund Burke to Charles Watson-Wentworth, 2nd Marques of Rockingham, 18 July 1768: 'Lord Shelburne still continues in administration, though as adverse and as much disliked as ever.' Burke declared in the House of Commons in 1782 that 'if lord

ting Portuguese Jesuit who was found guilty of involvement in a plot to assassinate King Jose I at Lisbon in 1758. It is significant that such a characterization was traced back to Shelburne's sometime friend John Wilkes.[4] The second problem is that when the range of possible members is considered, it becomes easy to find divisions.[5] A further difficulty is that members of Shelburne's entourage often themselves had interests in other political groupings of the time, and sometimes in consequence supplied conflicting advice concerning political conduct. A final difficulty is that Shelburne was notoriously vague in self-expression. The best-known example concerned British relations with North America. Shelburne considered himself a friend to North America but avowed on numerous occasions his opposition to the independence of the United States. When he finally accepted the inevitability of separation his self-justifications and tortuous claims to have been consistent amused his enemies and confused his friends.[6]

Shelburne was not a Catiline, or a Borgia in morals, it must not be ascribed to any thing but his understanding': cited in J.C.D. Clark, ed., Edmund Burke, *Reflections on the Revolution in France* (Stanford, CA, 2001), 216. See also Anon., 'Political Character of Lord Shelburne', *The London magazine, or, Gentleman's monthly intelligencer*, vol. 45, ed. Isaac Kimber and Edward Kimber (London, 1776), 577–9; John Adams reported on 25 May 1783, 'asked [David Hartley] what News from England? He said none. I told him I had heard that it was expected by some that Shelburne would come in. He said No. – I asked him why can't you coalesce with Shelburne as well as North? He said Shelburne is an Irishman, and has all the impudence of his nation. He is a parlaverer beyond all description. He parlavers everybody, and has no sincerity.' (John Adams, diary 41, Adams Family Papers).

4   Robert Heron, ed., *The letters of Junius: Stat nominis umbra, with notes and illustrations*, 2nd edn, 2 vols (London, 1804), I, 84–5. The poet Oliver Goldsmith was famously reported to have said to Shelburne: 'Do you know that I never could conceive the reason why they call you Malagrida, for Malagrida was a very good sort of man.' For one of many recollections of the anecdote, see Francis Hardy, *Memoirs of the political and private life of James Caulfield, Earl of Charlemont*, 2 vols (London, 1812), I, 344–5.

5   The range of visitors to Bowood is clear from Jeremy Bentham to Jeremiah Bentham, between 30 September 1781 and 2 October 1781 (Letter 416), *The Correspondence of Jeremy Bentham: Volume 3: January 1781 to October 1788*, ed. Ian R. Christie (London, 1971), 98–101; divisions are evident from Richard Price to Benjamin Franklin, 18 November 1782: 'Could my wishes have had any influence, our new ministers upon the first change would have immediately acknowledged the independence of America, and on this ground opened a negotiation for a general peace and made such concessions as would most probably have brought it about before this time. I have always delivered my Sentiments freely to Lord Shelburne on these Subjects. We have differed much in our opinions about them, but our friendship has continued.' *Benjamin Franklin Papers*.

6   John Cannon, 'Petty, William, Second Earl of Shelburne and First Marquess of Lansdowne (1737–1805)', ODNB. Shelburne's complicated position is clear from an entry in John Adam's diary, written at Paris, 14 September 1782: 'The Comte Montagnini de Mirabel, Min[ister] Plen[itpotentiary] of the King of Sardinia, asked what was the Principle of the indecision of G. Britain? Why don't they acknowledge your independence? They must have some intelligence, that is not public. – I answered I don't

Shelburne's relationships were equally complicated by the issue of patronage, and by the expectation that an act promoting an individual would afterwards result in support for other members of Shelburne's entourage.[7] The Bowood Circle can, as a result, be defined as those straightforwardly 'belonging to Lord Shelburne', without any reference to a party programme beyond Shelburne's evolving opinions.[8] Shelburne was, furthermore, avid for information, and often came across as the best-informed politician of his day.[9] A related approach to the Bowood Circle is to see it as a source of news and advice for Shelburne, and not necessarily either united or coherent. Josiah Tucker gave this impression when he recounted Shelburne's reading him 'one or two letters from a nobleman of the first consequence', before offering 'service' in return for Tucker becoming part of a stable of writers for Shelburne. Tucker refused, and made public the refusal in *Four Letters on important National Subjects* (1783) addressed to Shelburne, which were critical of the man and the politics imputed to him.[10]

Should attempts to define a Bowood Circle of shared political sentiment be abandoned in consequence? A negative answer derives from the fact that those who lived for decades at close quarters, such as Jeremy Bentham,

---

believe there is any Principle, or System in it. It is merely owing to their confusion. My Lord Shelburne, in compliance with the will of his master, refuses to do what all the world sees to be necessary. – Perhaps says the Comte they mean to annex certain conditions, to the acknowledgment of your independence. – But says I, what if we should annex conditions too? What if we should insist on an acknowledgement of our independence as a preliminary condition to entering into any Treaty or Conference? – Ay, says he, in that case you may have work enough.' John Adams, diary 33, *Adams Family Papers*.

[7]   For an example, see Bentham's anecdote about favours towards Lord Bristol: Diary of 28 September–3 October 1781 by Jeremy Bentham, 28 September 1781, *The Correspondence of Jeremy Bentham: Volume 3: January 1781 to October 1788*, 103–9.

[8]   Richard Brinsley Sheridan to Thomas Grenville, 21 May 1782 (Letter 82), *The Letters of Richard Brinsley Sheridan: Volume I*, ed. Cecil Price (Oxford, 1966), 147–8. The term was used about Richard Oswald of Auchencruive during the negotiations at Paris with France, Spain, and North America.

[9]   Thomas Park, *Royal and Noble Authors of England, Scotland and Ireland* (London, 1806), IV, 471–2: 'Lord Shelburne filled a large space in society as a statesman, an orator, and accomplished gentleman, an excellent landlord, a liberal patron of the arts, and a most amiable man in private life. He is thought to have possessed more political information than any other man of his time. There was scarcely a principal city on the continent of Europe, or in the United States of America, in which he had not one or more correspondents, from whom he collected every local event of importance, and often received intelligence which government had not the means of procuring.' See also Anon., 'One more Conjecture respecting the Author of Junius', *The Gentleman's Magazine, for December 1812*, ed. Sylvanus Urban, 499–501.

[10] Josiah Tucker, *Four Letters on important National Subjects* (London, 1783), 1–22. Tucker disagreed with Shelburne about the test acts for dissenting Protestants and about the role of the people in government, but shared Shelburne's view of colonies and free trade.

recalled that Shelburne did have 'fixed intellectual principles'.[11] Bentham's correspondence, of the early 1780s especially, identifies a body of individuals united around a political programme.[12] Contemporaries who were opposed to him often described Shelburne as the leading figure within a party with a singular identity. Burke had identified 'the Shelburne people' as a distinct grouping as early as 1769.[13] In the 1770s Burke claimed that this identity derived from the view that 'the people (always meaning the common people of London) were never in the wrong'.[14]

The best-known contemporary attempt to define the Bowood political programme is equally Burke's, in his attack on Shelburne's group, and Joseph Priestley more particularly, in *Reflections on the Revolution in France* (1790). Here the millenarian overtones of Priestley's *An History of the Corruptions of Christianity* (1782) were cited as evidence that Shelburne and the friends of the French Revolution wanted to see 'the fall of the civil powers', ending the Trinitarian alliance of church and state.[15] Burke was still more direct in a letter of 1790 where he declared that his intention in writing the *Reflections* had not been 'controversy with Dr Price, or Lord Shelburne, or any other of their set', but rather a complete refutation of their politics:

> … to set in full view the danger from their wicked principles and their black hearts. I intend to state the true principles of our constitution in church and state, upon grounds opposite to theirs. If any one be the better for the example made of them, and for this exposition, well and good. I mean to do my best to expose them to the hatred, ridicule, and contempt of the whole world; as I always shall expose such calumniators, hypocrites, sowers of sedition, and approvers of murder and all its triumphs. When I have done that, they may have the fields all to themselves; and I care very little how they triumph over me, since I hope

[11] Jeremy Bentham to Sir James Mackintosh, 1808 (Letter 1948), *The Correspondence of Jeremy Bentham: Volume 7: January 1802 to December 1808*, ed. J.R. Dinwiddy (Oxford, 1988), 464–6.

[12] Jeremy Bentham to George Wilson, between 15 September 1781 and 17 September 1781 (Letter 412), *The Correspondence of Jeremy Bentham: Volume 3: January 1781 to October 1788*, 82–9.

[13] Edmund Burke to Charles Watson-Wentworth, 2nd Marques of Rockingham, 9 July 1769, *Letters of Edmund Burke: A Selection*, ed. Harold J. Laski (Oxford, 1922), 54–8.

[14] Edmund Burke to John Bourke, 1st Earl of Mayo, 11 July 1776, *Letters of Edmund Burke: A Selection*, 211–13. Burke noted when Shelburne's faction had held power 'having overloaded the stomachs of their adherents, they were vomited up with loathing and disgust'. He went on to 'draw a useful lesson from the unprincipled behaviour of a corrupt and licentious people: that is, never to sacrifice his principles to the hope of obtaining their affection; to regard and wish them well, as part of his fellow creatures, whom his best instincts and his highest duties lead him to love and serve, but to put as little trust in them as in princes'. For similar claims, see Henry Goodricke, *Observations on Dr. Price's theory and principles of civil liberty and government* (York, 1776).

[15] Edmund Burke, *Reflections upon the Revolution in France*, ed. J.C.D. Clark (Stanford, Calif, 2001), 216.

they will not be able to draw me at their heels, and carry my head in triumph on their poles.[16]

Burke's linkage of the 'coffee-houses of Paris, and of the dissenting meeting houses of London' was itself based on a firm conviction that Shelburne represented an alliance between French *philosophes* and English Dissenters. There is much truth in this. Many of Shelburne's reform plans were as likely to be welcomed at the salons of Baron d'Holbach or Madame Helvétius, as they were at the dissenting academies of Warrington or Newington Green. But Shelburne's circle was not straightforwardly Unitarian and Dissenting, as the ever-more-evident tensions with Joseph Priestley reveal. Priestley had been recommended to Shelburne as a literary companion by Richard Price, and from 1773 lived at Bowood House in Wiltshire or Shelburne House in London, becoming 'a friend', and accompanying Shelburne abroad. It was after a visit to Paris in 1774 that Priestley completed the *Letters to a philosophical unbeliever*, inspired by a desire to refute the rejections of Christianity he found among the Parisian *philosophes*. In 1780 Priestley discerned that Shelburne was dissatisfied with his service. Although nothing specific was said, and although they parted amicably, Shelburne did not respond to subsequent attempts at contact by Priestley when both were in London.[17] Priestley later professed to have been uncomfortable living within Shelburne's elevated circle, where amusement was almost a profession. The deeper truth was that Priestley's increasingly millenarian political stance, based on the opinion that it was possible to move rapidly to a moralized world of Socinian Christian states, was at odds with Shelburne's preferred policy.[18] Shelburne opposed public controversy about religious beliefs, and was calling Priestley an 'Atheistical Christian' as early as 1786.[19]

---

[16] Edmund Burke to Sir Philip Francis, 20 February 1790, *Letters of Edmund Burke: A Selection*, 279–84.

[17] Joseph Priestley, *Memoirs of Dr. Joseph Priestley, to the year 1795: written by himself* (Northumberland, 1806), 72–5, 82–5.

[18] Benjamin Vaughan summarized the matter to Benjamin Franklin, 26 June 1780: 'Dr. Priestley & Lord Shelburne have parted, as far as I can understand, amicably. The truth is, the two characters were such as did not understand the one the other: The one did not comprehend enough the nature & merit of a speculative scholar, nor the other the situation and difficulties of a political actor.' *Benjamin Franklin Papers*.

[19] Shelburne to Richard Price, 19 December 1785, *Price Correspondence*, III, February 1786–February 1791, 101–4: 'There is nothing of which I am more convinced than that the effect of all church controversy as the world stands must be the making Christians Deists and Deists Atheists. To what else can the conceit which you say poor Dr Priestley has picked up in his flight. If it was to get the length of forming a sect, I know of no other name to give his followers except that of Atheistical Christians.' Shelburne said he 'never read thirty pages of any book whatever more happily expressed, or with which I was more captivated than I am with your seventh Sermon'. He was referring to Price's 'Of the Christian Doctrine as held by Trinitarians and Calvinists' in *Sermons*

Some sense of the division between Dissenters of Priestley's stamp and Shelburne's circle from 1780 onwards can be discerned in a letter from the lawyer George Wilson to his friend Jeremy Bentham of 1787. Wilson was seeking to inform Bentham about British affairs during the latter's long sojourn in Russia, and noted that 'everything teems with improvement'. By this he meant the consolidation of taxes, the opening of ports to the French, and the possible reform of tithes and the Poor Laws. Such schemes could be traced to there having been 'on all points of political economy, an evident change in public opinion within these ten years'. The ideas of Adam Smith's *Wealth of Nations* were stated to be one major cause, another was events in North America, and another 'the utter disgrace of the old thrones'. The point Wilson wanted to emphasize, however, was that the Dissenting way was not the right one for reform:

> The dissenters have failed in their attempt to get the Test Act repealed, but the division was respectable, and they are not discouraged. They are very angry with Pitt, whom they will probably no longer support as they did at the general election. Priestley has written him a letter, a printed one, I mean, full of rage against Pitt, the Trinity, and the Church Establishment – clever enough, and very bold, but very indiscreet, and certainly prejudicial to the cause. They are founding a college at Hackney, which is to rival and overthrow Oxford, and Cambridge; but I fear they have not heads to effect that good work. They are violent zealots in their way; and one article in the constitution of the new college is, that all the professors shall be dissenting parsons. Several eminent men among them have refused to subscribe on account of that clause.[20]

Priestley sought immediate reform, and believed the removal of abuses in church and state was possible by legislative means; infamously he likened his activities to 'laying gunpowder', with the expectation of 'an instantaneous explosion'.[21] With respect to international relations he was an ardent enemy to empire. Priestley wanted Britain to abandon even small dominions such as Gibraltar, and anticipated an upheaval across Europe against oppression in all states 'except Denmark and Sweden'. For such reasons he rejoiced in the French Revolution, which he believed derived from the same principles that had inspired the North American rebellion. The policy of the present 'race of kings' he considered 'remarkably similar to that of Pharaoh', and

---

on the Christian Doctrine (1787), which compared the extremes of 'Athanasianism and Calvinism' with 'Socinianism', and defended a middling Arian position.

[20] George Wilson to Jeremy Bentham, 24 April 1787 (Letter 589), *The Correspondence of Jeremy Bentham: Volume 3: January 1781 to October 1788*, 531–4.

[21] Joseph Priestley, *The importance and extent of free inquiry in matters of religion: a sermon, preached before the congregations of the Old and New Meeting of Protestant Dissenters at Birmingham. November 5, 1785. To which are added, reflections on the present state of free inquiry in this country* (Birmingham, 1785).

predicted 'their destruction in the manner predicted in the Scriptures, viz. with violence, and much consequent general calamity'. Priestley believed that Shelburne was of a similar opinion, arguing that 'Had [Shelburne] continued [Prime Minister] to this day, his liberal and enlightened policy would have saved England, and all Europe, the horrors of the present most ruinous and impolitic war [with revolutionary France]'.[22]

II

Priestley was wrong about Shelburne's opinions. Furthermore, Burke was mistaken in 1790 when he identified Priestley's apocalyptic politics with those of the Bowood Circle. Although Shelburne was tarnished with a Paineite brush after war broke out between Britain and France in 1792, the kinds of republican transformation of politics then envisaged, and envisaged by means of a war on Britain's constitution and social structure, was altogether alien to Bowood members. Their plans for perpetual peace made sense during the window of opportunity they perceived existed in the 1780s. Understanding Bowood politics entails returning to the aftermath of the Seven Years War. To this war Shelburne owed his rise, having so distinguished himself at Minden and Kloster Kampen that he was raised to the rank of colonel and appointed aide-de-camp to the king. Through knowledge of the court he became known to the First Lord of the Treasury, John Stuart, 3rd Earl of Bute, and was returned to the House of Commons as member for Wycombe. In 1762, before he could take his seat, he succeeded his father as Earl of Shelburne in the Irish peerage, and as Baron Wycombe in that of Britain.[23] Shelburne's view was that Britain had become over-extended despite its great victories during the Seven Years War. The resulting soaring national debt, and the successive controversies concerning the balance of constitutional powers within Britain, and the role of Britain in European politics, was tied, because of the war, to the question of whether Britain ought to maintain and to extend its global empire, or to allow it to decline. It was the latter question that Shelburne sought most ardently to address, and persuaded others to follow him. He became prominent in national argument from July 1766, when he served under William Pitt, 1st Earl of Chatham, as secretary of state for the Southern Department (until October 1768). His most significant memorandum foreshadowed later concerns, advocating giving the North American colonies much greater leeway with regard to setting their own western limits and trading policy, endowing them with

[22] Joseph Priestley, *Letters to the inhabitants of Northumberland and its neighbourhood, on subjects interesting to the author and to them* (Philadelphia, 1801), 26–9.
[23] John Norris, *Shelburne and Reform*, 1–17.

greater self-governance and reducing restrictions upon trade without jeopardising the integrity of the British empire.[24]

Shelburne believed he was living in an age of domestic and international crisis. This was a commonplace view, neatly expressed by David Hume in a letter reporting that Shelburne had informed him personally of the Earl of Chatham's resignation:

> Our administration is like a heap of loose stones, where, if you remove one, the rest will all tumble. This is the least of the numberless evils under which we labour. What do you think of our being such complete beggars as not to be able to subsist, and yet labouring under the jealousy and envy of all Europe, on account of our supposed power and opulence.[25]

Shelburne and his inner circle shared Hume's diagnosis of the evils of the day, epitomized by the likelihood of a debt-induced national bankruptcy, which was sometimes expected to prefigure a successful French invasion.[26] Unlike Hume, however, Shelburne and his friends believed that a solution could be found in the establishment of a sinking fund to deal with the debt, and the development of commerce in conditions of liberty domestically and internationally. Richard Price signalled such a prospect, when he speculated about the true interest of Britain with respect to North America in 1776:

> Had we nourished and favoured America with a view to commerce, instead of considering it as a country to be governed: Had we, like a liberal and wise people, rejoiced to see a multitude of free states branched forth from ourselves, all enjoying independent legislatures similar to our own: Had we aimed at binding

[24] Shelburne to the Lords of Trade, 5 October 1767, *Trade and Politics, 1767–1769* (Illinois, 1921), ed. Clarence Walworth Alvord and Clarence Edwin Carter, Western Policy, Collections of the State Historical Society, XVI, British Series, vol. III, 77–81.
[25] David Hume to William Mure, Baron Mure of Caldwell, 18 October 1768 (Letter 422), *The Letters of David Hume: Volume II*, ed. J.Y.T. Greig (Oxford, 1932), 187–9. See also John Burnby, *An address to the people of England, on the increase of their poor rates, dedicated to the earl of Shelburne* (London, 1780), ii–iii: 'the constitution of this kingdom seems in a galloping consumption, and unless an able physician is called in I fear it will dissolve, and leave not a wreck behind'; Shelburne, the physician, was praised for his 'prescription of liberties'.
[26] Benjamin Vaughan to Benjamin Franklin, 3 July 1778: 'We are certainly shockingly weak at this moment, and I believe it probable that the French may land and stay here for a season or so, though not permanently', *Benjamin Franklin Papers*. More broadly, see Istvan Hont, 'The Rhapsody of Public Debt: David Hume and Voluntary State Bankruptcy', in *The Jealousy of Trade: International Competition and the Nation–State in Political Perspective* (Cambridge, MA), 325–54; Michael Sonenscher, 'The Nation's Debt and the Birth of the Modern Republic: The French Fiscal Deficit and the Politics of the Revolution of 1789', *History of Political Thought*, 18 (1997), 64–103, 267–325; Michael Sonenscher, *Before the Deluge. Public Debt, Inequality, and the Intellectual Origins of the French Revolution* (Princeton, NJ, 2007).

them to us only by the ties of affection and interest; and contented ourselves with a moderate power rendered durable by being lenient and friendly, an umpire in their differences, an aid to them in improving their own free governments, and their common bulwark against the assaults of foreign enemies: Had this, I say, been our policy and temper; there is nothing so great or happy that we might not have expected. With their increase our strength would have increased. A growing surplus in the revenue might have been gained, which, invariably applied to the gradual discharge of the national debt, would have delivered us from the ruin with which it threatens us. The Liberty of America might have preserved our Liberty; and, under the direction of a patriot king or wise minister, proved the means of restoring to us our almost lost constitution.[27]

With the advent of war with the North American states, free trade would only succeed when it was tied to a commercial alliance with France, which was expected to bring peace to mainland Europe and allow gradual and relatively untroubled reform at home. Britain's dangerous thirst for empire would not be tenable in conditions of free trade, because global politics would begin to rely upon maintaining peace, by maintaining existing states involved in commerce, and because Britain's trade would fall relative to that of rival states, because it would no longer be artificially controlled by rapacious commercial companies. In short, Britain would no longer be able to afford an empire, and would no longer have a clear interest in sustaining one. This aspiration defined the politics of the Bowood Circle in the 1780s; by 1790, with the French Revolution in full flow, established positions regarding the likely future of Europe became uncertain, and remained so until after Shelburne's death.[28]

Shelburne had real hopes in the early 1780s that through peace with North America, Spain, and France, and by signing commercial treaties to establish free trade between these nations, a means could be discovered to return European states to Adam Smith's vaunted 'natural progress of opulence', which had been outlined as an ideal economic growth path for states in the third book of the *Wealth of Nations*. One of the great benefits of this policy, Shelburne believed, was that it would protect the independence of the existing states of Europe, so many of which were, like Poland, falling prey to larger neighbours in search of a British-style mercantile empire. Shelburne, following Dean Tucker, believed that the fears about the poorer states of Europe being able, because of lower wage costs, to undercut the prices of richer states like Britain were exaggerated. The argument that rich states would decline in conditions of natural liberty was widespread, made

---

[27] Richard Price, *Observations on the nature of civil liberty, the principles of government, and the justice and policy of the war with America* (Dublin, 1776), 98.

[28] Richard Whatmore, 'Etienne Dumont, the British Constitution and the French Revolution', *The Historical Journal*, 50 (2007), 23–47; Emmanuelle de Champs, Chapter 11 in this volume.

famous by Hume's essay 'Of Money' in his *Political Discourses* of 1752, and one of the main arguments in favour of the mercantile system.[29] Rather, in conditions of free trade Shelburne believed each state would specialize in particular branches of trade and thereby reap the rewards of greater commerce and wealth, untroubled by threats to national independence that had become illogical because they ruined trade. Revealing the full extent of Shelburne's aspiration is beyond this chapter. Here the example of Shelburne's capacity to bring together disparate groups is highlighted to illustrate the commercial politics of the Bowood Circle as they reached their apotheosis between 1783 and 1787. During these years Shelburne united physiocrats, *philosophes*, dissenters, projectors, and particular international groups such as the Genevan exiles of 1782 to advocate particular policies to establish the foundations for free trade and perpetual peace. The great benefit was seen to be maintaining the existing multitude of small and large states across Europe, rather than letting them collapse into antagonistic mercantile empires.

III

In a letter to Dugald Stewart, then professor of moral philosophy at the University of Edinburgh, Shelburne was candid about his debt to Adam Smith:

> I owe to a journey I made with Mr. Smith from Edinburgh to London [in the early 1760s], the difference between light and darkness through the best part of my life. The novelty of his principles, added to my youth and prejudices, made me unable to comprehend them at the time, but he urged them with so much benevolence, as well as eloquence, that they took a certain hold, which, though it did not develop itself so as to arrive at full conviction for some few years after, I can fairly say, has constituted ever since, the happiness of my life, as well as any little consideration I may have enjoyed in it.[30]

---

[29] Istvan Hont, 'The "Rich Country-Poor Country" Debate in Scottish Political Economy', in *Jealousy of Trade*, 267–324; 'The Rich Country-Poor Country Debate Revisited: The Irish Origins and French Reception of the Hume Paradox', in *Hume's Political Economy*, ed. Margaret Schabas and Carl Wennerlind (London, 2007), 222–342; Richard Whatmore, 'Adam Smith's Contribution to the French Revolution', *Past and Present*, 175 (2002), 65–89.
[30] William Petty, Lord Lansdowne, to Dugald Stewart, 1795 in *The Collected Works of Dugald Stewart*, 10 vols, ed. Sir William Hamilton (Edinburgh, 1858), X, 95. Shelburne's devotion to Smith is remarkable given his view that 'I can scarce conceive a Scotchman capable of liberality, but utterly incapable of impartiality. That nation is composed of such a sad set of innate, cold-hearted, impudent rogues, that I sometimes think it a comfort when you and I shall be [able] to walk together in the next world, which I hope

Shelburne's devotion to Smith was such that he presented his friends with copies of the *Theory of Moral Sentiments*, persuaded Smith to tutor his younger brother at Edinburgh, and sought out his opinion on particular issues of the day, such as Dalrymple's proposal for an expedition to the South Pacific in 1766–7.[31] Smith had evidently preached the benefits of natural liberty with respect to trade, and Shelburne learned of what became one of the central themes of the *Wealth of Nations*: the comparison between a natural path of economic development destroyed in Europe by feudalism, and the modern mercantile system, whose 'unnatural and retrograde order' prevented the full development of commerce at the same time as it caused war. The mercantile system owed it origins to the fact that the urbanization of Europe, which was a legacy of the Roman empire, had proceeded apace across the continent without any concomitant commercialization of agriculture. The promotion of natural liberty against the controls of the mercantile system was the solution.

Shelburne was ever a vociferous defender of commercial liberty, whenever peace could be guaranteed between states, and favoured neutrality during war as the surest way to the continued promotion of commerce. It was for this reason he attempted to persuade James Playfair to establish a journal called 'The Neutralist' and praised William Thomson's proposed weekly paper 'The Armed Neutrality', neither of which was ever launched.[32] While Smith was cautious and phlegmatic in his approach to practical reform, Shelburne believed in general moral principles 'as may embrace the Turk or

---

we shall as well as in this, we cannot possibly then have any of them sticking to our skirts.' (Shelburne to Richard Price, 30 November 1786, *Price Correspondence*, III, 93).

[31] Adam Smith to Shelburne, 21 February 1759 (Letter 28) and 12 February 1767 (Letter 101), *The Correspondence of Adam Smith*, ed. Ernest Campbell Mossner and Ian Simpson Ross (Oxford, 1987), 28–9, 122–4; Kirk Willis, 'The Role in Parliament of the Economic Ideas of Adam Smith, 1776–1800', *History of Political Economy*, 11:4 (1979), 505–44.

[32] Shelburne to Richard Price, 25 November 1786, *Price Correspondence*, III, 90. The benefits of neutrality were pressed upon Benjamin Vaughan by John Adams during the peace negotiations of 1783. Vaughan's cautious reply underlined the complicated relationship between support for a principle and contemporary reason of state politics: 'One of these first days of January I had a conversation with Mr. Benjamin Vaughan, upon the liberty of navigation as claimed by the confederated neutral powers and the Dutch. Shewed him the necessity England was in, of acceding to it, and the importance of doing it soon that they might have it to say, that they had arranged their affairs with the Dutch, as well as with the United States. He said he saw the importance, of pulling at the hairs one by one, when you could not pull out the whole tail at once. That he had written and would write again to my Lord Shelburne upon the subject: but says he you cannot blame us for endeavouring, to carry this point to market, and get something by it. We can not prevent the French from getting some territory in the East Indies more than they had and perhaps we may buy this of the Dutch for this point.' John Adams, diary 39, 1 January 1783, *Adams Family Papers*.

the Gentoo equally with the Christian'.[33] He was in consequence smitten by Anne-Robert-Jacques Turgot's idea of 'establishing certain fixed fundamental principles of law, commerce, morality and politics comprehensive enough to embrace all religions and all countries'. Shelburne's close friend and secretary Benjamin Vaughan translated Marie-Jean-Antoine-Nicolas de Caritat, marquess de Condorcet's *Vie de Turgot* (1786), which outlined Turgot's project. Shelburne wrote to Richard Price that he wanted him to make a reality of Turgot's vision:

> It is to the inculcating these principles I want you, my dear friend, to dedicate your whole time, to cry down war throughout the whole world, which nothing can ever justify, and to prove the advantages of peace, and the right which all countries have to require it of their sovereigns. If sovereigns are offended with each other, let them fight singlehanded, without involving their people in their silly quarrels. You have talents and character peculiarly adapted to give weight to these principles. Every one is sufficiently agreed about the existence of God and about his attributes, except some conceited men of letters, who are delighted to reason in the dark, and think themselves superior to the rest of the world, because they think they know what the rest of the world don't think worth knowing. I want you to keep better company?[34]

Shelburne continued to expound the principles he believed in until the end of his life:

> Providence has so constituted the world, that very little government is necessary. After the assembly at Philadelphia had sat a long time … considering what form of government they should adopt, Dr Franklin rose … to express his apprehension that if some plan was not speedily adopted, the people out of doors would learn a most dangerous secret, that things might go on very well without any positive form of government. How are all markets supplied? All the governments of Europe have been more or less occupied about the supply of their capitals, except London, which has never wanted. The grazier and the gardener know the amount of the demand ten times better than any legislator. What mischief has been done by legislating about corn, from which England even has not been exempt! Holland has left the corn trade entirely free, and has never felt what scarcity was. A negative government will not do in order to make conquests or to keep distant governments in dependence. But is that intended, or what good purpose of any kind does it answer.[35]

Such beliefs were the likely reason for Shelburne's friendship with the French

---

[33] Shelburne to Richard Price, 29 September 1786, *Price Correspondence*, III, 64.
[34] Shelburne to Richard Price, 22 November 1786, *Price Correspondence*, III, 86–7.
[35] Fitzmaurice, *Shelburne*, I, 81.

physiocrat André Morellet, whom he met in Paris in 1771, and who visited Bowood in 1772 and in 1782.[36] Morellet was a disciple of the philosopher Helvétius, who died at the height of his contemporary influence in 1772, and a member of Madame Helvétius's salon, which included the explorer Louis Antoine de Bougainville, the notorious atheist Paul-Henri Thiry, Baron d'Holbach, the soldier and philosopher François-Jean de Chastellux, Turgot, and Benjamin Franklin himself.[37] Neither Shelburne nor Morellet, who had met Smith at Paris in 1762, distinguished between Smith's politics and those of the second generation of French physiocrats associated with the reforming minister Turgot, whose short-lived ministry of August 1774 to May 1776 attempted a bonfire of economic controls upon trade. Morellet's impact upon Shelburne was recalled three decades later:

> I have not changed an atom of the principles I first imbibed from you and Adam Smith. They make a woeful slow progress, but I cannot look upon them as extinct; on the contrary, they must prevail in the end like the sea. What they lose in one play they gain in another.[38]

It was from Morellet that Shelburne learned the 'application of the principle of the liberty of trade to diverse questions of political economy'.[39] When Shelburne presented Morellet with a copy of Smith's *Wealth of Nations* in 1776, he immediately set about translating it.[40] When Morellet was elected to the Académie Française in 1786, a eulogy by the marquis de Chastellux reiterated Shelburne's acknowledgement of Morellet's influence upon him: 'It was your writings, your conversation, which were absolutely essential in clarifying for me the advantages of free trade, a valuable freedom which can reconcile all interests, and which ought to become a productive and shared source of prosperity for all nations' ['ce sont vos écrits, vos conversations qui ont le plus essentiellement contribué à m'éclairer sur les avantages de la

---

[36] Ibid., I, 429–33.

[37] André Morellet to Shelburne, 8 January 1772 (Letter 676). *Correspondance générale d'Helvétius, III, 1761–1774, Lettres 465–720*, ed. David Smith, Alan Dainard, Marie-Thérèse Inguenaud, Jean Orsini, and Peter Allan (Toronto and Buffalo, NY, 1991), 386–7; André Morellet to Shelburne 18 February 1777 (Letter 727), *Correspondance générale d'Helvétius, IV, 1774–1800/Lettres 721–855, suivies de lettres relevant des périodes des trois premiers volumes et découvertes depuis leur parution*, ed. David Smith, Jean Orsini, Marie-Thérèse Inguenaud, Peter Allan and Alan Dainard (Toronto and Buffalo, NY, 1998), 13–17.

[38] Shelburne to Morellet, 1802, Fitzmaurice, *Shelburne*, II, 430–1.

[39] André Morellet, *Mémoires inédits de l'abbé Morellet ... sur le dix-huitième siècle et sur la révolution*, 2nd edn, 2 vols (Paris, 1822), 277–9.

[40] Morellet's translation never appeared, as publishers would not print it on the grounds that there was already a translation in circulation by the abbé Blavet: see Morellet, *Mémoires inédits de l'abbé Morellet*, I, 243–6, II, 371.

liberté du commerce, liberté précieuse qui fait concilier tous les intérets, & qui doit devenir un jour la source féconde & commune de la prospérité des nations'].[41]

Chastellux's comment of 1786 is significant because it directly relates the liberty of trade to international relations. It was accompanied by the statement that Britain was now the imitator of France with regard to commercial principle, and that an era had been inaugurated that heralded peace between the two greatest commercial nations of the world rather than intermittent war. Reference to the application of the principle of liberty to political economy as a whole meant addressing the issue of international strife. Morellet's letters to Shelburne confirm this. Morellet saw the counterpart to the liberalization of the French grain trade attempted by Turgot to be what he termed 'cosmopolitan politics'. These amounted to realizing the project for perpetual peace of the abbé de Saint-Pierre.[42] With respect to North America, Morellet constantly reminded Shelburne that 'if England wanted to correct the problems of previous colonies, she could easily accomplish this, and in free trade she would even soon recover all the advantages of a monopoly for which she has paid so dearly' ['si l'Angleterre veut réparer ses fautes avec ses anciens colons, elle le peut facilement, et qu'elle recouvrera bientôt dans la liberté meme tous les avantages d'un monopole qu'elle a payé si cherement'].[43]

IV

If the first step for the Bowood Circle was the domestic liberalization of trade and the application of commercial principles to agriculture, the second

---

[41] François Jean Chastellux, *Discours prononcés dans l'Académie françoise, le jeudi 15 juin 1785 à la réception de l'Abbé Morellet* (Paris, 1785), 40–3.

[42] André Morellet, *Lettres de l'abbé Morellet de l'Académie française à Lord Shelburne, depuis marquis de Lansdowne, 1772–1803*, ed. Edmond Fitzmaurice (Paris, 1898), Morellet to Shelburne, 12 March 1776, 102; 30 December 1777, 130–5. Another Bowood Circle member, the physician Jon Ingenhousz, explained that perpetual peace might be secured by the use of air balloons: Jon Ingenhousz to Benjamin Franklin, 2 January 1784: 'If they can conduct the balloons in the same way as they do ships how could an army subsist when the enemy can throw force and destruction upon their scores and magazines at any time? How can an armed fleet attack any seacoast town, when the people of the country can swarm in the clouds and then fire upon it in the middle of the night? Do not you think that this discovery will put an end to all wars and thus force monarchs to perpetual peace or to fight their own quarrels among themselves in a duel?', *Benjamin Franklin Papers*.

[43] André Morellet to Shelburne, 1 April 1783 (Letter 788), *Correspondance générale d'Helvétius, IV, 1774–1800/Lettres 721–855, suivies de lettres relevant des périodes des trois premiers volumes et découvertes depuis leur parution*, 97–9.

was to establish an international community dedicated to freedom of trade between nations. Despite Turgot's failure, it explains why Morellet went to London in 1782 to negotiate with Shelburne on behalf of the French foreign minister Vergennes. In the aftermath of the protracted negotiations Morellet believed that he had helped to establish a new international order that rested upon mutual benevolence, itself founded upon enlightened self-interest, rather than upon egoism.[44] Having been secretary of state for home, colonial and Irish affairs under Rockingham, after the latter's death Shelburne served as First Lord of the Treasury from July 1782 to April 1783. As Parliament was in recess for five months of this period it gave Shelburne time to become directly involved in the diplomatic negotiations to end the North American war, aided by his emissary Richard Oswald and his private secretary Benjamin Vaughan. The new international order was inaugurated after a provisional treaty of peace was signed between Britain and the United States at Paris on 13 November 1782 and when on 20 January 1783 preliminary articles were signed with France and with Spain. The diplomatic work was deemed so significant that Shelburne persuaded Vergennes to give Morellet an annual pension after peace had been restored.[45] From Morellet's perspective, the Treaty of Paris of 1783 put right the diplomatic wrongs of the Treaty of Paris (1764) that had ended the Seven Years War and the Treaty of Aix-La-Chapelle (1748) that had put an end to the War of the Austrian Succession.

For Shelburne and his circle, in restoring peace between France and Britain the Treaty of Paris put an end to the post-1763 era of crisis. In underlining the costs and dangers of an expansive empire, it reminded the British that it was better to rely on trade rather than arms to sustain the state, and represented a warning against future colonization. Above all it was a chance for Europe to return to the natural progress of opulence, by dealing a heavy blow against the mercantile system of controlled trade, as Shelburne's friend Andrew Kippis underlined.[46] Shelburne in the House of Lords identified 'the era of Protestantism in trade', the argument being that the new principle of commercial liberty was better suited to Protestant states, and that the progress of trade would partner the progress of religion. Free commerce with North America was the best future for Britain:

> Monopolies some way or other, are ever justly punished. They forbid rivalry, and rivalry is of the very essence of the wellbeing of trade. This seems to be the era of Protestantism in trade. All Europe appear enlightened, and eager to throw off the vile shackles of oppressive ignorant monopoly, of that unmanly and illiberal principle, which is at once ungenerous and deceitful. A few interested Canadian

---

[44] Pierre-Edouard Lemontey, 'Eloge' in Morellet, *Mémoires inédits de l'abbé Morellet*, I, ix.
[45] Fitzmaurice, *Shelburne*, II, 264, Morellet, *Mémoires inédits de l'abbé Morellet*, I, 27.
[46] Andrew Kippis, *Considerations upon the provisional peace treaty with America and the preliminary articles of peace with France and Spain*, 2nd edn (London, 1783), 5, 79–81.

merchants might complain; for merchants would always love monopoly, without taking a moment's time to think, whether it was for their interest or not. I avow that monopoly is always unwise; but if there is any nation under Heaven, who ought to be the first that rejected monopoly, it is the English. Situated as we are between the old world and the new – and between the southern and northern Europe – all that we ought to covet upon earth was free trade, and fair equality. With more industry, with more enterprise, with more capital than any trading nation upon earth, it ought to be our constant cry – let every market be open – let us meet our rivals fairly – and we ask no more. It is a principle on which we have had the wisdom to act with respect to our brethren of Ireland, and, if conciliation be our view, why should we not reach it out also to America.[47]

After Shelburne resigned, on being defeated in the House of Commons on a motion censuring him for giving too much to the North Americans, Benjamin Vaughan exchanged letters with Franklin. In a summary of the Bowood Circle's hopes and expectations, Vaughan noted that the imperative was 'the overthrow of systems relative to English commerce' and that Shelburne had considered making England a free port:

You now see verified all that I said about binding down England to so hard a peace. It has put many good people into ill humour, and it has given a thousand pretexts to the bad people among us. But the overthrow of parties, is nothing to the overthrow of systems relative to English commerce, which was intended to be placed on a footing that would have been an example to all mankind, and probably have restored England to her pinnacle again. America I am sure we should have had as much of, as could be expected, upon the proposed systems of liberality. But however the ministry shall finally arrange itself, I cannot but hope on all hands, that we shall be more or less cured of our fighting and monopolizing notions and look to an American's Friendship. The boldness of my friend's conduct therefore has done infinite service to men's minds, as his conversation has done to the royal mind. You will take pleasure in hearing that he talked of making England a free port, for which he said we were fitted by nature, capital, love of enterprise, marine, connections, and position between the old and new world and the north and south of Europe; and that those who were best circumstanced for trade could not but be gainers by having trade open. Indeed I may now say to you with courage that I have scarcely seen or heard any thing of what has passed already, or was meant to take place hereafter, that I do not approve and applaud, as conducted upon grand principles. In short, I think that at last England will mend, not her parties indeed, but the proceedings of those who remain in office, whoever they may be.[48]

---

[47] Shelburne, *The Speech of the Right Honourable the earl of Shelburne, in the House of Lords, on Monday, February 13, 1783, on the Articles of Peace* (Ipswich, 1783), 4.

[48] Benjamin Vaughan to Benjamin Franklin, 25 February 1783, *Benjamin Franklin Papers*.

Shelburne later argued that 'the general system of the late peace' had extin-guished 'all mistaken ideas of rivalship'. Looking back from the perspective of a more adversarial stance towards which he saw developing in the after-math of the death of Frederick the Great, he claimed that 'never was there a period when animosity so soon subsided, when so few subjects of discussion, much less of dispute, had occurred with France as subsequent to 1782'.[49]

Although he left office prior to the negotiations, it was vital for Shelburne to see the peace treaty followed up by commercial treaties. That signed by William Eden and Gerard de Rayneval at Paris on 26 September 1786 was intended to 'adopt a system of commerce on the basis of reciprocity and mutual convenience, which, by discontinuing the prohibitions and prohibi-tory duties which have existed for almost a century between the two nations, might procure the most solid advantages, on both sides, to the national productions and industry'.[50] Shelburne was reported to be far from happy with the treaty. George Wilson and James Trail wrote, 'Lord Lansdowne sometimes says it is a pimping imitation of one of his great schemes – at others, that it is a very good treaty – and then, again, that it is a ruinous measure.'[51] In fact, Shelburne supported the Treaty, which he considered 'perfectly agreeable to my principles', and was pleased that Britain and France appeared to have adopted the principle of armed neutrality, following the model of the 'Treaty of Amity and Commerce' between Prussia and North America of 1785. Shelburne was concerned, however, that the public, being 'so ignorant and so changeable', would reject the treaty as going against national principle. It was an irony that William Eden now supported free trade with France while the year before he had vehemently refused it to Ireland. Shelburne admitted that he would be 'vastly troubled if it fails, for prejudice will get a new lease, and we shall be drove so far back in error'.[52] He realized that together the Treaty of Paris and the Anglo-French Commercial Treaty represented a transformed international world.

V

Shelburne was wholly behind a vision of an international politics in which empire was disparaged on the grounds that it went directly against national

---

[49] Shelburne, *The Substance of the Speech of the Marquis of Lansdowne, in the House of Lords, On the 14th of December, 1790; on the subject of the Convention with Spain, which was signed on the 28th of October, 1790* (London, 1790), 7.

[50] William Eden and Gerard de Rayneval, *Treaty of Navigation and Commerce between his Britannick Majesty and the Most Christian King. Signed at Versailles, the 26th of September, 1786* (London, 1786), 3.

[51] George Wilson, James Trail to Jeremy Bentham, 26 February 1787 (Letter 587), *The Correspondence of Jeremy Bentham: Volume 3: January 1781 to October 1788*, 526–7.

[52] Shelburne to Richard Price, 22 November 1786, *Price Correspondence*, III, 87–8.

self-interest. As this clashed with so much recent European history, which had seen all of the major states of Western Europe seek to expand and establish mercantile commercial empires, Shelburne was particularly interested in his endeavours for peace being recognized as a model for other European states. Europe's large states ought to be persuaded to engage commercially and on an equal basis with their smaller and weaker neighbours, rather than directing their trade or undermining their sovereignty. Such an idea was of course deemed to be the central message of the North American wars, which proved that a less-advanced state was better as a commercial ally than a miserable component of a commercial empire. But Shelburne was interested in the more direct message for Europe's states and an opportunity arose during the negotiations in London and in Paris, because Shelburne was also negotiating with Genevan rebels, who accused France of turning their state into part of a mercantile French empire. Shelburne wanted to present France as the opponent of popular liberties and national independence, but also to present Geneva as Europe's miniature North America. The story is little known, but the ideas expressed were prominent in the mid-1780s, and linked Shelburne's Bowood friends with Morellet's physiocrats and an active and influential group of exiled Genevans. The story reveals the extent to which contemporary interest in the rich-state/poor-state controversy including concern about its impact upon the map of Europe, and the possibility of maintaining the existing division of the continent into a multitude of forms of state, but living in peace rather than according to the dictates of reason of state politics.

In the 1760s British ministers were concerned that France might annex Geneva by taking advantage of the uncertain civil situation, which saw francophone patricians in the upper town at loggerheads with the *représentants* of the lower town.[53] The latter advocated a more popular constitution for the state and a greater distance between Geneva and France in international relations. By the later 1760s it was clear that France had usurped the cantons of Bern and Zurich in acting as Geneva's protector, and was interfering more and more in the civil affairs of the city. As Bernese troops paid for by France entered Geneva in 1766, the British accepted French policy, and more specifically the advice to 'trust [the French foreign minister] Choiseul'.[54] Yet British observers began to call for a moral foreign policy which defended liberty, and envisaged Britain as the scourge of tyrants wherever found. The Scottish geologist James Hutton made an impassioned

---

[53] Jean-Pierre Crommelin to Charles Lennox, 16 June and 26 June 1766, PRO, SP, 78/270; Henry-Seymour Conway to Charles Lennox, 1 April 1766, PRO SP 78/269.
[54] Henry-Seymour Conway to Charles Lennox, 9 May 1766, PRO, SP 78/270; Jean-Pierre Crommelin to Henry-Seymour Conway, 16 June 1766, PRO, SP 78/270; Charles Lennox to Henry-Seymour Conway, 22 June 1766, PRO, SP 78/270; Charles Lennox to Henry-Seymour Conway, 9 July 1766, PRO, SP 78/270.

appeal along these lines to Shelburne, whom he regarded as the minister responsible for European relations (even though the two secretaries of state shared European responsibilities between them). His view was that Geneva was on the verge of ruin, was being dominated by France, could not trust the cantons to defend Genevan independence, and in consequence had only Britain to turn to for rescue:

My neighbour's house, the finest house of its size in Europe is on fire, I beg your Lordship to send as many engines as you can to help extinguish it, and that your Lordship will pardon my thus breaking in upon you ... Your Lordship's noble and humane mind always a friend of legal liberty will value that virtuous people of Geneva whose beautiful state is on fire if I may use the term ... I am sorry that the Magistrates, who are most of them my good friends and whom I love and Honour have brought this French misery on their own Country ... I will only add the Swiss will never defend Geneva against France, only against Savoy for which they are more than a match, and want France to uphold them in the Pays de Vaud which they formerly conquered from Savoy and therefore will never disoblige France when France is at Peace with Savoy. My poor Heart will bless your Lordship & every friend of Geneva.[55]

Hutton went on to argue that it was a general principle of liberty 'that no weak state in Europe shall be overturned by any strong power', adding that Britain's merchants did not want to lose Geneva's trade, and Britain did not want to see such a fortified city under French command.[56] Other appeals followed. One identified Shelburne as someone 'known [for his] compassion for the oppressed assertors of their privileges and independence, in the ingenious, industrious, once flourishing protestant little republic of Geneva'.[57] Another, by Jean-Jacques Rousseau's friend Pastor Antoine-Jacques Roustan, appealed to Britain's commercial interests in preventing France from becoming dominant across Switzerland.[58] These were followed by a recommendation of Philip Stanhope, 2nd Earl Stanhope, who was William Pitt's cousin and living in the city for the good health of his second son Charles, to make Geneva a canton.[59] His rationale to Pitt was that France was dominating the republic and that Britain needed to counter

[55] James Hutton to Shelburne, 13 January 1767 (Letter A506), *Correspondance complète de Jean Jacques Rousseau: Tome XXXII: janvier–mars 1767*, ed. R.A. Leigh (Oxford, 1978), 272–4.

[56] James Hutton to Shelburne, 6 February 1767 (Letter A509), *Correspondance complète de Jean Jacques Rousseau: Tome XXXII: janvier–mars 1767*, 282–3.

[57] Jean Rodolphe de Vautravers to Shelburne, 12 February 1767, *Correspondence complete de Jean-Jacques Rousseau: Tome XXXII*, ed. R.A. Leigh (Oxford, 1978), 283–4.

[58] Antoine-Jacques Roustan to Shelburne, 15 January 1767, *Correspondence complete de Jean-Jacques Rousseau: Tome XXXII*, 275–9.

[59] Philip Stanhope to William Pitt, 2 February 1767, PRO 30/70/3/136.

such a development.[60] Neither Pitt nor Shelburne supported such an initiative, and pursued the policy of allowing France to sort out Geneva's internal difficulties, convinced as they were that France was not going to invade.[61] Within a year Shelburne was complaining to the French court about the annexation of Corsica, an action for which he was reportedly rebuked.[62] He was subsequently appealed to as a friend to Europe's small states, although it was equally clear that he would not support Britain going to war against France on the grounds of defending such states.[63]

Shelburne's views on small states evolved with his interest in Geneva. The city republic was increasingly seen to be dominated by France during the 1770s, and increasingly ripe for incorporation into France's empire. Shelburne's interest was stimulated by his friend Charles Stanhope, later to become 3rd Earl Stanhope, but at the time known as Lord Mahon, who was certain that the French threat to Genevan liberty had to be challenged.[64] In 1771 Mahon, when he was still living at Geneva, was given bourgeois status, elected to one of the branches of government, the Council of Two Hundred, and made commander of the *Tir de l'Arc* or company of archers.[65] Stanhope returned to England in 1774, and acted as the link between Shelburne and prominent Genevan exiles, such as the natural philosopher Jean-André Deluc, who visited Bowood in the same year.[66]

When unrest at Geneva in 1781 turned into revolution in 1782, reports were arriving in Britain from Turin of 6000 French troops and 4500 Sardinian soldiers marching towards Geneva, with the intention of restoring order and establishing a settlement guaranteed by these two powers, if necessary by massacre.[67] On 6 July 1782 it was reported that French, Sardinian, and Bernese troops had reinstated magistrates who had held their posts before

[60] Philip Stanhope to William Pitt, 19 December 1766, PRO 30/70/3/135.

[61] William Henry Nassau de Zuylestein, 4th Earl of Rochford to Shelburne, 22 January 1768 and 11 February 1768, PRO, SP 78/274.

[62] Edmund Burke, *Thoughts on the cause of the present discontents* (London, 1770), 53–6.

[63] James Boswell, *British Essays, in favour of the brave Corsicans: by several hands* (London, 1769), v–vi, 19–27.

[64] Gita Stanhope, *The Life of Charles, Third Earl Stanhope* (London, 1914), 1–20.

[65] A.C. Bennett, 'The Stanhopes in Geneva: A Study of an English Noble Family in Genevan Politics and Society, 1764–1774' (MA dissertation, University of Kent, 1992); G.M. Ditchfield, 'Stanhope, Charles, Third Earl Stanhope (1753–1816)', ODNB.

[66] Joseph Priestley, *Experiments and observations on different kinds of air* (London, 1774), 219. On Deluc in England and the court, see Clarissa Campbell Orr, 'Queen Charlotte as Patron: Some Intellectual and Social Contexts', *The Court Historian*, 6:3 (2001), 183–212; 'Charlotte of Mecklenburg-Strelitz, Queen of Great Britain and Electress of Hanover: Northern Dynasties and the Northern Republic of Letters', in *Queenship in Europe 1660–1815: The Role of the Consort*, ed. Clarissa Campbell Orr (Cambridge, 2004), 368–402.

[67] *The Annual Register, or a view of the politics, history and literature, for the year 1782* (London, 1783), 208.

the *représentant* uprising of 7 April, had poured eight hundred barrels of gunpowder into the Rhone, collected 14,000 armaments from the populace, imposed martial law, and forced those who had been granted bourgeois status since the revolution to return their liberty documents. Provisions were said to be scarce, and half the trees had been cut down 'under the pretence of protecting a freedom, which is now but an empty name'.[68] Whilst the newspapers endlessly commented upon the negative consequence of the alliance between France and Savoy, the European political situation precluded direct British involvement. In 1782 Britain was losing the war in the North American colonies, was heavily in debt, lambasted as an enemy to liberty, and widely seen to be falling behind France in the competition for international supremacy. Willoughby Bertie, the 4th Earl of Abingdon attempted to involve the British after the *représentant* commissioners asked him for additional help on 10 June 1782. He ultimately replied to them that there was nothing that the British could do because of their present situation, 'rent by divisions at home, and surrounded by enemies abroad'. 'Once', Abingdon reported, 'the fleets of England were the speaking trumpets of justice to the whole world', but Britain was now 'no longer in a capacity to speak to the enemies of the liberties of mankind in its wonted tone of authority'.[69] It is significant that the report on Abingdon's failure appeared in Kippis's *The New Annual Register.*

Shelburne did take action in 1782. He had long been aware of a project of Choiseul's to make a free port at Versoy on Lake Geneva, where 'toleration of religion is to be admitted', with the intention to 'destroy the republic'.[70] In 1782 negotiations were entered into with François D'Ivernois, a Genevan lawyer who, before his exile, had been publishing the Geneva edition of Rousseau's works, to 'secure a favourable reception for such families as were determined to quit Geneva, and not only a favourable reception but such positive encouragement & support as might reimburse their expenses, & lay the foundation of an establishment in this country'.[71] Such activity occurred

---

68 *British Magazine and Review* (London, 1782), 71. Review of 'An Historical and Political View of the Constitution and Revolutions of Geneva, in the Eighteenth Century. Written originally in French, by Francis D'Ivernois, Esq. LL. D. (late a Citizen of Geneva) and translated by John Farrell, A. M. in Boards, Cadell', *The English Review, Or, An Abstract of English and Foreign Literature*, vol. V (London, 1785), 162–5; Review of Brissot's 'Le Philadelphien à Genève', *English Review, or an abstract of English and Foreign Literature*, vol. IV (London, 1784), 129–33.

69 *The New annual register, or, General repository of history, politics, and literature*, ed. Andrew Kippis (London, 1783), 63–4.

70 William Henry Nassau de Zuylestein, 4th Earl of Rochford to Shelburne, 19 November 1767, *Correspondence complete de Jean-Jacques Rousseau: Tome XXXIV*, ed. R.A. Leigh (Oxford, 1979), 277.

71 Grantham, St James's to Mountstuart, 16 August, 1782 (No 7, draft), Bedfordshire and Luton Archives and Record Service, L 29/561/15.

despite the complaints of the Genevan magistrates.[72] Shelburne arranged for the Genevan exiles to set up a colony of watchmakers at Waterford in Ireland, with the expectation that a second Huguenot diaspora might do for the Irish economy what had been done for the English at the end of the seventeenth century. The Irish experiment was based on the Waterford colony enjoying the benefits of free commerce. It promised to be an example of economic power being used to show France the mistaken consequences of invading smaller neighbours and taking away the liberties of the citizens.[73] It was equally intended to show that free trade in Ireland would not undermine competitor mainland industries, and the positive consequences of economic development, led by Calvinists, for Ireland's Catholic peasantry.

In practice the Genevan economy did not collapse in the wake of a political migration, and the Waterford experiment failed because of problems in obtaining gold for the watches and men to fashion them. But François D'Ivernois, and his fellow Genevan exiles Etienne Clavière and Jacques-Antoine Duroveray, joined with the members of the Bowood Circle in seeking to persuade large states that increased commerce to rely upon peace, and that peace required the abandonment of contemporary notions of imperial or mercantile empire. This was the message of a series of public works and private letters by the Genevan exiles, who employed the hired pens of Honoré-Gabriel Riqueti de Mirabeau and Jacques-Pierre Brissot to further their cause.[74] The most important was written by D'Ivernois and translated into English as *An Historical View of the Constitution and Revolutions of Geneva in the Eighteenth Century*. It warned France that refusal to embrace free trade and to respect the independence of small states like Geneva would result in rabidly democratic patriot rebellions or in the dominion of a corrupt and servile aristocracy within a poor and economically collapsing state. As D'Ivernois put it, 'If [Geneva] ever loses her liberty, industry will take its flight along with it: Geneva shall then be but a dungeon of slavery, and the court of some opulent and depraved men: no longer will it fix the attention of philosophers; and if it be still inhabited, no industry, no citizen, no Genevese will be found amongst its inhabitants.'[75] More broadly, if the

---

[72] Syndics and Council of Geneva to Thomas Townshend, 18 December 1782, PRO, FO 95/8/12; Syndics and Council of Geneva to George III, 18 December 1782, PRO, FO 95/8/12 f. 637.

[73] Otto Karmin, *Sir Francis D'Ivernois 1757–1842. Sa vie, son oeuvre et son temps* (Paris and Geneva, 1920), 113–59.

[74] Honoré-Gabriel Riqueti de Mirabeau to Vergennes, 4 October 1782, *Mémoires biographiques, littéraires et politiques de Mirabeau*, 8 vols (Paris, 1834), IV, 114–40; Jacques-Pierre Brissot, *Le Philadelphien à Genève, ou lettres d'un Américain sur la dernière révolution de Genève, sa constitution nouvelle, l'émigration en Irlande, &c.* (Dublin, 1784).

[75] François D'Ivernois, *An Historical View of the Constitution and Revolutions of Geneva in the Eighteenth Century* (London, 1784), xviii.

small states of Europe succumbed to external aggressors, commercial decline would be precipitate.

Mirabeau arrived in England in 1784. With recommendations from Franklin, he was introduced to Benjamin Vaughan, and to Shelburne.[76] With help from the Genevan exiles he composed *Considérations sur l'Ordre de Cincinnatus, ou Imitation d'un pamphlet anglo-américain* (1785), which Samuel Romilly translated. This work, which included an exchange of letters between Richard Price and Turgot intended to warn against war or debt-induced bankruptcy, was among the most important statements of the dangers of mercantile empire, and of the need for free trade and peace between Britain and France.[77] It was followed by Morellet's friend the physiocrat Pierre-Samuel Dupont de Nemours's identical argument that the Eden Treaty 'is probably the only guarantee of peace between the two Empires' ['est peut-être le seul garant de la paix entre les deux Empires'] and that 'there can be no lasting war in Europe' ['nulle guerre ne peut être durable en Europe'].[78] Another member of the Genevan exile community, Jean-Louis De Lolme also wrote in favour of free trade and commercial treaties. With regard to the Eden Treaty he regretted that a more substantial treaty had been prevented 'since political jealousy proved too powerful for mercantile interest', but welcomed 'beneficial consequences from its opposition'.[79] Benjamin Vaughan's own summary of the Bowood position then appeared as *New and old principles of trade compared*, which argued that:

> ... it has certainly been the actual, property of the narrow [mercantile] system, to be devoted to wars of conquest and offence: while one of the chief objects of the free-trade system is to extinguish such wars, and to encourage such principles in our neighbours and in making generally, as shall lessen the frequency of the occasions even for wars of self-defence. There is scarcely one writer on free-trade, at the present day, who does not make this pacific turn more of a primary, than of a secondary, consideration. On the other hand, there was been scarcely one of our latter ruptures with France, or other nations, which has not, directly or indirectly, originated from systems of trade or colonization founded in monopoly. In short, estrangement and jealousy, violence and revenge, by whatever cause they

---

[76] See R. Hammersley, *The English Republican Tradition and Eighteenth-Century France: Between the Ancients and the Moderns* (Manchester, 2010), Chapter 11.

[77] Mirabeau, *Considerations On The Order Of Cincinnatus; To which are added, As well several original papers relative to that institution, As also A Letter from the late M. Turgot, Comptroller of the Finances in France, To Dr. Price, On the constitution of America; and An Abstract of Dr. Price's Observations on the Importance Of The American Revolution* (London, 1785).

[78] Dupont de Nemours, *Lettre à la chambre du commerce de Normandie, Sur le Mémoire qu'elle a publié relativement au Traité de Commerce avec l'Angleterre* (Rouen and Paris, 1788), 74–5.

[79] De Lolme, *An Essay containing a few strictures on the Union of Scotland with England; and on the present situation of Ireland* (London, 1787), 81.

are set in motion, tend to war; while liberal intercourse and exchanges seem to make the corner stones of peace and concord.[80]

VI

The Bowood Circle in the 1780s aimed to keep peace in Europe, maintain the current borders of states, and gradually dismantle the mercantile system, by means of political and commercial treaties enshrining the principle of free trade. This vision was dealt a blow when, soon after the September 1783 peace treaty was signed, an Order in Council excluded all North American citizens from Britain's West Indies trade. Benjamin Vaughan, who was a member of the Committee of West India Merchants and Planters, failed to have the order rescinded, and was warned by Franklin that 'England will get as little by the Commercial War she has begun with us as she did by the Military'.[81] When free trade with Ireland was challenged in Parliament, and when the demand for free passage through the River Scheldt by Joseph II of Austria threatened another European war, ideas about commercial peace began to appear utopian.[82] When Prussia invaded Holland in support of the besieged Stadholder in September 1787, a general war also beckoned because of France's support for the Dutch patriotic opposition. Pitt was prepared to fight France once again if intervention against Prussia took place, and began arming to this end.[83] Although France did not intervene, Richard Price warned Shelburne that 'France was likely to take measures to regain her weight which would open a new scene in Europe', risking war between Britain, Prussia. and Holland on one side, and France, Russia, and the Holy Roman Empire on the other.[84] Principled politics appeared impossible when short-term interests and domestic struggles for power were the norm. As Benjamin Vaughan wrote to Franklin, 'these late struggles have unhappily

---

[80] Benjamin Vaughan, *New and old principles of trade compared, or, A treatise on the principles of commerce between nations* (London, 1788), 2–3.

[81] Benjamin Franklin to Benjamin Vaughan, 26 July 1784, *Benjamin Franklin Papers*.

[82] Richard Price to Benjamin Franklin, 21 March 1785: 'We are just now alarmed here by the news that a war must take place on the Continent. I have hitherto been disposed to admire the [Holy Roman] Emperor; but I now execrate his conduct. Perhaps, however, this is a false alarm; and he will take more time for consideration before he suffers his ambition to involve Europe in blood. We talk of little here at present besides the propositions for establishing a perfect reciprocity in trade between this Kingdom and Ireland. These propositions have produced a violent clamour; and there is some danger that the ministry will be overthrown by them. It is obvious, that this gives little room for hoping that a liberal plan will be adopted with respect to the commerce of America.' *Benjamin Franklin Papers*.

[83] J.H. Rose, 'Great Britain and the Dutch Question in 1787–1788', *American Historical Review*, 14:2 (1909), 262–83.

[84] Richard Price to Shelburne, 10 November 1787, *Price Correspondence*, III, 152–4.

shown however, how little any of these people [Pitt, Fox, and Sheridan] are capable of grand political ideas or plans. They understand faction, and even that often but ill, but seem to know nothing of the new systems of general politics.'[85] The French Revolution for a short period presented new possibilities, but every initiative failed that sought to tie Britain and France together by commerce.[86] Shelburne turned to the Genevan exile Etienne Dumont, and to Jeremy Bentham, for new solutions to the eternal problems of establishing peace, justice between states small and large, and free trade.[87] Against many former members of the Bowood Circle, but alongside Charles Stanhope, Shelburne opposed war against revolutionary France, forever seeing it as a barrier to free trade, by entrenching aristocracies in the political and economic world.[88] He always looked back to the time, between his brief premiership and the British rearmament that accompanied the Prussian invasion of Holland, as a halcyon period for Europe, during which the Bowood Circle's commitment to reform and international peace by means of free trade were articulated, and ought to have been realized.

[85] Benjamin Vaughan to Benjamin Franklin, 4 March 1789, *Benjamin Franklin Papers*.

[86] Etienne Dumont, *Recollections of Mirabeau, and of the two first legislative assemblies of France* (Philadelphia, 1833), 202–3.

[87] R. Whatmore, 'Étienne Dumont et le Benthamisme: la démocratie dans les petits États', in 'Bentham et la France. Fortune et infortune de l'utilitarisme', *Studies of Voltaire and the Eighteenth Century*, ed. E. de Champs and J.-P. Cléro (Oxford, 2009), 111–27.

[88] Shelburne, Speech to the House of Lords, 17 February 1794, *The Annual Register, or a view of the politics, history and literature, for the year 1794* (London, 1799), 220–6; Charles Stanhope, *The Speech of Earl Stanhope, in the House of Lords, On Thursday the 20th of February, 1800, In support of his motion for Peace with the French Republic; Wherein he shews the ruinous tendency of the war* (London, 1800).

Index

STUDIES IN EARLY MODERN CULTURAL, POLITICAL AND SOCIAL HISTORY

.